The 4th International Symposium of
the Psychiatric Research Institute of Tokyo

ALCOHOLISM
AND
THE FAMILY

The 4th International Symposium
of the Psychiatric Research Institute of Tokyo

Place: Sasagawa Kinen Kaikan
Date: November 21 and 22, 1989

Executive Director: Tsuyoshi ISHII, M.D.

Director, Psychiatric Research Institute of Tokyo

2-1-8 Kamikitazawa, Setagaya-ku, Tokyo 156, Japan

Phone: 03-304-5701

Coordinator: Nobukatsu KATOH, M.D.

Director, Matsuzawa Hospital

2-1-1 Kamikitazawa, Setagaya-ku, Tokyo 156, Japan

Phone: 03-303-7211

Satoru SAITOH, M.D.

Head, Department of Sociopathology

The Psychiatric Research Institute of Tokyo

Organizing Committee: (The Psychiatric Research Institute of Tokyo)

Masato UNO, Director of Research

Shigeo KOSUGI, Director of Administration

Shinsaku KOYANAGI, Director of Technical Division

Kazuya YOSHIMATSU, Head, Department of Social Psychiatry

Takashi MOROJI, Head, Department of Psychopharmacology

Shohei OKABE, Head, Department of Clinical Psychology

Kenji KOSAKA, Head, Department of Neuropathology

Ken KADOTA, Head, Department of Neurochemistry

Yuji NAKATANI, Department of Sociopathology

Sponsoring Institute: The Psychiatric Research Institute of Tokyo (Tokyo, Japan)

The 4th International Symposium of
the Psychiatric Research Institute of Tokyo

ALCOHOLISM
AND
THE FAMILY

Edited by

SATORU SAITOH, M.D.
PETER STEINGLASS, M.D.
MARC A. SCHUCKIT, M.D.

Seiwa Shoten, *Publishers*
Tokyo

Brunner/Mazel, *Publishers*
New York

Library of Congress Cataloging-in-Publication Data

Tōkyō-to Seishin Igaku Sōgō Kenkyūjo. International Symposium (4th: 1989: Tokyo, Japan)
  Alcoholism and family / the 4th International Symposium of the Psychiatric Research Institute of Tokyo; edited by Satoru Saitoh, Peter Steinglass, and Marc A. Schuckit.
    p.   cm.
  Includes bibliographical references.
  Includes index.
  ISBN 0-87630-626-1
  1. Alcoholism—Congresses. 2. Family—Mental health—congresses. 3. Family psychotherapy—Congresses. I. Saito, Satoru. II. Steinglass, Peter. III. Schuckit, Marc Alan. IV. Title.
  [DNLM: 1. Alcoholism—congresses. 2. family—congresses. 3. Family Therapy—congresses. WM 274 T646a 1989]
  RC563.2.T64 1989
                              616.86'1—dc20
  DNLM/DLC   90-2644
  for Library of Congress   CIP

Published by
Seiwa Shoten Publishers
1-2-5 Kamitakaido, Suginami-ku
Tokyo, Japan

In collaboration with
BRUNNER/MAZEL, INC.
19 Union Square West
New York, New York 10003

CONTENTS

PREFACE

The science of the etiology and treatment of alcoholism has made notable progress in recent years. Since the early 1970s there have been growing inroads made concerning the relevance of hereditary factors in alcoholism. This has led to the presentation of various innovative hypotheses in this field. In conjunction with this there has been much discussion and study of the "alcoholic personality" and its possible characteristics. These may be considered the "longitudinal aspects" linked to the transmission of alcoholism.

However, there is yet another vital area, which may be considered the "horizontal aspect," i.e., the way in which communication patterns within the family, or their cultural backgrounds, contribute to both the maintenance of family homeostasis and the possibility of the intergenerational transmission of alcoholism. These studies have not only revealed the socio/interactional dynamics of the alcoholic family in both their "wet" and "dry" stages, but also offered significant implications for family treatment of the alcoholic family.

In Japan the problem of alcoholism had received only scant attention up to the mid-1970s, when the issue of housewives' alcoholism in the home hit the headlines. Nowadays, the Japanese cannot afford to ignore drinking problems within their society. The pure alcohol equivalent consumed annually by adults in Japan amounts to an average 6-7 liters per capita; 2-3% of adults are estimated to be alcoholics, with a present male/female ratio of 10:1.

This international symposium, sponsored by the Psychiatric Research Institute of Tokyo on November 21-22, 1989, brought together researchers engaged in both of the above areas, in order to create an open forum for both the exchange of new information and to act as a catalyst stimulating further innovative studies in this field.

Tsuyoshi Ishii
Director, Psychiatric Research Institute of Tokyo
Executive Director of the International Symposium
Nobukatsu Katoh
Director, Tokyo Metropolitan Matsuzawa Hospital
Head of the International Symposium Committee
Satoru Saitoh
Head, Department of Sociopathology Psychiatric Research Institute of Tokyo
Secretariat Director

CONTRIBUTORS

AMES, Genevieve M., Ph.D.
Study Director and Senior Research Scientist
Prevention Research Center
Pacific Institute for Research and Evaluation
2532 Durant Avenue
Berkeley, CA 94704
U.S.A.

ASAKA, Akio, M.D.
Professor
Yamanashi Medical College
1110 Shimokato Tamaho-cho
Nakakoma-gun, Yamanashi 409-38
Japan

BLACK, Claudia, M.S.W., Ph.D.
1590 South Coast Hwy
Suite #17
Laguna Beach, CA 92651
U.S.A.

BOHMAN, Michael, M.D.
Professor
The Department of Child and Youth Psychiatry
Umeå University, S-901 87 Umeå, Sweden

CLONINGER, Robert C., M.D.
The Departments of Psychiatry and Genetics
Washington University School of Medicine and
Jewish Hospital
216 South Kingshighway Blvd.
St. Louis, MO 63130
U.S.A.

DALBY, Anthony, C.Q.S.W.
Department of Sociopathology
Psychiatric Research Institute of Tokyo
2-1-8 Kamikitazawa, Setagaya-ku
Tokyo 156
Japan

ENDO, Yuko, B.A.
Chief
Harajuku Counseling Room
Affiliated to the Clinical Institute on Addiction
Problems (CIAP)
4-30-2 Jingu-mae
Shibuya-ku
Tokyo 150
Japan

GRANT, Marcus, Ph.D.
Senior Scientist
Division of Mental Health
WHO
1211 Geneva
27 - Switzerland

HARADA, Shoji, M.D.
Institute of Community Medicine
University of Tsukuba
Tennodai, Tsukuba
Ibaraki 305
Japan

HAYASHIDA, Motoi, M.D. Sc.D.
Philadelphia V.A. Medical Center
University of Pennsylvania
Philadelphia, PA 19104
U.S.A.

ICHIKAWA, Mitsuhiro, M.D.
Narimasu Kohsei Hospital
1-19-1 Misono
Itabashi-ku
Tokyo 175
Japan

ISHII, Tsuyoshi, M.D.
Director
Psychiatric Research Institute of Tokyo
2-1-8 Kamikitazawa, Setagaya-ku
Tokyo 156
Japan

KATOH, Nobukatsu, M.D.
Director
Metropolitan Matsuzawa Hospital
2-1-1 Kamikitazawa, Setagaya-ku
Tokyo 156
Japan

VON KNORRING, Anne-Liis, M.D.
The Department of Child and Youth Psychiatry
Umeå University
S-901 87 Umeå
Sweden

KOHNO, Hiroaki, M.D.
Director
National Institute on Alcoholism
National Kurihama Hospital
2769 Nobi
Yokosuka-shi 239
Japan

NAGANO, Kiyoshi, M.D.
Department of Sociopathology
Psychiatric Research Institute of Tokyo
2-1-8 Kamikitazawa, Setagaya-ku
Tokyo 156
Japan

NAKAMURA, Michihiko, M.D.
Associate Professor
Department of Psychiatry
Kyoto Prefectural University of Medicine
465 Kajii-cho
Kawaramachi dori
Hirokoji agaru
Kamigyo-ku
Kyoto 602
Japan

NISHIHARA, Kyoko, M.D.
Department of Psychophysiology
Psychiatric Research Institute of Tokyo
2-1-8 Kamikitazawa
Setagaya-ku
Tokyo 156
Japan

NISHIO, Kazumi, Ph.D.
Santa Rosa Institute
2455 Bennett Valley Road
Santa Rosa, CA 95404
U.S.A.

NOBUTA, Sayoko, M.A.
Harajuku Counseling Room
Affiliated to the Clinical Institute on Addiction
Problems (CIAP)
4-30-2 Jingu-mae
Shibuya-ku
Tokyo 150
Japan

NOGUCHI, Yuji, Ph.D.
Department of Sociology
Tokyo Metropolitan Institute of Gerontology
35-2, Sakae-cho
Itabashi-ku
Tokyo 173
Japan

NOMURA, Naoki, Ph.D.
Department of Sociopathology
Psychiatric Research Institute of Tokyo
2-1-8 Kamikitazawa, Setagaya-ku
Tokyo 156
Japan

SAITOH, Satoru, M.D.
Head, Department of Sociopathology
Psychiatric Research Institute of Tokyo
2-1-8 Kamikitazawa, Setagaya-ku
Tokyo 156
Japan

SCHUCKIT, Marc A., M.D.
Director
Alcohol Research Center
San Diego Veterans Affairs Medical Center and
Professor of Psychiatry
University of California, San Diego, School of
Medicine
San Diego, CA 92161
U.S.A.

SENOH, Eiichi, M.D.
Hasegawa Hospital
2-20-36 Ohsawa
Mitaka-shi
Tokyo 181
Japan

SIGVARDSSON, Sören, Ph.D.
The Department of Child and Youth Psychiatry
Umeå University
S-901 87 Umeå
Sweden

STEINGLASS, Peter, M.D.
Director
Ackerman Institute for Family Therapy
149 E. 78th Street
New York, NY 10021
U.S.A.

SUZUKI, Kenji, M.D.
Chief, Department of Psychiatry
National Kurihama Hospital
2769 Nobi
Yokosuka-shi 239
Japan

TAKEMURA, Michio, M.D.
Director
Clinical Institute on Addiction Problems (CIAP)
4-30-2 Jingu-mae
Shibuya-ku
Tokyo 150
Japan

TEZUKA, Ichiro, B.A.
Department of Sociopathology
Psychiatric Research Institute of Tokyo
2-1-8 Kamikitazawa, Setagaya-ku
Tokyo 156
Japan

VAILLANT, George E., M.D.
Raymond Sobel Professor of Psychiatry
Dartmouth Medical School
Hanover, NH 03756
U.S.A.

WHITTAKER, James O., Ph.D.
Professor Emeritus
The Pennsylvania State University
Middletown, PA
and
President
Whittaker & Whittaker Research Associates
3816 Copper Kettle Road
Camp Hill, PA 17011
U.S.A.

WHITTAKER, Sandra J., M.A.
Partner
Whittaker & Whittaker Research Associates
3816 Copper Kettle Road
Camp Hill, PA 17011
U.S.A.

INTRODUCTION

The recognition of the relevance of the topic of alcoholism and the family by an institution as prestigious as the Psychiatric Research Institute of Tokyo is most welcome. The development of a symposium on this topic demonstrates the importance of furthering our understanding of the impact that alcohol has on our patients and their families. It also highlights the increasing level of sophistication of alcohol-related research in the recent several decades.

The specific focus of this symposium and this volume is particularly challenging. The constellation and functioning of the family unit is diverse and is affected by multiple influences, including the overall society, the social stratum, levels of stress, and evidence of impaired functioning in any member of the family unit. The latter two forces are themelves dependent upon a variety of influences, including the pattern of substance use and related problems experienced by any family member. Thus, to propose an international symposium focusing not only on the family but on the impact that alcoholism can have on this most important institution is indeed a significant undertaking.

The success of this endeavor was apparent to all participants in Tokyo and is hopefully equally reflected in the pages that follow. The organizers from the Psychiatric Research Institute of Tokyo developed a working atmosphere in which clinicians and scientists were offered the opportunity of presenting their efforts and experiences in a manner in which mutual respect laid the groundwork for a full and often most exciting series of discussions. The formal presentations reflected in the chapters that follow were up-to-date, appropriately referenced, and presented in a manner that allowed for disagreement as well as for subsequent opportunities for all participants to learn new and helpful ways of understanding more about a highly complex problem.

Some of the papers clearly highlight biological aspects of the impact that alcoholism can have on the family structure. These are reflected in part by the family, twin, and adoption studies that demonstrate how an important part of the development and subsequent course of alcoholism appears to relate to biological and genetically transmitted factors. The chapters also point to the heterogeneity among alcoholics, with subsequent subgroups of individuals who appear to respond differently to the general atmosphere and to the specific family milieu in ways that focus our attention on environmental influences as well.

Other papers show how cultural and related social factors can impact on the development and course of alcoholism, and the manner in which this disorder changes interactions within the family. Thus, chapters in this volume give the reader the opportunity of understanding different perspectives on these interactions from the United States, Japan, Scandinavia, and other areas of the world. We are also given the opportunity to share some unique observations as they relate to subgroups within a major society, including Native Americans in the United States.

This data-oriented information is supplemented by important observational and experiential perspectives. Both clinical researchers and clinicians offer their unique experiences in working with men and women with alcohol problems. We learn about attempts to help families understand more about this complex and challenging disorder. These observations are an important counterpoint to the numbers and tables, and offer the opportunity to integrate both types of observations within a single text.

For all of these reasons, the readers of this volume are given the opportunity to assimilate a series of important observations coming from multiple perspectives. While each chapter focuses on alcohol and the family, we are able to understand more about these phenomena from data and observations gathered from sociologists, epidemiologists, biologists, psychiatrists, scientists who have developed unique ways to observe interactions among family members, and people with active clinical practices. It is our hope that this text will serve as a general introduction and as a nidus for gathering additional information for those readers who are interested in alcohol, the family, and their interactions.

Marc A. Schuckit, M.D.

PART I

GENETIC FACTORS OF ALCOHOLISM

In both this section and the next, the authors review the ways in which genetic and environmental factors contribute to the cause and/or development of alcoholism. We must pose the question: To what extent—and at what stage—may genetics interact with environmental influences?

Professor Marc Schuckit, Associate Professor Michihiko Nakamura, and Professor Asaka all address this challenging question in somewhat different ways.

Professor Schuckit and his team use biochemical and electrophysiological investigations. Professor Nakamura's group concentrates upon CNV (Contingent Negative Variation) paradigms within the electrophysiological field. Professor Asaka's methodology was the comparison of the life histories of monozygotic twins.

From these three reports, readers can gather information on a wide variety of approaches to this problem, and the extent to which answers have been uncovered, to date, regarding this question.

PART I: GENETIC FACTORS OF ALCOHOLISM

1

Alcoholism, A Familial Disorder: Genetic Aspects*

Marc A. Schuckit, M.D.

This paper discusses how genetic factors contribute to the familial nature of alcoholism. The importance of a genetic component to this disorder is supported by the fourfold increased risk for severe alcohol problems in close relatives of alcoholics, the high risk for identical twins of alcoholics, and the documentation of a high level of vulnerability among adopted-out children of alcoholics. Studies are now underway attempting to identify biologic factors that interact with the environment to produce the alcoholism risk. Among the leads is the documentation that sons and daughters of alcohol-dependent parents show a decreased intensity of reaction to modest doses of alcohol. The implications of these findings to the prevention and treatment of alcoholism are discussed.

I. INTRODUCTION

A) General Issues

Alcoholism is a familial disorder in many ways. *First*, the course of alcohol-related life problems affects mood, productivity, and episodes of violence, and, thus, impacts on the lives of most friends and relatives.[21] As a result, few alcoholics suffer their disorder alone. A *second* familial aspect of alcoholism rests with the *theory* that optimum treatment of the alcoholic cannot occur unless the entire immediate support system, including the family unit, joins in therapy.

The present paper focuses on a *third* way in which alcoholism is familial. For many years, alcoholism has been demonstrated to cluster in certain fam-

*This work was supported by the Veterans Affairs Research Service and NIAAA Grant 05526.

ily groups,[3] a finding which could be the result of genetic and/or environmental factors. The strong familial component has contributed to the development of studies evaluating if the patterns might reflect underlying genetic factors. This search has proceeded through several steps of increasing complexity as is described in the next section.

B) The Search for Genetic Factors in Alcoholism

Alcoholism indeed runs strongly within families.[3],[19] The risk for developing this serious disorder is increased at least fourfold in close family members of alcoholics. Most data also indicate that if the original identified alcoholic has no obvious major preexisting psychiatric disorders (i.e., he has primary alcoholism), the illness most likely to be observed in that family is alcoholism itself.[17],[18],[24] Also consistent with the importance of a genetic predisposition is the probability that the risk for developing alcoholism increases with the number of alcoholic relatives, even if those alcoholics had never lived with the individual while he or she was growing up. For example, alcoholism in a grandfather appears to add significantly to the alcoholism risk.[8] Finally, the more severely alcoholic the individual is (e.g., whether he or she has been hospitalized or not), the greater the likelihood a close family member will develop alcoholism.

This constellation of findings has justified the next type of investigation, *twin studies*,[14] with results that have generally supported the importance of genetic factors. Partanen and colleagues[12] in Finland documented a greater similarity for many drinking characteristics for identical twins when compared to fraternal pairs. The classical twin study focusing on severe and pervasive alcohol-related life problems (i.e., alcoholism) reported that the risk for alcoholism was twice as high in the identical twin of an alcoholic than in a fraternal twin, with the latter demonstrating a level of similarity that was equivalent to that of same-sexed full siblings.[7] Those results were similar to several earlier investigations and have been supported by later studies (e.g., 2,14). However, one recent investigation began with individuals who fulfilled criteria for alcoholism but who were selected from a general *psychiatric* hospital population, and generated data inconsistent with a genetic influence.[10]

The preponderance of data from the family and twin investigations justifies making the efforts needed in *adoption* studies. If alcoholism is genetically influenced, then the sons and daughters of alcoholics should be at exceptionally high risk for this disorder, even if they were adopted out and raised by nonalcoholics.[19],[20] All modern adoption studies have documented that alcoholism in the biological parent predicts the likelihood of alcoholism in the children, even in individuals who were raised by nonalcoholics.[2],[6],[27] An interesting sidelight has been the lack of evidence that being reared by an alcoholic increases the risk at all beyond what would be predicted from the illness in the biological parent alone.

In summary, one familial attribute of alcoholism is the manner in which it clusters within families. There is evidence from family, twin, and adoption studies to support the contention that this familial aspect of alcoholism includes a genetic component. The next section briefly reviews the methods with which our own and other laboratories have approached a next logical step in the search for genetic factors impacting on alcoholism.

II. SUBJECTS AND METHODS:
The Search for What Might Be Inherited

A) Some General Issues

The data outlined above are informative in multiple ways. First, the fact that no modern study shows a 100% risk for alcoholism in the identical twins of alcoholics underscores the importance of environmental factors. Second, there is *no* clear evidence that alcoholism is inherited as an autosomal dominant disorder with complete expression or penetrance. For example, no study has shown that half of the sons and daughters of severely alcoholic men or women will demonstrate the disorder themselves. Thus, it is possible that the genetic factor either involves a limited number of dominant genes with incomplete expression (i.e., the gene might be passed on following a dominant mode of inheritance but other factors impact on whether the disorder itself develops), or that multiple genes are required in order for the clinical syndrome to develop (an example of polygenic inheritance). In any event, the search for genetic factors impacting on alcoholism is likely to be complex, and different types of genetic factors might exert their influences in different families. It is, thus, unlikely that research will identify a single alcoholic gene that always expresses itself.

For these and other reasons, the search for a genetic influence might best begin by focusing on relatives of carefully defined severe and more "classical" cases. The more homogeneous the population under study, the greater the chance that a specific set of genetic influences interacting with environment within that family cluster might be identified. Therefore, our work focuses on the 70% or so of severe alcoholics who have no major preexisting disorder, a group we label as primary (i.e., simple or classical) alcoholics.[15],[19],[24]

These individuals developed their first major life problems from alcohol before any evidence of psychotic disorders such as schizophrenia, severe personality disorders such as the antisocial personality disorder, or severe affective disturbances such as major depressive disorder or manic depressive disease. This emphasis on primary alcoholism is in recognition of evidence that the antisocial personality disorder, schizophrenia, manic depressive disease, and so on each have unique genetic influences that may be distinct from those operating in alcoholism. Carrying out genetic studies in families of patients with multiple genetically influenced disorders may make it impossible to identify genetic factors unique to alcoholism itself.

Despite these complexities, the adoption investigations and a significant proportion of the twin studies still demonstrate the probable importance of genetic influences in alcoholism. Support for such factors is strong enough to justify a search for the specific manifestations of genetic factors that might interact with environment to cause the final clinical picture. There are a number of ways that such a search might be carried out. The most powerful approach would involve longitudinal investigations of sons and daughters of carefully defined primary alcoholics, when these children were adopted out close to birth and raised without knowledge of their biological parents' problems. However, gathering such a sample would be difficult and expensive, especially because these individuals must be brought to a laboratory where they can be evaluated at multiple times during their lives before the alcoholism actually develops.

As a result of these considerations, our laboratory has opted to study a large number of individuals who are at high risk for the future development of alcoholism, most classically sons of alcoholic fathers. Because the data cited above indicate that their alcoholism risk is no different whether they were raised by alcoholics or not, we focus on nonadoptive samples. The next section presents the study methods used in our research with sons of alcoholic fathers and appropriate controls. This is followed with an overview of the results of the studies generated by our group.

B) Methods for Studying Populations at High Risk for Alcoholism

Our work has proceeded through three phases. In Phase 1, the selection and identification of a sample, questionnaires are mailed to 18- to 25-year-old men who are either students or nonacademic personnel at our university and affiliated hospitals.[16],[19],[22] This structured instrument gathers information on demography, alcohol and drug use histories, and associated problems, as well as the psychiatric histories for both subject and all first-degree relatives. From this sample, drinking young men who have an alcoholic father (sons of alcoholic mothers are excluded to avoid any fetal-alcohol effects) are identified as the family history positive (FHP) or high risk group. For each man, a family history negative (FHN) individual is chosen matched on demography and drinking history. The information gathered from the questionnaire is evaluated through a personal interview as well as by an analysis of relevant blood markers that might be elevated in the context of heavy drinking, such as gamma glutamyl transferase.[23]

In Phase 2, FHPs and FHNs are invited individually to the laboratory where they are tested. All subjects undergo a *baseline* evaluation of various personality attributes, physical condition, and some electrophysiological measures. The latter include background cortical electroencephalograms (EEGs) for determination of the amount of power in the slower wave forms, including alpha, as well as event-related potential (ERP) paradigms looking specifically at the latency and amplitude of the positive wave at 300 milliseconds after the stimulus (the P3). The specific methodologies for all of these baseline evaluations have been described in other papers.[4],[5],[16],[19],[20],[30]

The second attribute for evaluation in Phase 2 occurs through observations of body functioning and feelings *following challenges* with placebo, two different doses of ethanol (0.75 ml/kg and 1.1 ml/kg of ethanol mixed as a 20% by volume solution and consumed over a 7- to 10-minute period), or two different doses of diazepam (0.12 and 0.20 mg/kg of diazepam infused intravenously over 7 minutes).[31] In each of the test conditions, subjects are subsequently evaluated every 30 minutes for blood alcohol or drug levels, subjective feelings, drug- or ethanol-induced changes in hormones, changes in cognition and motor performance, and changes in some of the electrophysiological characteristics.

Phase 3 of the series of studies began in March of 1989. All 470 FHP and FHN subjects evaluated in the laboratory over the prior decade are now being followed up 8 to 12 years after their initial evaluation. Each individual will undergo a one-hour structured face-to-face interview determining the drug and alcohol use pattern since testing, any drug- and alcohol-related problems, as well as any psychiatric disorders occurring in the interim. Similar interviews are also being carried out with at least one additional informant (usually a spouse), and bloods and urines are gathered for evaluation of state markers of heavy drinking as well as of drug blood levels at the time of testing.[23]

The next section presents a brief overview of some of the results of Phase 1 and Phase 2. Information from Phase 3 will be available in approximately 5 years.

III. RESULTS OF STUDIES OF POPULATIONS AT HIGH RISK

The data generated from our laboratory over the past decade have been divided into baseline evaluations and the results of the alcohol and diazepam challenges. The former have demonstrated few impressive personality differences between FHPs and FHNs, as well as an overall high level of similarity between the two family history groups on most cognitive and psychomotor tests.[19],[29] These levels of baseline equivalence include relatively sophisticated measures such as the Category Test of the Halstead Reitan Test Battery as well as similarities at baseline in the levels of body sway or static ataxia.

One interesting series of results relating to differences at baseline focuses on electrophysiological measures. First, while some sets of subjects have demonstrated a trend for lower amplitudes of the P3 wave of the ERP in FHPs, no statistically significant differences between FHPs and FHNs on this measure have been observed.[13] This finding is distinct from those reported by some other laboratories,[1] but differences may reflect the test methods used as well as the relatively high level of cognitive functioning of the subjects typically tested by our group.

The two family history groups have shown some differences on a second electrophysiological measure in our work, the results of the background cortical EEGs. Recently we have carried out a series of studies in conjunction with the Scripps Clinic and Research Foundation. As described elsewhere, these evaluations have revealed less beta activity at baseline as well as evidence of fewer post-ethanol changes in EEG stability for FHP subjects.[4],[5]

The most consistent findings from our work are those generated from the repeated evaluations *following the ethanol challenges*. Despite identical average blood alcohol concentrations (BACs) for FHPs and FHNs following ethanol and even after controlling for any effects of placebo, the FHPs have consistently demonstrated less intense reactions to the alcohol. These have included the demonstration of less intense response in subjective feelings after drinking, less change in hormones known to be affected by alcohol, and less intense changes on two electrophysiological measures.

The first evidence of a decreased intensity of reaction to alcohol in the FHPs came from an evaluation of their self-reports of subjective feelings of intoxication using an analog-type scale.[16],[19] Asked to rate their feelings of "high," drug effect, sleepiness, and so on every half hour after consuming the beverage, as a group the FHPs demonstrated lower levels of alcohol effect throughout most of the experimental session. These results have been corroborated in most samples of young adult men and women evaluated in both the United States and elsewhere.[16],[19],[20]

The dampened effect of alcohol on motor performance was evaluated with repeated measures of the level of ethanol-induced increases in body sway.[19] Despite similarities on this measure at baseline and significant increases in sway after drinking for both family history groups, the FHPs have repeatedly been shown to have less post-ethanol increases in this measure, a finding consistent with their own self-reports of feelings of intoxication. Similar results have also been reported in women and in at least one additional laboratory.[9]

In order to avoid the possibility that conscious or subconscious expectations might lead the child of an alcoholic to feel that he or she should either behave differently or report different feelings, our group searched for more biological measures of intensity of response. We have focused on three hormones known to be likely to change with relevant doses of alcohol: prolactin, cortisol, and adrenocorticotropin hormone (ACTH). For all three hormones the FHPs as a group have been shown to demonstrate less change than the FHNs.[25],[26],[28]

Regarding alcohol, we have utilized both background cortical EEG and ERP paradigms in order to evaluate the family group differences on the intensity of electrophysiological changes following an alcohol challenge. As has been reported recently, once again the results point toward less intense response for the FHPs. First focusing on the latency of the P3 wave in the ERP paradigm, FHPs returned to baseline condition much more rapidly despite equivalent BACs for the two family history groups.[30] Regarding background cortical EEGs, the ability of ethanol to destabilize or unsynchronize the EEG was significantly less evident in the FHPs than the FHNs.[5]

Finally, in a separate study we have demonstrated that the decreased reaction to ethanol does not appear to be true for diazepam.[31] This lack of generalizability of the phenomenon to a benzodiazepine has been documented for post-drug effects on subject feelings, body sway, and hormones.

IV. DISCUSSION

This paper has described one way in which alcoholism can be viewed as a familial disorder. The introduction documents how alcoholism clusters within families with the result that close relatives of alcoholics have a fourfold increased risk for the disorder themselves. These data encouraged investigators to expand their efforts by applying the methods from family and twin studies to the alcoholism field. The latter indicate that the children of alcoholics are at fourfold increased risk for alcoholism, even when they have been adopted out and raised without knowledge of their biological parents' problems.

At the same time, the data have also consistently indicated that genetics explains only one part of the risk. It is likely that alcoholism is a multifactorial disorder where genetic factors interact with other familial and non-familial forces to result in the final appearance of the clinical syndrome that we label as alcohol abuse or dependence. This paper has focused mostly on the biological aspects, but the complex interaction of forces contributing to alcoholism must be recognized.

Based upon the genetic results, an active search is now underway attempting to identify those genetically controlled biological factors that might contribute to the alcoholism risk. This paper has presented one approach, efforts that focus on careful study of children of alcoholics before the alcoholism develops in an effort to identify factors that might contribute to the future risk. These young men and women are then followed over time in order to determine the relationship between their earlier life characteristics and the later development of alcohol-related life problems.

Used as an example of the type of work going into the familial nature of alcoholism as it relates to a genetic predisposition, studies emanating from our laboratory demonstrate just one of many possible approaches. Exciting work is also going on through evaluations of increasingly sophisticated ERP paradigms as applied to children of alcoholics, baseline cognitive and psychomotor functioning as it might relate to some samples of individuals at high risk for alcoholism, the possible relationship of enzyme types and activity levels as they relate to risk, and the relationship between personality characteristics and the future development of alcoholism. Space constraints do not allow for a presentation of the full picture of these interesting studies, each of them would in itself be suitable material for the types of information presented here.

Through a combination of this type of studies it is hoped that the identification of some of the components of a biological predisposition toward this familial disorder might have potentially important practical results. *First*, knowing more about those factors that place one at enhanced risk might help clinicians and scientists to develop more appropriate prevention strategies. *Second*, longitudinal evaluation of individuals who carry the biological predisposition as evidenced through the presence of a biological marker but who do not themselves later develop alcoholism could yield important clues to the social and environmental factors that might be manipulated in an attempt to minimize the risk. *Finally*, it is probable that not all alcoholics suffer from the same disorder but, rather, that there are important subgroups. These divergent populations might develop their alcohol-related life problems through different mechanisms; thus, studies of genetic factors in alcoholism might help identify unique subgroups with specific treatment needs. This, in turn, might markedly improve our ability to develop effective and efficient rehabilitation programs.

REFERENCES

(1) Begleiter H, Porjesz JB, Bihari B, et al.: Event-related brain potentials in boys at risk for alcoholism. *Science* 227:1493-1496 (1983).
(2) Cadoret RJ, Troughton ED, O'Gorman TW: Genetic and environmental factors in alcohol abuse and antisocial personality. *J Stud Alcohol* 48:1-8 (1987).
(3) Cotton NS: The familial incidence of alcoholism: A review. *J Stud Alcohol* 40:89-116 (1979).
(4) Ehlers CL, Schuckit, MA: EEG response to ethanol in sons of alcoholics. *Psychopharm Bull* 24:434-437 (1988).
(5) Ehlers CL, Schuckit, MA: Evaluation of EEG alpha activity in sons of alcoholics. *Am J Psychiatry*, in press (1989).
(6) Goodwin DW: Alcoholism and genetics. *Arch Gen Psychiatry* 42:171-174 (1985).
(7) Kaij L: *Studies on the Etiology and Sequels of Abuse of Alcohol.* Lund, Sweden: University of Lund, Department of Psychiatry (1960).
(8) Kaij L, Dock J: Grandsons of alcoholics. *Arch Gen Psychiatry* 32:1379-1381 (1975).
(9) Lex B, Lukas S, Greenwald N, et al.: Alcohol-induced changes in body sway in women at risk for alcoholism. *J Stud Alcohol* 49:346-356 (1988).
(10) Murray RM, Clifford C, Gurling HMD, et al.: Current genetic and biological approaches to alcoholism. *Psychiatr Dev* 2:179-192 (1983).
(11) Martin NG: Twin studies of alcohol consumption, metabolism and sensitivity. *Aust Drug Alc Rev* 7:9-12 (1988).
(12) Partanen J, Bruun K, Markkanen T: *Inheritance of Drinking Behavior: A Study on Intelligence, Personality, and Use of Alcohol of Adult Twins.* Helsinki, Finland: Finnish Foundation for Alcohol Studies (1966).
(13) Polich J, Bloom FE: Event-related brain potentials in individuals at high and low risk for developing alcoholism: Failure to replicate. *Alcohol Clin Exp Res* 12:368-373 (1988).
(14) Schuckit MA: Twin studies on substance abuse. In Gedda L, Parisi P, Nance W (eds), *Twin research 3: Epidemiological and Clinical Studies*, New York: Alan R. Liss, pp. 61-70 (1981).
(15) Schuckit MA: The clinical implications of primary diagnostic groups among alcoholics. *Arch Gen Psychiatry* 42:1043-1049 (1985).
(16) Schuckit MA: Genetics and the risk for alcoholism. *JAMA* 254:2614-2617 (1985).
(17) Schuckit MA: Overview: Epidemiology of alcoholism. In Schuckit MA (ed), *Alcohol Patterns and Problems*, p. 142. New Brunswick: Rutgers University Press (1985).
(18) Schuckit MA: Alcoholism and affective disorders: Genetic and clinical implications. *Am J Psychiatry* 143:140-147 (1986).
(19) Schuckit MA: Biological vulnerability to alcoholism. *J Couns Clin Psychol* 55:301-309 (1987).
(20) Schuckit MA, Gold E, Risch C: Serum prolactin levels in sons of alcoholics and control subjects. *Am J Psychiatry* 144:854-859 (1987).
(21) Schuckit MA: *Drug and Alcohol Abuse A Clinical Guide to Diagnosis and Treatment.* New York: Plenum Press (1989).

(22) Schuckit MA, Gold E: A simultaneous evaluation of multiple markers of ethanol/placebo challenges in sons of alcoholics and controls. *Arch Gen Psychiatry* 45:211-216 (1988).

(23) Schuckit MA, Irwin M: Diagnosis of alcoholism. *Medical Clinics of North America* 72:1133-1153 (1988).

(24) Schuckit MA, Monteiro MG: Alcoholism, anxiety and depression. *Br J Addict* 83:1373-1380 (1988).

(25) Schuckit MA, Gold E, Risch C: Serum prolactin levels in sons of alcoholics and control subjects. *Am J Psychiatry* 144:854-859 (1987).

(26) Schuckit MA, Gold E, Risch C: Plasma cortisol levels following ethanol in sons of alcoholics and controls. *Arch Gen Psychiatry* 44:942-945 (1987).

(27) Schuckit MA, Goodwin DA, Winokur GA: A study of alcoholism in half siblings. *Am J Psychiatry* 128:1132-1136 (1972).

(28) Schuckit MA, Risch SC, Gold E: Alcohol Consumption, ACTH level, and family history of alcoholism. *Am J Psychiatry* 145:1391-1395 (1988).

(29) Schuckit MA, Butters N, Lyn L, et al.: Neuropsychologic deficits and the risk for alcoholism. *Neuropsychopharm* 1:45-53 (1987).

(30) Schuckit MA, Gold E, Croot K, et al.: P300 latency after ethanol ingestion in sons of alcoholics and in controls. *Biol Psychiatry* 24:310-315 (1988).

(31) Schuckit MA, Hauger RL, Monteiro MG, et al.: Response of 3 hormones to diazepam challenge in sons of alcoholics and controls. *Alcholism; Clinical and Experiented Research* (in press).

2

CNV of Substance Use Patients with Alcoholic Father

Michihiko Nakamura, M.D.
Kyoko Nishihara, M.D.
Kiyoshi Nagano, M.D.
Satoru Saitoh, M.D.

We recorded the CNVs from 12 patients with Substance Use Disorder under a sequence of 5 recording conditions including the conventional CNV paradigms with and without motor response. The patients were divided into two groups according to their family history. The patients with alcoholic fathers (FHP) were more depressive and hypersensitive at the CNV recording day than those without alcoholic fathers (FHN). The reaction time under the two response conditions was significantly shorter for the FHP patients than that for the FHN group. The CNV magnitude reduced under the second response condition for the FHP group. These findings suggest that the substance use patients with alcoholic fathers may reduce arousal level through repetition of a simple task to bring on depression in emotion and then motivation. We speculate that an arousal reduction with behavioral automatization may be influenced by some genetic factors.

I. INTRODUCTION

The event-related potentials (ERPs) such as a P300 have been applied to children at risk for developing alcoholism. The ERP studies were provoked by the facts obtained from many investigations on alcoholic families, including the studies on twins and adopted children.[4] Begleiter et al.[2] observed the reduced amplitude of P300 in the high-risk sons as compared with those without alcoholic parents. Thereafter, Polich and his colleagues[9],[10],[11],[12] intensively investigated the genetic effects on auditory and visual P300s of individuals with and without alcoholic parents. However, they could not confirm those effects reported by Begleiter. On the other hand, Elmasian et al.[3] reported the diminished P300 after ingestion of alcoholic beverages in subjects with alcoholic families. However, Polich and Bloom[13] failed to confirm the results of Elmasian by using placebo beverages instead of alcohol. Schuckit[14] reported through the investigation of alcoholic influences on P300 that the individuals with alcoholic fathers showed faster recovery of P300 latency after intake of a high dose of alcohol.

The CNV, which was discovered by Walter et al.,[17] develops during a fixed foreperiod reaction time task using two separate stimuli and a motor response for the second stimulus. The CNV is interpreted in the psychological terms such as expectancy, motivation, attention/arousal,[16] but we have paid much attention to a dynamic aspect of the CNV since 1975.[5] Then we[6],[8] have studied recovery of CNV magnitude after deprivation of a motor response in anorexic and depressive patients as well as normals. Changes of the CNV magnitude after the motor deprivation were divided into two patterns, excessive and inadequate recoveries. The pattern of excessive recovery was associated with the endogenomorphic type of depression and the bulimic type of anorexia nervosa, while another pattern related no with the opposite types, namely, neurotic and restricting, respectively. Furthermore, we[7] observed an inverted-U relation between the CNV magnitude and the extroversion score of Maudsley Personality Inventory (MPI) for normals and we also found a shift of the inverted-U relation toward the introversive side after the motor deprivation.

These findings suggest that the excessive recovery of the CNV may indicate a hyperarousal state on the basis of Eysenck's thesis that an introvert has cortically hyperarousal level as compared with an extrovert. Thus, we applied the CNV recovery test to the psychoactive substance use patients in order to reveal the difference in the learning pattern of the CNV between the patients with and without alcoholic parents and in order to investigate the genetic influences on arousal state of the second generation.

II. SUBJECTS AND METHOD

1. Subjects

Twelve naive patients, ranging in age from 16 to 48 years old, participated in this study under control of informed consent. Their dependent substances were organic solvents such as paint thinner (7 patients), brom (1 patient), amphetamines (5 patients) and alcohol (1 patient), as shown in Table 1. Their clinical diagnoses were Alcohol Dependence (303.90), Amphetamine Delusional Disorder (292.11), Inhalant Dependence (304.60),

TABLE 1.
Patient Profiles

Case	Sex	Age	DSM-III-R	Diagnosis	Duration (years)	Alcoholic Father
1	M	28	304.90	Polysubstance Dependence	>2	no
2	M	28	304.90	Polysubstance Dependence	>2	no
3	M	23	304.60	Inhalant Dependence	>2	yes
4	M	21	304.60	Inhalant Dependence	8	yes
5	M	21	304.60	Inhalant Dependence	6	no
6	M	27	304.60	Inhalant Dependence	7	no
7	M	37	292.11	Amphetamine Delusional Disorder	20	yes
8	M	16	304.60	Inhalant Dependence	2	no
9	M	18	304.60	Inhalant Dependence	>2	no
*10	M	31	304.60	Inhalant Dependence	15	yes
11	M	28	292.11	Amphetamine Delusional Disorder		
			304.40	Amphetamine Dependence	7	yes
12	F	29	303.90	Alcohol Dependence	8	no
13	M	48	292.11	Amphetamine Delusional Disorder	>10	?

*Failure of the CNV recording due to GSR contamination

Polysubstance Dependence (304.90) according to DSM-III-R.[1] The duration of dependence was at least 2 years or more and its longest duration was 20 years. The mental states at the recording day were estimated by State-Trait Anxiety Inventory (STAI), Maudsley Personality Inventory (MPI), Cornell Medical Index (CMI) and a brief interview by one psychiatrist (M.N.). All patients were estimated to have right-handedness by using 7 different inventories.

The patients were divided into two groups according to their family history. Four patients had alcoholic fathers and one had an elderly brother with amphetamine dependence in addition to his alcoholic father. These 5 patients were gathered as a family history positive (FHP) group. The other patients had families with neither alcoholism nor other mental disorder, so that they were grouped as a family history negative (FHN). One patient (case #13) could not be classified according to family history because of unreliable information due to early death of his parents.

2. CNV Recording

The EEGs were recorded with a time constant of 5 sec from six scalp sites of Fz, Cz, Pz, Oz, C3, and C4 by reference to the linked earlobes according the international 10-20 electrode placement system. The conventional CNV paradigm was used: namely, a warning stimulus (S1) was 1 KHz tone-pip of 100 msec duration and an imperative stimulus (S2) was 2 KHz tone which followed 2 sec after S1. The CNVs were obtained in a sequence of 5 experimental conditions of Stimuli, Control response, Nonresponse, Recovery response and Discrimination. A button pressing was required immediately after S2 as soon as possible under the Control and Recovery response conditions, whereas no button pressing was asked for under the conditions of Stimuli and Nonresponse. Under the Discrimination condition, the patient was asked to count mentally the occurrence of S2 with a long duration of 1500 msec but to ignore the S2 with a short duration of 200 msec. Each condition consisted of 2 blocks, and 20 trials per block were presented at an irregular interval over 10 sec. The EEGs were converted into digital data at a sampling interval of 5 msec and were stored on a hard disk of a minicomputer (VAX 11/750) in addition to an FM tape . The artifact-free trials were selected automatically according to programmed criteria for artifact rejection and were averaged every condition per subject by using a minicomputer.

3. Measurement and Statistics

The mean CNV magnitude was measured segmentally every 100 msec from S1 to 1 sec after S2. The segmental CNV amplitude does not only enable us to estimate the magnitude, but also to evaluate the waveform. The reaction time was measured as a delay time from S2 onset to a button pressing under both the response conditions. Since this report concerns the learning pattern of the CNV, the CNVs under two response conditions were mainly analyzed. The EEG data of one patient (case #10) were missed because of remarkable contamination of GSR. The two-way analysis of variance (ANOVA) was used for a statistical treatment.

III. RESULTS

1. Psychological Tests

There were no remarkable differences in age, duration of dependence, and clinical diagnosis between the FHPs and the FHNs, but the duration of dependence tended to be longer for the FHPs than for the FHNs. The STAI and the MPI also showed no significant difference between the FHPs and the FHNs, though both the patients showed increased scores on trait-anxiety and neurotic tendency of MPI, as shown in Table 2.

As a whole, the patients showed relatively high scores on the following

TABLE 2.
Comparison of Psychological Tests between FHP and FHN Patients

	With Alcoholic Father (FHP)	Without Alcoholic Father (FHN)	Statistical significance
STAI I pretest	39.0± 4.3	36.3± 4.3	n.s.
I posttest	38.4± 4.3	39.1± 8.0	n.s.
II	48.6± 9.3	49.7± 6.7	n.s.
MPI E	21.6±13.2	27.3±11.7	n.s.
N	33.2± 8.7	33.3± 7.5	n.s.
L	7.6± 2.6	7.3± 5.6	n.s.
CMI Past Hx	2.8± 1.5	1.0± 0.6	P = 0.0239
Depressive	3.0± 2.1	0.2± 0.4	P = 0.0322
Hypersensitive	4.6± 1.1	2.3± 1.6	P = 0.0283

TABLE 3.
Comparison of Reaction Time (msec) between FHP and FHN Patients

Response Condition	With Alcoholic Father (FHP)	Without Alcoholic Father (FHN)	Total
Control	205.0±47.8	243.7±59.5	229.6±58.3
Recovery	194.9±39.2	249.2±73.8	229.4±68.4
Total	199.9±43.5*	246.4±66.7*	229.5±63.3

*Bonferroni t = 4.303, df = 128, P = 0.00003

items of the CMI: fatigue (2.583, 36.9%), frequency of illness (2.917, 32.4%) and skin (2.917, 32.4%), hypersensitivity (3.417, 57.0%), aggression (4.583, 50.9%), and maladaptation (4.750, 39.6%). The psychic complaints of the CMI revealed statistically significant correlations between depression and tension (r = 0.576, t = 2.229, df = 10, 0.0499) or hypersensitivity (r = 0.667, df = 2.834, df = 10, P = 0.0177), and between tension and hypersensitivity (r = 0.879, t = 5.833, df = 10, P = 0.0002). Furthermore, the FHPs had significantly higher scores on past history (t = 2.714, df = 9, P = 0.0478), depression (Welch t = 2.942, df = 5.31, P = 0.0322), and hypersensitivity (t = 2.609, df = 9, P = 0.0566) than the FHNs had.

2. Behavioral Findings

The mean reaction time did not reduce at the Recovery response condition as compared with that at the Control response condition , but the FHP patients showed significantly shorter reaction time under both the response conditions than the FHNs (Table 3). The two-way ANOVA using condition

(Control and Recovery response conditions) vs genetic influence (with and without alcoholic father) showed the significant difference in genetic influence (F = 18.520, df1 = 1, df2 = 128, P = 0.00003) but neither in condition (F = 0.000) nor in interaction (F = 0.516).

3. CNV Findings

Two-way ANOVA using recording site (Fz, Cz, Pz, Oz, C3 and C4) vs genetic influence for each segmental CNV amplitude was performed under each response condition, as shown in Table 4. The significant differences were as follows: under the Control response condition, the genetic influence was observed in only one segment of 400-500 msec, but site effect was found in the segments 0-200 msec, 500-700 msec and 2100-2300 msec; under the Recovery response condition, the genetic influence appeared in the segments of 0-400 msec, 600-1400 msec, 1800-1900 msec, 2300-2500 msec, 2900-3000 msec and 3100-3300 msec, and the site effect occurred in the segments of 0-200 msec and 2100-2300 msec. The segments of 0-400 msec and 2000-2400 msec included the evoked potentials in response to S1 and S2, respectively, so that the parietal CNV segments of 200-400 msec and 2200-2400 msec, comparably to the P300, were analyzed by two-way ANOVA using condition vs genetic influence. The segments of 200-300 msec and 2200-2400 msec did not reach a significant level but the segment of 300-400 msec showed a statistical significance for genetic influence (F = 4.606, df1 = 1, df2 = 18, P = 0.04574) and the FHPs had more positive amplitude (1.054 + 2.901 μV) than the FHNs had (− 1.284 + 2.020 μV).

Figure 1 shows the changes of the segmental CNV amplitude between the Control and Recovery response conditions for the FHPs and for the FHNs. The FHN group did not show any difference in segmental CNV amplitude between two response conditions at all recording sites (Fig. 1A), but the FHP group significantly reduced the segmental CNV amplitude under the Recovery response condition, especially at Cz and Oz. Table 5 (p.21) indicates the results of two-way ANOVA of difference in the segmental CNV amplitude between the Control response condition and the Recovery response condition. The significant differences were as follows: genetic influence was observed in the segments of 0-200 msec, 500 − 1500 msec, 1600 − 2100 msec, 2200 − 2600 msec, 2700 msec and 2900 − 3200 msec, but neither the site effect nor the interaction effect appeared in any segment.

IV. DISCUSSION

The present results are briefly summarized here. The results of the psychological tests showed that the patients with alcoholic fathers (FHP) might

TABLE 4.

Two-Way ANOVA of Segmental CNV Amplitude under Response Condition

Segment after S1 (msec)	Control Site F	P	Response Condition Genetic F	P	Interact F	P	Recovery Site F	P	Response Condition Genetic F	P	Interact F	P
<S1>												
− 100	2.61	0.03	—	—	—	—	4.27	0.00	7.11	0.01	—	—
− 200	8.41	0.00	—	—	—	—	7.53	0.00	12.27	0.00	—	—
− 300	—	—	—	—	—	—	—	—	5.77	0.02	—	—
− 400	—	—	8.29	0.01	—	—	—	—	5.85	0.02	—	—
− 500	—	—	—	—	—	—	—	—	—	—	—	—
− 600	3.50	0.01	—	—	—	—	—	—	—	—	—	—
− 700	2.94	0.02	—	—	—	—	—	—	7.63	0.01	—	—
− 800	—	—	—	—	—	—	—	—	8.45	0.01	—	—
− 900	—	—	—	—	—	—	—	—	10.44	0.00	—	—
−1000	—	—	—	—	—	—	—	—	10.18	0.00	—	—
−1100	—	—	—	—	—	—	—	—	5.88	0.02	—	—
−1200	—	—	—	—	—	—	—	—	9.55	0.00	—	—
−1300	—	—	—	—	—	—	—	—	4.90	0.03	—	—
−1400	—	—	—	—	—	—	—	—	4.59	0.04	—	—
−1500	—	—	—	—	—	—	—	—	—	—	—	—
−1600	—	—	—	—	—	—	—	—	—	—	—	—
−1700	—	—	—	—	—	—	—	—	—	—	—	—
−1800	—	—	—	—	—	—	—	—	—	—	—	—
−1900	—	—	—	—	—	—	—	—	4.83	0.03	—	—
−2000	—	—	—	—	—	—	—	—	—	—	—	—
<S2>												
−2100	—	—	—	—	—	—	—	—	—	—	—	—
−2200	2.81	0.03	—	—	—	—	2.64	0.03	—	—	—	—
−2300	3.17	0.01	—	—	—	—	2.62	0.03	—	—	—	—
−2400	—	—	—	—	—	—	—	—	5.24	0.03	—	—
−2500	—	—	—	—	—	—	—	—	5.26	0.03	—	—
−2600	—	—	—	—	—	—	—	—	—	—	—	—
−2700	—	—	—	—	—	—	—	—	—	—	—	—
−2800	—	—	—	—	—	—	—	—	—	—	—	—
−2900	—	—	—	—	—	—	—	—	—	—	—	—
−3000	—	—	—	—	—	—	—	—	5.09	0.03	—	—
−3100	—	—	—	—	—	—	—	—	—	—	—	—
−3200	—	—	—	—	—	—	—	—	5.37	0.03	—	—
−3300	—	—	—	—	—	—	—	—	4.36	0.05	—	—
−3400	—	—	—	—	—	—	—	—	—	—	—	—
−3500	—	—	—	—	—	—	—	—	—	—	—	—

Note:

−: not significant

df: df1 = 5, df2 = 54 for Site and Interact; df1 = 1, df2 = 54 for Genetic.

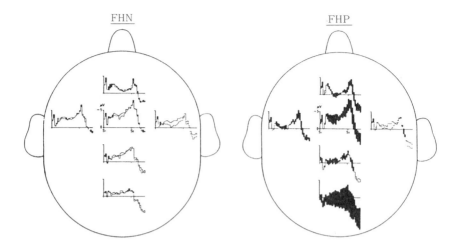

Figure 1.   Mean Segmental CNV Amplitudes under Control and Recovery Response Conditions in FHP and FHN Patients.

The FHN patients did not show any significant difference in the segmental CNV amplitude between the Control and Recovery response conditions at all recording sites, while the FHP patients significantly reduced the segmental CNV amplitudes under the Recovery condition, especially at Cz and Oz, as compared with those at the Control condition.

be more depressive and hypersensitive than those without alcoholic fathers (FHN). However, FHP and FHN patients did not differ in other clinical findings from each other, though the FHP group tended to be longer in duration of dependence than the FHN group. The parietal segment of 200 – 300 msec including P300 was larger for the FHPs than that for the FHNs. The FHP group responded to S2 faster than the FHN group, but both the groups were not different in reaction time between the two response conditions. On the other hand, the FHP group had rather higher CNV magnitude under the control response condition than the FHN group had, but the FHP group showed dissociation between the behavioral performance and the brain slow potential under the Recovery response condition, resulting in much smaller segmental CNV amplitudes than those of the FHN group.

Effects of psychoactive substances on the CNV are summarized in Shagass's review.[15] Generally speaking, the CNV decreases with alcohol and sedatives or depressants while the CNV increases with excitants and antidepressants. However, these effects are sometimes bidirectional, suggesting that the psychological properties of the subject may have an important role in developing the CNV.

TABLE 5.
Two-way ANOVA of Amplitude Difference between Control
and Recovery Response Conditions

Segment after S1 (msec)	Site (df1 = 5, df2 = 51)		Genetic (df1 = 1, df2 = 51)		Interact (df1 = 5, df2 = 51)	
	F	P	F	P	F	P
<S1>						
− 100	—	—	8.00	0.01	—	—
− 200	—	—	4.96	0.04	—	—
− 300	—	—	—	—	—	—
− 400	—	—	—	—	—	—
− 500	—	—	—	—	—	—
− 600	—	—	5.51	0.03	—	—
− 700	—	—	5.63	0.03	—	—
− 800	—	—	12.44	0.00	—	—
− 900	—	—	7.60	0.01	—	—
− 1000	—	—	12.93	0.00	—	—
− 1100	—	—	6.21	0.02	—	—
− 1200	—	—	18.19	0.00	—	—
− 1300	—	—	8.28	0.01	—	—
− 1400	—	—	4.46	0.04	—	—
− 1500	—	—	6.03	0.02	—	—
− 1600	—	—	—	—	—	—
− 1700	—	—	8.66	0.01	—	—
− 1800	—	—	5.55	0.03	—	—
− 1900	—	—	5.88	0.02	—	—
− 2000	—	—	7.54	0.01	—	—
<S2>						
− 2100	—	—	11.71	0.01	—	—
− 2200	—	—	—	—	—	—
− 2300	—	—	13.37	0.00	—	—
− 2400	—	—	14.94	0.00	—	—
− 2500	—	—	10.91	0.01	—	—
− 2600	—	—	5.86	0.02	—	—
− 2700	—	—	—	—	—	—
− 2800	—	—	6.17	0.02	—	—
− 2900	—	—	—	—	—	—
− 3000	—	—	4.57	0.04	—	—
− 3100	—	—	4.37	0.05	—	—
− 3200	—	—	7.19	0.01	—	—
− 3300	—	—	—	—	—	—
− 3400	—	—	—	—	—	—
− 3500	—	—	—	—	—	—

It is difficult to conclude whether the present results obtained from the relatively small number of patients reflect direct effects of psychoactive substance on the central nervous system or not, but we would point out several interesting findings . The first is that the segment including a parietal P300 after S1 reduced in amplitude for the FHNs. The previous reports, as mentioned in this introduction, concerns with the "normal" individuals at high risk for alcoholism. Then we cannot simply compare our results with theirs but we can point out some possibility that the genetic factors influence on the development of P300. The second, the results of the CNV recovery pattern and reaction time, as described in our previous paper,[7] suggest that the FHP patients are apt to show too faster habituation or automatization, resulting in a downward shift of arousal level and then probably in depression of mood. The third, the recovery pattern of the FHPs resembled the patients with the non-endogenomorphic or "neurotic" depression[8] and those with the restricting or "hysterical" type of anorexia nervosa.[6] This suggests that the style of addiction in the FHPs may be different from that in the bulimia nervosa. On the other hand, the FHN patients maintained the same level of the CNV magnitude after the Nonresponse condition and this stable pattern was common in the normal adults as reported in the previous paper.[5],[7] The pattern of inadequate CNV recovery observed in the FHP patients is likely to be influenced by some genetic factors though we could not reveal the clinical manifestations except depression and hypersensitivity. Thus, we can conclude that there are at least two different types of substance use patients, one has normal pattern of the CNV recovery without alcoholic family history while the other shows depression of arousal and mood in the family history.

REFERENCES

(1) American Psychiatric Association: *Diagnostic and Statistical Manual of Mental Disorders. 3rd Edition-Revised.* Washington, D.C.: American Psychiatric Association, p. 567 (1987).
(2) Begleiter H, Porjesz B, Bihari B, et al.: Event-related brain potentials in boys at risk for alcoholism. *Science*, 225: 1493-1496 (1984).
(3) Elmasian R, Neville H, Woods D, et al.: Event-related brain potentials are different in individuals at high and low risk for developing alcoholism. *Proc Natl Acad Sci USA*, 79: 7900-7903 (1982).
(4) Goodwin DW: *Alcoholism. The Facts.* New York: Oxford Univ Press (1981).
(5) Nakamura M, Fukui Y, Kadobayashi I, et al.: Effects of motor-response-deprivation on contingent negative variation (CNV). I: Normal adult data. *Folia Psychiat Neurol Jpn*, 29: 321-328 (1975).
(6) Nakamura M: A behavior neurophysiological study of anorexia nervosa. *J Kyoto Pref Univ Med*, 88: 1033-1043 (1979).

(7) Nakamura M, Iida H, Takahashi S, et al.: Recovery of CNV area after non-response condition: inverted-U relation with arousal. *Folia Psychiat Neurol Jpn*, 35: 159-165 (1981).

(8) Nakamura M, Iida H, Fukui Y, et al.: Melancholia and excessive CNV recovery after nonresponse condition. *Folia Psychiat Neurol Jpn*, 36: 81-88 (1982).

(9) Polich J, Bloom FE: P300 and alcohol consumption in normals and individuals at risk for alcoholism. A preliminary report. *Prog Neuro-Psychopharmacol Biol Psychiat*, 10: 201-210 (1986).

(10) Polich J, Bloom FE: P300 from normals and adult children of alcoholics. *Alcohol* 4: 301-305 (1987).

(11) Polich J, Burns T, Bloom FE: P300 and the risk for alcoholism: family history, task difficulty, and gender. *Alcoholism: Clin Exp Res*, 12: 24B-254 (1988a).

(12) Polich J, Haier R, Buchsbaum M, et al.: Assessment of young men at risk for alcoholism with P300 from a visual discrimination task. *J Study Alcohol*, 49: 186-190 (1988b).

(13) Polich J, Bloom FE: Event-related brain potentials in individuals at high and low risk for developing alcoholism: failure to replicate. *Alcoholism Clin Exp Res*, 12: 368-373 (1988c).

(14) Schuckit MA, Gold EO, Croot K, et al.: P300 latency after ethanol ingestion in sons of alcoholics and in controls. *Biol Psychiatry*, 24: 310-315 (1988).

(15) Shagass C: Contingent negative variation and other slow potentials in adult psychiatry. In Hughes JR, Wilson WP (eds), *EEG and Evoked Potentials in Psychiatry and Behavioral Neurology*, pp. 149-167. Stoneham, MA: Butterworth (1983).

(16) Tecce JJ: Contingent negative variation (CNV) and psychological processes in man. *Psychol Bull*, 77: 73-108 (1972).

(17) Walter WG, Cooper R, Aldridge VJ, et al.: Contingent negative variation: an electric sign of sensori-motor association and expectancy. *Nature* (London), 203: 380-384 (1964).

3

Drinking Behavior and Lifestyles in Twins

Akio Asaka, M.D.

Although alcohol dependence may be influenced by genetic factors, psychosocial factors also play a significant role in its development. The present study clarifies the effects of the psychosocial and environmental factors that contribute to alcoholism. The study includes: (1) a case study on twin patients; (2) genetic and/or environmental analysis on twins' drinking behaviors; and (3) an analysis of twins' lifestyles, focusing on drinking behavior. It is suggested that positive adjustment of the milieu surrounding the patient is essential and effective for both the treatment and prevention of alcohol dependence.

I. INTRODUCTION

Drinking behavior, including alcohol dependence, is, of course, influenced by biological and/or psychosocial factors. Thus, it is not beyond comprehension that alcohol dependence can be said to be a biopsychosocial disorder. This article deals with genetic and/or psychosocial aspects of drinking behaviors in order to clarify the cause of alcohol dependence and to get some hints for its treatment.

This paper comprises three parts:

(A) A case study
(B) Analysis of genetic and psychosocial factors on drinking behaviors
(C) Lifestyle and health status in twins

II. PART A: A CASE STUDY
Five Pairs of Twins with Alcohol Dependence

Subjects and Methods

Subjects were obtained through an initial and a second survey, and then a final investigation.

The initial survey:

This was commenced in 1983 by a postal questionnaire, distributed to psychiatric hospitals and/or clinics within Japan known to have 100 or more beds. The aim was to locate and register twin patients who had been diagnosed as having various types of mental disorders. There were at that time 1,316 hospitals throughout Japan, with a total of 272,720 beds. This brief questionnaire was sent to each, asking if they had twin patients as either in- or outpatients. Eight-hundred and twelve hospitals replied to the questionnaire (61.7%). Of these, 113 informed us that they had such cases and agreed to cooperate with our survey.

The second survey:

The next step was to contact the above 113 hospitals by telephone, to get more information concerning the number of twins and tentative diagnoses and/or zygosity. The results obtained showed that within 14 hospitals there were 15 pairs of twins, of which at least one suffered from alcohol dependence; a further 99 hospitals indicated 112 cases of twins with other mental disorders.

The final investigation:

Five twins were finally selected from among a short list of 15 pairs. The final investigation consisted of personal interviews, zygosity diagnosis and referencing medical records. Zygosity diagnosis consisted of examining genetic markers such as ABO blood groups, MN blood groups, ear wax, MDH (mid-digital-hair) and fingerprints. They were also requested to answer the KAST (Kurihama Alcoholism Screening Test, see Table A and Appendix 1). ALDH2 activity was also examined via hair roots. Brief summaries of five twin cases are described in the text, including family history, past history, and present illness. The diagnosis was ascertained by ICD-9, DSM-III, and the criteria of alcohol dependence made by the Committee of Ministry of Health and Welfare.

TABLE A-1.

A Part of Questionnaire concerning "Sensitivity of Alcohol" (TAST) in F, "Motivation of Drinking" in G and "Problem Drinking Behaviors" (KAST) in H.

Survey on Pattern of Alcohol Consumption and Its Relation to Alcohol Sensitivity

A) Are you male or female?

B) How old are you? _____ years old.

C) May I have your height _____ and weight _____ ?

D) Not counting small tastes, how old were you when you started drinking alcoholic beverages? _____ years old.

E)-1 How often do you have alcoholic beverages?
        1. Nearly every day
        2. 1-4 times a week
        3. 1-3 times a month
        4. 1-11 times a year
        5. Have never drunk alcohol

 -2 When you drink alcoholic beverages, how much do you have?
        Beer   _____ Bottles (Large Bottles)
        Wine   _____ Glasses
        Liquor _____ Glasses
        others _____

F) When you drink an alcoholic beverage, do you experience

	Always	Sometimes	Never
1. Facial flushing	3	2	1
2. Flushing elsewhere on the body	3	2	1
3. Itchiness	3	2	1
4. Dizziness	3	2	1
5. Drowsiness	3	2	1
6. Anxiety	3	2	1
7. Headaches	3	2	1
8. Pounding in the head	3	2	1
9. Sweating	3	2	1
10. Palpitations	3	2	1
11. Nausea	3	2	1
12. Cold and shivery	3	2	1
13. Dypsnea (difficulty breathing)	3	2	1

G) People drink for many different reasons. Please answer how important it is for you to drink with respect to the following reasons.

	Very important reason	Somewhat important reason	Not an important reason
1. Drinking is good for celebration.	3	2	1
2. I drink because there is not anything else to do.	3	2	1
3. Drinking is a part of good diet.	3	2	1
4. I like the feeling of getting high or drunk.	3	2	1
5. It is what most of my friends do when			

we get together.	3	2	1
6. Drinking helps me to forget about my worries and problems.	3	2	1
7. Drinking gives me more confidence.	3	2	1
8. I drink when I feel tense and nervous.	3	2	1
9. I drink to be sociable.	3	2	1
10. I drink because I like the taste of alcoholic beverages.	3	2	1

H) Have you ever had the following experiences?

	Yes	No
1. My drinking has impaired an important relationship	2	1
2. Impossible to resolve 'I won't drink today'	2	1
3. I've been called 'a drunkard'	2	1
4. I've drunk myself into a stupor	2	1
5. Amnesia ('blackout') about the previous evening's events	2	1
6. On my days off I start drinking during the morning	2	1
7. I've missed important appointments because of a hangover	2	1
8. I've been treated for diabetes, liver or heart trouble	2	1
9. I've experienced sweating, tremors, insomnia or frustration when without alcohol	2	1
10. Drinking is necessary during my work	2	1
11. Unable to get to sleep without alcohol	2	1
12. Usually drink over 3 GO of sake during evening meal	2	1
13. I've been detained by the police because of my drinking	2	1
14. I get angry when I'm drunk	2	1

Results and Discussion

At the second survey stage, with regard to alcohol dependence, it was noted that the concordance rate among MZ was 0.77 (probandwise) and 0.67 (pairwise) respectively.

The case studies of the final five pairs are as follows:

Twins #1: 45-year-old males (Figure A-2)

Born as the 4th and 5th sibs of 7 siblings. Birth weight was nearly 2000 gr for both Mr. A (the firstborn) and Mr. B (second born), although Mr. A weighed slightly more than Mr. B, who was seen to have neonatal asphyxia.

They were born in S City in Hokkaido. Their older brother had died young, so they were raised somewhat protectively by their parents. Following graduation from the same department of the same university, Mr. A held several jobs in different companies related to finance. Mr. B entered an insurance company, moving between several of their branch offices around Hokkaido. Both married at the same time and at the same age, 29. Mr. A divorced at 33, Mr. B at 31. Mr. A stopped working at 35, and Mr. B at 30, and neither

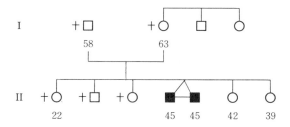

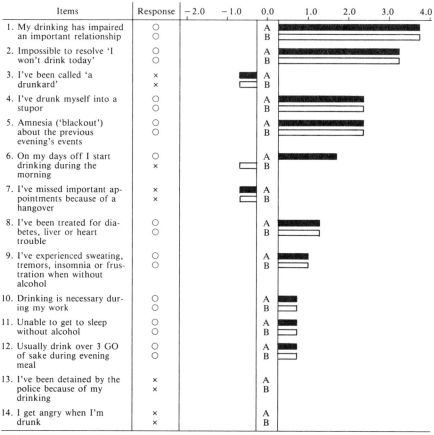

Items	Response	−2.0	−1.0	0.0	1.0	2.0	3.0	4.0

1. My drinking has impaired an important relationship — ○ A, ○ B
2. Impossible to resolve 'I won't drink today' — ○ A, ○ B
3. I've been called 'a drunkard' — × A, × B
4. I've drunk myself into a stupor — ○ A, ○ B
5. Amnesia ('blackout') about the previous evening's events — ○ A, ○ B
6. On my days off I start drinking during the morning — ○ A, × B
7. I've missed important appointments because of a hangover — × A, × B
8. I've been treated for diabetes, liver or heart trouble — ○ A, ○ B
9. I've experienced sweating, tremors, insomnia or frustration when without alcohol — ○ A, ○ B
10. Drinking is necessary during my work — ○ A, ○ B
11. Unable to get to sleep without alcohol — ○ A, ○ B
12. Usually drink over 3 GO of sake during evening meal — ○ A, ○ B
13. I've been detained by the police because of my drinking — × A, × B
14. I get angry when I'm drunk — × A, × B

Total   Mr. A: 15.6   Probability   Mr. A: Severe problem-drinker
         Mr. B: 13.5   Mr. B: Severe problem-drinker

Figure A-1.   Pedigree and KAST scores of Twin Case 1.

held further employment after that time.

Both were very close to each other throughout childhood and into adulthood. They stated they often felt insecure when apart and that if one was sick or psychologically depressed, the other used to exhibit the same symptoms.

Both Mr. A and Mr. B started drinking at the age of 18, during various club activities at the university. Mr. A got a part-time job at a beer garden, allowing him more opportunity to drink. When Mr. A was 33 years old, his mother suffered an apoplexy, and he had to look after her and support her in her work. He was extremely anxious, psychologically stressed, and complained of insomnia. He began drinking heavily, even in the morning. His mother died the following year, which caused him to drink even more severely. He was admitted to a psychiatric hospital for the first time at the age of 34, and had six further repeat admissions.

Meanwhile, Mr. B had been transferred to several branch offices around Hokkaido by his company. The frequent loneliness meant that he drank compulsively. At 30 he received treatment for liver dysfunction as an outpatient, but because he didn't curb his drinking he was then admitted to a university school's department of neuropsychiatry. He divorced at that time, and was later readmitted three more times to this department.

Both Mr. A and Mr. B showed they were ALDH2 nondeficient. The KAST scores were 15.6 and 13.5 respectively. Both were classified as severe problem drinkers. Zygosity diagnosis indicated the possibility of being MZ: $Pr(M) > 0.9795$.

Twins #2: 65-year-old females (Figure A-3)

Born as the 4th and 5th of 8 siblings. Their father was a heavy drinker. Their next older sister was burnt to death in infancy in an accident caused by their drunken father. Their uncle was also a severe problem drinker who was killed by a friend during a drunken brawl. Ms. A's husband and the husband of Ms. A's daughter were also problem drinkers.

They were born and brought up in a rich farming family until they were eight. At that time their father was cheated out of his farm and lands by a friend. They were forced to leave their junior high school and also had to start work as servants in many different places. Ms. A returned home at 21 and at age 23 she married a fisherman who had very little economic security and who was a problem drinker. At age 28, she had a daughter. From age 30 to 45, she returned to work as a maid in K's restaurant and then had several different part-time jobs. Her husband then had a gastrectomy, so she was forced to remain at home to care for him.

Ms. B returned home at age 23, shortly after commencing work at T's restaurant as a maid. She started cohabiting with a man at the age of 27,

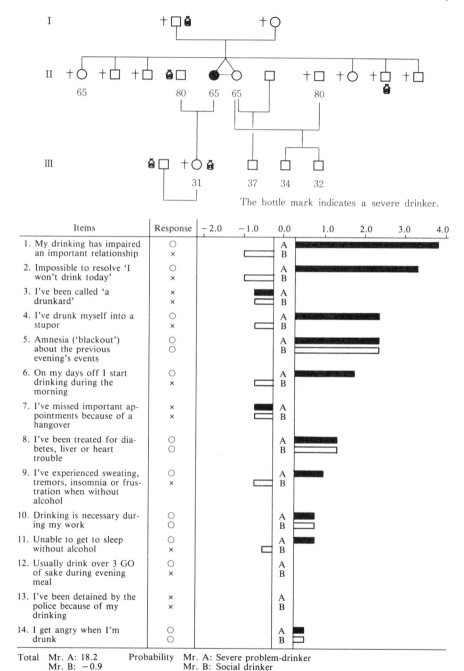

The bottle mark indicates a severe drinker.

Items	Response		A/B	Score
1. My drinking has impaired an important relationship	○ ×		A B	
2. Impossible to resolve 'I won't drink today'	○ ×		A B	
3. I've been called 'a drunkard'	× ×		A B	
4. I've drunk myself into a stupor	○ ×		A B	
5. Amnesia ('blackout') about the previous evening's events	○ ○		A B	
6. On my days off I start drinking during the morning	○ ×		A B	
7. I've missed important appointments because of a hangover	× ×		A B	
8. I've been treated for diabetes, liver or heart trouble	○ ○		A B	
9. I've experienced sweating, tremors, insomnia or frustration when without alcohol	○ ×		A B	
10. Drinking is necessary during my work	○ ○		A B	
11. Unable to get to sleep without alcohol	○ ×		A B	
12. Usually drink over 3 GO of sake during evening meal	○ ×		A B	
13. I've been detained by the police because of my drinking	× ×		A B	
14. I get angry when I'm drunk	○ ○		A B	

Total   Mr. A: 18.2   Probability   Mr. A: Severe problem-drinker
          Mr. B: −0.9   Mr. B: Social drinker

Figure A-2. Pedigree and KAST scores of Twin Case 2.

and had a child by him. They married and then divorced when she was 30, and she looked after the child. She married again at 31 and her new husband knew Ms. A's husband's friends. He wasn't a hard worker, but didn't drink and was a gentle man. She had two more children during this marriage.

Ms. A began to drink at the age of 30, and Ms. B at age 38. Ms. A sometimes drank too much because of her husband's violence. At the age of 58 she had a furious row with her husband over a trivial matter and drank so much that she was taken to the psychiatric hospital. Thereafter she drank daily. She was readmitted at the age of 63. Ms. B, however, sometimes drank at home with her adult children.

Both Ms. A and Ms. B tested positive for ALDH2. Their KAST scores were 18.2 for Ms. A and -0.9 for Ms. B. Ms. A was classified as a severe problem drinker. Zygosity was classified as MZ. The probability of being MZ: $Pr(M) > 0.9794$.

Twins #3: 30-year-old males (Figure A-4)

The 3rd and 4th of 4 siblings. There were no complications at birth. Their father and two elder brothers were all heavy drinkers, all having been previously admitted to hospital at some time because of alcohol dependence.

Both graduated from special schools, so did not take up regular employment. Their parents divorced when the twins were both 17 years old. At around age 20, Mr. A had a job on a street stall. He abused stimulant drugs at about 26 and was imprisoned for a year. Mr. B, at age 17, got work with a transportation company. A year later he also had a street stall. He started to commit fraud at age 20, which was followed by four occasions of stealing, violence, etc.

Drinking began for Mr. A at 20 years old, with work friends, but he didn't have opportunity to drink much. His boss on the street stall also allowed him no chance to drink. However, Mr. B started drinking at 17 with friends and continued to drink. His consumption of alcohol increased rapidly; during days off he drank in the mornings. He was first admitted to hospital at 22 years old, being hospitalized six times.

ALDH2 was active for Mr. B but we couldn't obtain any of Mr. A's hair roots. KAST score for Mr. A was -6.1, and for Mr. B was 17.0. Mr. B was diagnosed as severe problem drinker. These twins were diagnosed as monozygotic, and the probability of being MZ: $Pr(M) > 0.9796$.

Twins #4: 48-year-old males (Figure A-5)

Born as the 6th and 7th of 7 siblings. There were no complications at birth. Customarily, people within their local community drank, but not so heavily.

Mr. A graduated from school and went on to be a craftsman in a woodworking shop. He married at 21 and had 2 children. He divorced at 35. Before then he had to resign from work because of his drinking. Mr. B, after

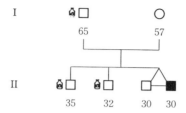

The bottle mark indicates a severe drinker.

Items	Response	−2.0	−1.0	0.0	1.0	2.0	3.0	4.0
1. My drinking has impaired an important relationship	× ○			A B				
2. Impossible to resolve 'I won't drink today'	× ○			A B				
3. I've been called 'a drunkard'	× ○			A B				
4. I've drunk myself into a stupor	× ○			A B				
5. Amnesia ('blackout') about the previous evening's events	× ○			A B				
6. On my days off I start drinking during the morning	× ○			A B				
7. I've missed important appointments because of a hangover	× ×			A B				
8. I've been treated for diabetes, liver or heart trouble	× ×			A B				
9. I've experienced sweating, tremors, insomnia or frustration when without alcohol	× ○			A B				
10. Drinking is necessary during my work	× ×			A B				
11. Unable to get to sleep without alcohol	× ○			A B				
12. Usually drink over 3 GO of sake during evening meal	× ○			A B				
13. I've been detained by the police because of my drinking	× ○			A B				
14. I get angry when I'm drunk	× ○			A B				

Total Mr. A: −6.1   Probability   Mr. A: Social drinker
       Mr. B: 17.0   Mr. B: Severe problem-drinker

Figure A-3.   Pedigree and KAST scores of Twin Case 3.

graduation, worked in the family's milk business for four years and then got a job at a blood bank up to the age of 20. He married at 25 and opened a small restaurant.

Their parents also ran a small hotel, and the home atmosphere enabled them to first start drinking around 16 years old. Mr. A liked alcohol and indulged more and more. He was often absent from work without warning. He was admitted to a hospital at age 23 for the first time. He eventually had to leave his job, and was soon divorced. From the age of 45 he had repeated admissions to hospital because of drink.

Mr. B also drank heavily at times, the motive being unclear. At 33, while he was running his restaurant, there was a tragic accident when an employee's daughter, of whom Mr. B was very fond, fell into a cauldron of boiling water and died. From this time on Mr. B drank very severely and was soon hospitalized. He rapidly repeated admissions, usually monthly.

ALDH2 was nondeficient type for both brothers. KAST score was 19.0 for Mr. A and 18.9 for Mr. B, both being considered severe problem drinkers. Zygotic diagnosis indicated they were monozygotic twins, probability being: Pr(M) # 0.9623.

Twins # 5: 64-year-old males (Figure A-6)

Seventh and 8th of 8 siblings. Their oldest brother was a heavy drinker and died in an accident during heavy drinking. Another elder brother was a heavy drinker who died in a mental hospital. His son also drank heavily.

They did poorly at primary school. They worked mainly as farm laborers. Mr. A left home at 33 and went to Kyoto, and then Kawasaki, Hamamatsu, Chiba and Shizuoka, eventually returning home (Miyazaki) at age 47. Mr. B had a similar life course, but had lived mostly around Miyazaki Prefecture. They had lived together since they were 59 years old and neither married.

Both Mr. A and Mr. B began to drink at age 20, their employer customarily paying them by alcohol or food, instead of money.

At age 60 they suffered from ischias, but only Mr. B stayed absent from work to drink every day. Mr. B was admitted to a psychiatric hospital at age 62.

ALDH2 activity was found in both. KAST score was -4.5 for Mr. A and 8.0 for Mr. B, with Mr. B clasified as a severe problem drinker. They were diagnosed as MZ, the probability being: Pr(M) > 0.9663.

1. Process of Case Findings

It is well known that differences of alcohol consumption exist among different areas of prefectures of Japan. This is said to be a reflection of the "social disapproval or tolerance accorded to drinking behavior in each region."

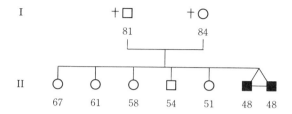

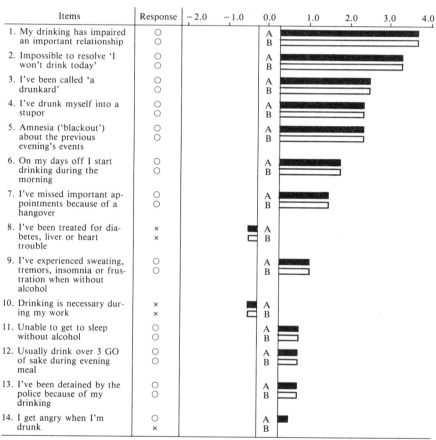

Figure A-4.   Pedigree and KAST scores of Twin Case 4.

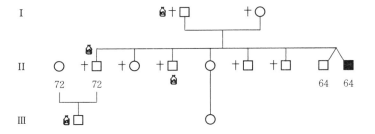

The bottle mark indicates a severe drinker.

Items	Response	−2.0	−1.0	0.0	1.0	2.0	3.0	4.0
1. My drinking has impaired an important relationship	× ×			A B				
2. Impossible to resolve 'I won't drink today'	× ○			A B				
3. I've been called 'a drunkard'	× ○			A B				
4. I've drunk myself into a stupor	× ○			A B				
5. Amnesia ('blackout') about the previous evening's events	× ○			A B				
6. On my days off I start drinking during the morning	× ×			A B				
7. I've missed important appointments because of a hangover	× ×			A B				
8. I've been treated for diabetes, liver or heart trouble	× ○			A B				
9. I've experienced sweating, tremors, insomnia or frustration when without alcohol	× ○			A B				
10. Drinking is necessary during my work	× ×			A B				
11. Unable to get to sleep without alcohol	× ×			A B				
12. Usually drink over 3 GO of sake during evening meal	× ○			A B				
13. I've been detained by the police because of my drinking	× ○			A B				
14. I get angry when I'm drunk	× ○			A B				

Total   Mr. A: −4.5   Probability   Mr. A: Social drinker
        Mr. B: 8.0   Mr. B: Severe problem-drinker

Figure A-5.   Pedigree and KAST scores of Twin Case 5.

It is interesting to note that twin cases of alcohol dependence showed mainly among those areas of comparatively large amounts of alcohol consumption (table not shown). These results suggested the differing social attitudes towards drink, mentioned above.

2. ALDH2 Phenotype

Through examination of hair roots, we found that all cases of alcohol dependence showed non deficiency type of ALDH2 activity. This shows a good biological basis for alcohol dependence, in agreement with previous reports.

3. Environmental Factors and Alcohol Dependence

(a) Three pairs of twins discordant concerning the diagnosis of alcohol dependence:
  i) Twins #2
     The character and life history of each twin were almost alike. They began drinking later in life, Ms. A at 30 and Ms. B at age 38. At this time both were working in different restaurants as waitresses. Ms. A's drinking was a means of relieving the stress of her husband's violence, which habit seemed to lead to dependence.
     However, Ms. B stated that she was very happy that her fiance did not drink any alcohol. Therefore, it was suggested that the discordance between the pair's alcohol dependence was caused by their husbands' differing attitudes towards drinking behavior. There are some reports that female alcoholics often had husbands who were themselves heavy or problem drinkers.
  ii) Twins #3
     The biggest difference between the pair's life histories was the character of their employers. Mr. A's employer was strict, refusing any drinking at work. Mr. B got many opportunities to drink and drank heavily under the lax eye of his employer. Another big difference is that Mr. A lived a little distance away and was closely involved with his mother, while Mr. B lived with his father, a heavy drinker. It is thought that they were heavily influenced by the person with whom they most closely associated, i.e., their mother or father.
  iii) Twins #5
     There was little information about their life histories, but Mr. A left home 10 years earlier than Mr. B. Mr. A had more chance to adapt to his social environment. After returning home and then living together, Mr. A had to look after them both. This gave Mr. B op-

portunity to drink, whereas Mr. A was unable to because of the need to maintain themselves. Both suffered from ischias, Mr. A consulted the hospital, whereas Mr. B consulted the bottle, sedating his pain without medical treatment. The different ways in which each adapted to his life situation created their different roles in life.

(b) Two sets of twins concordant concerning diagnosis of alcohol dependence:

i) Twins #1

In this pair, Mr. A's first admission to hospital was 4 years before Mr. B's. Mr. B had to move frequently because of his job, and this isolation from family caused him great loneliness. This was causal in enhancing his drinking. On the other hand, Mr. A was living with his mother, who somewhat prevented him from indulging in drinking. However, upon her death he began to increase both the frequency and volume of drinking. Thus, it seems that living alone or living with the family determined the time of first admission.

ii) Twins #4

Ten years' difference between first admission was also seen as a major difference between this pair. Up to the death of the little girl, Mr. B had been drinking but not hospitalized, but this tragedy directly related to his first admission. It had been partly his relaxed attitude to drink that had allowed his family to look after him at home up to this point. However, in comparison, Mr. A's violence towards his family when drunk was very different—such as threatening with kitchen knives and chasing after them. The varying behaviors during their drunken state seemed to create the reason for the difference between the pair's admission time.

4. Conclusion of Case Study

As mentioned above, the person who was in close relation with the patients seemed to be significant in regard to manifestation of their alcohol dependence or their time of admission. These "significants" included the co-twin, spouses, parents or seniors. It was revealed that not only genetic but also psychosocial factors—in particular, human relationships surrounding the patients—played a vital role in the pathogenesis of alcohol dependence.

III. PART B: ANALYSIS OF GENETIC AND PSYCHOSOCIAL FACTORS ON DRINKING BEHAVIORS

Subjects and Methods

The first investigation:

Questionnaires were mailed in April – July of 1980, to 862 twin individuals entered in the "Tokyo 12-year-old Twin Registry." These were all applicants for the junior high school affiliated with the University of Tokyo. The questionnaire included gender, age, height, weight, occupation, past history, family history, smoking and drinking habits, etc. Answers were received from 119 sets of twins, consisting of 104 MZ (42 male-male and 62 female-female) and 15 DZ (9 same-sex and 6 opposite-sex).

The second investigation:

Forty-six (37 MZ and 9 DZ) out of the 119 pairs consented to participate in the examination of "adults' diseases." The examination consisted of insulin-loaded, blood pressure, blood uric acid, cholesterol, triglyceride, and so on. During this occasion a more detailed questionnaire of drinking habits was requested, containing the following categories: "drinking patterns," "sensitivity to alcohol," "motives for drinking," "problem drinking behaviors." We used "TAST," (the University of Tokyo ALDH2 Screening Test, created by ourselves) (see Apendix 2) to determine "sensitivity to alcohol." "KAST" (Kurihama Alcohol Screening Test) was used to determine "problem drinking behaviors." Table A-1 indicates these parts of the questionnaire.

Results and Discussion

Smoking and drinking habits are shown in Table B-1. We thought it remarkable that there was not one pair in which one drank every day, while the other never drank at all. Considering smoking, complete discordance was seen in 13 pairs. Such differences indicate that genetic factors were more involved in drinking habits than in smoking habits. Table B-2 shows these patterns. Intraclass correlation coefficients of MZ were significantly higher than zero, with regard to the frequencies and volumes of both smoking and drinking behaviors, whereas these were not significant in DZ, random or unrelated pairs. Also within the MZ they were calculated separately, whether they were living together or apart, or single or married, but any remarkable differences were not recognized. Results suggested that genetic factors influenced drinking or smoking behaviors and were more prominent in drinking behavior.

TABLE B-1.
Drinking and Smoking Habits in MZ

		Drinking habits in 104 MZ		
			B	
		none	*sometimes*	*every day*
	none	19	8	0
A	sometimes	9	56	2
	every day	0	3	8

		Smoking habits in 104 MZ		
			B	
		none	*sometimes*	*every day*
	none	68	4	4
A	sometimes	1	3	1
	every day	9	1	14

TABLE B-2.
Intraclass Correlation Coefficients in Drinking and Smoking Habits

Zygosity	*drinking frequency*	*drinking volume*	*smoking frequency*	*smoking volume*
MZ	0.6366**	0.4394**	0.5635**	0.3916*
	n = 104	n = 70	n = 104	n = 98
DZ	0.2718	0.7738	0.3327	0.2058
	n = 15	n = 5	n = 15	n = 15
Random pair	− 0.1255	− 0.1184	0.1184	0.2353
	n = 119	n = 67	n = 119	n = 113

* $p < 0.05$ ** $p < 0.01$

TABLE B-3.
Intraclass Correlation Coefficients with respect to "Drinking Pattern"

Zygosity	*Duration time*	*Frequency*	*Volume*
MZ (n = 37)	0.942***	0.781***	0.531***
DZ (n = 9)	0.924***	0.444	0.207

*** $p < 0.001$

TABLE B-4.
**Intraclass Correlation Coefficients with respect to
"Sensitivity of Alcohol (TAST)"**

Zygosity	Aldehyde	Overdrinking	Alcohol
MZ (n = 37)	0.731***	0.402***	0.144
DZ (n = 9)	0.372	0.195	0.581

*** $p < 0.001$

TABLE B-5.
Intraclass Correlation Coefficients with respect to "Motivation of Drinking"

Zygosity	Eager for drunkenness	Smooth relationship	Enjoy taste
MZ (n = 37)	0.206	0.445**	0.497**
DZ (n = 9)	0.444	0.218	0.097

**$p < 0.01$

The next step was the analysis of the second-step data. Table B-3 shows drinking patterns. Intraclass correlation coefficients were calculated, after standardization of each value by gender. As shown in the table, the values of duration of years' drinking, those of frequency (times per week), and those of volume (pure ethanol) are all significantly high among MZ. However, only one item—duration—is significant in the DZ.

Table B-4 shows the results of "sensitivity to alcohol." The following procedures were undertaken to obtain these figures: first, principal component analysis of 13 TAST items was carried out among 1,829 subjects from the general public. Three principal components—"aldehyde," "overdrinking," and "alcohol." Each factor score was given to twin individuals and, after standardization, intraclass correlation coefficients were again calculated. As shown in the table, the three factors are all significantly higher in MZ but not DZ. Regarding "motives for drinking," in principal component analysis of ten items, three items were extracted: "keen desire to get drunk," "helps me to relate well with others," and "enjoy the taste." In a repeat of the above process, intraclass correlation coefficients were calculated as shown in Table B-5. Three factors were also taken from KAST, these being "general problems," "social problems," and "dependence problems." Results are shown in Table B-6.

The final analysis was performed only with MZ, using multiple regression analysis. First, percent deviation (PD) was calculated on each item of 4

TABLE B-6.

**Intraclass Correlation Coefficients with respect to
"Problem Drinking Behaviors (KAST)"**

Zygosity	General problems	Social problems	Dependence
MZ (n = 37)	0.395*	0.775***	0.247
DZ (n = 9)	0.077	0.271	0.010

* $p < 0.05$ *** $p < 0.001$

TABLE B-7.

**Multiple Regression Analysis of Percent Deviation
[(1A − B1/(A + B)]*100 of each item**

Dependent variable
   A. Category
      "problem drinking behavior" (KAST)
      1. general problems
      2. social problems
      3. dependence

Independent variables
   B. Category (biological basis)
      "drinking pattern"
      1. duration time
      2. frequency
      3. volume
   C. Category (genetic basis)
      "sensitivity to alcohol" (TAST)
      1. aldehyde
      2. overdrinking
      3. alcohol
   D. Category (psychosocial basis)
      "motivation of drinking"
      1. eager for drunkenness
      2. smooth relationship
      3. enjoy taste

categories, and analysis was made using each factor of the three "KAST" items as dependent variable, and each factor of the categories "drinking pattern," "TAST" and "motives for drinking" as independent variables. At the significant level ($P = 0.05$) of F value, the independent variable "keen desire to get drunk," from the "motives for drinking" category, was the most appropriate when the dependent variables were "general problems" or "dependence symptoms" from the KAST category, as is shown in Table B-7. The results indicated a stronger association between the problem-drinking behaviors and motives for drinking (i.e., psychosocial basis) than that between problem drinking behaviors and drinking patterns (i.e., biological basis) or "TAST" (genetic basis). These results suggest that problem drinking patterns were evidently caused by psycho social factors rather than by biological or genetic factors.

IV. PART C: LIFESTYLE AND HEALTH STATUS IN TWINS

Subjects and Methods

This study started in April 1989 and is still in progress. It originally aimed to clarify the risk factors for the development of osteoporosis and/or arteriosclerosis. Questionnaires were sent to the twins, who are members of the "Tokyo 12-year-old Twin Registry" and partly overlapped with subjects already described in III: Part B. Up to now, 123 pairs of twins, consisting of 92 MZ and 13 DZ, have replied. The above diseases are, of course, caused by genetic as well as environmental factors such as nutrition, exercise, lifestyle and so forth. Biological examinations such as bone mass density, pulse wave velocity (degree of arteriosclerosis) and other laboratory examinations are being carried out. The questionnaire considers lifestyle (18 items), subjective physical symptoms (23 items), subjective mental symptoms (18 items using Zung's SDS slightly modified), eating habits (19 items) and the milieu in which they're living, and so forth. We will present the study of lifestyles, health status and a study focusing upon drinking behaviors in this section.

From the 18 lifestyle questions the following were selected: (1) Do you smoke? (2) Do you drink? (3) Do you eat breakfast every day? (4) How long do you sleep each night? (5) How much leisure time do you have? (6) How many times do you exercise? (7) Do you consider your diet carefully?

Depending upon the answers, points were awarded from 0 (bad) to 1 (good) and total sum was calculated, from 0 to 7. The value was named as Health Practice Index (HPI). Objective or laboratory data is, however, not yet available for health status. Thus, this was derived from two parts, using subjective physical symptoms including 23 items, and subjective mental symptoms (Zung's SDS) (18 items) slightly modified. The sum total of these 23 items was named Subjective Physical Index (SPI) and Subjective Mental Index (SMI) respectively.

Results and Discussions

First of all, a lifestyle analysis was performed. By computing Cramer's V coefficients of raw scores of each item, comparison was made between

TABLE C-1.
Cramer's V Coefficients of Lifestyle

	MZ	DZ
Smoking habit	0.377***	0.378***
	(n = 109)	(n = 13)
Drinking habit	0.464***	0.509***
	(n = 109)	(n = 14)
Breakfast	0.463***	− 0.217
	(n = 104)	(n = 14)
Sleeping time	0.252***	0.551***
	(n = 104)	(n = 14)
Own leisure time	0.093	0.025
	(n = 98)	(n = 13)
Exercise	0.131*	− 0.037
	(n = 106)	(n = 14)
Balance of nutrition	− 0.056	− 0.120
	(n = 104)	(n = 14)
Total Health Practice (THP)	0.359***	0.503**
	(n = 92)	(n = 13)

** p < 0.01   *** p < 0.001

TABLE C-2.
Intraclass Correlation Coefficients of Standardized HPI, SPI and SMI

	MZ	Living apart MZ	Living together MZ	DZ
HPI	0.272***	0.203*	0.366***	0.191
	(n = 92)	(n = 65)	(n = 27)	(n = 13)
SPI	0.588***	0.576***	0.606***	0.047
	(n = 96)	(n = 63)	(n = 28)	(n = 11)
SMI	0.328***	0.366***	0.082	0.184
	(n = 101)	(n = 74)	(n = 27)	(n = 14)

*p < 0.05   ***p < 0.001

MZ and DZ in each item. Table C-1 indicates the results. It was particularly remarked upon that smoking habits, drinking habits, duration of sleep and also HPI are higher in both MZ and DZ, particularly drinking habits. So, it may be said that drinking habits are surely influenced by genetics, even if comparing several health practices.

In general, HPI was higher in females than in males. HPI score was standardized by gender as well as SPI and SMI. Intraclass correlation coefficients of the standardized HPI, SPI and SMI are all significantly higher in MZ but not in DZ, as shown in Table C-2. After the MZ were further divid-

TABLE C-3.
**Absolute Difference between the pair as to HPI (ZHPI),
SPI (ZSPI) and SMI (ZSMI)**

	ZHPI	ZSPI	ZSMI
DZ	0.806 (n = 13)	1.204 (n = 11)	0.879 (n = 14)
MZ	0.906 (n = 92)	0.602 (n = 96)	0.953 (n = 101)
	p = 0.686	p = 0.0041**	p = 0.660
Apart MZ	1.037 (n = 65)	0.593 (n = 68)	0.956 (n = 74)
Together MZ	0.591 (n = 7)	0.624 (n = 28)	0.954 (n = 27)
	p = 0.0181*	p = 0.8210	p = 0.9895

*p < 0.05   **p < 0.01

TABLE C-4.
Pearson's correlation coefficients among ZHPI, ZSPI and ZSMI

	ZSPI	ZSMI
ZHPI	0.238	0.128
	p = 0.020*	p = 0.208
ZSPI		0.060
		p + 0.557

ed into two groups, i.e., living together or living apart, intraclass correlation coefficients were computed for each (also Table C-2). As shown, significant values are seen in both groups excepting SMI.

Next, the absolute difference between the pair was calculated, and these were entitled ZHPI, ZSPI and ZSMI. Table C-3 indicates the values of MZ and DZ with regard to these. Significant difference between MZ and DZ was only recognized in ZSPI, suggesting genetic influence on subjective physical complaints. In only MZ, comparisons between the groups living together and living separately showed a significant difference only in ZHPI. This indicates that the intraclass difference of health practice was higher in those living separately

Table C-4 shows Pearson's correlation coefficients that indicate the three values of these twin individuals. Intraclass difference of Health Practice Index significantly correlated with that of Subjective Physical Index. Therefore, further analysis was conducted in order to clarify which health practice items closely relate to subjective physical symptoms. Following this, multiple regression analysis was carried out, using ZSPI as dependent variable and each item of 7 ZHPI as independent variables. Multiple regression analysis indicated only three items were meaningful, that is—in order of importance—leisure time, duration of sleep and enough exercise. So, consumption or nonconsumption of alcohol beverage does not play an important role in health status according to subjective physical symptoms. As no objective physical symptoms are available at present, final conclusions must await its utilization.

In the analysis of this section, it was tentatively concluded that health status, although estimated subjectively, was connected with rather more than only drinking practices.

V. SUMMARY

Genetic factors are, needless to say, the basis of the cause of alcohol dependence. However, psychological and/or social factors also play an important role in the development of alcohol dependence, clarified to some extent by the present study. This study included "A case study on twin patients," "Genetic and/or environmental analysis on twin drinking behaviors" and "An analysis of twins' lifestyles, focusing upon drinking behavior." Thus, it is suggested that positive adjustment of the milieu surrounding the patient is essential and effective for both the treatment and prevention of alcohol dependence.

APPENDIX 1.
Kurihama Alcoholism Screening Test (KAST)

	Answer	Score
1. My drinking has impaired an important relationship	yes	3.7
	no	−1.1
2. Impossible to resolve 'I won't drink today'	yes	3.2
	no	−1.1
3. I've been called 'a drunkard'	yes	2.3
	no	−0.8
4. I've drunk myself into a stupor	yes	2.2
	no	−0.7
5. Amnesia ('blackout') about the previous evening's events	yes	2.1
	no	−0.7
6. On my days off I start drinking during the morning	yes	1.7
	no	−0.4
7. I've missed important appointments because of a hangover	yes	1.5
	no	−0.5
8. I've been treated for diabetes, liver or heart trouble	yes	1.2
	no	−0.2
9. I've experienced sweating, tremors, insomnia or frustration when without alcohol	yes	0.8
	no	−0.2

10. Drinking is necessary during my work	often	0.7
	sometimes	0.0
	seldom	−0.2
11. Unable to get to sleep without alcohol	yes	0.7
	no	−0.1
12. Usually drink over 3 GO of sake during evening meal		
	yes	0.6
	no	−0.1
13. I've been detained by the police because of my drinking		
	yes	0.5
	no	0.0
14. I get angry when I'm drunk	yes	0.1
	no	0.0

Total Score	Evaluation
≤ 2	problem drinker
> 2	normal drinker

APPENDIX 2.
TAST
Tokyo University ALDH2-Phenotype Screening Test

When you drink alcoholic beverages, what symptoms do you experience?
Please select the appropriate answer for each item.

How to detect your ALDH2 phenotype.
① Write down the coefficient you selected in each checking area.
② You can get your TAST score by totaling all coefficients.
③ If your TAST score is . . .

positive, then you are ALDH2-positive type.
negative, then you are ALDH2-negative type.

Subjective Symptoms	always	sometimes	never	checking area
Facial flushing	−10.04	5.2	8.95	
Flushing elsewhere on the body	−0.43	−2.98	1.20	
Itchiness	3.37	−3.89	0.38	
Dizziness	−0.58	−1.27	0.25	
Drowsiness	0.31	0.36	−1.03	

Appendex 2 (continued)

Anxiety			
	0.00	− 4.11	0.10
Headaches			
	− 0.79	0.07	0.01
Pounding in the head			
	0.83	0.62	− 0.24
Sweating			
	− 3.25	1.43	− 0.44
Palpitations			
	− 1.88	0.04	0.26
Nausea			
	− 10.07	0.19	0.03
Cold and Shivery			
	8.15	− 2.42	0.14
Dyspnea (difficulty breathing)			
	− 4.34	2.69	− 0.19

Your TAST score →

REFERENCES

(1) Beloc NB and Breslow L. Relationship of physical health status and health practices. *Prev Med* 1: 409-421 (1972).
(2) Dean K. Social support and health: Pathways of influence. 1: 133-150 (1986).
(3) Harada S, Agarwald DP and Goedde HW. Possible protective role against alcoholism for aldehyde dehydrogenase deficiency in Japan. *Lancet* ii: 827 (1982).
(4) Saito S and Ikegami N. Kast (Kurihama Alcoholism Screening Test) and its applications. *Jap J Study Alcohol* 13: 229-237 (1978).
(5) Schuckit MA. Two types of alcoholism in women. *Arch Gen Psychiat* 20: 301-306 (1969).
(6) Yamada K, Asaka A, Norioka T and Takeshita T. Questionnaire for detecting the phenotype of low Km ALDH (ALDH2). in *Biomedical and Social Aspects of Alcohol and Alcoholism*, Kurihama K, Takada A and Ishii H eds, 481-484 (1988).
(7) Zung WWK. A self-rating depression scale. *Arch Gen Psychiat* 12: 63-70 (1965).

Part I: Discussion

(*Chairperson*) *Professor Bohman*: Thank you for your presentation which is an excellent survey of the problems of the genetics of alcoholism and poses many interesting questions. I would like to ask if you think there may be a special gene to be identified, behind this susceptibility to alcoholism.

Professor Schuckit: Pharmacogenetic factors are very important in how we react to most drugs. For example, some people are more sensitive to anticholinergic medications, while others are very sensitive to antihistamines. These differences appear to be genetically influenced. Therefore, it would not be surprising if there was a group of genes that impact upon how we react to alcohol.

My guess would be that this is not an abnormal gene but a group of genes that everybody has. However, I believe there is a distribution of normal genes—a Guassian curve—and that there is a threshold below which an intensity of response to alcohol places you at high alcoholism risk. So, I don't necessarily believe there is an alcoholic gene. I believe that there are a limited number of genes that influence your reaction to alcohol and put you at high risk for problems in a heavy drinking society.

Question: Usually, alcoholics don't become red in the face when they drink. However, certain Japanese people do flush heavily. What about the sons of such Japanese alcoholics?

Professor Schuckit: This is a wonderful question, and you have many experts on this phenomenon in Japan, including Dr. Harada. Approximately one half of Japanese people have an absence of the mitochondrial form of aldehyde dehydrogenase. Thus, when they drink, their levels of acetaldehyde, the first breakdown product of alcohol, must become higher before the aldehyde dehydrogenase enzyme destroys the acetaldehyde. That, of course, contributes to a facial flushing and, sometimes, a rapid beating of the heart. Some important data, again demonstrated by Drs. Harada, Suzuki, and others, show that the rate of alcoholism among Japanese who flush appears to be a good deal lower than in nonflushers. So you have a genetic factor that impacts upon continuation of drinking.

In my own work I studied Caucasian and non-Jewish men, for a variety of reasons. While there are some data from Britain to say that a mild level of flushing may be observed in some Caucasians, I believe that the level of flushing is so mild that it probably has no major impact on the alcoholism risk in Caucasians.

Dr. Asaka: This is a question about your Discriminant Function Analysis with FHP and FHN. You carried out an analysis between FHP and FHN and you mentioned "floating" and "body sway" and ACTH. You mentioned that 80% was the level of accuracy of the analysis. My question is: How many independent variables did you use in that analysis? Among the variables used, which one contributed most highly in the analysis?

Professor Schuckit: I think that is a most important question. I will refer you to the March 1988 issue of *Archives of General Psychiatry* where we published the paper. In putting the study together, we limited the number of variables in the DFA to those appropriate for the number of FHP/FHN pairs. We didn't say, for example, that we had 60 men in that analysis; we said we had 30 pairs. Therefore, we picked a number of variables we thought were appropriate in a DFA dealing with 30 people.

The variables are not independent of each other, because all of them demonstrate less response in the sons of alcoholics. It was not possible to pick items that were totally independent. However, in a Principal Components Analysis that followed the DFA, we found it was likely that, in order to discriminate best between the groups, one needed some aspects of subjective feeling, some aspects of body sway, and also prolactin and cortisol.

My guess is that all three were needed, not because they were totally different, but rather because the men differed in which system was least sensitive to alcohol. So, some men could be picked up best by the hormones, whereas other men with a similar phenomenon could be picked up better by the body sway. I must also say that the DFA does not impress me as much as whether the follow-up will show that we are indeed able to predict who becomes alcoholic.

(*Chairperson*) *Professor Bohman*: May I ask Dr. Schuckit if he has some further comment upon his first, and very lucid, presentation on the basic problems of the genetics of alcoholism?

Professor Schuckit: I think the three presentations complemented each other in making some basic points. The twin studies demonstrate that genetic factors are involved, but show how complicated the issues can be. The study on CNV demonstrated that whatever it is that's inherited to increase one's risk, it might be manifested in different ways in different systems. Also, there might be various forms of factors that increase the risk, perhaps indicating subgroups of alcoholics. So I think that the three papers complemented one another in demonstrating both the importance of genetics and also the complexity of the interaction between genetics and the environment.

Question: Dr. Schuckit, could you tell us why you chose only Caucasian men for your research purposes?

Professor Schuckit: In putting together a study, as we did in 1975, knowing that we wanted to have the largest number of people possible for follow-up, it was important to avoid the complexities caused by having subgroups. Therefore, one had to make a decision between studying something in a way that might have wide generalizability and thus risking not finding anything because of too much heterogeneity within the samples, or saying, "You can never study everybody so at least describe carefully the population, and make it as large and *relatively* homogeneous as possible." So I had to choose: Do I include Blacks, Mexican-Americans, Asians, and Caucasians? And within, let's say, Asians, do I subdivide people—Korean, Chinese, Japanese, the three major groups in my area? There would be too many groups, so I chose Caucasians.

For similar reasons I felt I had to choose men or women. I could have studied both, but then I would run the risk that what is increasing the risk in men might be different in women. Personally, I don't think it is, but if I'm wrong I could ruin 20 years of work. So, I focused only on men because men have the greater chance of expressing alcoholism in the future.

I have read recently that the difference in Japan between men and women on expression of alcoholism may be as high as tenfold. In the United States, it's double or triple. So why not study the group that has the greater chance of showing the disorder? I had to select age groups, etc., but the choice was based on having a relatively homogeneous population. If I'm right, then others will apply this to other populations.

Question: Dr. Asaka, you explained the interaction of environmental and genetic aspects and showed us a type of guide map. I think you attach much importance to social factors, but I would like to ask you about the life histories.

You say there wasn't much difference between your cases, but I think the key persons related to each patient played a very important role, according to your survey. However, as to the influence of psychosocial factors, as far as the manifestation, further development of, or lapsing back into alcoholism is concerned, I think we should think of it in that fashion. I believe the lifestyle is a concept that doesn't have a lot of longitudinal studies, at present, but KAST, I believe, shows the difference with time. Variables don't have the longitudinal factor, but KAST results include longitudinal factors. So, maybe we cannot combine them together in a simple manner to conclude that there are social or psychological factors. Would you elaborate upon this?

Dr. Asaka: This is a very important matter, and also a very difficult question to answer. My studies looked at a cross-sectional part only and not at the longitudinal aspects. Thus, my study lacks this longitudinal aspect. However, the process up to the manifestation of alcoholism has been studied.

We haven't conducted a complete follow-up study after that stage. So, as to how to tackle this, I think it is necessary to combine both the longitudinal and other aspects to come up with the multidimensional approach. We are now in the process of finding out what sort of approach this should take. I'm sorry not to be more specific in my answer.

(*Chairperson*) *Professor Bohman*: Dr. Schuckit, I've one more question please: You state that you don't want to have subtypes, but there's a contradiction here because we know that alcoholism is a very heterogeneous phenomenon! Might it not be difficult, then, to really assess that you have no subtypes?

Professor Schuckit: I didn't mean to say that I *wouldn't* have subtypes. However, to get the sample as homogeneous as possible, it's a good idea to avoid major differences such as men/women, racial groups, too huge an age range, etc. Your question is quite correct, i.e., that *within* alcoholics, and their sons, there *must* be subtypes. For example, even if alcoholism were autosomal dominant and coming down from one side of the family, the genotype at most could be seen in one half of the sons, while the other half won't have it.

Your question also raises another issue. *You* will be presenting some lovely data, I'm sure, on the possible importance of Type 1 and Type 2 alcoholism. In our sample, our fathers had many Type 2 characteristics—something like 20% or 25% of the fathers had their first alcohol problems before the age of 25; as many as 60% of the fathers had received alcoholism treatment. If we take Type 1/Type 2 as a continuum and rate the alcoholic fathers on that continuum, on the TPQ the sons of Type 2-like alcoholics looked similar to the sons of men who had more Type 1 characteristics. However, we continue to look at this important *potential* subdivision and, as we follow our population up, we'll evaluate more about the relationship between potential Type 1/Type 2 characteristics and the later development of alcohol and drug and mental health problems. But your question very much points out that even within the sons of alcoholics and within the sons of nonalcoholics there *must* certainly be heterogeneity.

Dr. Claudia Black: I did want to say, Dr. Schuckit, how much I appreciate your work and how important it has been throughout the world. Also, to begin your work with children from alcoholic homes in 1975, to find the sample that you did, and to be able to maintain contact with that sample is a wonderful statement about you and your staff, especially since we recognize how much people from chemically dependent families move around; they're very hard to follow!

Not only do the families move in terms of the parents, but also the children have been very hard to find. Finally, children and people with such problems have only begun to be more willing to be identified—or self-identify themselves—since the 1980s. Thus, this study, beginning as it did in 1975, is to be commended.

I was curious about what you said concerning the percentage of these subjects who had parents who had been involved in an alcoholism recovery or treatment program.

Professor Schuckit: Somewhere around 60% of the sons had alcoholic fathers who had enough trouble so that they had either sought treatment or been in A.A. At least, there's been some self-identification of the father.

Dr. Claudia Black: Although I know this isn't your particular area of research, I'm interested as well in any differences among *daughters* of alcoholics, daughters of mothers as well as daughters of fathers. Can you summarize whether or not there are similarities and/or differences?

Professor Schuckit: I can at least respond to the intensity of reaction to alcohol in daughters of alcoholics. Barbara Lex did some research with Jack Mendelson and Nancy Mello at Harvard using a Cambridge sample of mostly blue-collar subjects. This relatively small study showed significantly less intense response to alcohol for the daughters of alcoholics, especially on the motor performance tasks. Because of the size of her sample, one can't be sure what's going on, but I am reassured, considering how difficult all of this is to do, to find that a major theme—the decreased reaction to alcohol—is being replicated at all.

Henry Begleiter's work was also mentioned earlier. He also replicated the decreased response in men as measured by changes in P300 latency. However, in response to your question, women are harder to study. This is because the alcohol challenge can be affected by birth control pills and by phase of the menstrual cycle. So, you can choose the men, match them on quantity and frequency and other background, and test them on *any* day. However, if you test daughters, you have to add another layer of control here, which is very difficult. But even with that, the preliminary studies that are statistically significant say there's a similar phenomenon in daughters.

(Chairperson) Professor Bohman: I think that Dr. Nakamura's paper has some relevance in the discussion, and the findings are related to Begleiter's. This gives us opportunity to discuss personality, cognition, and such factors. Dr. Nakamura, perhaps you could say something that would help us start the discussion.

Dr. Nakamura: I've nothing extra to add to what I presented. However, significance of the relationship between arousal levels and alcoholism is rather ambiguous. From the data that I presented today, this area can include aspects of personality of the alcoholism, as well as regulation of the central nervous system as an arousal function, in my interpretation. This isn't limited to substance use, but extends also to alcoholism. Thus, the CNV can be the basic functions for the interpretation of the biological response to substance abuse and alcoholism.

Question: My name's Yamada, from Kurihama Hospital. In relation to Dr. Nakamura's presentation, Dr. Schuckit previously mentioned that there's a "floating" or "high" sensation or body sway. That's a rather subjective sensation. Therefore, I would ask if these items are to be interpreted psychologically or as a physiological condition related to the central nervous system. Perhaps either Dr. Nakamura or Dr. Schuckit might like to answer this question?

Professor Schuckit: I would be interested in Dr. Nakamura's comments as well, but please notice it isn't just a matter of subjective feelings. We began with those because they were the easiest to study. We then went into more motor-performance tasks. But those also bothered us because we were afraid that what we were observing was related to psychological expectations. Thus, we have also demonstrated that after alcohol the sons of alcoholics show less change in background cortical EEG stability—a physiological measure— demonstrated a less persistent change in P3 latency, and showed either less intense or less long-lasting chagnes in cortisol, prolactin and ACTH. All these findings indicate that the phenomenon being observed *must* have some biological component.

That is not to say that one can be certain there is no psychological aspect. However, at least part of what we're observing must have a physiological basis. It also is likely that what we're observing is relatively protean, non-specific, because the data indicate it is not likely to be specific for dopamine or norepinephrine beecause too many systems are involved. It's more likely to be something as relatively simple as whether the cell membrane has a higher or lower level of resistance to alcohol or whether prostaglandins or second-messenger changes following the cell membrane effects are showing greater or lesser sensitivity.

However, I think that the *breadth*, the wide array of results, and all of those biological components indicate that some biological mechanism is highly likely to be involved.

Dr. Nakamura: As to the psychological and biological effects, it is very difficult to differentiate between the two. These two processes interact and overlap so much, or else they are supplementary to each other. Therefore, the CNV or Dr. Schuckit's data, cannot be explained by only one theory.

There are many physiological or biological factors involved behind the scenes here. In total, they express themselves psychologically in different ways. One of the biological aspects is the CNV, which has been proposed by myself.

(*Chairperson*) *Professor Bohman*: I think Dr. Asaka's twin study highlighted many problems regarding the biological, social, and environmental aspects. In a way, as Dr. Schuckit mentioned, this complements the other two presentations. Dr. Asaka, do you have any further comments about your paper, some discussion point for the audience?

Dr. Asaka: I don't have anything to add to my presentation. However, I found the two other speakers' presentations very interesting, and I'd like to ask them the following question concerning ERP, P3 and CNV in connection with schizophrenia. If there are very closely related family members with this disease, I have heard that it is possible for other family members to exhibit similar diseases. Whether those findings are considered traits—personality traits—or states, I believe genetic factors play more of a role in the traits. Would either of you comment on whether you feel such behaviors would be considered traits or states?

Dr. Nakamura: This is a very difficult question to answer. Either CNV or P300 can be used as a genetic marker, because we can find common items in the family members.

I have received data concerning a family with anorexia nervosa. The CNV of the patient and family members show some common findings, so I think there should be some familial aspect in the CNV. I don't know if we can say it's genetic or not, but some familial components certainly do exist.

I also found more data concerning body weight changes in anorexia nervosa and I have compared the CNV recording with changes of the weight. After four weeks and after three months we conducted the CNV recording. However, although the body weight recovered quite well, the CNV recovery did not change. So, I think this stability may reflect a kind of trait, instead of a state. That is my belief.

(*Chairperson*) *Professor Bohman*: Are there any other questions or comments?

Professor Steinglass: Perhaps this is the time to ask all of the panelists to do a little speculating about the future. You've all given us several messages today. Perhaps I might be allowed to summarize these?

First of all, I heard that findings regarding biological risk factors for the development of alcoholism have reached a stage in which all three of you are very excited about the work that you're doing, and very excited about the findings you're sharing with us today.

Second, I think you are all in agreement in saying that you are doing research about a highly complicated condition that probably has multiple factors as determinants, both in terms of onset and in terms of course.

Third, to some extent there was the hint that the most exciting part of the research may unfold in the longitudinal data just beginning to emerge that have predictive or prospective elements to them.

Now with those three general comments in mind, I ask you to speculate a bit about the future. First of all, do you feel the field has reached a level of maturity at which we're actually ready to take on integrative studies that combine biological and psychosocial variables in the same design?

Second, if you were to bet some money on which biological variables you would like to see incorporated in that design, biological risk factors, which ones would you select?

(*Chairperson*) *Professor Bohman*: Thank you for your challenge! Dr. Schuckit?

Professor Schuckit: In answer to your first question: Yes! You summarized things well!

In answer to your second question: Yes, we have reached a point where people who are doing family studies had best also gather the genetic data and begin to analyze the data separately for people with and without various levels of potential biological contribution to what's being observed. We have reached a point where those of us doing work in the biological sphere can no longer ignore the psychosocial and family aspects that have been shown in your own work and the work of others.

It is time to begin to integrate more. Of course, this can be very difficult to do—very expensive, very time-consuming. However I think for us to make major steps forward we need to take some of the biological markers, take a look at people who carry various loadings of the potential biological markers, and *within them* observe those who do develop problems and those who don't, gathering as rich a data set as possible regarding family and psychosocial factors.

Regarding the biological factors: Marcus Grant is working with the WHO on a study which may develop into a focus on some of the biological markers. In the United States, the National Alcohol Institute is also funding a project that will focus on some markers.

Among the more prominent mrkers would be the P300, as well as some of the background cortical EEG components, especially as they relate to fast and slow alpha-rhythms. A third potential marker, although one that makes me uncomfortable for a variety of reasons, is monoamine oxidase activity levels—a very nonspecific marker with a wide range of normal values. Adenylate cyclase is is another enzyme-type system that is being evaluated. Also, several laboratories, including that of Shirley Hill in Pittsburgh, have identified a number of blood proteins that would be worth looking at. Of course, we must also measure alcohol and aldehyde dehydrogenase isoenzyme patterns. The studies that hopefully will be done in conjunction with the World Health Organization, as well as the one being done in the United States, all are trying to take advantage of those five or six markers.

Dr. Nakamura: As to the future, when we use these kinds of biological markers, it is possible for us to prevent the development of alcoholism by discriminating or screening the high-risk individual. It may be possible to come up with a preventive or effective system. For instance, I have talked about arousal level for some genetic factors to be involved in alcoholism; it may be possible to develop an effective system for the future.

Dr. Asaka: Concerning the study on twins: In Japan, the Twin Registry is not conducted as in your country, Dr. Bohman. Therefore, a prospective study is very difficult to conduct in this country. I believe that a Registry of Alcoholic Patients is also difficult for the same reasons. Because of this system, we have a problem in Japan in that it is impossible to register alcoholic patients. It may be necessary to improve our system, with the cooperation of researchers, government officials and family members.

(*Chairperson*) *Professor Bohman*: Before the discussion ends, I'd like to make a personal comment.

Alcoholism and alcohol abuse are functions of the total consumption of alcohol in the general population. Total consumption is a function of prices, taxes, availability, customs, culture and fashions, etc. Given this knowledge, it is interesting, and also astonishing, that several television channels in Japan advertise alcoholic beverages, with the aim of promoting and increasing alcohol consumption. Advertising alcoholic beverages in the media is certainly not restricted to Japan; it is present in almost all so-called developed countries. On the other hand, governments—with the support of WHO—are trying to minimize alcohol consumption. Most governments officially declare that they want to decrease consumption by at least 25%. So, citizens live in a paradoxical "schizophrenic" situation, with contradictory messages. One message goes to the head. The other, most important message, goes to the heart and to the stomach.

Minimizing the availability of alcohol beverages may be the best way to prevent alcoholism. People have to be educated about the rationale of such a policy. The problem is that the alcohol industry may not be ready to accept this rationale. While waiting for a change, we have to realize that a substantial minority of the inhabitants of our countries will, in the future, get into serious trouble because of alcoholism. At special risk are people with the extremes of Type 1 and Type 2 personalities.

PART II

GENETIC FACTORS OF ALCOHOLISM: CLINICAL ASPECTS

In this section, there is further consideration of the question posed concerning the relationship between genetic and environmental factors in alcoholism, this time from a clinical point of view.

Professors Bohman, Cloninger and colleagues, using the results of adoption studies among children of alcoholics in Sweden, have developed a classification of the subtypes of people experiencing alcoholism. They discuss personality traits associated with these subtypes, and their biochemical origins.

Professor Vaillant conducted a long-term follow-up study concerning the onset and course of alcoholism, with several different cohorts of patients. He concluded that while genetic factors must not be excluded in the search for the onset of alcoholism, it seemed that environmental factors in fact had more influence with regard to the chronicity of the disease.

Professor Harada's report, focusing upon a Japanese population, might seem somewhat constrained, but the results have clinical importance. He reported earlier that approximately 40% of Japanese drinkers are deficient in ALDH (a type of isozyme of ALDH2). Such drinkers all show symptoms of flushing, palpitations, hypertension, etc., due to the pattern of their metabolic processes when ingesting alcohol. He concluded that only a small proportion of this group will go on to become alcoholics. Now, Professor Harada offers relevant data on molecular and biological studies (DNA analysis). His research pinpoints the locus of the ALDH2 deficiency in a specific chromosome, thus confirming the hereditary nature of this phenomenon.

4

Steps Towards a Classification of Alcoholism: Lessons from Adoption Studies

Michael Bohman, M.D.
Robert C. Cloninger, M.D.
Sören Sigvardsson, Ph.D
Anne-Liis von Knorring, M.D.

Recent genetic and epidemiological research towards a pathophysiological model of alcoholism has led to the hypothesis that there are two distinct subtypes of alcoholism. These subtypes may be distinguished in terms of alcohol-related symptoms, personality traits, ages of onset, and patterns of intrafamilial inheritance. Type 1 alcoholism is characterized by anxious, passive-dependent personality traits and rapid development of tolerance and dependence on the anti-anxiety effects of alcohol. This leads to loss of control, difficulty terminating binges once they start, guilt feelings, and liver complications following socially encouraged exposure to alcohol intake. In contrast, Type 2 alcoholism is characterized by antisocial personality traits and persistent seeking of alcohol for its euphoriant effects. This leads to early onset of an inability to abstain entirely, as well as fighting and arrests when drinking. Empirical findings about sex differences, ages of onset, associated personality traits, and longitudinal course are described in a series of adoption studies in Sweden.

Supported by grant B85-25X-07368-04C from the Swedish Medical Research Council. Address requests for reprints to Dr. Bohman. Partly appeared in *Advances in Alcohol and Substance Abuse*, 1989.

59

INTRODUCTION

Susceptibility to alcoholism is familial, but its distribution cannot be explained by either genetic or environmental factors alone. Well-designed studies of adoptees, half-siblings, and twins do implicate genetic factors in the development of at least some forms of alcohol abuse. But the results of pedigree research are incompatible with simple genetic Mendelian inheritance. In addition, there are large group differences in the prevalence of alcoholism due to sociocultural influences. Both consumption and complications have varied widely from one historical era to another and currently vary from country to country, between social classes, between persons of different occupation, religions affiliation, age or sex.

These observations strongly suggest that the susceptibility to alcoholism is neither entirely genetic, nor entirely environmental, nor simply the sum of separate genetic and environmental contributions. Rather, specific combinations of predisposing genetic factors and environmental stressors appear to interact before alcoholism develops in most persons. However, the nature of this interaction has been a mystery for two major reasons: (1) the clinical heterogeneity of alcohol abuse and (2) the confounding of genetic and environmental influences within families.

Alcohol abuse is a heterogeneous set of behaviors that includes any pattern of ethyl intake that causes medical and/or social complications. For example, some alcoholics are socially well adjusted as teenagers, work regularly as young adults, but later drink with increasing frequency until prolonged binges lead to marital and work problems and perhaps withdrawal symptoms when intake is reduced. Others start to abuse alcohol as teenagers, develop an antisocial lifestyle with repeated delinquency or criminality and frequent social complications. Within any particular family the syndrome is often similar in its pattern and severity. However, families differ in both genetic and sociocultural background, so the cause of familial differences remain ambiguous.

Children are influenced by both their genes and the environments provided by their parents. Therefore, to disentangle gene-environmental interactions, children separated from their biological relatives at an early age and reared by unrelated adoptive or foster parents must be studied.

Recent adoption studies in Sweden have identified subtypes of alcoholics who differ in alcohol-related symptoms, personality traits, and pattern of inheritance.[7],[5] Many past studies had treated alcoholism as if it were a single discrete entity despite the repeated observation that core symptoms of dependence, social and/or family problems, and depressive symptoms are only weakly correlated with one another. Also alcoholism is associated with antisocial personality traits in some families, but not in others. Similarly antisocial traits are characteristic of most alcoholics with onset in adolescence or early adulthood, but only a minority of those with later onset.[11] In contrast, passive-dependent personality traits have been found to increase the risk of later alcoholism in some longitudinal studies.[18] Hence alcoholism appears to be heterogeneous in its causes, course, and clinical features.

Findings about the inheritance of alcoholism and related disorders have been instrumental in defining current approaches to the classification of alcoholic subtypes. Progress in defining different types of alcoholism will be described by describing the actual sequence of research results obtained in collaborative studies carried out in Sweden and the United States. Key findings of clinical or etiological importance will be emphasized.

THE STOCKHOLM ADOPTION STUDY

In the mid-sixties Bohman initiated a large-scale study of all adopted children who had been born to single women in Stockholm, Sweden, from 1930 to 1949. These were 862 men and 913 women of known paternity who had been adopted by nonrelatives in the first few months of life, and the average age at separation was 4 months.[3],[5],[7] Information about alcohol abuse, psychopathology, and medical treatment was available for the entire lifetime of the adoptees and their double set of parents from hospitals, clinics, and several registers that are systematically maintained in Sweden. Identification of alcohol abuse using these sources has been found to identify about 70% of alcoholics.[18] Alcoholics identified in this way are fairly representative of Swedish alcoholics in general in personality disorders or traits compared to other alcoholics.[13] Hence adoptees and their parents were identified as alcohol abusers if they were ever registered with the Swedish Temperance Boards for alcohol abuse, treated for alcoholism in institutions, hospitals or clinics, or diagnosed as alcoholic by a psychiatrist.

One basic assumption of our investigation was that adoption is an opportunity to reverse the "negative social heritage" of the adoptees, whose biological parents often had low socioeconomic status and a much higher frequency of alcohol abuse or criminality than the general population. Thus 32.4% of 1775 biological fathers and 4.7% of 1775 biological mothers were known to have been alcohol abusers at the time of follow-up. (The corresponding percentages for registered criminality among biological fathers and mothers were 29% and 6.4%). In fact, the risk of alcohol abuse and criminality in the adoptees was only about half that of their fathers.[3] There was also a good agreement between the occupational status among adoptees and the general population.[4]

TABLE 1.

Inheritance of Susceptibility to Alcohol Abuse in the Stockholm Adoption Study

Alcohol abuse in biological parents		Alcohol abuse in adoptees			
Father	Mother	Sons		Daughters	
		N	%	N	%
No	No	571	14.7	577	2.8
Yes	No	259	22.4	285	3.5
No	Yes	23	26.0	29	10.3
Yes	Yes	9	33.3	22	9.1

It is reasonable to conclude that adoption as social measure greatly reduced the risk of social incompetence among the adopted individuals in the Swedish population. However, it was obvious from our preliminary analyses that alcohol abuse in the biological parents was associated with a substantial increased risk of alcohol abuse in their adopted-away children. The risk of alcohol abuse was studied in the children when they were 23-43 years of age. As shown in Table 1 the adopted-away sons were more likely to be alcohol abusers if either their biological father or mother had been registered for alcohol abuse than if neither parent had been registered for alcohol abuse. However, the adopted-away daughters were more likely to be alcohol abusers only if their biological mother had been registered for alcohol abuse, not if neither parent or only the biological father had been registered for alcohol abuse. This sex difference suggested that some types of alcohol abuse might be heritable primarily in men; whereas other forms may be heritable in both men and women.[7],[5]

Cross-fostering Analysis of Adopted Men

In the next step of our analysis of heterogeneous groups of alcohol abusers, we first provisionally subdivided the adopted men according to their frequency and severity of registered abuse, as suggested by Kaij.[13] We distinguished adopted men who had "mild abuse" (one registration only), "moderate abuse" (two or three registrations and no treatment) and "severe abuse" (a diagnosis of alcoholism and/or treatment for alcoholism, including compulsory treatment in an institution for alcoholics or supervision according to the Temperance Act, or three or more registrations by the Temperance Board).

The biological parents of the "moderate abusers" were found to differ significantly from those of the other abusers: Their fathers more often had teenage onset of both criminal behavior and severe alcohol abuse. We called this father-son inherited alcoholism Type 2 or "male-limited alcoholism." In contrast, the biological fathers of the other abusers usually had later adult onset of mild to severe alcohol abuse without criminal behavior. This was true also whether the severity of abuse in the adoptee was mild or severe (Type 1 alcoholism). Furthermore, the biological mothers of this type of alcoholism had a substantial increased risk of alcohol abuse; whereas the biological mothers of the Type 2 alcohol abusers had no excess compared to the mothers of nonalcoholic adoptees. The only observed difference in the backgrounds of the mild and severe Type 1 alcohol abusers was in the occupational status of their biological and adoptive parents: Severe abuse was more likely to occur in those with predisposition to low occupational status.

These findings suggested that there were genetic differences between Type 1 and Type 2 alcohol abusers, but not between mild and severe Type 1 abusers. In other words, the differences between mild and severe alcohol abusers were largely determined by environmental exposure variables, not by genetic factors.

The importance of postnatal environmental factors on severity of Type 1 alcohol abuse was examined in a cross-fostering analysis of the 862 adopted men. In this analysis the risk of disorder in adoptees is considered as a consequence of different combinations of biological parent background and postnatal environmental experience, which is illustrated in Table 2 for alcohol abuse in the 862 adopted men. The risk of severe abuse increased twofold in sons who had both Type 1 biological background and low occupational status in their adoptive home. Likewise the risk of mild abuse was dependent on both the genetic and the environmental background. Accordingly, Type 1 alcoholism has also been called "milieu-limited" alcoholism.

On the other hand Type 2 alcoholism was highly heritable from father to

TABLE 2.
Cross-fostering Analysis of Mild and Severe Type 1 Alcoholism

Is Genetic Background Type 1?	Is Environmental Background Mild or Severe?	Male Adoptees Observed		
		Total N	% With Mild Abuse	% With Severe Abuse
No	—	448	6.5	4.2
Yes	No	237	7.2	6.3
Yes	Mild	91	15.4*	7.7
Yes	Severe	86	4.7	11.6*

* Abuse is increased only given both genetic and postnatal predisposition (p < .05).

TABLE 3.
Cross-fostering Analysis of Type 2 Alcohol Abuse in Men

Is genetic background type 2?	*Is environmental background type 2?*	*Male adoptees observed*	
		Total N	*% with type 2 abuse*
No	No	567	1.9
No	Yes	196	4.1
Yes	No	71	16.9[a]
Yes	Yes	28	17.9[a]

[a]Risk is significantly increased in those with type 2 genetic background compared to others (p < 0.01).

son, regardless of external circumstances (Table 3). The risk in sons of Type 2 fathers was increased about ninefold compared to the risk in sons to other fathers, including those with either Type 1 or no alcoholism.

VALIDATION OF THE TYPOLOGY: CROSS-FOSTERING ANALYSIS OF ADOPTED WOMEN

So far our suggested typology was tentative. But in order to test the validity of the distinction between the suggested two types of alcoholism that we had developed in the studies of adopted men[7] we carried out tests of predictions in adopted women.[5] We had predicted that biological parents of Type 1 alcoholism would have an excess of adopted-away daughters with alcohol abuse, a prediction based on the findings that mothers of Type 1 alcoholics had often been alcoholics, but not those of Type 2 alcoholics.

In order to test this prediction, we classified the biological parents of the adopted women, using a multivariate discriminant function derived from the male sample. That is, we classified the biological parents of women according to several characteristics that had distinguished the two types of male alcoholics, such as age of onset of alcohol abuse and associated criminality. Thus, we classified the biological parent backgrounds in exactly the same way regardless of sex of the adoptee. Then we checked to see what behaviors were actually observed in the adopted women. In Tables 4 and 5, behaviors of daughters of Type 1 and Type 2 biological families are summarized. As predicted the Type 1 background daughters were more likely to be alcohol abusers than were Type 2 or other daughters.

We also found that the Type 2 background daughters were likely to have prominent somatization as evidenced by their excessive physical complaints and sick leave disability.[6] The Type 2 background daughters had frequent and diverse physical complaints, such as headaches, backaches, and

TABLE 4.

**Psychopathology in the Adopted-out Daughters of Type 1 Biologic Parents
and of Nonalcoholic Biologic Parents**

| | Classification of daughters[a] | | |
Observed psychopathology[b]	*Type 1 (N=110) row %*	*Low risk (N=282) row %*	*Significance level P*
Alcohol abuse	7.3	2.5	<0.05[c]
Criminality only	0	1.4	NS
Somatization only	16.3	16.3	NS
Other disability	13.6	15.2	NS

[a]Classification of the biologic parents of the women was based on discriminant analysis of an independent sample of parents of adopted men.
[b]The classification system for adoptees was hierarchical, proceeding from alcohol abuse to other psychiatric disability. Thus criminality only indicates criminality and no alcohol abuse with or without somatization or other disability; somatization only indicates neither alcohol abuse nor criminality.
[c]Risk is increased compared with low-risk daughters.

TABLE 5.

**Psychopathology in the Adopted-out Daughters of Type 2 Biologic Parents
and of Nonalcoholic Biologic Parents**

| | Classification of daughters[a] | | |
Observed psychopathology[b]	*Type 1 (N=105) row %*	*Low risk (N=282) row %*	*Significance level P*
Alcohol abuse	4.8	2.5	NS
Criminality only	2.9	1.4	NS
Somatization only	26.7	16.3	<0.05[c]
Other disability	13.3	15.2	NS

[a]Classification of the biologic parents of the women was based on discriminant analysis of an independent sample of parents of adopted men.
[b]The classification system for adoptees was hierarchical, proceeding from alcohol abuse to other psychiatric disability. Thus criminality only indicates criminality and no alcohol abuse with or without somatization or other disability; somatization only indicates neither alcohol abuse nor criminality.
[c]Risk is increased compared with low-risk daughters.

stomachaches. This is consistent with other studies showing an association of Briquets syndrome or somatization disorder with antisocial personality and alcoholism in men in the same family.[9] Given the same genetic predisposition, men usually express Type 2 alcoholism and women usually express somatization. Somatization in women and Type 2 alcoholism in men are associated with antisocial personality traits.[9]

PERSONALITY AND ALCOHOLISM SUBTYPES

So far our analyses of the adoptees and their two sets of families does not indicate any simple and direct mode of inheritance of alcohol abuse. Rather, our studies suggest that the transmission between generations of alcoholism to a large extent is associated with personality factors, which are continuously distributed in the population. In fact Type 1 and Type 2 alcoholics seem to differ by being at opposite extremes of the same dimensions of heritable personality factors. Thus the genetics of different alcohol-related syndromes are at least partly a question of the heritability of various personality variables.[10]

The alcohol-related symptoms and personality traits of individuals with different alcoholic subtypes were directly measured in nonadoptee clinical samples in Sweden.[15] Type 2 alcoholic men were found to be more impulsive, extraverted and sensation-seeking subtypes than Type 1 male or female alcoholics. They were also found to have low platelet monoamine oxidase activity in thrombocytes.

In a further step in our analyses of the adoptee cohort, we were able to identify men and women at high risk for alcoholism by selection of adoptees with different forms of anxiety of somatization.[9] Cognitive anxiety refers to frequent anticipatory worrying associated with complaints of weakness and fatigue, but infrequent headaches, backaches, and other bodily complaints. Cognitive anxiety is associated with passive-dependent personality traits, including (1) high harm avoidance (that is, cautious, apprehensive, pessimistic, inhibited, shy, and fatigable; (2) high reward dependence (i.e., eager to help others, emotionally dependent, warmly sympathetic, sentimental, sensitive to social cues, and persistent); (3) low novelty seeking (i.e., rigid, reflective, loyal, orderly, and attentive to details).

In contrast, individuals with *somatic* anxiety or somatization have the reverse configuration of personality traits, which is characteristic of antisocial personality, including: (1) low harm avoidance (i.e., confident, relaxed, optimistic, uninhibited, carefree, and energetic); (2) high novelty seeking (i.e., impulsive, exploratory, excitable, disorderly, and distractible), (3) low reward dependence (i.e., socially detached, emotionally cool, practical, tough-minded, and independently self-willed).

Individuals with either cognitive or somatic anxiety were at increased risk for alcoholism. However, adoptees with cognitive anxiety had fewer criminal biological parents than in the general population (as expected for the Type

1 alcoholism). In contrast, adoptees with somatic anxiety had more criminal biological parents than in the general population (as expected for Type 2 alcoholism).

PERSONALITY IN CHILDHOOD AS PREDICTOR OF ALCOHOLISM IN YOUNG ADULTHOOD

In order to test our suggested scale of personality in the development of alcoholism, we reanalyzed an ongoing prospective longitudinal study of children who were registered for adoption in Stockholm in a two-year period during the 1950s. At age 11, 431 children had been followed up for a detailed behavioral assessment including a semi-structured interview with their class teachers.[2],[8] This assessment permitted rating of the three dimensions of personality, suggested by Cloninger[10]: i.e., harm avoidance, novelty seeking, and reward dependence, independent of any other information about their later behavior. Independently, records about alcohol abuse (and criminality) were obtained about 16 years later (age 27-28 years).

We predicted that abuse would be primarily Type 2, that both antisocial personality configuration (i.e., high novelty seeking, low harm avoidance and low reward dependence) and the anxious personality configuration (high reward dependence, high harm avoidance and low novelty seeking) would increase alcohol abuse in adult age. In addition we predicted that most early onset alcoholics would have the antisocial personality configuration. We also predicted that the probability of alcohol abuse would increase exponentially with the population mean on these three personality dimensions.

All of these predictions were confirmed as summarized in Table 6 about the 233 men. On the basis of childhood personality alone, we were able to distinguish groups of boys who varied in their later risk of alcoholism from 4% to 75%.[11] In addition, we could distinguish boys who committed only property crimes from those who committed crimes of violence: Criminality in general was associated with high novelty seeking, but violent criminality also required low harm avoidance.[16]

These results from our adoption, clinical and longitudinal studies in Sweden have been recently confirmed in the St. Louis Family Study, USA. In this study the Type 2 syndrome, which is characteristic of men in families of male alcoholics, is distinguished by individuals with onset of persistent alcohol-seeking behavior ("inability to abstain entirely") before age 25 years, fights while drinking, arrests for reckless driving while drinking, and treatment for alcohol abuse. In contrast, the Type 1 syndrome, which is characteristic of men related to female alcoholics, is distinguished by onset after age 25 years of loss of control, guilt feelings, binges, and liver disease. Heritability of

TABLE 6.
**Quantitative Perrsonality Deviation and Non-Linearity of Risk
for Later Alcohol Abuse**

Childhood Personality Rating	# Boys	% Alcohol Abuse	Risk Ratio*
Harm Avoidance			
+2 or +3	21	14	1.6
+1	49	8	0.9
0	99	9	1.0
−1	39	18	2.0
−2 or −3	25	28	3.1
Novelty Seeking			
+2 or +3	65	25	2.3
+1	24	4	0.4
0	101	11	1.0
−1	27	0	0.0
−2 or −3	16	13	1.2
Reward Dependence			
+2 or +3	30	20	2.5
+1	67	12	1.5
0	89	8	1.0
−1	29	17	2.2
−2 or −3	18	22	2.8

* Risk ratio is the ratio of the risk in the specified group to the risk of average individuals.

alcoholism in the Type 2 families was 88%, and that in Type 1 families was 21%,[12] estimates similar to those obtained in the Stockholm Adoption Study.

DISCUSSION

The series of studies that we have described here has defined a consistent set of distinguishing characteristics for two subgroups of alcoholics. The distinguishing features are summarized in Table 7. Type 1 alcoholics have personality traits that make them susceptible to anxiety. In response to the anti-anxiety effects of alcohol, they may rapidly become tolerant and dependent and have difficulties terminating drinking binges once they have started ("loss of control"). The Type 2 alcoholics have antisocial personality traits: They persistently seek alcohol for its euphoriant effects ("inability to abstain").

These differences in clinical features and patterns of inheritance are associated with other neurophysiological and psychopharmacological differ-

TABLE 7.

Distinguishing Characteristics of Two Types of Alcoholism

Characteristic Features	Type of Alcoholism	
	Type 1	Type 2
Alcohol-related problems		
Usual age of onset (years)	After 25	Before 25
Spontaneous alcohol-seeking (inability to abstain)	Infrequent	Frequent
Fighting and arrests when drinking	Infreqeunt	Frequent
Psychological dependence (less of control)	Frequent	Infrequent
Guilt and fear about (alcohol dependence)	Frequent	Infrequent
Personality Traits		
Novelty seeking	Low	High
Harm avoidance	High	Low
Reward dependence	High	High

ences summarized elswhere.[10] For instance, abstinent Type 2 alcoholics and their sons have augmenting perceptual reactance to stimulation by increasing intensity, as well as a reduced amplitude of the late positive component (P3) of the event-related brain-wave potential.[1]

Despite the differences among Type 1 and Type 2 alcoholics, there often is still overlap in symptoms, particularly in treatment samples. Our results suggest that two opposing processes predispose to alcohol abuse, not that there are two discrete nosological entities. Risk of alcoholism is a quantitative variable, not a dichotomy or a trichotomy.

Starting our adoption studies 25 years ago with very general and broad questions about the transmission or prevention of the "social heritage," our studies have now clearly shown that alcoholism "runs in families" and that there are genetic differences between different subtypes of alcoholics. The genetic transmission seems be related to personality traits, which are normally distributed in the population and moderately inherited. On the other hand, our results do not answer questions about, for instance, the biological variability of dependence, addiction, tolerance, or other facilitating or protecting factors which may be independent of the suggested personality factors.[17]

REFERENCES

(1) Begleiter H, Porjesz B, Bihari B, et al: Event-related brain potentials in boys at risk for alcoholism. *Science* 225: 1493-1496 (1984).

(2) Bohman M: A comparative study of adopted children, foster children and children in their biological environment born after undesired pregnancies. *Acta Paediatrica Scandinavica suppl* 221: 5-38 (1971).

(3) Bohman M: Some genetic aspects of alcoholism and criminality. *Arch Gen Psychiatry* 35: 269-276 (1978).

(4) Bohman M, von Knorring A-L: Psychiatric illness among adults adopted as infants. *Acta Psychiat Scand* 60: 106-112 (1979).

(5) Bohman M, Sigvardsson S, Cloninger CR: Maternal inheritance of alcohol abuse: cross-fostering analysis of adopted women. *Arch Gen Psychiatry* 38: 965-969 (1981).

(6) Bohman M, Cloninger CR, von Knorring A-L, et al: An adoption study of somatoform disorders. III. cross-fostering analysis and genetic relationship to alcoholism and criminality. *Arch Gen Psychiatry* 41: 872-878 (1984).

(7) Cloninger CR, Bohman M, Sigvardsson S: Inheritance of alcohol abuse: cross-fostering analysis of adopted men. *Arch Gen Psychiatry* 38: 861-868 (1981).

(8) Cloninger CR, Sigvardsson S, Bohman M: Childhood personality predicts alcohol abuse in young adults. Alcoholism, *Clinical & Experimental Research* vol 12: 494-505 (1988).

(9) Cloninger CR: A unified biosocial theory of personality and its role in the development of anxiety states. *Psychiatric Developments* 3: 167-226 (1986).

(10) Cloninger CR: Neurogenetic adaptive mechanisms in alcoholism. *Science* 236: 410-416 (1987).

(11) Cloninger CR, Sigvardsson S, Bohman M: Childhood personality predicts alcohol abuse in young adults. Alcoholism. *Clinical and Experimental Research* 4: 494-505 (1988).

(12) Gilligan SB, Reich T, Cloninger CR: Etiologic heterogeneity in alcoholism. *Genetic Epidemiology* 7: 395-412 (1987).

(13) Kaij L: *Alcoholism in Twins*. Stockholm, Almqvist & Wiksell (1960).

(14) Kaij L: Biases in a Swedish social register of alcoholics. *Social Psychiatry* 5: 216-218 (1970).

(15) von Knorring A-L, Bohman M, von Knorring L, Oreland L: Platelet MAO activity as a biological marker in subgroups of alcoholism. *Acta Psychiat Scand* 72: 51-58 (1985).

(16) Sigvardsson S, Bohman M, Cloninger CR: Structure and stability of childhood personality: prediction of later social adjustment. *Child Psychol Psychiat* 6: 929-946 (1987).

(17) Tabakoff B, Hoffman PL: Genetic and biological markers of risk for alcoholism. In Kiianma K, Tabakoff B & Saito T: *Genetic Aspects of Alcoholism*. Helsinki. The Finnish Foundation for Alcohol Studies, vol 37 (1989).

(18) Öjesjö L: Prevalence of known and hidden alcoholism in the revisited Lundby population. *Social Psychiatry* 15: 81-90 (1980).

PART II: GENETIC FACTORS OF ALCOHOLISM:
CLINICAL ASPECTS

5

Prospective Evidence for the Effects of Environment upon Alcoholism

George E. Vaillant, M.D.

This article reports multivariate analyses of data from a 33-year prospective study of the 456 nondelinquent controls from the Gluecks' delinquency study. The data suggest that presence or absence of South European ethnicity (perhaps as a result of attitudes toward alcohol use and abuse) and the number of alcoholic relatives (perhaps more due to heredity rather than environment) accounted for most of the variance in adult alcoholism explained by childhood variables. Premorbid antisocial behavior also added significantly to the risk of alcoholism. However, an unstable family environment was a more important predictor of whether an individual loses control of alcohol at an early age and/or has multiple symptoms, than whether he has many alcoholic relatives.

I. INTRODUCTION

Alcoholism involves illusions. Many of these illusions stem from trying to see a very complex disorder in simple black and white terms. Investigators have sometimes oversimplified the social and genetic contributions to alcoholism. In this paper I shall use longitudinal, prospective study of community samples to illustrate the fact that both environment and genes may make important and quite different contributions to alcoholism.

Prospective studies are gradually teaching psychiatrists the astonishing fact that most of the psychopathology seen in alcoholics is the result, not the cause, of alcohol abuse.[14],[17],[28],[29] Put differently, alcoholism is the horse, not the cart, of mental illness. The relationship between sociopathy and alcoholism, however, remains less clear. Marc Schuckit has succinctly summarized the etiological possibilities that might link alcoholism and sociopathy.[22]

The three possibilities are: first, that sociopaths abuse alcohol as but one symptom of their underlying antisocial personality; second, that alcoholics manifest sociopathic symptoms as a consequence of primary alcohol dependence; and third, that there may be a common factor that leads both to alcoholism and sociopathy. Clearly, a prospective design is essential to elucidate the correct possibilities.

Which of Schuckit's three possibilities is confirmed will depend in part upon how the clinical sample is originally selected. In the prospective studies of both Robins[21] and the McCords,[17] the antecedents of alcoholism and sociopathy appeared to be very similar. An antisocial adolescence often preceded adult alcohol abuse. Both studies, however, were limited by their initial focus upon a relatively antisocial group of school children.[20],[21] One in four of the boys in Robins' sample later met her criteria for sociopathy, and only one in 12 was classified as a "primary" alcoholic. Thus, in her study much alcohol abuse seemed a consequence of childhood antisocial behavior and Schuckit's first possibility seemed most likely.

In contrast, in the prospective studies of college samples[14],[28] which tend to exclude antisocial adolescents, the causal sequence was reversed and adult sociopathic behavior was almost always a consequence of alcohol abuse. In these instances, Schuckit's second possibility seems more tenable.

By examining a more heterogeneous sample, I wish to suggest that both Schuckit's first two possibilities are correct but that the second possibility occurs more often than the first. I shall test a model that suggests that sociopathy—to the extent that it precedes alcohol abuse—may be a result of nonspecifically disorganized, and unhappy, childhoods. The model suggests that alcoholism—to the extent that it precedes antisocial behavior—may depend upon quite different childhood factors—namely, familial alcoholism and attitudes toward alcohol use.

Bohman's careful cross-fostering study suggests a similar model.[2] Bohman studied criminality and alcoholism in 2,000 adoptees and in their biological parents. There was a strong association between alcohol abuse in biological parents and alcohol abuse in their adopted-away children. There was not a strong association between criminal behavior in biological parents and criminal behaviour in their adopted away children. The implication from Bohman's and many other studies is that genetic factors play a definite etiological role in alcoholism. There is abundant evidence from other studies that disorganized families play a specific role in sociopathy;[7],[17],[21] this paper will suggest that that is not true for a majority of alcoholics.

My sample was the 456 controls used by Sheldon and Eleanor Glueck[7],[8] in their classic study of juvenile delinquency. When they were 12-16 years old, these men were selected from inner-city Boston schools for study. The only criteria for selection were that the controls be matched with delinquents remanded to reform school in terms of IQ, ethnicity, and high-crime neighborhood residence. Thus, the sample was largely drawn from socially disadvantaged families; 61 percent of their parents were foreign born and the mean IQ of the subjects was 95.

In order to assemble evidence about alcoholism, criminality, mental illness, and social dependency, the Glueck research team interviewed the men, their parents, and their teachers. The Gluecks checked criminal records, mental health records, and social service records for all first-degree relatives. The men were reinterviewed at age 25; they were reinterviewed at age 32, and they were reinterviewed at age 47. At age 47 only four of the 456 could not be located and 400 were still alive and fully cooperative with the research.

The study design was to establish lifetime prevalence (up to age 47) of alcoholism and, of equal importance, to establish naturalistic patterns of recovery from alcoholism. The advantages of our design are fivefold. First, unlike clinical samples it was possible to include *all* the alcoholics in a community cohort. Second, unlike clinical samples, we could ensure that each alcoholic had an equal chance of getting counted. (Most clinical studies oversample the most chronic, relapsing alcoholic.) Third, we could keep track of recovered alcoholics as well as of those who were sick. Fourth, we could contrast our sample with naturalistically matched conrols. Fifth, the mental and social adjustment of our sample was studied before as well as after they began to drink alcoholically. Most clinical samples are severely biased in one or more of these respects.

Alcoholism was measured with three separate scales, none of which proved to be superior to another.[31] These scales were Cahalan's Problem Drinking Scale,[4] the American Psychiatric Association DSM-III criteria for alcohol abuse and alcohol dependence, and the Problem Drinking Scale[28]—a modified version of the Michigan Alcoholism Screening Test (MAST)[24] that capitalized on our available longitudinal data. Of the 456 men in the study, 256 could not be described as problem drinkers by any definition. One hundred and sixteen had four or more different symptoms of alcohol abuse; of these 116 men, 71 men also met the DSM-III[1] criteria for alcohol dependence.

When one contrasts the alcohol dependent adults with adults with no drinking problems, it appeared as if alcoholism was a social illness reflecting and presumably caused by social disadvantage. Thus, Table 1 illustrates that the alcoholics were several times more likely to be unemployed, and personality disordered, and five times more likely to belong to the lowest social class. However, Table 1 also reveals that attributing causal significant to these differences is probably an error. The childhood of these two groups of men

TABLE 1.

Adult Variables that Are More a Result than a Cause of Alcoholism

	Social Drinkers (n = 260)	Alcohol Dependent Drinkers (n = 71)
Adult Variables		
Lowest adult social class (V)	4%	21%
10+ years unemployed	4%	24%
Never completed high school	56%	41%
HSRS <70	24%	51%
Corresponding Childhood Variable		
Lowest parent's social class (V)	32%	30%
Multi-problem family membership	11%	14%
IQ <90	28%	30%
Childhood emotional problems	32%	30%

Note: HSRS = Health Sickness Rating Scale (15)

TABLE 2.

Relationship between Parents' Culture and Development of Alcohol Dependence

	Culture of Parents		
DSM-III Classification	Irish (n = 75)	Other[a] (n = 193)	Mediterranean (n = 130)
No alcoholic abuse	59	58	86
Alcohol abuse without dependence	13	19	10
Alcohol dependent	28	23	4

Note: Values are in percentages; DSM-III = Diagnostic and Statistical Manual of Mental Disorders (1). p < .001 by chi-square test.
[a]Canadian, American, Northern European

did not reveal significant differences in social class or economic dependency. Alcoholism leads to social disadvantage more often than the reverse.

Although the men themselves were native born and shared a common social environment, the cultural mores of their parents (61% of whom were foreign born) differed greatly. Such differences in parental ethnicity were highly correlated with the men's subsequent use of alcohol. Table 2 contrasts the culture in which the men's parents were raised with the likelihood of the development of alcohol dependence among the men themselves. The 75 men of Irish extraction were seven times more likely to manifest alcohol dependence than the 130 men of Italian, Syrian, Jewish, Greek, or Portuguese extraction.

Admittedly, the relationship between alcohol use and culture is extremely complex,[10],[11],[16],[25] but in this study the relationship is reduced to a single common denominator—cultural characteristics of alcohol use that empirically affect the likelihood of alcohol dependence. Thus, ethnicity was crudely scaled to contrast cultures that forbid drinking in children but condone drunkenness in adults with those cultures that teach children how to drink responsibly but that forbid adult drunkenness.[12],[18] Mediterranean cultures allow children to drink alcohol but have strong sanctions against drunkenness in adults. Conversely, the Irish and North American cultures forbid drinking in adolescence, have flirted with total prohibition for a century, but give tacit or explicit approval to drunkenness in male adults. For purposes of statistical depiction, other Northern European countries were assigned an intermediate position. Jellinek[12] points out in some detail that although France teaches children responsible drinking, it also condones drunkenness and alcohol use independent of meals.

The interaction between parental culture and familial alcoholism was interesting. Among men of Irish extraction the presence of alcoholic relatives only slightly increased the risk of alcohol dependence in the subjects: Many Irish subjects with alcoholic relatives became lifelong teetotalers. Among other ethnic groups (both among the Southern Europeans in whom alcohol abuse was rare and among the Northern Europeans and old Americans in whom it was common), alcohol dependence ocurred five times as often in men with several alcoholic relatives as it did in men with no alcoholic relatives.

In this study, childhood environmental weaknesses were defined on a continuous 25-item scale. Boys having 10 or more items were considered to come from multi-problem families. Representative items were: Mother either delinquent or alcoholic, boy described self as indifferent to mother, father arrested multiple times, father physically cruel towards subject, boy made eight moves or more, family was known to nine or more social service agencies. Childhood environmental weaknesses correlated with future risk of alcohol abuse, but this risk exactly paralleled incidence of parental alcohol abuse. By this I mean that future alcoholics have troubled childhoods because they have alcoholic parents. In Table 3, of the 45 men who had *few* childhood environmental weaknesses but did have an alcoholic father, 29% became alcohol dependent. Of the 56 men with many environmental weaknesses but *no* alcoholic parent, only 9% became alcohol dependent. In other words, the observed differences between alcoholics and nonalcoholics in environmental weaknesses can be explained using a genetic rather than environmental model.

Social disadvanage is *not* a major cause of alcoholism. In the present study, alcoholism could be predicted just as well by the number of alcoholic ances-

TABLE 3.

**Proportion of Men Developing Adult Alcoholic Dependence when
Multi-Problem Family Membership and Paternal Alcoholism Are Covaried**

Childhood Environmental Weaknesses	Father Not Alcoholic	Father Is Alcoholic
0-5 Problems	n = 194	n = 45
	12% alcoholic	29% alcoholic
6-10 Problems	n = 42	n = 71
	10% alcoholic	28% alcoholic
10+ Problems	n = 14	n = 33
	7% alcoholic	27% alcoholic

tors who did *not* live with the patient as it could by alcoholic parents who did live with the subjects. Thus, this study corroborated the cross-fostering studies that have suggested alcoholic relatives contribute to alcoholism in probands through genetic rather than through environmental influence.[9]

The evidence cited thus far in this paper points away from childhood environment playing a critical role in alcoholism. But such evidence has led to another illusion, namely, that "hereditary" alchoholism may be different from alcoholism in individuals without alcoholic relatives. Work by Cloninger and other researchers[3],[5],[6],[27] has suggested that alcoholics with heavy genetic loading may reflect "primary" or "process" alcoholism and be analogous to juvenile diabetes or process schizophrenia. This hypothesis is based on the clinical observation that in alcoholics with many alcoholic relatives alcoholism begins earlier, has a worse prognosis, and is more severe. On the other hand, alcoholism that occurs in individuals without known alcoholic relatives has a relatively good prognosis, begins later, and is less severe.

It has been suggested that this latter alcoholism is "secondary" or "acquired" and is analogous to "reactive schizophrenia" and adult-onset diabetes. Certainly, if one studies Skid Row, socially deviant alcoholics, they tend to have many alcoholic relatives and to have begun early. In contrast, late-onset middle-class alcoholics often have better social adjustment and have fewer alcoholic relatives. Why? The difficulty with such studies is that they are cross-sectional and are not drawn from community samples but from clinical samples. These studies, as the introduction of this paper suggests, are subject to many sources of bias.

Figures 1 – 3 offer three contrasting composite pictures of alcoholics derived from community samples. The first figure was produced by superimposing the life histories of all the 116 problem drinkers in the Gluecks'[7],[8] sample. By age 31 over 50% had become alcoholic, but age of onset was *not* correlated with genetic loading, and by age 47, 50% had recovered. Figure 2 shows the drinking careers of the 25 problem drinkers from Figure 1 who also met Lee Robins' criteria for sociopathy.[21] Clearly, the sociopaths' alcoholism began early. But what distinguished the sociopaths in Figure 2 from the other alcohol abusers in Figure 1 was not that they had greater loading of alcoholism in their ancestors, but that they had had very unstable childhood environments.[30]

Figure 3 shows the superimposed alcoholic careers of 25 alcoholics from a socioeconomically very different cohort of "normal" Harvard College sophomores also prospectively followed for 40 years.[27],[29] These men were socially advantaged, highly educated, and had relatively stable childhoods. Even with heavy genetic loading, they did not lose control of their alcohol use until relatively late. Perhaps as a function of superior social supports and an absence of sociopathic traits, the college sample rarely "hit bottom"

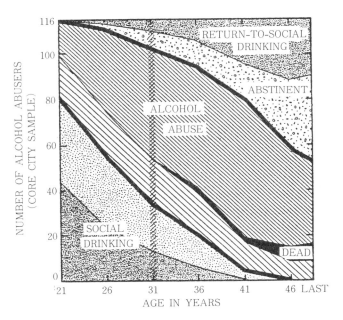

Figure 1. Composite life course of alcohol use and abuse among the 116 Core City men ever classified as alcohol abusers. Stippled area refers to the proportion drinking asymptomatically: light stippling indicates diagnostic uncertainty. Diagonal lines reflect men with 4+ symptoms of alcohol abuse: widely spaced diagonal lines indicate diagnostic uncertainty. The crosshatched line at age 31 is intended to accentuate differences in age of onset of alcohol abuse in the different samples in this and the following figures.

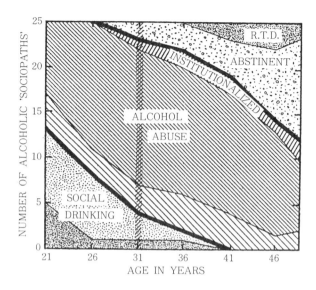

Figure 2. Composite life course of alcohol use and abuse among the 25 surviving inner city alcohol abusers who met Robins' criteria for sociopathy. Interpretation as in Figure 1.

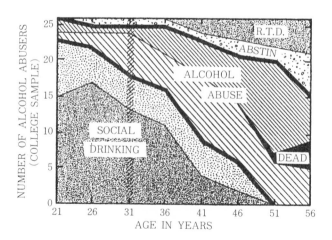

Figure 3. Composite life course of alcohol use and abuse among the 26 college alcohol abusers. Interpretation as in Figure 1. Abstin. = abstinence as defined in the text. R.T.D. = return to asymptomatic drinking after having met the criteria for alcohol abuse.

so badly that they were willing to sustain the prolonged abstinences seen in Figure 1. Certainly, the long-term prognosis of the college sample was inferior to that of the inner city men. Yet their genetic loading was less. In contrast to the college sample, the sociopaths were far more disadvantaged and far more symptomatic, yet their long-term prognosis was also better. Of course, it must be remembered that these findings came from a 40-year study and, in clinical studies, social disadvantage and multiple symptoms uniformly predict poorer prognosis over the next *one* or *two* years.

The point of the three figures is to suggest that environment may be more important than genes in determining the *course* of alcoholism if the disease does develop. Table 4 illustrates this implied role of environment more clearly. For the inner city men, the number of alcoholic relatives was not correlated with the age of onset of their alcoholism. Rather, it was alcoholics raised in unstable environments who were most likely to lose control of their drinking *early*. Alcoholic parents were associated with early onset of alcoholism only if they lived with their child.

It is known that unstable childhood leads to delinquency, that delinquents abuse drugs of many sorts, and that delinquents are more likely than nondelinquents to manifest alcoholism. Similarly, alcoholics with known alcoholic relatives often—as a result of living with these relatives—grow up in disrupted, conflict-ridden homes and are likely, when young, to engage in antisocial behavior for environmental as well as genetic reasons. In addition, Daniel Weinberger[32] has reminded us that the same genetically transmitted illness (e.g., Huntington's chorea) can present very differently if it first occurs in young rather than middle-aged individuals. Put differently, Cloninger[6] suggests that Type II alcoholics are high in novelty seeking, low in harm avoidance and in reward dependence, whereas Type I alcoholics are low in novelty seeking and high in harm avoidance and reward dependence. Although such differences may depend on genetic differences in neurotransmitters, these same contrasts are observed when middle-aged fathers argue with their genetically similar adolescent sons over motorcycles, study habits, and mountain climbing.

In short, advocates of Type I and Type II alcoholism have not seriously considered the possibility that both types of alcoholism may have similar genetic transmission. However, *age of onset* of alcoholism, which may affect clinical symptoms, may be environmentally, not genetically, determined. The conclusion to be drawn from Table 4 is not that there are two kinds of alcoholism. Rather, genetic loading is an important predictor of *whether* an individual develops alcoholism, but an unstable environmental loading is an important predictor of *when* an individual develops alcoholism. Since a common means of having an unstable childhood is to have an alcoholic

TABLE 4.

Association of Environmental and Hereditary Factors with Age of Onset of Alcoholism

	Age of onset of alcoholism[a]			
	9 – 19 years	*20 – 30 years*	*31 – 46 years*	*Total*
Total Sample (n = 109)	18%	37%	45%	100%
No Alcoholic Relatives (n = 31)	19%	32%	49%	100%
Many Alcoholic Relatives (n = 33)[b]	15%	42.5%	42.5%	100%
Multiproblem Childhood (n = 16)	44%	37%	19%	100%
Incohesive Family (n = 33)	33%	49%	18%	100%
Alcoholic Parents (in Environment) (n = 30)	27%	43%	30%	100%

[a]Defined as the year an individual developed his fourth symptom on a 16-item Problem Drinking Scale (28).

[b]Alcohol abuse was estimated separately for parents and for relatives who did not live with the subject. "Alcoholic relatives" here reflected a combination of both scales and meant that at least two relatives showed *minor* evidence of alcoholism (two or more convictions for alcoholism, mention of alcoholism in official records, or strong suspicion in the case record) or one relative with *major* evidence (two or more criteria for minor evidence and evidence of chronicity).

TABLE 5.

Contribution of Selected Premorbid Variables to Number of Alcohol-Related Problems and Sociopathic Behaviours

	Alcohol-related problems		Sociopathic behaviors[a]	
Variable	*% explained variance*	*beta weight*	*% explained variance*	*beta weight*
Alcoholism in heredity	7.6	.19	1.3	.05
No Mediterranean ethnicity[b]	3.5	.20	1.0	.11
School behavior problems[b]	3.0	.18	8.0	.30
Childhood environmental weaknesses	.1	.05	2.1	.07
Poor infant health	.1	.10	2.9	.17

[a]See Robins[21]

[b]To minimize the variance that they could explain, these two variables were entered into the multiple regression after the other four variables.

parent, confusion arises in people's minds as to the relative roles of heredity and environment in the course of alcoholism.

Table 5 examines the independent contribution to the total number of alcohol-related problems for each of the potential etiological variables identified. Alcoholic heredity, school behavior problems, and not being brought up in a Mediterranean culture (entered into the multiple regression analysis as a dummy variable) each made an important contribution to the explained variance in subsequent alcohol problems. If the number of alcoholic relatives is controlled, multi-problem families are not associated with an increased number of alcoholic related problems, but they are associated with an increased number of antisocial problems.

I do not wish to imply that in adult life other environmental variables do not possess etiological importance. This paper, of course, reports on only a single cohort of inner city male alcoholics from a single city. By excluding the more severe delinquents, the Glueck sample minimizes the contribution of premorbid social deviance to alcoholism. Demographic variables,[4] occupation,[19] social peer groups,[13] legal availability,[26] societal instability[18] attribution and expectancy effects,[16] and other, as yet unidentified, factors certainly contribute independent variance to the development of alcohol dependence. The purpose of this paper is simply to provide balance to the environmental-genetic complexity of the etiology of alcoholism.

Acceptance of this paper's conclusions requires confirmation in other samples and settings. To confirm the paper's hypothesis definitively, it would be necessary to conduct a cross-fostering study. In such a study men, born of alcoholic parents, who were raised in a stable family by nonalcoholic parents, would be predicted to develop alcoholism, with late onset and only moderate severity. Men, born of nonalcoholic parents who were raised in disrupted alcoholic families would be less likely to develop alcohol dependence, but if they did, it would be predicted that they would develop alcoholism younger and be more symptomatic, thus resembling the hypothetical "process" or "primary" alcoholic.

REFERENCES

(1) American Psychiatric Association: *Diagnostic and Statistical Manual of Mental Disorders*. Washington D.C: American Psychiatric Association Press (1980).

(2) Bohman, M: Some Genetic Aspects of Alcoholism and Criminality, *Arch General Psychiatry* 35: 269-276 (1978).

(3) Buydens-Branchey, L, Branchey, MH, and Noumair, D: Age of alcoholism onset: I. Relationship to psychopathology. *Arch Gen Psychiatry* 46: 225-230 (1989).

(4) Cahalan, D, and Room, R: *Problem Drinkers A National Survey*. San Francisco: Jossey-Bass (1970).

(5) Cloninger, CR, Bohman, M and Sigvardsson, S: Inheritance of Alcohol Abuse: Cross-Fostering Analysis of Adopted Men. *Arch Gen Psychiatry*, 38: 861-868 (1981).

(6) Cloninger CR: Neurogenic adaptive mechanisms in alcholism. *Science*, 236:

410-416 (1987).

(7) Glueck S and Glueck E: *Unraveling Juvenile Delinquency*. New York: The Commonwealth Fund (1950).

(8) Glueck S, and Glueck E: *Delinquents and Non-Delinquents in Perspective*. Cambridge, Mass: Harvard University Press (1968).

(9) Goodwin DW: Alcoholism and heredity. *Arch Gen Psychiatry*, 36: 57-61 (1979).

(10) Greely A and McReady WC: *Ethnic Drinking Subcultures*. New York: Praeger (1980).

(11) Heath DB: A critical review of ethnographic studies of alcohol use. In RJ Gibbons (Ed.), *Research Advances in Alcohol and Drug Problems* (Vol 2). New York: Wiley (1975).

(12) Jellinek EM: *The Disease Concept of Alcoholism*. New Haven, Conn: Hillhouse Press (1960).

(13) Jessor R and Jessor SL: Adolescent development and the onset of drinking. *Quarterly Journal of Studies in Alcoholism*, 36: 27-51 (1975).

(14) Kammeier, M.L., Hoffman, H., and Loper, R.G.: Personality Characteristics of Alcoholics as College Freshman and at Time of Treatment. *Quarterly Journal of Studies on Alcohol*, 34: 390-399 (1973).

(15) Luborsky L: Clinicians' Judgements of Mental Health. *Arch. Gen. Psychiatry*, 7: 407-417 (1962).

(16) Marlatt GA and Rohsenow DJ: Cognitive processes in alcoholic use: Expectancy and the balanced placebo design. In NK Marlow (Ed.), *Advances in Substance Abuse Behavioral and Biological Research*. Greenwich, Conn: Jai Press (1980).

(17) McCord W, and McCord J: *Origins of Alcoholism*. Stanford: Stanford University Press, (1960).

(18) Pittman DJ and Synder CR: *Society, Culture and Drinking Patterns*. New York: Wiley (1962).

(19) Plant ML: *Drinking Careers*. London: Tavistock (1979).

(20) Powers E and Witmer H: *An Experiment in the Prevention of Delinquency*. New York: Columbia University Press (1959).

(21) Robins LN: *Deviant Children Grown Up: A Sociological and Psychiatric Study of Sociopathic Personality*. Baltimore: Williams and Wilkins (1966).

(22) Schuckit MA: Alcoholism and Sociopathy—Diagnostic Confusion. *Quarterly Journal of Studies on Alcohol*, 34: 157-164 (1973).

(23) Schuckit MA: The Clinical Implication of Primary Diagnostic Groups among Alcoholics. *Arch Gen Psychiatry*, 42: 1043-1049 (1985).

(24) Selzer ML: The Michigan Alcoholism Screen Test: The Quest for a New Diagnostic Instrument. *Amer J. Psychiatry*, 127: 1653-1658 (1971).

(25) Stivers R: *A Hair of the Dog*. University Park: Pennsylvania State University Press (1976).

(26) Terris, MA: Epidemiology of cirrhosis of the liver: National mortality data. *Amer J of Public Health*, 57: 2076-2088 (1967).

(27) Vaillant, GE: *Adaptation to Life*. Boston: Little Brown (1977).

(28) Vaillant, GE: Natural history of male psychological health: VIII. Antecedents of alcoholism and "orality." *American Journal of Psychiatry*, 137: 181-186 (1980).

(29) Vaillant, GE: *The Natural History of Alcoholism*. Cambridge, Mass: Harvard University Press (1983).

(30) Vaillant, GE: Natural History of Male Alcoholism V: Is Alcoholism the Cart or the Horse to Sociopathy. *Brit J. Addiction*, 78: 317-326 (1983).

(31) Vaillant, GE, Gale, L, and Milofsky ES: Natural history of alcoholism: II. The relationship between different diagnostic dimensions. *Journal of Studies of Alcoholism*, 43: 216-232 (1982).

(32) Weinberger DR: Implications of normal brain development for the pathogenesis of schizophrenia. *Arch Gen Psychiatry*, 44: 660-669 (1987).

6

Genetic Polymorphism of Aldehyde Dehydrogenase in Orientals as Genetic Marker of a High-Risk Group of Alcoholism

Shoji Harada, Ph.D.

It has been suggested that a deficiency in ALDH2 isozyme may provide protection against alcoholism. In this paper, the genotypes of $ALDH_2$ locus were determined in healthy Japanese and the acetaldehyde metabolism after alcohol intake was investigated using a gas chromatography technique. The gene frequencies of $ALDH_2^1$ and $ALDH_2^2$ were compared between healthy controls and alcoholic patients. The individuals possessing the homogenous genotypes of $ALDH_2^2$ showed strong sensitivity to alcohol due to a higher formation of blood acetaldehyde after alcohol intake.

I. INTRODUCTION

Human NAD-dependent aldehyde dehydrogenase (ALDH, EC:1.2.1.3) consists of four different components using separation techniques such as electrophoresis and isoelectric focusing.[1],[2] Our previous studies demonstrated that the faster migrating component (ALDH2, E2, ALDH I) shows genetic polymorphism (normal and deficient in isozyme bands) in Oriental populations and that the deficiency of ALDH2 isozyme is responsible for the higher acetaldehyde level and flushing symptom after alcohol[3],[4] intake. Subsequent studies indicated that the frequency of the deficiency was significantly lower in alcoholics than that of healthy controls.[5] The data suggest that individuals deficient in ALDH2 isozyme may lead to protection against alcoholism. Recent studies on the basis of molecular biology revealed that the cause for the isozyme deficiency is a structural mutation leading to the synthesis of inactive and unstable protein.[6] Moreover, the determination of the genotypes of $ALDH_2$ locus is now possible using the advanced techniques for DNA analysis.[7],[8]

II. MATERIALS AND METHODS

Genomic DNA was isolated from the blood samples of 41 unrelated healthy Japanese, 12 pairs of twins families and 52 alcoholic patients according to the method of Blin and Stafford.[9] The blood ethanol and acetaldehyde levels were measured in 41 healthy Japanese using gaschromatograph with head space system (Perkin Elmer) according to the method reported by Mizoi et al.[10]

The DNA target sequences containing the point mutation responsible for ALDH2 normal and deficiency were amplified according to the polymerase chain reaction (PCR) technique.[11] The PCR amplification was performed in the 100 μl reaction mixture containing 10 mM $MgCl_2$, 200 μM dNTP, geratine 200 μl/ml, 1μM primer 1 and 2, 1 μg denature DNA and 2 units of thermostabile Taq polymerase (SCS Ltd.) using an instrument of heat block (Perkin Elmer Cetus). Thirty-five cycles of amplification were made at 50°C for 2 mins. on the step of annealing, at 70°C for 2 mins. on the extension and at 90°C for 1.5 min. on the denaturing. Two different primers, namely primer 1: 5'-CCACACTCACAGTTTTCACTT and primer 2: 5'-CAAAT-TACAGGGTCAACTGCT produced by a Beckman DNA synthesizer were used to amplify the target sequences in the region of exon 12.[12]

For the slot-blot hybridization, 5 μl of amplified product was denatured with 0.4 M NaOH and 25 mM EDTA in a final volume of 200 μl and heated for 2 min at 95°C followed by cooling on ice. Samples were loaded on to a nylon filter (Zetaprobe, Biorad) using slot blotter (Minifold II, Schreicher and Schuell). After baking at 80°C for 1 hour, the filter was prehybridized in the buffer containing 5 x SSPE, 5 x Denhard and 0.5% SDS for 1 hour at room temperature.

Filters were subjected to stringent hybridization of allete-specific oligonucleotide prepared with DNA synthesizer. Each oligonucleatide (ALDH$_2^1$: 5'-GTTTTCACTTCAGTGTATGCC, ALDH$_2^2$: 5'-GGCATACA-CTAAAGTGAAAAC)[8] were phosphorylated at their 5-termini with [γ-^{32}P]ATP and polynucleotide kinase.[13] After prehybridization, probes were added and hybridized at 50°C for 2 hours. Filters were rinsed twice in 5 x SSPE and 0.1% SDS for 60 min at 55°C for probe ALDH$_2^1$ and at 50°C for probe ALDH$_2^2$. The autoradiogram was exposed for 3 to 6 hours with a single intensification screen.

III. RESULTS AND DISCUSSION

The ALDH^2 genotypes of DNA extracted from blood samples could be determined using PCR method and slot-blott hybridization with synthesized oligonucleotide probes. In Figure 1, genotyping of ALDH$_2$ 1, ALDH$_2$ 2-1 and ALDH$_2$ 2 could be clearly determined. Recent study on the relationship of enzymatic activity and ALDH 2 genotypes indicated that a heterotetramer forming with the subunits of ALDH$_2$ 1 and ALDH$_2$ 2 have no enzymatic activity in autopsy liver samples.[8] The same results were obtained in the present study on the isozyme analysis of hair roots lysates and on the genotypes of DNA. Namely, only the homozygous genotypes of ALDH$_2^1$ showed an enzymatically active band.

The study on the genetic model concerning ALDH 2 genotypes was performed using the samples from the families of twins. As shown in Table 1, the inheritance of two alleles (ALDH$_2^1$ and ALDH$_2^2$) are well consistent with Mendelian heredity.

On the basis of this finding, the gene frequencies of ALDH$_1^2$ and ALDH$_2^2$ were investigated among the 41 healthy controls and 52 alcoholics. As shown in Table 2, ALDH$_2$ 1, ALDH$_2$ 2-1 and ALDH$_2$ 2 in the healthy controls were 58.6%, 34.1% and 7.3%, respectively. On the other hand only two individuals showed ALDH 2 isozyme deficiency in alcoholics and their genotypes were ALDH$_2$ 2-1. The gene frequency of ALDH$_2^2$ in alcoholics was significantly lower than that of healthy controls. These results confirmed our previous study on ALDH isozyme in hair roots using isoelectric focusing.

Our previous data indicated that the concentrations of blood acetaldehyde after alcohol intake were significantly higher in the individuals showing the deficiency of mitochondrial isozyme (ALDH 2) than those of the normal. In this study the subjects showing isozyme deficiency could be differentiated as heterozygout or homozygout by PCR method. Therefore, the blood acetaldehyde concentrations after alcohol intake were compared among the groups of three different genotypes forming with combination ALDH$_2^1$ and

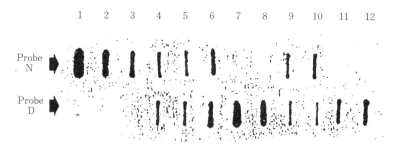

Figure 1.   Genotypes of two alleles at ALDH$_2$ locus.
N: ALDH$_2^1$ probe, D: ALDH$_2^2$ probe. 1,2,3 indicate ALDH$_2$ 1 genotype.
4,5,6,9,10: ALDH$_2$ 2-1, 7,8,11,12: ALDH$_2$ 2.

TABLE 1.
Genetic Study of ALDH in Twins and Parents

	Parents		*Monozygous*	
	(F)	*(M)*	*(A)*	*(B)*
1)	N ×	ND	ND	ND
2)	D ×	ND	ND	ND
3)	ND ×	ND	ND	ND
4)	N ×	N	N	N
5)	D ×	ND	ND	ND
6)	ND ×	N	N	N
7)	N ×	ND	N	N
8)	ND ×	N	N	N
9)	N ×	N	N	N
	(F)	*(M)*	*Dizygous*	
10)	N ×	ND	N	ND
11)	N ×	N	N	N

N: ALDH$_2^1$/ALDH$_2^1$, ND: ALDH$_2^1$/ALDH$_2^2$, D: ALDH$_2^2$/ALDH$_2^2$, F: Father, M: Mother, A,B: Twins

TABLE 2.
Genotypic Distribution at ALDH$_2$ Locus of Healthy Controls and Alcoholics

Genotypes	*ALDH$_2^1$/ALDH$_2^1$*	*ALDH$_2^1$/ALDH$_2^2$*	*ALDH$_2^2$/ALDH$_2^2$*	*Total*
Controls	24 (57%)	14 (34%)	4 (9%)	42
Alcoholics	18 (90%)	2 (10%)	0 (0%)	20

Controls: ALDH$_2^1$ = 0.74, ALDH$_2^2$ = 0.36
Alcoholics: ALDH$_2^1$ = 0.95, ALDH$_2^2$ = 0.05

ALDH$_2^2$ genes (ALDH$_2$ 1, ALDH$_2$ 2-1, ALDH$_2$ 2) in healthy controls.

As shown in Figure 2, the homozygous genotype of ALDH$_2$ 1 showed the lowest concentration (4.9 ± 1.7 μM). The subjects showing heterozygous genotypes of ALDH$_2$ 2-1 had lower concentration (24.6 ± 8.4 μM) than that of homozygous genotype of ALDH$_2$ 2 (71.2 ± 32.3 μM).

Consequently, the individuals possessing the homogenous genotype of ALDH$_2^2$ showed strong sensitivity to alcohol due to a higher formation of blood acetaldehyde after alcohol intake. We obtained the data (data were not shown) indicating that the phenotypes of ADH2 locus may also a important role for blood acetaldehyde concentration. These studies will be published elsewhere.

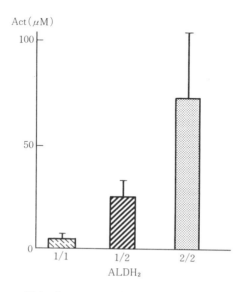

Figure 2. Blood acetaldehyde concentration after alcohol intake among three different genotypes of ALDH₂ locus.

REFERENCES

(1) Harada, S., Agarwal, D.P., Goedde, H.W.: Electrophoretic and biochemical studies of human aldehyde dehydrogenase isozymes in various tissues. *Life Sci.*, 26: 1771-1780 (1980).

(2) Harada, S., Misawa, S., Agarwal, D.P., Goedde H.W.: Liver alcohol dehydrogenase and aldehyde dehydrogenase in the Japanese: Isozyme variation and its possible role in alcohol intoxication. *Am. J. Hum. Genet.*, 32: 8-15 (1980).

(3) Harada, S., Agarwal, D.P., Goedde, H.W.: Aldehyde dehydrogenase deficiency as cause of facial flushing reaction to alcohol in Japanese. *Lancet*, ii: 982 (1981).

(4) Harada, S., Agarwal, D.P., Goedde, H.W.: Mechanism of alcohol sensitivity and disulfiramethanol reaction. *Substance and Alcohol Actions/Misuse*, 3: 107-115 (1982).

(5) Harada, S., Agarwal, D.P., and Goedde, H.W.: Possible protective role against alcoholism for aldehyde dehydrogenase deficiency in Japan. *Lancet*, ii: 827 (1982).

(6) Impraim, C.G., Wang, Yoshida, A.: Structual mutation in a major human aldehyde dehydrogenase gene results in loss of enzyme activity. *Am. J. Hum. Genet.* 34: 837-841 (1982).

(7) Yoshida, A., Wang, G., Deve, V.: Determination of genotypes of human aldehyde dehydrogenase locus. *Am. J. Hum. Genet.*, 35: 1107-1116 (1983).

(8) Hsu, L.C., Bendel, R.E., Yoshida, A.: Direct detection of usual and atypical alleles on the human aldehyde dehyderogenase 2 locus. *Am. J. Hum. Genet.*, 41: 996-1001 (1987).

(9) Blin, N., Stafford, D.W.: A general method for the isolation of high molecular weight DNA from eukaryotes. *Nucleic Acid Res.*, 3: 2303-2308 (1976).

(10) Mizoi, Y., Ijiri, I., Tatsuno, T. et al.: Relationship between facial flushing and blood acetaldehyde levels after alcohol intake. *Pharmacol. Biochem. & Behav.*, 16: 303-311 (1979).

(11) Saiki, R.K., Gelfand, D.H., Stoffel, S. et al: Primer directed emzymatic amplification of DNA with a thermostabile DNA polymerase. *Science* 239: 487-491 (1988).

(12) Hsu, L.C., Bendel, R.E., Yoshida, A.: Genomic structure of human alcohol mitochondrial aldehyde dehydrogenase gene. *Genomics* 2: 57-65 (1988).

(13) Maniatis, T., Fritsh, E.F., Sambrook, J.: *Molecular cloning: a laboratory manual*, Cold Spring Harbor, NY: Cold Spring Harbor Laboratory (1982).

Part II: Discussion

(*Chairperson*) *Professor Schuckit*: We have been fortunate today to hear two opposite ends of the spectrum of the kind of work that can be done. First, Dr. Bohman introduced us to the information about the adoption studies supporting genetics and showed us a theory about how alcoholics might fall on a continuum between Type 1 and Type 2. This is a theory that is presently being evaluated with some data consistent, some data inconsistent, but it is a potentially viable focus for more research.

Dr. Vaillant's paper, sharing the findings from his impressive, long-term follow-up study, has also been vital in indicating the pressures that environmental factors may bring to bear upon genetic influences already present, and the enigma of how the two influences affect each other within the drinker.

We also heard from Dr. Harada, about where his kind of work with genetics in alcoholism may lead us. Within different ethnic groups, it may be that we will begin to use some of the very impressive molecular genetic approaches to learn more about which types of genes might be involved.

Now, I would like to open the discussion with a question. Dr. Harada, do we have any information on what gene is involved for control of ALDH1?

Dr. Harada: The new nomenclature is ALDH2—a mitochondrial enzyme which is regulated by the gene located on chromosome 12. This enzyme consists of a tetramer, the subunit of which is regulated by the gene possessing 1.5 kb as cDNA consisting of 12 exons.

(*Chairperson*) *Professor Schuckit*: It would be interesting to see, especially among the Japanese who have the mitochondrial enzyme, whether the other factors—such as reaction to alcohol or the other potential markers—play an important role. Now you have two different major subtypes of people, based on their enzyme patterns, and it may be that some of the things that have now been studied in Caucasian populations may be important within the subgroup of Japanese who have ALDH1.

Professor Ishii (*P.R.I.T.*): Your data are very impressive and I'm wondering whether the personality traits are different between the two groups or not. Dr. Bohman stated that in Caucasians there were two kinds of personality traits in alcoholism. So I was wondering if there are any personality differences between the two groups—those people deficient or nondeficient in the enzyme. Have you studied that kind of difference?

Dr. Harada: I have not yet conducted such a study. I believe Dr. Asaka may know the difference.

Dr. Asaka: We have obtained a study concerning differences in motivation of drinkers, but haven't yet conducted such studies as you mention. We need cooperation between clinicians and basic researchers.

Professor Bohman: I'd be very astonished if there were difference, because I think these must be absolutely independent genetic traits. They don't belong to the same biological systems. That is my hypothesis.

Dr. Harada: Yes, if they drink alcohol, they might show different symptoms, but in the normal state they don't show any difference. I think there are many other kinds of factors, such as those stated by Dr. Bohman. The fact that people who have low activity of aldehyde dehydrogenase cannot metabolize the acetaldehyde effectively is only one of the biological factors controlling alcohol consumption. The acetaldehyde makes them feel very unhappy or in terrible condition. Such a symptom plays a protective role against alcohol abuse.

Question: A question to Dr. Harada, please: Your study not only includes alcoholism but is also related to the origin of nations of human races. As far as I know, American Indians are very vulnerable to alcohol. So I think your study also relates very well to the origin of races. It didn't appear in your presentation, but is it true that the American Indians also show much deficiency in ALDH?

Dr. Harada: Yes, it is true that my study is related to the origin of races. About 12,000 years ago, the first American Indians crossed over the Bering Sea to reach the American Continent. On the second migration, about 6000 years ago, they reached all the way into North America. The third time, 3000 years B.C., Eskimos, for example, moved to the Arctic regions. So these were the earlier ones who went to South America about 12,000 years ago, and then to North America.

When we look at Latin America, a number of Indians living there show very high frequency of ALDH deficiency and don't, I believe, consume a lot of alcohol. However, American Indians in North America, who may be of a different origin because they immigrated at a later time, have a very low frequency of deficiency, perhaps as low as 10%. Therefore, the North American Indians have a greater problem with alcoholism compared to these in Latin America.

We are at the moment planning a further study as regards Eskimos, to compare with the past data that we have about their alcohol consumption and ALDH. It seems, at this stage, that there are only a small number of ALDH-deficient type Eskimos.

(Chairperson) Professor Schuckit: As co-chair, I don't know whether I should

comment or not. Michael Bohman and I have many things in common, but one of the things we tend to *disagree* about is the accuracy of the present Type 1/Type 2 theory. I only wish people would realize that, while I'm not quite sure whether you (Professor Bohman) and Bob Cloninger are right or if I'm right in what I'm seeing, it is important to know there are people who are disagreeing.

Part of the problem, of course, is philosophical and relates to whether you view the true "antisocial personality disorder" as a separate illness. *I* do for a variety of reasons. Therefore, in our work—I'm not talking about the studies you've heard today—we will include actual alcoholics who have many antisocial traits, but who don't meet criteria for antisocial personality disorder. Those latter individuals are excluded.

Once those severe antisocial personality disorder people are excluded, in our work with alcoholics as well as in the work of others, there is great difficulty replicating the monoamine oxidase data. There is also difficulty replicating predictions made on personality, as well as on clinical course. So we have two groups of people working very hard. Only time will tell which group is right.

In the meantime, though, the theory that Professor Bohman has developed with Bob Cloninger emphasizes important things. It shows that both genetics and environment are important; it emphasizes that there may be certain subgroups with different levels of sensitivity to genetic factors; and it begins to hypothesize how neurotransmitters in the brain might be tied in. But I think we have a way to go before we are certain.

Professor Bohman: These two types (Types 1 and 2) have to be seen as prototypes of alcoholism, related to the personality traits described in my lecture, i.e., extremes of normally distributed personality traits, underlying a high risk to develop alcoholism. The "Type 1 personality" seeks alcohol as a means of relaxation or as a drug against anxiety or worries. The Type 2 personality seeks to get excitement, to get a "kick" out of life, by drinking or other activities. Some of the Type 2 alcoholics may grow out of their habit when drinking ceases to give them the same excitement or reward as at the beginning of their career, as shown in Vaillant's longitudinal study.

The problem with young Type 2 abusers is that they often get into social troubles, lose jobs or drop out of education, or get in trouble with the police. They may, as a consequence, have less opportunity to enter a normal, socially acceptable career. However, if they happen to live in an upper or middle class family with a good social network, they may be protected from social decline. They may develop into extroverted, energetic personalities, seeking excitement in unusual jobs or sports, i.e., adapting to life in a socially acceptable way.

In itself these personality variables are not good or bad, but simply adaptive mechanisms, which react to different environmental conditions. However, the widespread use of alcohol is certainly an environmental condition which puts these personality types at risk.

Dr. Asaka: Dr. Harada talked about ALDH today and Dr. Bohman mentioned risk factors or biological factors. You referred to ADH, also, as being a predecessor of ALDH in your presentation. Would Dr. Harada care to comment on ADH from the viewpoint of molecular biology?

Dr. Harada: Although I did not comment today about how the different ADH phenotypes influence the effects of alcoholism, we have studied the relationship between ADH and alcoholism. There was no significant difference among the two groups, namely alcoholics and healthy controls, concerning ADH phenotypes. However, we did obtain another interesting result: Independently of the ADH phenotype, the concentration of blood acetaldehyde is influenced by ALDH types. Thus, individuals showing a homozygous type of ALDH deficiency experience very bad symptoms following alcohol ingestion, due to having the slowest acetaldehyde metabolization speed.

PART III

ALCOHOLIC FAMILIES AND MENTAL HEALTH

This third section presents a discussion of the status of mental health services available to alcoholic families.

Firstly, Dr. Grant of the WHO (Senior Scientist in the Division of Mental Health) discusses this topic from an international perspective and summarizes the situation as it relates to various countries' programs for families with alcoholic-related problems. He also introduces the concept of the need for a multicenter study to identify ways to strengthen coping methods in the family.

Dr. Senoh's report informs us of the situation of public health centers in Tokyo, and particularly points out the need for Tokyo's mental health centers to become the major focus for future community-based psychiatric services. He outlines the work of the health center with regard to the alcoholism problem, indicating services available for the affected individual and his family.

James and Sandra Whittaker indicate the ways in which alcohol abuse and alcohol dependency have ravaged the native American Indian and Alaskan Eskimo populations. They present the results of their observational anthropological research. Their stimulating report is a reminder that alcoholism is a disease requiring the most urgent attention, at all levels of intervention.

7

International Perspectives on Alcoholism and the Family: An Overview of WHO Activities

Marcus Grant, Ph.D.

The first part of this paper consists of an international review of the world literature on the effects on children and adolescents of excessive drinking by their parents. The second part describes a proposed WHO initiative, stimulated by the conclusions of the international reviw of the literature. The proposal is for a multicenter, multinational study designed to identify, understand and strengthen natural family coping methods for dealing with alcohol and drug abuse so that these can be applied in primary health care settings.

INTRODUCTION

This paper is in two sections. The first consists of an international review of the world literature on the effects on children and adolescents of excessive drinking by their parents. This review comprises one section of a much more extensive review "Alcohol and Family Health: An International Review of the Effects and Outcomes of Excessive Drinking," which was prepared by myself with Dr. Martin Plant of Edinburgh and Dr. Jim Orford of Exeter. The full text is available from the Mental Health Program of the World Health Organization.

The second (and briefer) section of the paper describes a proposed WHO initiative, stimulated by the conclusions of the international review of the literature. The proposal is for a multicenter, cross-national study designed to identify, understand and strengthen natural family coping methods for dealing with alcohol and drug abuse so that these can be applied in primary health care settings.

In the literature, the harmful or dependent use of alcohol is described by many different terms. These include "alcoholism," "alcohol abuse," "alcohol dependence," and "problem drinking." Authors from different disciplines and from different countries use a wide range of labels which are often undefined. Accordingly, this paper employs several different terms since these were employed in some of the references that are cited.

EFFECTS ON CHILDREN AND ADOLESCENTS

In recent years there has been an upsurge of interest in the possible effects upon children and adolescents of having a parent with a drinking problem. Most of the research in this area comes from Eastern Europe and the United States. Apart from a study of the short- and long-term effects of parental drinking problems in Sweden,[1],[2] there are only scattered studies from Western Europe and, apart from a small amount of work from Japan and some interest in the fetal alcohol syndrome in Australia, little work on this topic appears to have been conducted outside of Eastern Europe and the United States. In many areas, research into the children of people with severe alcohol problems is an emerging or recent scientific concern.

Research from Eastern Europe

In Bulgaria, there has been a considerable interest in the effects upon children of having a parent who drinks excessively. Research in that country has been summarized by Boyadjieva.[3] Stankoushev and co-workers[4] noted a higher rate of "neurotic behavior" and memory and attention disturbances among children with an "alcoholic" parent than among controls. Four years later, in 1978, another Bulgarian study by Christozov and co-workers[5] investigated 50 children, ages 4 to 15 years, with an "alcoholic" father; these researchers attributed the high rate of "neuroticism" which they found among these children to three pathogenic mechanisms: immediate stress, frustration and deprivation.

In the early 1980s, Toteva reported the findings of a study of 220 children ages 5 to 15 years[6],[7] in an unpublished dissertation, *Psychological Disturbances and Social Disadaptation in Children with Alcoholic Parents*. This group of children, each of whom had a parent (usually the father) who had been treated for "alcoholism," was compared with a control group of 110 children of healthy parents. "Neurotic" disturbances were found in 56% of the larger group compared with 22.5% of the controls; antisocial behavior was registered in 23% of the study children vs only 3% of the control group; suicidal tendencies were found in a substantial minority of the children of treated alcoholics, and four children had attempted suicide.

Testing for intelligence, memory, and attention showed, according to Boyadjieva,[3] that 60% of children with an "alcoholic" parent had IQs below 75, and 53% had disturbances in short-term memory. In a thesis and a review, Boyadjieva[3],[8] has developed the theory that the presence in the family of a father with a drinking problem is a major stress factor for children, slowing normal development, leading to lowered self-esteem and inferiority complexes and, hence, in many cases to identity crises. The connection between parental "alcoholism" and childhood "neurotic disorders" has been further investigated by Toteva.[9]

Shurygin[10] reported a major USSR study of 74 children (ages from less than 1 year to 16 years) in 52 families in which the father was suffering from chronic "alcoholism" and had received treatment. "Psychogenic" disorders were almost six times as frequent in the study group compared with a control group of equal size. Twenty-eight were diagnosed as suffering from one or another variant of "patho-characteristological development." Shurygin describes in detail how the disorders, and in particular the two commonest variants, grew out of the microsocial environment of the family. In 10 cases, an "inhibited" variant was noted. In the early stages, behavioral peculiarities were apparent only in the presence of the father: Children avoided their fathers totally or refused to go home. Later, this behavior was generalized to the school, where teachers noticed increased pensiveness and silence among the children, who avoided the company of peers. As Shurygin puts it, such behavior is justified in the following way.[10]

"I see what sort of father my friend has, how everything is peaceful with them. Then I go home and cry. Why are my mother and I so unhappy? So now I do not go to see my friend, and yes, I am ashamed of my father" (translated from Russian).

Eight children displayed the "temporary-excitable" variant, which began with sullen, unwilling, and threatening behaviors, again specifically in the presence of the father. Once again, this behavior developed and generalized and, unless the problem was resolved by death or departure of the father, or by his cure, the child developed symptoms of "social-pedagogic neglect" with a tendency to antisocial forms of behavior. A proportion of the children in Shurygin's study were followed over 2 years or more, and if such a resolution of the family problem did occur, a reversal in the child's behavior was observed. The inhibited children become more active, lively, tender, and accessible, and the "temporary-excitable" children become more balanced in mood, with the frequency of their outbursts lessening and their behavior becoming more easily corrected.

Shurygin's investigation was confined to what he termed the microsocial factor in the generation of childhood disorders. However, he pointed out that most Russian researchers have considered biological and microsocial factors jointly. He cited work suggesting that parental drinking problems may be linked with the development of childhood epilepsy, as well as with mental retardation. Several researchers, he pointed out, are examining the morphological and functional changes in the generative cells of parents as one of the probable reasons for the "inferiority" of the offspring. In a review, Boyadjieva[3] also cited work from the USSR suggesting a high frequency of abortions and the possibility of damage prior to birth (the fetal alcohol syndrome). Other Russian workers have also suggested that parental "alcoholism" may be one factor related to childhood convulsions.[11]

In Poland, according to Boyadjieva, there have been few studies of children in "alcohol" families. Strzembosz[12] found maladjustment in 64% of children in families in which the mothers had drinking problems, and in another study,[13] a correlation was found between the duration of alcohol abuse and the degree of psychological disturbance in the children. In another Polish study, broken homes and criminal behavior resulting from "alcoholism" were discovered in the backgrounds of 80% of a sample of 50 8- to 16-year-old boys residing in a child custody center in Warsaw.[14] A study from the 1960s by Borzova[15] reported the results of administering tests, questionnaires, and interviews to 50 6- to 14-year-olds from "alcohol" families who were attending a month's reeducational camp. A higher than expected incidence of "neurotic" symptoms and lower than expected intelligence levels were reported, and 82% of the children showed strong attachment towards their mothers and minimal or no positive relation to their "alcoholic" fathers.

In Yugoslavia, there has been a greater interest in marriage and marital therapy for problem drinkers than in the effects of drinking problems upon children. However, Dordevic and Dukanovic[16] pointed to the frequent behavior and learning problems experienced by the children of 100 "alcoholics" at the Treatment Institute in Belgrade. "Alcoholism" as one of a number of negative factors in the background of epileptic schoolchildren in comparison with nonepileptic controls has also been reported from Yugoslavia.[17] Boyadjieva[3] cited a recent Yugoslavian study[18] of suicidal tendencies among the children of women "alcoholics" who had attempted suicide themselves.

In Czechoslovakia, there has been a long-standing interest in the effects of parental drinking problems on children. Freiovai[19] studied more than 500 families with a "morally impaired" child between 9 and 16 years old who was placed in a reeducation facility. In 27% of the families, "alcoholism" was found in one or both parents, and among 47 families with more than 1 child in the facility, 53% had one or both parents "alcoholic." Similarly, Koznar and co-authors[20] found "alcoholism" along with incomplete and disharmonious families, mental illness, and criminal behavior more common in the family backgrounds of adolescents with antisocial behavior problems than in the backgrounds of those with "neurotic" problems or learning difficulties.

Matejcek[21],[22] examined intelligence, school performance and general adjustment in 200 children whose fathers had been registered at the Anti-Alcoholism Counseling Center in Prague. On intelligence testing, Matejcek found a difference of 7 IQ points in favor of the comparison group (almost wholly accounted for by a difference of 8 points on verbal intelligence), in the oldest of the three age groups only (the 13- to 15-year-olds). There was no difference in parents' assessments of the child's IQ, which in many cases were felt to be unrealistic. Teacher's assesments were much closer to the formal IQ test results. Pediatricians' ratings of intelligence (above average, average, below average) and schoolmates' nominations of most intelligent, most gifted, and quickest children both showed significant differences in favor or the comparison group. Children from "alcoholic" families were less likely to be chosen as "best friends" on a sociometric test. On a test of maladjustment, the difference between group means was significant overall, was particularly significant for the 9- to 11-year-olds, was less significant for the 4- to 6-year-olds; the difference was not significant for the oldest age group. In a regression analysis, the most important variable predictive of maladjustment was gender; boys showed higher scores than girls.

Other studies from Eastern Europe include a Czechoslovakian study of gypsy and nongypsy special schoolchildren in Western Bohemia;[23] a high rate of unfavorable family circumstances, including "alcoholism," especially amongst the gypsy children, was noted. From Slovenia, there is a report of several differences in the family lives of 4- to 8-year-olds who dropped out of school in comparison with control children, one factor being higher rate of parental "alcoholism."[24] Finally, to complete the review of studies on this subject from Eastern Europe, Boyadjieva[3] found a small number from Eastern Germany; the most conclusive appears to have been one reported in the mid-1960s by Partnitzke and Prussig.[25] They investigated 120 children with "alcoholic" fathers and found three times the rate of "neuroticism" than that among a control group of children. A second study by Farkasinszky and coworkers[26] found that children with "alcoholic" parents had an increased level of anxiety, as well as "psychopathic" character and "social maladaptation."

Research from Western Europe

From Western Europe, which, on the whole, has contributed rather less to research on the effects of parental drinking problems on young children and adolescents, there are occasional reports suggesting that sons of parents with drinking problems are particularly at risk of antisocial behavior. For example, the records of a child psychiatric clinic in West Berlin showed boys with "alcohol" fathers to be particularly likely to be diagnosed as having conduct disorders while both boys and girls with "alcohol" parents were likely to have emotional problems, especially if the problem drinking parent was the mother.[27]

Mader[28] reported a high rate of family "alcoholism" among "adolescent criminals" in Austria, and from Switzerland Fanai reported that adolescents with "personality disorders" had a higher than average number of psychiatrically abnormal persons in their families, particularly "alcoholics," who made harmonious family life impossible.[29]

Of greater interest is a study from Zurich by Schmidt and co-workers[30] in which parental "alcoholism" is listed as one of 9 psychosocial risk factors that differentiated 300 11-year-olds with learning difficulties from a contrast group of 200 children of the same age who were in the top third of their classes academically. Children in the first group had had the start of their schooling postponed, or had had to repeat a class, or had been admitted to special classes or educated in special schools or homes for the handicapped.

In France, suicide and attempted suicide were considered in relation to having a parent with drinking problems. A family history of "alcoholism" was one of the five risk factors for adolescent suicide attempts among more than 500 14- to 19-year-olds who had been hospitalized after a suicide attempt in Lyon, Strasbourg, or Paris. Angel and co-workers[31] and Marcelli[32] found parental "alcoholism" to be one possible factor in the etiology of suicide attempts among children under 12 who constituted 10-15 percent of all suicide attempts by children and adolescents in France. In yet another study, 10 of 130 adolescent suicide attempters had an "alcoholic" parent. No control data were reported to enable this statistic to be interpreted.[33] Another study indicated that one or both parents of 35 "drug addicts" who had made at least one suicide attempt were "alcoholics" or users of psychotropic drugs.[34] Finally, in a further study, "alcoholism" and conflict were found to be more frequent among the parents of 38 6- to 16-year-old suicide attempters in comparison with a group with psychosomatic problems.[35]

De Mendonca[36] carried out a study in Portugal that was published in French; de Mendonca was concerned with the effects upon children when only the father had a drinking problem. He compared two groups of 100 children each from the district of Coimbra; one group had "alcohol" fathers and the other did not. In all cases, the mothers were free of drinking problems and mental illness. The fathers in the first group had all attended an "alcoholism'' treatment center, and the results were based on interviews with the mothers. The control group was chosen from the same residential area. Unfortunately, some considerable differences between the two groups of families make interpretation difficult. Compared with the control group, children in the paternal "alcoholism" group were older (median ages 8-9 vs 6-7); 96% of their families were in low socioeconomic classes IV and V on a 5-point scale, compared with 32% of the controls. De Mendonca argued that this disparity was due to "social drift," that the original levels of the two groups were similar, and that the alcohol group families were larger (median number of children four vs two).

The two Coimbra groups differed greatly in terms of the mothers' reports of their children's early development and adjustment. In the paternal "alcoholism" group, breast feeding was more likely to have been prolonged to 1 year or more after birth (57% vs 35%). Developmental delays (in first teeth, first steps, first words, and first sentences) were much more common; sphincter control was more often delayed; infantile illnesses were reported (infectious, allergic, and neuropsychiatric); progress at school was much more likely to be poor (76% vs 14% had to retake at least 1 year); and later neuropsychiatric symptoms of one kind or another were universal (vs 24% of controls). Anxiety, fear at night, anxiety crises, and insomnia were some of the commonest symptoms.

Although most children in both groups were under 10 years old, and the oldest only 12 to 13, mothers reported that 74% of the study group and 55% of the controls drank alcohol regularly. In the control group, a reason frequently cited was that wine was a form of nourishment and was good for the child. In the paternal "alcoholism" group, 25% of mothers stated that the child was imitating its father, and 16% said that the father forced the child to drink.

De Mendonca attributed the differences he found partly to the child's anxiety which was a reaction to the family atmosphere of conflict created by the father's drinking. However, he also took into account the toxic effect of the child's own alcohol consumption and, in general, was conscious of the etiological complexity of the matter.[36]

> In our opinion the neuropsychlogical problems that we came across in the children of alcoholic fathers resulted from hereditary, social and psychological factors, which combined together cause certain basic deficiencies, be they organic or functional, in the child's nervous structures, onto which there grow, very exaggerated psychological manifestations of emotional imbalance. All these disturbing factors abound in the households where there is an alcoholic father [translated from the French].

De Mendonca also formed the opinion that in some families the birth of the children had revealed conflicts in the parents' relationship which had hitherto been lying dormant and that, in many instances, the mothers had a profound need for emotional compensation, which they found in their children, towards whom they established a very restrictive and protective relationship. These observations need to be placed against the prevailing conservative traditions of the region which dictated that wives rarely worked outside the home and families rarely split up.

Considerable interest in the disadvantages that result from parental drinking problems has been shown by Swedish researchers. Nylander[1] compared 229 children from 141 families in which the fathers were "alcoholics" with 163 control children. The groups were carefully matched, and the children were between 4 and 12 years old. Those in the study group, as in de Mendonca's[36] and in many other studies, showed more frequent signs of mental ill health and a wider variety of symptoms than did the controls: 27% of boys and 30% of girls showed "mental insufficiency." Anxiety neuroses and depression were the commonest diagnoses, and rates were equally high among the three age groups: 4-6, 7-9, and 10-12 years. Apart from definite psychiatric diagnoses, stress symptoms such as headaches, stomachaches, and tiredness were very common, and children had often been investigated for physical conditions without an underlying organic reasons being confirmed. Their teachers considered that 48% of the school age children vs 10% of the control children exhibited problems. Among the 7- to 9-year-old boys, as many as 74% with "alcoholic" parents showed difficulty in adjusting.

Although there appear to have been no special studies of this subject in Japan, occasional mention has been made of a possible link between parental drinking problems and the well-being of Japanese children. For example, one study of depressive symptoms among 14- to 22-year-olds claimed to establish a link between the depression of the "behavior disorder" type (as opposed to depression of inhibited, anxious, or withdrawn types) and families with dominant fathers or disorganized families with mentally ill or "alcoholic" parents.[37] Another decribes a single case of childhood psychosis in which the father had a serious drinking problem.[38] In another report, "alcoholism" in one or both parents was cited as one of several family background factors leading to juvenile delinquency,[39] and again the father's "pronounced tendency towards alcoholism" is mentioned as the first of a number of factors differentiating a sample of families in which a majority of siblings were delinquent in comparison with families of similar socioeconomic status, but without delinquency.[40]

Evidence from the rest of the world appears to be sparse. A notable exception is a study by Cassorla[41] of attempted suicide in Brazil. Broken homes, poor relationships between parents, and physical and mental diseases and "alcoholism" in the family were all found to be higher among 50 12- to 27-year-olds who had recently attempted suicide, in comparison with both normal and psychiatric controls.

A great deal of research has been carried out on this subject in North America and Britain. This has been reviewed by several author[42]-[45] and will only be summarized here.

In general the results of this work in North America and Britain have been in line with that from studies elsewhere such a those by Nylander,[1] de Mendonca,[36] and Matejcek.[21],[22] A higher risk of some ill effects — including negative attitudes toward the problem-drinking parent and to the parents' marriage, reading retardation and loss of concentration at school, and temper tantrums and fighting seems to be a universal finding for young children. In studies of adolescents, the results are less consistent, with the occasional finding of no difference between probands and controls,[46] but most studies have reported a raised risk of ill effects, including delinquency or antisocial behavior, anorexia nervosa, and drinking and drug problems.[45] One study from Ireland found that violence was important in distinguishing those families in which paternal alcohol problems were associated with childhood developmental problems from families without such difficulties.[47]

LONG-TERM EFFECTS — USE OF FAMILY HISTORIES

A multitude of reports from clinical settings in Britain and North America have shown that excessive drinkers are particularly likely to report having a parent who had an alcohol problem.[48],[49] Similar reports have come from many other countries including Chile,[50] Iceland,[51] Hungary,[52] Yugoslavia,[53] and the USSR.[54] For example, in the study by Helgason and Asmundsson,[51] 70 men under 30 years of age who had been convicted for public drunkenness at least twice within 1 month and who lived in the Reykjavik area were matched for age, school attended, examination success, and intelligence with 70 controls. Each man was asked about family background, and a number of their mothers were contacted to check the answers. Significantly more fathers of the "alcohol abusers" than of the controls were reported to have been "excessive drinkers" (37% vs 13%), and significantly fewer were abstainers (17% vs 34%). The authors also commented that their data suggested more psychiatric symptoms among mothers, although the mothers had not been recognized as ill (the rate of excessive drinking among mothers was negligible). Significantly more "abusers" had experienced changes in family structure during childhood, mostly as a consequence of divorce that was often related to the father's excessive drinking (53% vs 23%, at least one such change; 21% vs 9%, two or more changes; 12% vs 3%, three or more changes).

Djukanovic and co-workers[53] reported on the retrospective accounts of 100 married male "alcoholics" attending a treatment unit in Belgrade, Yugoslavia. Although the absence of a control group makes it difficult to interpret the results, the authors noted that 27% of these men reported having lost one or both of their parents through death before the age of 18; that more than half had lost one or both by death, separation, or divorce; that a third had experienced frequent changes of guardians during childhood and early adolescence and that substitute parents were often inadequate; that 75% reported that their relationships with parents were characterized by destructive conflict; that in 75% of cases one or more members of the parental family were "excessive drinkers" and in 42% were "alcoholic"; and that 38% of the parental families exhibited other "social-pathological phenomena" (mainly criminality, suicide and suicide attempts).

It is frequently suggested that total abstinence in the parental home, or a combination of abstinence in one parent and excessive drinking in another, may foster later excessive drinking by children.[55] There appears to be little convincing evidence to support this view. However there is some evidence from studies from Britain[48],[56],[57] that the reverse may hold true, namely that excessive drinking in a parent is followed by an increased incidence of total abstention or very light drinking in the offspring. Hughes and co-workers[56] also found that abstaining, like excessive drinking, ran in families.

From the work of McCord and McCord in 1960[58] and Robins in 1966[59] onwards to Vaillant's 1983 work,[57] *The Natural History of Alcoholism,* evidence has accumulated from studies in the United States that alcohol problems and criminality, both in the proband's generation and in the previous generation, are linked in complex ways. A 1983 Finnish review by Pulkkinen[60] on the predictability of criminal behavior concluded that the "pathogeneses" of "alcoholism" and criminality are complex and are interlinked developmental processes. A recent study from Yugoslavia[61] claims to distinguish primary and secondary "psychopaths" (a term that has ceased to have much currency in the English language literature) among "chronic alcoholics," and relates that categorization to a family history of "alcoholism." It has been found that soldiers who resigned from the Yugoslav Army were more likely to have parents with "alcoholic," "psychopathic," and marital problems than were controls.[62] In another Yugoslav study,[63] an unfavorable family atmosphere with one parent "alcoholic" was reported in 50% of a sample of soldiers who committed delinquent acts while drunk.

Interrelationship among family history, "antisocial personality," and gender were examined by Lewis and coworkers[64] in a study of more than 400 referrals to the psychiatric department of a hospital in Missouri in the

United States. Of this sample, 36% of men and 10% of women received a diagnosis of "alcoholism." The multivariate statistical procedure used (stepwise logistic modeling) found gender, "antisocial personality," and a family history of "alcoholism" to be the variables that were most predictive of "alcoholism." Among men, those with antisocial perssonality who were not "alcoholic" were no more likely to have a family history of "alcoholism" than were those without either diagnosis, but the same was not true for women. A family history of "alcoholism" was just as common (55%) among women with antisocial personality alone as it was among those who had a diagnosis of "alcoholism" (52%). Lewis and co-workers suggest that "alcoholism" and "antisocial personality" may be etiologically independent in men, but not in women.

The suggestion that the process of intergenerational transmission may be different for women and for men is supported by two other recent studies from the United States. In the first,[65] a history of drinking problems among parents (especially fathers) and siblings was more common among a sample of women with a diagnosis of "borderline personality disorders" than among women with diagnosis of "schizophrenia" or "bipolar disorder." Interestingly, if the samples in the three studies are combined, a family history of drinking problems was not related to the extent of a woman's own drinking. In the second study,[66] a link between familial "alcoholism" and "bulimic anorexia" among women was suggested.

Another, and more recent, line of research in the United States[67] has suggested a link between family histories of excessive drinking (particularly in male members) and family histories of depression (particularly in female members). A French study has also found significantly more "alcoholic" men and depressed women in the family histories of "alcoholic" men than of controls. The same difference was noted in the family histories of depressed women when these were compared with controls.[68]

The possibility that women with alcohol problems may have more negative factors in their family histories than do men with drinking problems is also raised by Bevia's[69] study of the families of women "alcoholics" in Spain. Over three-quarters of the women in his sample described childhoods "full of negative experiences,"[69, p.231] and 30% had lived in "intensely alcoholic families." [69, p.231] He implied that these negative family experiences were greater than those found in comparable samples of men with drinking problems, although the data presented are not sufficient to establish this. A recent British study by Latcham[70] found a positive family history of "alcoholism" in 73 of 190 male "alcoholics" (32 fathers, 6 mothers, 23 brothers, 1 sister, 2 grandparents, 8 uncles, 1 aunt), but in as many as 26 of 27 women (7 fathers, 3 mothers, 11 brothers, 4 uncles, 1 son).

In the United States, Midanik[71] has reported the prevalence of "alcoholism" and problem drinking among first degree relatives of respondents in a national population survey. Women with alcohol problems, whether alone or in conjunction with depressive symptoms, reported higher rates of "alcoholism" or problem drinking in their immediate families (fathers, mothers, brothers, sisters) than did men. The author suggested that women are more influenced by the home environment or, alternatively, that a more severe family history of "alcoholism" is the necessary condition for women to eventually manifest alcohol problems. However, women overall more often reported positive family histories than men, which suggested to the author that women might be using a less restricted definition and might, therefore, be more likely to classify their relatives (particularly male relatives) as "alcoholics" or problem drinkers.

Other work in the retrospective tradition which suggests a familial link between drinking and other kinds of psychiatric and psychological problems has been reported in recent studies from the United States and in work from Yugoslavia, Czechoslovakia, and Switzerland. A 1985 report from the United States[72] is of interest because it mentions an increased risk of anxiety disorders in the blood relatives of probands with "alcoholism." This increased risk was linked to the presence of both an alcoholic problem and an anxiety disorder in the probands, suggesting to the authors that then "alcoholism" might have resulted from the self-medication of anxiety symptoms. Another USA study[73] found a link between reported parental or drinking problems and reports of drinking problems, depression, and "personality disorders" among a sample of more than 600 opioid addicts. Those with parental drinking problems also reported more disrupted childhoods.

Pozarnik[74] compared the childhood recollections of more than 200 "schizophrenic" patients with those of a large sample of the general population of Yugoslavia. Family discord and an accumulation of two or three unfavorable family factors, of which "alcoholism" plus poor financial and housing conditions was the commonest combination, were found at a higher rate (6% vs 38%) among the "schizophrenic" sample. In a study from Czechoslovakia[75] 100 "deprived" women, who were investigated for suspected prostitution and venereal disease, were compared with 100 married women attending a prenatal clinic. The "deprived" group more often reported the absence of a father during their upbringing and more often described dissension in the families. Thirty percent reported at least one "alcoholic" parent.

A recent report from the United States by Price and co-workers[76] picks out parental fighting and excessive drinking as dominant themes in the childhood memories of a sample of 28 teenage male prostitutes. Finally, from

Switzerland there is a report that parental "alcoholism" was one of a number of background factors among patients seeking help with marital troubles.[77]

Among those who have themselves developed drinking problems in adult life, an association between an early onset or degree of severity, or both, of these problems, and a family history of excessive drinking has frequently been reported. Among white male patients hospitalized for the treatment of "secondary alcoholism" in Cape Town, South Africa, age of onset was negatively associated with the severity of parents' drinking habits.[78] Retrospective research of this kind has been carried on apace in recent years in the United States. For example, in three studies[79-81], a family history of alcohol problems was found to be linked with early onset of drinking problems among adults. Volicer and co-workers[80] found that family history was linked with severity of alcohol problems, and there were few differences between those with fathers and those with fathers and those with mothers who had drinking problems. The highest level of problems was among those who had two parents with alcohol problems. Stabenau[82] found that a family history of alcohol problems was associated with a greater frequency of symptoms among "alcoholic" inpatients. Alterman and Tarter[83] found a greater frequency of family alcohol problems (60%) among "alcoholic" inpatients with a history of "brain injury" (unconsciousness following trauma) than among those without (35%).

The possibility that birth order might excited interest from time to time. However, findings are highly inconsistent (a positive finding linking penultimate birth order with alcohol problems among women in West Germany,[84] but a negative finding from Iceland, for example[51]). Work in the alcohol field[85] and beyond it,[86] has shown how very complex the apparently simple question of birth order turns out to be. Research has rarely controlled for size of family, spacing of children, or gender of siblings.

Finally in this section mention should be made of the much smaller amount of work carried out on the family histories of spouses of drinkers. For example, Nici[87] has produced some confirmatory evidence for the long-held view that daughters of problem drinkers are subsequently more likely to marry problem drinkers than are other women, and Djukanovic and co-workers,[53] in the study already referred to, have reported that wives of male "alcoholics" under treatment in Belgrade are as likely to have disturbed childhood backgrounds as are their husbands. Of the wives in their sample, 39% had lost one or both of their parents through death before the age of 18; many were exposed to emotional frustration during childhood and adolescence, in particular having been discriminated against by their mothers; and excessive drinking existed in 55% of their parental families and "alcoholism" in

24%. As noted before, the absence of a control group in this study makes interpretation difficult.

PROPOSED WORLD HEALTH ORGANIZATION STUDY ON NATURAL FAMILY COPING METHODS

Although it is impossible to quantify the overall contribution of alcohol and drug abuse to family ill health (affecting both child and adult members of families, in both the short and long term), it is probably very considerable indeed. The results are likely to be widespread and the cost in human and financial terms very great, particularly as the link between family ill health and alcohol or drug abuse is often unidentified by health workers.

It is therefore proposed to initiate a multicenter cross-national study with the following two principal aims:

  i) To study naturally occurring alcohol/drug coping methods within families in a number of contrasting areas of the world, to identify commonalities and differences across sociocultural groups, genders and family relationships.

 ii) As a result of the information obtained, to develop and provide an initial test of one package of methods which can be used within primary health care settings, again in a number of contrasting areas, for supporting and strengthening these naturally occurring methods in families where a problem has already been identified.

These aims have been developed on the basis of the conclusions reached in reviews of the international literature on alcohol and family (including the one presented above), as well in as those research studies which have focused on responses to alcohol-related problems. One such focus of research on alcohol abuse in the family has been concerned with the ways family members naturally respond to alcohol problems in the home, and the tactics and strategies they adopt in an attempt to control them or their consequences. More recently similar information has started to become available on the ways in which family members naturally respond when there is a problems of drug abuse in the family. Most of the coping responses described are highly similar in the cases of alcohol and other drugs.

As the concept of family "coping" is so central to this proposal it requires a little closer definition at this point. The concept of coping, as that term is used here, is a broad one, embracing the full range of responses which family members report making as a consequence of being in close contact with, and being affected by, drinking or drug use by a family member which is seen as being excessive. It includes actions that are deliberately taken with an end in view: for example, refusing to allow injecting in the home, not lending money, being especially encouraging towards the drug user or drinker, seeking outside help. But it also includes reactions that the relative is aware of having made whilst recognizing that they may not be functional for her/himself or for the drinker or drug user: for example, being too terrified to do anything, keeping out of the way as much as possible, starting an argument, covering up for the drinker or drug user. It covers not only actions, but also reactions of a cognitive and/or emotional kind: for example, blaming oneself, adopting the attitude that responsibility for change lies with the user, being constantly worried about what the drinker is doing. What these diverse elements of "coping" have in common is that they occur naturally and can be reported to outsiders who are interested in understanding or helping. They are natural resources for treatment and prevention.

The natural family coping approach differs from some other perspectives on alcohol, drugs, and the family because it does not assume that excessive alcohol or drug use is a symptom of disfunction in the family system as a whole nor that use is functional for the family in some way. The coping approach assumes that family members are responding to a stress which is not of their own making. However, the approach acknowledges that some ways of coping may be maladaptive for the well-being of the individual coper, and some may play a part in maintaining the excessive alcohol or druge use.

"Coping," as a concept to be employed in this research is principally an individual-level variable. Its assessment is in the first place conducted with individuals and conclusions will be drawn about how individual family members cope. The data to be collected will sometimes, however, allow statements to be made about how two or more family members interact over coping (e.g., a mother who is trying to be confrontative is not supported by her husband whom she perceives to be avoiding coping with their son's drug use), or about how a whole family is coping (e.g., all members are avoiding the problem, or the family is chaotic in its coping because each member is taking a different stance).

If the general relevance of these ideas can be more firmly established, they offer one of the most important ways forward for the prevention and treatment of alcohol and drug problems. Not only are many of the problems associated with these substances problems of family health with major impact in the family setting, but also it is often the family of a person who is abusing a drug that is first alert to the problem and motivated to do something about it. Most health workers have not known of the natural coping potential within the family for prevention in this area, and have not felt in a position to offer help which could encourage and build upon these natural resources. The proposed research will involve a major extension of the family coping line of research, in an attempt to confirm the coping methods that naturally exist and those that constitute the more effective preventive methods.

The reviews referred to above also identified the primary health care setting as one in which many alcohol problems present, frequently in the form of physical, emotional, or social problems amongst child or adult relatives.

The view that primary health care may be one of the most appropriate settings in which to respond to alcohol problems in the family is supported by the report of the WHO project on the Management of Alcohol-Related Problems in General Practice. Combining information from the 14 centers that contributed data, Family Problems achieved the second rank among 12 alcohol-related problems in terms of frequency of occurrence of problems in general practice, and ranked first in terms of the frequency with which practitioners provided help. A comment from one of the collaborators in the WHO Community Response to Alcohol-Related Problems project was: "The family therefore seemed to be the battleground where drinking problems are most commonly addressed. This is of particular concern when the role of women is undergoing rapid change. The changed habits and attitudes of women may prove crucial in predicting a socializing influence of the family as far as drinking norms are concerned in future years."

The emphasis on primary health care in this proposal is in keeping with the adoption of primary health care as a strategy to be pursued by WHO Member States towards the goal of Health for All by the Year 2000. The definition of primary health care adopted must reflect the different patterns of health services, broadly defined, found in different areas of the world.

REFERENCES

(1) Nylander, I.: Children of alcoholic fathers. *Acta Paediatr Scand* 49: (Supp. 121) (1960).
(2) Rydelius, P.: Children of alcoholic fathers: their social adjustment and their health status over 20 years. *Acta Paediatr Scand*: (Supp. 286) 10-85 (1981).
(3) Boyadjieva, M.: *Alcoholism and the family: review of the literature in some socialist countries.* Prepared for the World Health Organization, Division of Mental Health, Geneva (1984).
(4) Stankoushev, T., Chinova, L., and Rasboinikova, E.: On some peculiarities in the psychological development and behaviour of children with alcoholic parents. *Pediatria* (Sofia) 13: 25-29 (1974).
(5) Christozov, C., Achkova, M., and Shoilekova, M.: Psychological transformation of the father's alcoholism into the picture of child neuroses. In *Alcoholism and smoking medizina and fizkultura*, edited by A. Maleev (cited by Boyadjieva), pp. 93-97 (1984).
(6) Toteva, S.: Neurotic symptoms in children of alcoholic parents and the suicidal risk of children of alcoholics. *Bulletin NINPN* (Sofia) 10: 104-109 (1982a).
(7) Toteva, S.: On the suicidal risk in children of alcoholics. *Bulletin NINPN* (Sofia) 10: 85-92 (1982b).

(8) Boyadjieva, M.: Crisis situation in youth. *Narodna Mladej*, Sofia (1979).
(9) Toteva, S.: A katamnestic follow-up study of children with neurotic disorders brought up in a family with one parent suffering from alcoholism. *Nevcol Psikhiatr Neurokhic* (Sofia) 24: 10-14 (1985).
(10) Shurygin, G.I.: Concerning a psychogenic pathological personality formation in children and adolescents in families with fathers suffering from alcoholism (in Russian). *Zn Nervropatol Psikhiatr* (Moskva) 10: 1566-1569. (1978).
(11) Antonov, I. P., and Shan'Ko, G. G. Convulsive states in children (in Russian). *Abstract No. 05455 Psych. info*, undated.
(12) Strzembosz, A.: Stopian przytosowania spolecznego dzieci alkoholicow z waszawy objetych przed iv laty postepowaniem opiekunczym (in Polish). *Problemy Alkoholizmu* 26: 11-14 (1979).
(13) Gerkowicz, T.: Wplyw alkoholizmu rozicon na zdrourie dziecka (in Polish). *Problemy Aloholizmu* 23: 7-8 (1976).
(14) Drecka, M., Mazurczak, M. and Puzyuska, E.: Psychiatric and psychological characteristics of children remaining in the child custody center in Warsaw (in Polish). *Psychiatrica Polska* (Warsaw) 10: 403-412 (1976).
(15) Borzova, E. Problems of mental development of children in the alcoholic family. *Psychologia a Patopsychologia Dietata* 3: 153-160 (1967-68).
(16) Dordevic, M., and Dukanovic, B.: Effect of alcoholism on emotional relations in the family (in Serbo-Croat). *Sociologija* 16: 473-488 (1974).
(17) Plavcc, S., and Vukadinovic, M.: Some problems of schooling and social status of epileptic children in the schools of the Crnomerec community (in Serbo-Croat). *Neuropsihijatrija* 24: 49-53 (1976).
(18) Veseb, C.: Suicidal attempts in women alcoholics. *Alkoholizam Godina* (Belgrade) 13:79 (1983).
(19) Freioval, E.: Alcoholism of parents and moral impairment of school age youngsters. *Czeskoslovenskai Psychiatrie* 62: 188-192 (1966).
(20) Koznar, J. Matyek, G., Uhrova, A.: Results of a retrospective study of the family conditions of problem children in counselling (in Czech). *Czeskoslovenska Psychologie* 23: 365-374 (1979).
(21) Matejcek, Z.: Children in families of alcoholics, I. The rearing situation (in Czech). *Psychologija i Patopsychologia Dietata* 16: 303-318 (1981a).
(22) Matejcek, Z.: Children in families of alcoholics, II.. Competence in school and peer group (in Czech). *Psychologija i Patopsychologia Dietata* 16: 537-560 (1981b).
(23) Machova, J., and Gutvirth, J.: Family environment of special school children (in Czech). *Psychologija i Patopsychologia Dietata* 116: 352-360 (1981).
(24) Sterle, V.: School and home (in Slovack). *Clovek-Sola-Delo* 3: 13-16 (1970).
(25) Partnitzke, K. H., and Prussig, O.: Kinder alkohol such Eigerettern, *Psychiat Neurol Med Psychol* 18: 1-6 (1966).
(26) Farkasinszky, T., et al.: Entwicklungsstörungen den Persönlichkeit bei Kindern Alkoholiker. *Alcoholism* 9:3-8 (1973).
(27) Steinhausen, H., Gobel, D., and Nestler, V.: Psychopathology in the offspring of alcoholic parents. *J Am Acad Child Adolesc Psychiatry* 23: 465-471 (1984).
(28) Mader, R.: Alcoholism in adolescent criminals: a comparative study from 1965/66 to 1969/70. *Acta Paedopsychiatirica* 39: 2-11 (1972).
(29) Fanai, F.: Progress and prognosis of degeneration: catamnesias of adolescents with disturbed social behaviour. *Psychiatria Clinica* 2: 1-13 (1969).

(30) Schmidt, W., et al.: Genetical, medical and psychosocial factors as cause of learn-
     ing difficulties in a cohort of 11-year-old pupils, Winterthur study (in German),
     Acta Paedopsychiatrica 49: 9-45 (1983).
(31) Angel, P., Taleghani, M., Choquet, M., and Courtecuisse, N.: An epidemio-
     logical approach to suicide attempts by adolescents: some answers from the en-
     vironment (in French), *L'Evolution Psychiatrique* 43: 351-367 (1978).
(32) Marcelli, D.: Suicidal attempts of the child: statistical and general epidemiolog-
     ical aspects (in French). *Acta Pacdipsychiatrica* 43: 213-221 (1978).
(33) Duche, D., et al.: Attempts at suicide by adolescents (in French). *Revue de Neu-
     tropsychiatrie Infantile et d'Hygiene Mentale de l'Enfance* 22: 639-656 (1974).
(34) Braconnier, A., and Olievenstein, C.: Attempted suicide in actual drug addicts
     (in French). *Revue de Neuropsychiatrie infantile et d'Hygiène Mentale de L'En-
     fance* 22: 677-693 (1974).
(35) Moullembre, A., et al.: Essay on suicide: a theoretical and a clinical approach
     (in French). *Bulletin de Psychologie* 27: 804-943 (1973).
(36) de Mendonca, M.M.: Etude pediopsychiatrique sur des enfants de père alcoo-
     lique. *Revue de Neuropsychiatrie Infantile* 25: 411-428 (1976).
(37) Nishimura, R., Masui, R., Tsuno, R., and Ushijima, S.: Depressive states in
     adolescents (in Japanese). *Kyushu Neuropsychiatry* 29: 85-92 (1983).
(38) Murata, T., et al.: A case report and conference discussion concerning a boy
     suffering from a psychogenic psychosis (in Japanese), *Jpn J Child Psychiatry*
     17: 223-235 (1976).
(39) Takei, M., Sei, T., Kikuchi, T., and Hosae, T.: The relationship between delin-
     quent formation space on juvenile delinquency and the family with special refer-
     ence to the approach frame. *Jpn J Criminal Psychology* 10: 52-62 (1974).
(40) Ishihara, T., and Ikegawa, S.: Family structure associated with offences in
     brothers and sisters (in Japanese). *Jpn J Criminal Psychology* 10: 41-52 (1974).
(41) Cassorla, R.M.: Family characteristics of youngsters attempting suicide in Com-
     pinas, Brazil: a comparative study with normal and psychiatric youngsters (in
     Portuguese), *Acta Psiquiatr Psicol Am Lat* 30: 125-134 (1984).
(42) El Guebaly, N., and Offord, D.: The offspring of alcoholics: a critical review,
     Am J Psychiatry 134: 357-365 (1977).
(43) El Guebaly, N., and Offord, D.: On being the offspring of an alcoholic: an
     update. *Alcoholism* (New York) 3: 148-157 (1979).
(44) Wilson, C.: The impact of children. In *Alcohol and the family*, edited by J.
     Orford and J. Harwin, Croom Hel, London, pp. 151-167 (1982).
(45) Velleman, R., and Orford, J.: Intergenerational transmission of alcohol
     problems: hypotheses to be tested, In *Alcohol-related problems: room for
     "manoeuvre,"* edited by N. Krasner, J.S. Madden, and R.J. Walker, John Wiley
     and Sons, Chichester, pp. 97-113 (1984b).
(46) Kammeier, M.: Adolescents from families with and without alcohol problems.
     QJ Stud Alcohol 32: 364-374 (1971).
(47) Keane, A., and Roche, D.: Developmental disorders in the children of male al-
     coholics. In *Proceedings of the 20th Institute on the Prevention and Treatment
     of Alcoholism,* International Council on Alcohol and Addictions, Manchester,
     Lausanne, pp. 82-90 (1974).
(48) Velleman, R., and Orford, J.: *Adult children of problem drinking parents.* Fi-
     nal report to Department of Health and Social Security (UK), Department of
     Humanities and Social Studies, University of Bath, Bath, United Kingdom

(1984a).
(49) Cotton, N.S.: The familial incidence of alcoholism: a review. *Stud Alcohol* 40: 89-116 (1979).
(50) Kattan, L., et al.: Characteristics of alcoholism in women and evaluation of its treatment in Chile (in Spanish). *Acta Psiquiatr Pricol Am Lat* 19: 194-204. Abstract No. 11368 Psycinfo (1973).
(51) Helgason, T., and Asmundsson, G.: Behaviour and social characteristics of young social alcohol abusers. *Neuropsychobiology* 1: 109-120 (1975).
(52) Laszlo, C.: The internalization of deviant behaviour patterns during socialization in the family (in Hungarian). *Demografia* 13: 386-393 (1970).
(53) Djukanovic, B., et al.: Family history of alcoholics and their spouses (in French). *Revue d'Alcoolisme* 24: 245-250 (1978).
(54) Paschenkov, S.Z.: Specificity of familial forms of alcoholism (in Russian). *Sovetskaijy Meditsinu* 11: 76-79 (1976).
(55) Pele. 1.: Aietopathogenic elements of alcoholism (in French). *Acta Psychiat Belg* 80: 138-148. Abstract No. 81042315 Excerpt. Med. (1980).
(56) Hughes, J., Stewart, M., and Barraclough, B.: Why teetotallers abstain. *Br J Psychiatry* 146: 204-205 (1985).
(57) Vaillant, G.: *The natural history of alcoholism.* Harvard University Press, Cambridge, MA, 1983.
(58) McCord, W., and McCord, J.: *The origins of alcoholism.* Stanford University Press, Palo Alto, CA, 1960.
(59) Robins, I.: *Deviant children grow up: a sociological and psychiatric study of sociopathic personality,* Williams & Wilkins, Baltimore, 1966.
(60) Pulkkinen, L.: Predictability of criminal behaviour (in Finnish), *Psykologia* 18: 3-10 (1983).
(61) Cmelic, S., and Brankovic, M.: Da li je alkoholizan hereditarho oboyenje? (in Serbo-Croat, English abstract), *Soc. Psihijat* 10: 57-60 (1982).
(62) Kapor, G., Vujosevic, K., and Brankovic, M.: Sociomedical factors influencing resignations from the army (in Serbo-Croat) *Vojnosanitetski Pregled* 31: 79-83 (1974).
(63) Kandic, B., Joviccvic, M., and Vujosevic, K.: Forensic and psychiatric aspects of expertise of military personnel delinquency performed in the state of acute drunkenness (in Serbo-Croat). *Vojnosanitetski Pregled* 26: 227-230 (1969).
(64) Lewis, C.E., Rice, J., and Helzer, J.E.: Diagnostic interactions: alcoholism and antisocial personality, *J Nerv Ment Dis* 171: 105-113 (1983).
(65) Loranger, A.W., and Tulis, E.H.: Family history alcoholism in borderline personality disorder. *Arch Gen Psychiatry* 42: 153 (1985).
(66) Collins, G.B., et al.: Alcoholism in the families of bulimic anorexics. *Cleveland Council Quarterly* 52: 65-67 (1985).
(67) Winokur, G.: Depressive spectrum disease: description and family study. *Comp Psychiatry* 13: 3-8 (1972).
(68) Bourgeois, M., and Penaud, F.: Alcoholism and depression: statistical inquiry into familial antecedents of depression and alcoholism in a group of alcoholic men and depressed women (in French), *Annales Medico-Psychologiques* 2: 686-690 (1976).
(69) Bevia, F.J.O.: La familia de la mujer alcoholics. *Actas Luso-Espanolos de Neurolg y Psychiatria y Cliencias Afines* 4: 227-238 (1976).
(70) Latcham, R.: Familial alcoholism: evidence from 237 alcoholics, *Brit J Psychiatry*

147: 54-57 (1985).

(71) Midanik, L.: Familial alcoholism and problem drinking in a national drinking practices survey. *Addict Behav* (Oxford) 8: 133-141 (1983).

(72) Merikangas, K.R., et al.: Familial transmission of depression and alcoholism. *Arch Gen Psychiatry* 42: 367-372 (1985).

(73) Kosten, T.R., Rounaville, B.J., and Kleber, H.D.: Parental alcoholism in opioid addicts. *J Nerv Ment Dis* 173: 461-469 (1985).

(74) Pozarnik, H.: Family circumstances of preschizophrenic patients (in Serbo-Croat). Abstract No. 79032238. Excerpt *Med Pschijat Panas* 9: 495-499 (1977).

(75) Sipova, I., and Nedoma, K.: Family setting and childhood in socially and sexually deprived women (in Czech), *Czeskoslovenska Psyckiatrie* 68: 150-153 (1972).

(76) Price, V., Scanlon , B., and Janus, M.: Social characteristics of adolescent male prostitution. *Victimology: An International Journal* 9: 211-221 (1984).

(77) Lobos, R.: Sociopsychiatric aspects of marital troubles (in German), *Schweitzer Archiv Neurologie, Neurochirurgie und Psychiatrie* 109: 367-397 (1971).

(78) Abelsohn, D.S., and van der Spuy, H.I.J.: The age variable in alcoholism. *J Stud Alcohol* 39: 800-808 (1978).

(79) Schuckit, M.A.: Subjective responses to alcohol in sons of alcoholics and controls. *Arch Gen Psychiatry* 41: 879-887 (1984).

(80) Volicer L., Volicer, B.J., and d'Angelo, N.: Relationship of family history of alcoholism to patterns of drinking and physical dependence in male alcoholics. *Drug Alcohol Depend* 13: 215-222 (1984).

(81) Cook, B.L., and Winokur, G.: A family of familial positive vs familial negative alcoholics, *J Nerv Ment Dis* 173:175 (1985).

(82) Stabenau, J.R.: Implications of family history of alcoholism, anti-social personality, and sex differences in alcohol dependence, *Am J Psychiatry* 141: 1178 (1984).

(83) Alterman, A.E., and Tarter, R.E.: Relationship between familial alcoholism and head injury. *J Stud Alcohol* 46: 256-258 (1985).

(84) Malhotra, M.K.: Familial and personal correlates (risk factors) of drug consumption among German youth. *Psychological Abstracts* (Psychinfo) Abstract No. 25814, vol 71, October 1984.

(85) Blane, H.T., and Barry, H.: Birth order and alcoholism: a review. *Q J Stud Alcohol* 34: 837-852 (1973).

(86) Kock, H.L.: Some emotional attitudes of the young child in relation to the characteristics of his siblings. *Child Development* 27: 393-426 (1956).

(87) Nici, J.: Wives of alcoholics as "repeaters." *J Stud Alcohol* 40: 677-682 (1979).

8

The Results of a Survey on Counseling at Public Health Centers in Tokyo

Eiichi Senoh, M.D.

Sayoko Nobuta, M.A.

Public health centers in Tokyo were studied with regard to their offered levels of care and general attitudes toward alcoholic families. Questionnaires were sent to public health nurses in charge of mental health and alcohol counseling. It was found that the Public Health Centers' interest regarding the alcohol problem is quite high. Positive and active involvement of the public health nurses in the alcohol problem may be related to the fact that the method of handling patients has changed in emphasis from that of treating only the patient to that of involving the family members. It also became clear that the Public Health Centers were the only officially recognized places in the community where the families of alcoholic patients can receive consultation free of charge.

I. INTRODUCTION

This study focuses on the process of a family being identified as having an alcohol problem and becoming the object of treatment and research. The most important institute in this process is the Public Health Center as it is the window which identifies the family. The Public Health Center is also the center of local mental health and is expected to play an important role in the network therapy of alcoholism.

The Mental Health Law implemented in 1988 states, "The Public Health Center implements medical care for those suffering from mental health problems and protects them" as well as "should maintain and promote the mental health of nationals." We can interpret this statement as a symbol of the shift from the policy of medically caring for the person himself/herself who is suffering from an alcohol problem to a more active involvement in the mental health of individual members of the alcoholic's family.

At present, in addition to our respective workplaces, we are involved in alcohol addiction consultation in metropolitan Public Health Centers. The fact that alcoholics are dealt with by these local public health centers is quite natural considering that those suffering from alcoholic problems and their families come from local areas and finally recover in the same areas.

From another viewpoint, we can guess the actual local alcoholism situation by the current situation of the Public Health Centers' alcohol consultations. From the above understanding of the basic problem, we have studied the actual situation of Public Health Center alcoholism consultation and the consciousness of the public health nurses all over Tokyo. We also related the results of the above studies to the situation of the Mental Health Center, which is the core of local mental health, with regard to alcohol problems. The following section describes the method and results of our study.

II.   THE OBJECTIVE AND METHOD OF THE STUDY

Objective

We studied all of the Public Health Centers and Health Consultation Centers (a total number of 110) with regard to whether they offer specialized alcoholism counseling and the content and number of cases handled, if any. This was done by sending written questionnaires mainly to public health nurses who are in charge of mental health or alcohol counseling. We sent the questionnaires out on the last day of July 1989 and collected them by August 15. We also requested these public health nurses to describe "questions and problems from their position as those in charge of alcohol addiction consultation," or "how they can involve themselves in the solution of the problem."

Results

We were able to collect 95% of the questionnaires. The results were computed in three different geographical areas of 23 Metropolitan wards: East, West, and the Tama area.

1. The health centers' overall situation.   The number of Public Health Centers offering alcohol addiction counseling with an independent budget set aside for this purpose is 12 in the 23 Metropolitan wards, East (25.5%); 8 in the 23 Metropolitan wards, West (24.0%); and 8 in the Tama area (27.6%) respectively. Before 1980 only 2 of these centers offered counseling. Another 14 began between 1981 and 1984, and 12 between 1985 and 1989. One is planned to open in 1990.

More Public Health Centers in the 23 Metropolitan wards began consultation even before 1984, while in the Tama area the majority of Public Health Centers offering this service began doing so after 1985. As for consultation frequency, 11 centers conducted consultations once a month; 12 centers twice a month; 3 centers three times a month; 1 center four times a month; 1 center every other month; and 1 center intermittently.

However, 4 out of 5 Public Health Centers in Itabashi Ward offer consultation, and some of them four times a month. A similarly high frequency can be seen in Nakano Ward as well. In 14 Public Health Centers, specially assigned public health nurses are in charge of the consultation while in 11 centers public health nurses take turns in offering consultations. In 4 centers, other arrangements have been adopted. Outside specialists participated in the consultation in 27 centers. The types of outside specialists can be divided into medical doctors in 21 centers, psychological consultants in 3 centers, P.S.W.'s in 3 centers, nursing staff in 4 centers, self-help group members in 2 centers, and another in 1 center.

In most cases, both group therapy and individual consultation are adopted.

The average numbers in group therapy comprise less than 5 in 3 centers, 6-10 in 13 centers, 11-20 in 11 centers, and over 20 in 1 center. The number of group therapy participants is greater among centers in the 23 Metropolitan wards.

2. The contents of consultation in areas where alcohol addiction consultation is not implemented.   We recorded the monthly number of requests for alcoholism counseling received by those Public Health Centers also offering other counseling. In most cases the number was less than 10 . In 6 centers in the 23 Metropolitan wards, East, and in 3 centers in the 23 Metropolitan wards, West, the number of cases was between 11 and 20. In 1 center, each month had between 21 and 30 and over 30. As a whole, we can conclude that the consultation frequency is higher in the 23 Metropolitan wards compared to other areas.

3. The nurses' awareness of the significance of alcoholism counseling.   We asked the public health nurses to what degree they consider this consultation helpful to local mental health. The majority in all the areas stated that it was "very meaningful." Public health nurses in the 23 Metropolitan wards appreciated the service more than those in the Tama area. We compared the evaluation of the public health nurses in both the implementation area and nonimplementation area.

As the result, we found that the public health nurses in the nonimplementation districts of the Tama area evaluated the meaning of consultation relatively low, while even in the non-implementation areas in the 23 Metropolitan
wards the public health nurses tended to highly appreciate the service.

*4. The degree of public health nurses' interest in the alcohol addiction
problem.*   We studied to what degree individual public health nurses are interested in the alcohol addiction problem by area. The interest was the highest
in the 23 Metropolitan wards, East, followed by the 23 Metropolitan wards,
West, and the Tama area in this order. Comparing the implementation and
nonimplementation areas, we found that the public health nurses in the
nonimplementation districts of the Tama area have relatively negative opinions, while there was no significant difference in opinions between the implementation and non-implementation areas.

5. Relationships with the Mental Health Center.   We asked the public health
nurses how the individual Public Health Centers utilized the Mental Health
Center which coordinates local mental health issues. We found that many
Public Health Centers utilized the Mental Health Center by participating in
the training programs organized by the Mental Health Center as well as introducing the patients' families to their education programs.

In the 23 metropolitan wards, the number of Public Health Centers which
participated in the supervision (case study group meetings) was much greater compared to that in other areas. In the Tama area, the number which never
participated (i.e., no relationship between the Public Health Centers and the
Mental Health Center) was 8.

*6. The problems the public health nurses in charge of alcohol addiction con-
sultation face and their role consciousness with regard to alcohol-related
problems.*   We requested the public health nurses to answer our questionnaires in three different levels such as: a) issues related to alcohol addiction
consultation; b) issues related to team work in the Public Health Centers;
and c) issues related to the local community. In the first category, public
health nurses expressed their opinions as to how to motivate patients under
the present situation in which the number of consultation requests is small.
Their main wishes were to learn the techniques of family intervention, have
more opportunity to study various cases, and increase the frequency of consultation.

In the second category, difficulty in the method of organizing a team with
public health nurses in charge of the area, insufficient time due to a great
number of duties, and discrepancies in opinions of supervisors were conspic-

uous expressions of opinions. In the third category, most opinions stated that they wish to have more coordination with social welfare office case workers, that they wish to establish a local medical institute dedicated to alcohol-related problems, that there was difficulty in organizing a team with medical specialists such as medical doctors at mental hospitals due to their rather low awareness, and that there is a need for communication with the local self-help group. As a whole, the majority described the difficulty of organizing coordination with other institutions.

In the Tama area where a great number of mental hospitals are located, some public health nurses stated that there is no clear relationship between the role of hospital treatment and that of the Public Health Centers. Some public health nurses expressed their wish to alter society, saying that there is a need to control advertising and automatic vending machines as well as establishing a temporary refuge for the patients' families.

Most of the public health nurses stated that the role of the Public Health Centers is to educate, advertise and publicize the problem of alcohol addiction. Some insisted that they should further expand the role of the Public Health Centers as the social resource related to the alcohol problem.

The conspicuous opinion in Tama and the 23 Metropolitan wards' area was that the role of the Public Health Center is to be the local care system coordinator and promoter of network therapy. Some emphasized their role as the primary center for discovery of problems as they implement resident health checks and the 3-year child health checks in the community and discover alcohol problems in the background. Some suggested that Public Health Centers cooperate with health education in schools so that they can start alcohol education earlier.

We can see the impact of their daily activities dealing with people suffering from alcohol problems, as well as their involvement with self-help groups such as Japan Sobriety Party and AA. However, the most influential must be the supervision of specialists in alcoholism. These external specialists seem to play an important role as the supervisors of these public health nurses.

III. SUMMARY AND CONSIDERATION

It is hoped that their addictive behavior will be cured.

Pursuing the idea that the local community should be allowed a clear say in developing alcohol abuse treatment programs, Mr. Noda, along with others, has been holding such forums concerning treatment of alcohol abuse in Takatsuki, Osaka. A group has been formed in which medical doctors hired on contract basis, specialist mental health counselors, hospital specialists and self-help group members are all actively involved. The health center has been working hard to coordinate all related institutions.

Dr. J. Shore introduced community care treatment for the alcoholic.

It is now 10 years since Public Health Centers have been engaged in alcoholism prevention and treatment activities. Reports, supported by research, have specified that the counseling services for problem drinkers in the Tokyo Metropolitan areas be placed under the auspices of the public health centers.

Dr. Saitoh indicates, in a report on the Setagaya Public Health Center, the effectiveness of the two-hour counseling sessions concerning the dangers of alcohol abuse. These are held four times a month. Participants consist of problem drinkers and their families, medical hospital staff, community health nurses, social welfare staff, and self-help group members.

These meetings are not structured, but rather are staged along the lines of an "encounter group." There is no prearranged discussion or comment. Participants may sit in the pleasant environment and openly discuss whatever is on their minds. Approximately 60% of visitors requesting counseling are the family members of problem drinkers, which clearly indicates that the public finds the health center of great value for holding such community-based groups.

Dr. Saitoh proposes that alcoholism can be dealt with via the "personal-relation model," which advocates the use of family-oriented discussions for the reformation of distorted personal and family relationships and a consequent improvement in their addictive behaviors.

Mr. Iwasaki has developed, in the health center, a three-tier program regarding alcohol problems. The first stage is *Introduction*, where people in need of assistance are introduced to medical personnel and self-help groups. Secondly, *Facility Rental* assists self-help groups to rent rooms in medical centers, thus increasing the development of such groups for those in need of them. Thirdly, *Consultation*: depending upon their needs, people may visit individual counselors or attend group therapy sessions.

Mr. Iwasaki has also changed the focus of assistance from the abuser to the family, and aims to bring about changes in the identified patient's behavior patterns via interaction with family members.

A health center nurse, Mr. Akashi, points out that the heavy burden of numerous one-to-one consultations can be alleviated by changing to group therapy sessions.

Mr. Miyasato has been holding "alcohol abuse family sessions" for both abusers and their families, in the mental health center. These group therapy and education-oriented sessions attract a range of participants, from normal, social drinkers through people experiencing alcohol dependency syndrome. Meaningful results have been seen in terms of prevention of alcoholism, as well as in early discovery and alleviation of the disease.

From the results of the answers collected through these multiple-choice questionnaires, we have considered how the Public Health Centers can deal with families with alcohol problems from the mental health viewpoint and its meaning in this process. The first point is that the Public Health Centers' consciousness regarding the alcohol problem is quite high and they have a very positive attitude. Looking at this in more detail, however, we found unevenness in various local areas. In short, in the 23 Metropolitan wards' East area the public health nurses highly appreciated the role of Public Health Centers.

Similarly, in the same area, the Public Health Centers have a close coordinating relationship with the Mental Health Centers.

The background of this unevenness in various areas is that the Shitaya Mental Health Center, the only one in Tokyo, is located in the 23 Metropolitan wards, East. Thus, there is a history and tradition of cooperation between the two centers.

On the other hand, in the 23 Metropolitan wards, West, it has been only a short period of time since the Chubu Mental Health Center was founded and began alcoholism counseling service.

In the Tama area, it will be several more years before the Tama Mental Health Center opens.

TABLE 1.

Alcohol Addiction Consultation at Public Health Centers

	Number of Implemented Public Health Centers	*Prior to 1980*	*[3] 1981 – 1984*	*[4] After 1985*
23 Metropolitan wards: East	12	1	8	3
23 Metropolitan wards: West	8	1	4	3
Tama area	9	0	2	7

TABLE 2.

Frequency of Alcoholism Counselling Offered by Public Health Centers

	4 times per month	*3 times per month*	*twice per month*	*once a month*	*every other month*	*twice year*
23 Metropolitan wards: East	0	1	6	4	0	0
23 Metropolitan wards: West	1	1	3	3	1	0
Tama	0	1	3	4	0	1

TABLE 3.
The Number of Average Consultation Cases per Month

	0-10	*22-20*	*21-30*	*31-*
23 Metropolitan wards: East	11	6	1	1
23 Metropolitan wards: West	14	3	0	0
Tama	18	1	0	0

TABLE 4.
The Evaluation of Alcoholic Consultation

	Very meaningful	*Con- siderable*	*Some- what*	*Not meaningful*
23 Metropolitan wards:				
East, implemented group	10	1	1	0
Not-implemented group	17	2	1	0
23 Metropolitan wards:				
West, implemented group	8	0	0	0
Not-implemented group	9	2	1	1
Tama, implemented group	6	1	1	0
Tama, not-implemented group	10	4	4	0
Total	60	10	8	1

TABLE 5.
Interest of Individual Public Nurses on the Alcohol Addiction Problem

	Very interested	*Considerably interested*	*Somewhat interested*	*Not very interested*
23 Metropolitan wards:				
East, implemented group	9	3	0	0
Not-implemented group	12	6	1	0
23 Metropolitan wards:				
West, implemented group	4	4	0	0
Not-implemented group	7	4	2	0
Tama, implemented group	5	4	0	0
Tama, not-implemented group	6	10	1	0
Total	43	31	4	0

Another factor of the positive and active attitude of the public health nurses in Tokyo toward the alcoholism problem is that the method of handling the patients has changed in emphasis from that of treating only the patient himself/herself to that of involving all of the family members — in other words, introducing the concept of the family systems theory and developing family intervention techniques.

By adopting the concept of family systems theory, public health nurses should be able to discover alcohol problems such as an alcoholic father as the background of a case of a child with asthma who is under consultation.

Or, they might find the alcoholic father in the process of giving consultation to a child who refuses to go to school.

The last point to be made is the fact that the Public Health Center is the only official institution in the community where the family of alcoholic patients can receive consultation free of charge. We can position the Public Health Center offering alcoholism counseling as the place where the alcoholic family as a family system can gradually and surely recover. In this sense, we can position the Public Health Centers as the institutes which function as intermediates between the alcoholic family and mental health.

There has been considerable, well-documented, change concerning the historical understanding and view of alcohol dependency syndrome. Japan has traditionally viewed chronic alcoholism as stemming from an individual's lack of willpower. This led to the dismal result of long-term hospitalization for such individuals, even for many years following World War II. Theoretically, from the "model theory" perspective, this could have been considered the "moral and legal model."

Following the establishment of specialist alcoholism wards in the Kurihama National Hospital in 1963, Jellinek brought forth the "disease model" definition of alcohol dependency syndrome.

Questionnaires have shown that caretakers have been those principally involved in community care services, using both family intervention techniques and networking, alongside merely passively introducing the alcoholic client to specialist hospitals.

Chart A indicates the historical changes in mental health concepts concerning alcoholism:

Chart A: The evolution of alcoholism models

Past:	Chronic alcoholism	Moral model
Present:	Alcohol dependency syndrome	Disease model
Future:	Alcohol-related problems	Systems model

REFERENCES

(1) Shore JH and Kofoed L. Community intervention in the treatment of alcoholism. *Alcoholism* 8: 151-159 (1984).
(2) Saitoh S. Rupture of disease-model in community mental health activities — An evaluation of the disease, concept of alcohol dependence syndrome. *Seishin Igaku* 30: 701-708 (1988).

(3) Saitoh S, Noguchi Y and Ikegami N. Report on community based program at Setagaya Health Center. In: *Biomedical Aspects of Alcohol and Alcoholism.* (Eds.) Kameda T, Kuriyama K and Suwaki H. 165-195. Osaka: Aino Hospital Foundation. Gendaikikakushitsu Publishing (1985).

(4) Noda T, Kawata A, Ando T, et al. Survey on the actual conditions of alcoholics in a satellite city — Takatsuki City — and a follow-up study — in relation to a community support system. *Japanese J Alcohol and Drug Dependencèe* 23: 26-52 (1988).

(5) Iwasaki M, Endo S, Matsumoto F, et al. On the effectiveness of a group-meeting for alcoholics and their families — Introduction of a community care program held by a public health center. *Japanese J Alcohol and Drug Dependence* 23: 130-139 (1988).

(6) Miyasato K, Yamashiro A, Sugimoto Y, et al. Prevention and intervention program of alcohol dependence: Educational and group-psychotherapeutic approach. *Seishin Igaku* 30: 537-545 (1988).

9

Alcoholism and the Native American Family

James O. Whittaker, Ph.D.
Sandra J. Whittaker, M.A.

Studies by the authors of Native American populations over the past 30 years have revealed alcoholism rates that appear to be the highest in the world. In some groups it is virtually impossible to find any adult over 18 years of age who is not an alcoholic or recovering alcoholic. Alcoholism and, more recently, poly-substance abuse have threatened the fabric of family life, lead-ing to substantially increased divorce rates, separation, child abuse, beatings, suicides, and cases of fetal alcohol syndrome.

Even the most remote of Alaska's towns — those on the shores of the Arctic Ocean, unreachable except by air — have been af-fected by both alcoholism and drug abuse. Poverty alone is not the cause. In fact, some evidence suggests that more money alone would simply exacerbate the problem. Multiple causes suggest there is no single simple solution. Rather, multifaceted efforts from every possible resource sustained over time offer the best hope of restoring sobriety and family integrity to the Native American.

INTRODUCTION

As 1989 draws to a close, the plunder of our planet increases unabated. A huge oil spill in Prince William Sound, Alaska, has killed thousands of animals, fouled hundreds of miles of pristine wilderness, endangered the econ-omy of the region for years, and contributed — as we will see in this paper — to the accelerated destruction of the Native population in the area. There was less than a "one in a million chance" of this kind of disaster, we were told by the oil companies who wanted to develop the Arctic oil fields.

Drilling for oil on the north slope of Alaska, they said, would "benefit the native population" as well as "reduce America's dependence on foreign oil." But in reality, as we shall see, the "benefits" to the Eskimo and other

Native Alaskan peoples have taken the form of increased alcohol abuse, family disintegration, violence, and finally drug dependence. Most of the oil, we might add, is being sold outside the United States.

The situation is no better in the so-called "Lower 48." Alcoholism, alcohol abuse, and overall cultural genocide have never been greater threats to the indigenous population of North America. We hear of the plight of "endangered species" such as the African elephant which humans have been busily hunting into extinction for their ivory. At the same time, drift net fishing in the Pacific threatens many species. "Don't worry," we are promised, "these species can replenish themselves." But the threat is also to the native peoples of North America where lives depend on these resources from the sea.

The plunder of our planet threatens not only many species like the elephant, rhino and walrus, but also human groups such as the Sioux, Cheyenne, and Crow, as well as the Aleut, Tlingit and Inupiat. "Ecosociology" is a term which we will hear more often in the next century. The interdependence of human life and the environment is something we cannot take for granted as we have in the past. Ignorance of this interdependence will truly be at the peril of not only native groups but the entire human species as a whole.

SUBJECTS

In this paper we will summarize our work with indigenous peoples in North America, work that extends back about 30 years. In this period, two extensive surveys of alcohol use were conducted on the same native population (Standing Rock Sioux Tribe) involving 392 subjects.[18],[19],[21] In August of 1989, we returned to the same Tribe for an extensive update of the situation, and more recently — in September — we traveled 3000 miles in Alaska to review the situation among native groups there.

Our work began in 1960 on the Standing Rock Sioux Reservation in North Dakota. At that time we undertook the *first* extensive systematic survey of alcohol on an American Indian reservation. Using Indian interviewers who were themselves members of the Tribe involved, we constructed an in-depth interview schedule which was administered to 208 Indians over 15 years of age and about equally divided between male and female.[18],[19]

Twenty years later we conducted the first systematic follow-up of an Indian Tribe, interviewing some 184 subjects (both male and female) over 15 years of age. Again, the same procedure was used, involving Indian interviewers who were members of the Tribe.[20],[21]

In the intervening time since 1980, we have been involved in the investigation of biomedical factors (ALDH I and II) in both the Standing Rock Sioux Tribe and Navajo groups in Arizona. This work was in collaboration with

Professor Harada of Tsukuba University in Japan and Professor Goedde of the University of Hamburg in Germany.[7] Recently we have attempted to collect data for Dr. Asaka. Dr. Satoru Saitoh's work and Dr. Asaka's work on alcoholism have been inspiration and models.[8],[15]

METHODS

In the 1960 study, we devised an interview schedule consisting of 94 (mostly open-ended) questions divided into five parts. The five parts were: (1) pattern of drinking; (2) motivation to drink; (3) social context of drinking; (4) knowledge about alcohol and its effects; (5) results of drinking. Many of the questions had been utilized in studies of drinking among white subjects and provided us with a basis of comparison. Other questions evolved from extensive discussions with various members of the Tribe and with non-Indians involved with the Tribe in one capacity or another.[18],[19]

In the 1980 follow-up study, we used many of the same questions since the purpose was to assess changes in drinking behavior that might have occurred over 20 years. In addition, however, we initiated some new questions intended to elicit information concerning the absence of certain behavioral symptoms of alcoholism we had noted in the 1960 study. We also included, at the request of the Tribal Chairman, questions about the use of drugs on the reservation.[20],[21]

RESULTS

Before presenting the results of our work, a few words about the cultural background of the Sioux are important. These are genetically Mongoloid peoples whose ancestors probably crossed the land bridge from Siberia to Alaska 12,000 years ago. Nomadic and warlike before contact with whites, they lived in the upper Great Plains in what are now Minnesota and Nebraska. Obtaining horses from the Spanish explorers in the 17th century, they became more mobile and moved west into the Dakotas and southern Manitoba. As far as we know they never had any intoxicating beverages, nor did they brew any before contact with white fur trappers and traders in the 18th century.

The society was communal and matriarchal with extended families. Women were mainly responsible for child rearing, cooking, and making clothing. Men were warriors and hunters. Bravery, generosity (sharing), and stoicism were, and *still are,* important values in this culture — especially for men but also for women. Living in one of the harshest climates in the world where temperatures often plunge to 40 below zero degrees Fahrenheit and the winters are long, they survived quite well for centuries before contact with whites.

Then Indians were introduced to alcohol by white traders who bartered whiskey for furs. Early on there were stories of Indians' bizarre and violent behavior when given alcohol. In fact the massacre of White settlers by drunken Indians in the late 19th century led to a Federal law prohibiting the sale of alcohol to Indians. That law was in effect until 1953.

An early accommodation with whites led to the signing of several treaties between the great Sioux Nation and the U.S. government. Among these was one guaranteeing the Sioux perpetual sovereignty over the Black Hills in South Dakota. That treaty was broken when an Army Colonel named Custer led an exploratory party into the Black Hills and discovered gold. In 1868, the Standing Rock Sioux Reservation was established in what is now southern North Dakota and northern South Dakota. Over a million acres of land that whites considered largely worthless was set aside for the Tribe along the banks of the Missouri River.

Attempts to force the Sioux to remain on the Reservation however, were largely unsuccessful. So-called "hostiles" refused to comply, and with Sitting Bull (member of the Standing Rock Tribe) they moved west into Montana. In 1876, Col. Custer encountered the largest single encampment of Indians in American history on the Little Big Horn River in eastern Montana. The rest of the story is well known.

The Custer massacre was really a turning point in the history of the Sioux for it marked the end of traditional Indian life and the beginning of the tragedy that continues to this day. By 1881, the Army had killed many Indian people, including women and children, and the remainder had submitted against their will to Reservation life. Forcing these people into sedentary dependency, in many respects, caused the alcohol problems we see today. Especially for men, the Reservations have been a disaster for they made it impossible to continue the traditional Sioux way of life. Warfare against other tribes ended and hunting also ended for all practical purposes when, in a 10-year period, some four million buffalo were butchered — sometimes only for their tails which could be used as flyswatters. Outlets for aggression vanished; activities which enhanced self-esteem disappeared. Missionaries stamped out Indian religions and tuberculosis and other diseases killed thousands.

Despised, discriminated against, denied any kind of meaningful economy, forced to live on handouts, many Indians turned to alcohol. And increasingly, in the early part of this century, bootleggers provided alcohol. No one really knows how serious the problem was before 1953, however, because consuming alcohol was illegal and there were no studies. As we said, our work in 1960 was the first in which the problem of Indian alcoholism was examined extensively and with the cooperation and encouragement of the Tribe involved.

RESULTS OF THE 1960 STUDY

Our 1960 study revealed a staggering alcohol problem. More Indian males drank at that time than white males regardless of age. But more importantly, they tended to heavy consumption and frequent drinking. Fewer women drank than men, but among younger women it was apparent that alcohol problems were increasing.

Comparing Indian and white drinking revealed some interesting differences regardless of sex: (1) Indians drank more frequently (3 or more times per week was the norm); (2) Indians drank greater amounts at each sitting (drinking large amounts until the supply was gone was common); (3) Drinking was virtually always in groups.

Signs of alcoholism — both behavioral and physical — were common. Behavioral signs have tended to be less reliable indicators because of cultural differences. Morning drinking, blackouts, compulsive drinking, DT's and binges, however, were certainly very evident. We estimated the rate of alcoholism to be 5 times that in the white population.

Comparing respondents and their parents of the same sex, it was apparent that alcohol problems had increased significantly over the preceding generation in both men and women. About twice as many women reported drinking as in the previous generation and the greatest increase was in the number of regular drinkers. Almost *5 times as many* women were regular drinkers as in the previous generation.

Some 68% of the drinkers had been arrested for public intoxication and other offenses. Child abuse and neglect were rampant and increasing. In the month we were there, 70 children were placed in foster homes because of neglect or abandonment by parents.

Many families were beginning the process of disintegrating. But pressure was still very great on women to remain with their husbands regardless of their behavior. Disapproval of female drunkenness also mitigated against females matching males drink for drink. Finally women still had the major responsibility for child rearing. [18],[19],[20]

RESULTS OF THE 1980 STUDY

Twenty years later, our results revealed an absolutely unmitigated disaster on this Indian reservation. It is hardly an exaggeration to say that by 1980 that there were only three groups on the reservation — alcoholics, recovering alcoholics, and children. Our estimate is that the incidence of alcoholism was (and still is) the highest of any group in the world and that it has led to increased disintegration of family and Tribal life.

Our data from the 1980 study indicate that 50% of the men over 40 years of age are alcoholics and that 25% of the women in this age group are alcoholics. Based on our findings concerning the physical symptoms of alcoholism, we categorically reject the contention of some investigators who maintain that Indians do not become alcoholics.

To summarize our findings — "40% of the men drinkers and 16% of the women drinkers characterized themselves as 'alcoholics,' and of those who said they did not drink, 50% of the men and 18% of the women described themselves as 'recovered alcoholics.'" About 38% of the men drinkers and 22% of the women drinkers said that they became inebriated the last time they drank — up slightly from the results in 1960. Some 62% of the male drinkers and 40% of the female drinkers reported that drinking had caused them problems such as losing friends, bankruptcy, divorce, arguments, marital disharmony, fights, and arrests.

Signs of various stages of alcoholism were present: 62% of the drinkers reported blackouts, 15% reported increasing frequency of blackouts, 22% (19% of the men and 25% of the women) reported secret drinking, 17% preoccupation with alcohol, 23% avid drinking, 72% guilt feelings, 70% inability to stop drinking once they started, 87% changing drinking patterns to try to control drinking, 18% dropping friends, 7% quitting jobs, 90% geographic escape, 28% protecting their liquor supply. Also, 15% reported hospitalization for drinking, 37% some morning drinking (up from 25% in 1960), 10% drinking regularly before breakfast, 16% prolonged intoxication, 10% alcoholic psychoses. Further, 25% reported loss of tolerance to alcohol, 12% recourse to non-ethyl alcohol, 18% tremors, 10% delirium tremens, 52% (74% of the men and 28% of the women) arrests for intoxication, 20% spending all their money on alcohol, and 38% of the men and 11% of the women divorce or separation because of drinking.

In this culture we have seen that alcohol abuse has become commonplace. Familial alcoholism is often seen where there is social alienation, an alcoholic father, instability and economic hardship, and low parental occupational levels.[5],[6] Also, the reference group is of great importance in drinking behavior.[4]

NATIVE POPULATIONS IN ALASKA

Sixteen percent of the population in Alaska is native — Indian, Eskimo, and Aleut. But whether Athapascan Indian, Tlingit, Inupiat, or other, all of these cultural groups have problems with alcohol abuse today. The problem is reflected in a rash of suicides and violent deaths punctuated by rapes, beatings, and child abuse. Recently the *Anchorage Daily News* (January 1988) published an extensive series of articles on the problem — a series which won the Pulitzer Prize.[2] In that series, they report that "Alaskan Natives are four times as likely to commit suicide as other Alaskans; Alaskan Native men between the ages 20 and 24 are 10 times more likely to kill themselves than non-Natives nationwide; fetal alcohol syndrome, where a pregnant woman's drinking damages her unborn child, is $2^1/2$ times more common among Native women than non-Natives. Natives comprise 16% of the population, but make up 34% of the prison inmates".[2]

In September of this year, we visited an Arctic town, a predominantly Eskimo community on the shores of the Arctic Ocean. It cannot be reached by road, only by air from Prudhoe Bay. Yet, as isolated as it is, alcoholism is rampant, and more recently cocaine and other hard drugs have become an equally important problem. Suicides, family break-ups, beatings, rapes, fights, FAS, and other signs of alcohol and drug abuse have become common.

Unemployment is low in this town and incomes are high. The group owns the land of the Prudhoe Bay oil fields and receives more than a million dollars a year in land taxes. Jobs are plentiful and family incomes of several thousand dollars a month are not uncommon. So those who believe that alcoholism and drug abuse are caused simply by substantial economic deprivation in Native communities should take a look at somewhere a substandard economy is not the case. All things being equal, increasing incomes alone is likely to increase substance abuse.

The same thing can be seen in other Native communities. In English Bay, Alaska, for example, oil from the 11 million gallon spill at Prince William Sound and money from Exxon has changed life for better or worse. Binge drinking has risen dramatically among the Aleut population on the Kenai Peninsula. Money earned cleaning up oil has made life easier in some respects for the moment, but many Natives say it has not made life better.

Like the Arctic community we spoke of, no roads lead into or out of English Bay. It is cut off from the rest of the world by a fortress of glaciers, active volcanoes and the big moat of Cook Inlet. Only six people have full-time jobs, including three in the school. Before the spill, everybody lived off the bounty of the sea. The only money that came into the village before the spill was for sales of surplus salmon at the end of the season. By early this summer, everybody in the village above 18 years of age was working for Exxon at wages of $16.00/69.00 per hour. Ten-foot skiffs were rented out at $300.00 per day. One person in the village said," It was like a typhoon came in and emptied out the village." "Everything changed overnight. We gained a lot of money, but we lost a lot of family closeness and our own food.''[2] The village, which had had a strong sobriety movement for the last six years, is now seeing a lot of villagers who have "fallen off the wagon," including an alcohol counselor. Some traditional activities continue. Some salmon, according to newspaper reports, are being harvested and hung to dry. A seal was recently killed and shared by the Natives. But as winter approaches, many smokehouses are empty.

IMPACT ON THE FAMILY

The statistics we do have all underscore the devastating nearly overwhelming magnitude of the problems facing the Native American family due to alcohol/substance abuse. If anything, we probably see underreporting in many areas. Much of this is due to cuts in research money available from the U.S. Federal Government during the Reagan years. Some is due to the fact that there are so many areas to investigate and the territory to cover is both vast and, in many cases, remote. Language differences contribute to the difficulties. So do cultural sensitivities. There is still a great reluctance to speak out on these matters to "outsiders." In addition, many Native Americans do not like to discuss these things freely even among themselves. In some cases, irresponsible researchers have simply used the alcohol problem to enhance their own careers by presenting their results in a sensationalistic way without regard for the feelings of the people from whom they gathered the information. Still, scientists have been able to gather enough to help the people begin to truly understand the outline and nature of the "monster."

There is no area of Native family life that has not been adversely affected by alcohol abuse. The mortality rate alone is still more than four times the rate among all Native Americans as compared with non-Natives.[9],[12] It is most probably higher if the deaths from heart disease, homicides, suicides, cerebrovascular disease, diabetes mellitus, and accidents, many of which may have an alcohol-related component, were to be factored in.

With the increase seen over the past two decades in women who have become alcoholics, there has been a concomitant increase in the incidence of fetal alcohol syndrome and fetal alcohol effect. The syndrome was not well-defined and recognized by the scientific community until about 10 years ago. The impact of the diminished lives of these children will be felt for years. The stress on families and the expense of caring for these tragically impaired youngsters will require support from every quarter. In 1985, the Indian Health Service trained large numbers of their people to begin to deal with just this one problem on a national level.[9],[10],[11],[12]

Among families rendered dysfunctional by alcohol and, sometimes, polysubstance abuse, recent research points clearly to increased alcohol and drug intake by adolescents.[10] In one report from Alaska, of the suicides investigated, 72% were related to alcohol. Homicides were estimated to be 84% alcohol-related, and among 15-to-34-year-olds, 70% of all deaths involved alcohol.[10, p. 52] Other serious family difficulties reported by newspapers include runaways, outplacement of children from the home, school dropouts and teenage pregnancies. In addition, some cases of child abuse and child molestation have been noted.

Domestic violence is most probably underreported, but the Indian Health Service has estimated that from one-fourth to one-half of the violent incidents, beatings, and fights are caused by alcohol abuse.[12]

ATTACKING THE PROBLEMS CAUSED BY ALCOHOL ABUSE

After hearing such numbing statistics, one may well ask, "Is anything being done to effectively combat this scourge?" There is, in fact, a great deal being done at every level. Whole Native communities have begun to make these problems their number 1 priority. The Cheyenne River Sioux Tribal Council resolved two years ago that they had declared "war on all that is

TABLE 1.

Alcoholism Deaths and Mortality Rates

Age-Adjusted Rates per 100,000 Population for Indians and
Alaska Natives in Reservation States and for U.S. All Races
1978-1985

	Number of Deaths		*Age-Adjusted Rates and Their Ratio*		
Calender Year	*Indian and Alaska Native*	*U.S. All Races*	*Indian and Alaska Native*	*U.S. All Races*	*Ratio of Indian to U.S. All Races*
1985	281	15,844	26.1	6.2	4.2
1984	316	15,706	30.0	6.2	4.8
1983	293	15,424	28.9	6.1	4.7
1982	298	15,596	30.7	6.4	4.8
1981	338	16,745	35.8	7.0	5.2
1980	382	17,742	41.3	7.5	5.5
1979	398	17,064	45.1	7.4	6.1
1978	437	18,490	54.4	8.1	6.7

In 1985, age-adjusted death rates specifically attributable to alcoholism (10, p. 4) were 4.2 times greater for American Indians/Alaska Natives than for U.S. All Races.

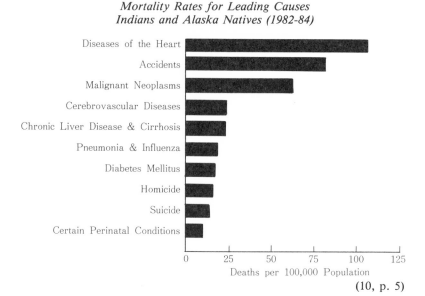

Mortality Rates for Leading Causes
Indians and Alaska Natives (1982-84)

(10, p. 5)

Figure 1.   Alcoholism has long been recognized as a major health problem for American Indian/Alaska Native people. It continues to be identified as a major factor in accidents, chronic liver disease, homicides and suicides. As the following chart indicates, these conditions are among the leading causes of death for American Indians and Alaska Natives.

associated with alcohol and drug abuse and, further, to work toward an alcohol and drug free reservation by the year 2000".[16] The Standing Rock Sioux at their annual Pow-Wow this year declared their pride to all attending in having an alcohol and drug-free event. A dance honoring sobriety was performed. A film called "The Honor of All" about the Alkali Lake Indian Band in Canada and their 14-year struggle from nearly 100% alcoholism among adults to more than 90% sobriety is having a major impact in all Native American communities where it has been shown.[1] Alaskan villages are refusing to let any cargo be off-loaded from airplanes without inspection to see if alcohol is aboard. Individuals are continuing their fight to become and remain substance-free.

There is also a profound recognition by the Indian Health Service that treatment ultimately must be multifaceted, community based and (more importantly) operated, and must target early prevention and intervention.

We are also seeing a renaissance of Native American pride in their diverse cultures and religions which serve to raise the self-esteem of all. AA has be-

gun to be adapted to Native American needs and philosophies and has started to enjoy success. Diet, nutrition, and exercise programs are springing up
on Reservations. In some communities, sobriety has been made a condition
to run for public office. Women's groups, various nonprofit and church organizations have opened shelters and safe-houses and are sponsoring group
meetings to discuss alcohol-related problems. Schools have begun prevention programs and the mass media have become involved. Treatment programs for adolescents are on the rise. The potential for making a real dent
in the mountain of misery is now apparent. We must add, however, that
all of these valiant attempts do not address the poverty and severe economic
straits in which most tribes find themselves. The lack of pride, sense of use-
lessness, and depression which come from unemployment are not about to
disappear, nor will the harsh, remote, and desolate physical characteristics
of many of the Reservations. We can expect all of the problems we have
reported in this paper to be with us for some time to come.

CONCLUSION AND NEED FOR FURTHER RESEARCH

As we have seen, there is no question that alcohol and drug abuse are continuing to have a devastating impact on Native American families. Given
the magnitude and extent of the problems experienced by these diverse peoples, much more research and many more treatment and prevention programs
need to be funded by the Federal government. In many areas, we still do
not know much more than the broad outlines of the severe disruption to the
social fabric which is being suffered. We know enough only to see that the
monster of alcoholism and that of polysubstance addiction are not yet tamed
for Native America.

We need to know what effects various programs now in place are produc-
ing as their efforts are brought to bear on alcohol abuse. Are individuals
and families becoming alcohol free and are they maintaining their sobriety?
Are fewer youngsters experimenting with addictive substances? Are families
breaking up at a slower rate? Is the divorce rate falling? Is suicide becoming
less common? Has the incidence of domestic violence abated? Do we see less
child abuse, alcohol-related deaths, dropouts, teenage pregnancies? How are
community and school-based mental health programs doing? A willingness
to adjust programs according to the answers to questions such as these will
enhance results.

Further research and the sharing of such information in forums such as
this enable all of us to keep from reinventing the wheel. But if we have learned
anything, we have learned that regardless of culture, the family is the absolutely critical institution. We have learned that alcoholism and polysubstance

abuse destroy not only the fabric of the family but poison the entire society. We have learned that treatment of the individual alone is insufficient. It appears that multifaceted efforts from every possible resource sustained over time offer the best hope of restoring mental health and family function to our Native Americans and their communities.

In short, all the disciplines concerned must intensity their efforts and cooperation.

REFERENCES

(1) Alkali Lake Indian Band. *The Honor of All* (video documentary), Phil Lucas Productions, Inc., Issaquah, WA (1987).

(2) *Anchorage Daily News*. A People In Peril (Pulitzer Prize winning series on Alcoholism among Native Alaskans) (Jan. 1988).

(3) Chi, I., Kitano, H., & Lubben, J. Male Chinese Drinking Behavior in L.A. *J. Stud. Alcohol* 49: 21-26 (1988).

(4) Chi, I., Lubben, J., & Kitano, H. Differences in Drinking Behavior among Three Asian-American Groups, *J. Stud. Alcohol* 50: 15-24 (1989).

(5) Cotton, N. The familial incidence of alcoholism: A review, *J.Stud. Alcohol* 40: 89-116 (1979).

(6) Glenn, S. and Parsons, O. Alcohol Abuse and Familial Alcoholism: Psychological Correlates in Men and Women, *J. Stud. Alcohol* 50: 116-128 (1989).

(7) Goedde, H., Agarwal, D., Harada, S., Whittaker, J., et al. Aldehyde Dehydrogenase Polymorphism in North American, South American and Mexican Indian Populations. *Am. J. Hum. Genet.* 38: 395-399 (1986).

(8) Imaizumi, Y. & Asaka, A. Mortality Rate of Alcoholics in Japan, Medico-Biological, Psychological and Socio-cultural Studies of Alcoholism: Intensive Approach on Ethnic Differences. Proceedings of International Joint Meeting, Tsukuba, pp. 1-9 (1982).

(9) Indian Health Service. *IHS Alcoholism/Substance Abuse Prevention Initiative.* Vanderwagen, C., Mason, R., & Owan, T., Eds. Rockville, MD: IHS (1986).

(10) Indian Health Service. *IHS School/Community-Based Alcoholism/Substance Abuse Prevention Survey.* Rockville, MD: IHS (1987).

(11) Indian Health Service. *Prevention, The Leap to Wellness.* Rockville, MD: IHS (1988).

(12) Indian Health Service. *A Progress Report on Indian Alcoholism Activities*, Rockville, MD, 4-5 (1988).

(13) Pandina, R. & Johnson, V. Familial Drinking History as a Predictor of Alcohol and Drug Consumption among Adolescent Children, *J. Stud. Alcohol* 50: 245-254 (1989).

(14) Rhoades, E., Mason, R., Eddy, P. et al. *The Indian Health Service Approach to Alcoholism among American Indians and Alaska Natives.* Public Health Reports, Nov-Dec 103-6, 621-627 (1988).

(15) Saitoh, S. Epidemiological Research on Alcoholism in Japan, Medico-Biological, Psychological and Socio-cultural Studies on Alcoholism: Intensive Approach on Ethnic Differences, Proceedings of International Joint Meeting, Tsukuba (1982).

(16) Tribal Resolution No. 313-87-CR, Cheyenne River Sioux Tribe. (Nov. 4, 1987).

(17) Welte, J. & Barnes, G. Alcohol use among minority groups;, *J.Stud. Alcohol* 48: 329-337 (1987).

(18) Whittaker, J. O., Alcohol and the Standing Rock Sioux Tribe, I. The pattern of drinking. *Q.J.Stud. Alcohol* 23: 468-479 (1962).

(19) Whittaker, J.O. Alcohol and the Standing Rock Sioux Tribe, II. Psychodynamic and cultural factors in drinking, *Q.J.Stud. Alcohol* 24: 80-90 (1963).

(20) Whittaker, J.O., Alcohol use and the American Indian — Some Socio-cultural Lessons about the Nature of Alcoholism, *Brit. J. Alcohol and Alcoholism* 14: 140-147 (1979).

(21) Whittaker, J.O. Alcohol and the Standing Rock Sioux Tribe, A Twenty-Year Follow-Up Study, *J.Stud.Alcohol* 43-3, 191-200 (1982).

(22) Whitaker, J.O. & Whitaker, S. J. *Psicologial, 4th ed.,* Nueva Editorial Interamericana, Mexico, Spain, Brazil, (1985).

Part III: Discussion

(*Chairperson*) *Dr. Kohno*: We have heard the speakers and would like to take up questions one by one. The first presentation was by Dr. and Mrs. Whittaker. What questions have we for them?

Dr. Nomura (*P.R.I.T.*): Dr. Whittaker, as an anthropologist myself, may I say how much I admire your project. I was thinking, as you spoke, that years ago Ruth Benedict studied three primitive cultures, including two Indian tribes on the American Continent. She termed one a very megalomanic tribe, Kwakiutl, which she called the "Plains Indians," in contrast to the other tribe, the Zuni, whom she described as quiet or repressed. In your study, you combined all the American Natives, including the Alaskan Eskimos, but do you still find some ethnic differences in the tribes? If so, how much are Benedict's findings still supported—or not supported—at this moment by your empirical studies?

Professor Whittaker: That's a good point. Certainly, the tribes aren't the same! I didn't mean to give this impression. I'm aware that there are cultural differences between, say, the Southwestern tribes, such as the Navaho and the Hopi, and the Plains Indians tribes that we're talking about. In some cases, there are very large differences. However, regardless of cultural differences, alcoholism seems to cut across all. Fifteen or twenty years ago, researchers used to say that the alcoholism rates are very low among tribes like the Zuni, for example, but that's not true today. In fact, some even denied that there was alcoholism among American Indians. "Alcohol abuse," they said, but not "alcoholism."

After our research in 1960, there were many researchers who did work in the Southwest among the Navaho, Hopi, Zuni, and other tribes. Some Caucasian researchers came back and said, "We don't see some of the symptoms that we see in white alcoholics, such as 'guilt feelings.' Therefore, the Indians are not alcoholics." However, when you look at the mortality rates from cirrhosis and see that five times as many Indians are dying from cirrhosis as whites, there is *prima facie* evidence of alcoholism that is undeniable!

Concerning the question of whether Ruth Benedict's conclusions are valid today, I think there's still validity in terms of cultural differences that contribute to alcoholism. For example, the incidence of alcoholism, suicide, juvenile suicide, family discord, and all the rest of it among the Sioux is highly predictable. In fact, given the culture and economic conditions, it is exactly what I would predict. Some people say, "Isn't Indian alcoholism genetic?

There must be biological factors that predispose these people to drink to excess!" But let's face it: When you put people in circumstances in which these people are forced to live, what would you expect? I would expect exactly what we see. I would be surprised to see anything else! The behavior is *very predictable*, given the circumstances of internalizing aggression because there are no outlets for aggression; the stoicism; the teaching of endurance; suffering in silence; and being raised in a culture where there is an enormous amount of frustration without any outlets for aggression. Alcoholism, suicide, marital problems—I would expect them all.

Dr. Ishii (P.R.I.T.): Dr. Whittaker, your presentation was both shocking and impressive. You explained a little about the reservation system in North America. Isn't this actually a form of discrimination against these tribes? Also, people living in the reservations don't have anything worthwhile to live for; there is no hope for them. I think that was the origin of the development of alcoholism in these people. Therefore, given the discrimination against them, we surely have to stimulate them to know a better way of life . Perhaps you could let us know what kinds of actual programs are in operation at the moment to solve these problems.

Professor Whittaker: That's a good point. You know, there's a saying, "The only good Indian is a dead Indian!" Every American knows that phrase, even children! So the Indians are raised in a society in which it is conveyed that "Indians are no good!" What I was trying to bring out in my presentation was that here were Indians, such as the Sioux—a very proud people, very independent, very self-sufficient—who survived for centuries in a harsh part of the world and did it very well. The men had only two main activities: hunting and fighting. They were great warriors. All of a sudden, whites came along and said, "You can't be yourselves anymore. Now you have to stay in one place (something the Sioux *never* did), you can't hunt buffalo, you can't engage in warfare anymore. At the same time, missionaries were telling these people that their religious beliefs were no good, thus implying, "You are no good." Let me tell you about the early attempts to make white men out of Indians.

My wife and I live close to Carlisle, Pennsylvania, the site of the famous Indian school. At the turn of the century, Indians were brought from all over the West to Carlisle—men and women, girls and boys. They were taught: 1) You can't speak Indian languages. Whether, you are Dakotah, Navaho, or whatever, you all must speak English; 2) Young men must cut off their long hair. No native-Indian braids are allowed; 3) You can't dress like an Indian. You must dress like a white man; 4) You all need to learn useful trades: Young men must learn carpentry, young women must learn sewing, embroidery, and so on.

These were all alien to the Indians and, to some extent, they were all *use-less* skills for life on the reservation. In other words, the message that was conveyed was "There's something wrong with you as you are. You have to change!" So, if you have a whole generation raised like this, what happens to the self-image? To self-esteem? What happens?

In the past there were studies done with Negro children in the United States in which they were asked which types of dolls they preferred to play with. The Negro children characteristically preferred the *white* dolls. What does that suggest about the self-image? Somehow, it suggests that there's something wrong with being Black! That Black wasn't "beautiful." By the same token, the message to the Indians was that they were not beautiful, not acceptable.

Nowadays, we're beginning to see some of the traditional Indian religious beliefs and ceremonies—for example, the Sun Dance (the manhood-initiation ceremony for young men in the Sioux tribe)—beginning to return. It was performed secretly for some time because missionaries disapproved of the Sun Dance since it involved mutilation—according to the missionaries, a horrible "heathen ceremony!" Now the Sioux are performing it much more openly and they are beginning to train Indians to be medicine men again. We're *beginning* to see some pride in being Indian.

There are Indian schools in which the history books say nothing about Indian history. Only *white* heroes, from George Washington onwards, are mentioned, but nothing about Indian heroes! Can you imagine teaching Indian children nothing about their own people or their own history? We also gave the same message to Black people, as if to say, "Oh, the Blacks never did anything important. You have to learn *white* history."

Now, we're beginning to teach children something about their own tribal background, their own leaders, their own culture so as to help them develop some pride in being Indians. And that's a big part of the solution, I think, to help them realize that being themselves, being Indian, is something to be proud of. We've achieved this with Black people now, I think, or I hope we have. Perhaps we should now concentrate on teaching the Indian that it's *great* to be Indian, that you should be *proud* of being a Sioux, Navaho, Hopi, or whatever.

Professor Bohman: The question of original populations, conquered and surviving in their own country, is serious and raises ethical dilemmas. In the northern part of the Scandinavian countries and the Soviet Union, the people known as the Laponians have been living since probably before the present majority entered this part of the world. They have survived in spite of hundreds of years of discrimination by the present majority in the circumpolar region. However, they have managed, also, to adapt to the majority culture. Perhaps not in an entirely successful way, but they have been able to retain some of their identity, culture, and their language. Alcoholism has also been a problem, but not to the extent that was described by Dr. Whittaker.

Professor Whittaker: We're discussing only a few minority groups, but I'm sure you're better able to answer this than I am. For example, this is a problem not only in North America, but worldwide. You find these minority groups everywhere suffering discrimination, racism, etc. For example, the Australians have an enormous problem with their Aboriginal population. We know there are similarities that cut across all of these groups. New Guinea is another place this is happening and there are big problems with alcoholism there.

Dr. Grant: Perhaps I can comment on this from a global perspective. In China, in New Zealand, in Australia, in most of the countries of Latin America (for example, in Peru, Colombia, Argentina), in the Soviet Union, in other countries around the world, including the Nordic countries, as we've just heard, there are situations in which a minority group has for various reasons found itself in a position of being oppressed. And curiously, the minority group has often found itself also to have rather high prevalence of substance abuse problems. This is not always alcohol. The Australian Aborigines, for example, although they do abuse alcohol, are primarily affected by petrol and solvent abuse. In Latin America, clearly, the major form of substance abuse is with the coca leaf rather than with alcohol. But whichever the substance, it is clear that one way in which minority groups are suffering even more is through the consequences of the use of psychoactive substances—a use begun, perhaps, in the belief that this would alleviate their suffering in some way.

One area of great interest to us in WHO is whether there are possibilities to take action in this area from an international perspective that are not possible for any single nation. It may be very difficult for a nation with a long history of dealing harshly with a particular group to perform an about face and behave in a different way. For example, I know that my colleagues who are Australian Aborigines would have found it very difficult had there been a white Australian talking about Aboriginal substance abuse problems here; they would have been deeply offended by that.

There are important differences between cultures in the response that they make and in the accommodation they're coming to, which may make it rather difficult for effective solutions to be found at a national level. It may be, however, that the *commonalties* across nations are sufficiently strong to be able to come up, as it were, with a version of the Declaration of Human

Rights that refers specifically to the situation. Certainly, this is something that we're pursuing very actively in WHO. I was fascinated to hear Dr. Whittaker's presentation. I think this is an enormously important area, and one which we ignore at our peril.

(*Chairperson*) *Dr. Kohno*: Thank you very much. It is believed that we don't have this kind of racial problem in Japan, but we actually have the Ainu Tribe problem in the North of Japan, as indicated by Dr. Ishii.

Question: I'd like to take a bit of exception. I think there is more of a problem in Japan than you're acknowledging. There's a myth that Japan is a completely homogeneous culture. I think that is a myth in many ways. I'd like to ask Dr. Senoh to comment on the different areas of Tokyo where there is a greater concentration of Koreans—or Japanese who are descended from Koreans who were brought over during the War—or Burakumin. I think the incidence of alcoholism will be higher in those areas.

Dr. Senoh: We have not conducted epidemiological research of the alcohol consumption for Koreans living in Japan. As far as I know from my clinical experience, I don't find any racial difference for alcohol consumption but we *should* pay much more attention to this kind of problem. We shouldn't pretend it doesn't exist, but rather we should acknowledge that Japan also has this sort of problem and be working to solve it.

Professor Saitoh (*P.R.I.T.*): I think this is a very important issue, but there are difficulties in studying it. We cannot make any definitive comment on this problem. Those from overseas countries, such as the Southeast Asian countries, are rather deprived in the socioeconomic situation, so they are prone to drug or substance abuse. In any event, we think it's essential for us to have some formal research or survey for the racial problem, but at present we don't have any plan at all.

(*Chairperson*) *Dr. Kohno*: Thank you. Although this problem is quite important, we would like to move on to the next presentation, by Dr. Senoh. Are there any questions or comments on Dr. Senoh's presentation?

(*Chairperson*) *Professor Steinglass*: I think what we're hearing is the very important issue of the tremendous variance that occurs based on the behavioral and social context of, first of all, drinking, and, secondly, treatment approaches. Perhaps if we can just underscore that point and hold on to it, I'm sure that we will press our presenters for more details in terms of their speculations about why there are these dramatic differences from one setting to another, even though the condition, supposedly, is the same.

Question: Dr. Senoh, the use of the public health center is quite different from area to area, I'd like to know the level of awareness held by the community as to the role played by the public health center?

Dr. Senoh: We didn't have a survey as to he awareness of the community of the role of the health centers regarding alcoholism consultation. One way of communication is via bulletins issued by the health centers to all local citizens, indicating at which centers and at what times they can receive alcoholism consultation. However, I'm not sure to what *extent* the community knows the existence of such consultation services at public health centers.

Dr. Genevieve Ames: I would just like to make a comment on what Dr. Whittaker said, and then I'd like to ask Marcus Grant something:

There is considerable research on alcohol and drug use among American Indians in the United States right now; much of it is being done by anthropologiests. Also, there are treatment programs on some of the larger reservations that are funded by the Indian nations themselves.

One of the major problems with indigenous populations in the United States—in integrating them into American society—is that the leaders of the Indian nations and many of their citizens do not want to move from their reservation. Some reservations have prospered from mining and oil lands. Most American Indians have the right and the opportunity to integrate into American society. For example, there's a local American Indian population working and living in Los Angeles. There is a study now being conducted on the drinking in that population. Many Los Angeles Indians go back and forth to their reservation on weekends.

We've had so many recent immigrant and migrant populations in the United States that are rapidly integrating that we wonder why the oldest one is the least integrated into American society. Perhaps one answer is that they have their own lands, their own nations, and their own government. Some may be inhibited from integration by natural cultural boundaries. I also would have to take some issue with the phrase you quoted as a typical American saying: "The only good Indian is a dead Indian." I think it is somewhat *passé*.

Professor Whittaker: On, I agree! But everyone *knows* the phrase, and in many parts of the West people still believe it.

Dr. Genevieve Ames: I think the older generation may know of the phrase, but I rarely hear it among younger people.

I would now like to comment on Dr. Grant's statement that researchers in Western nations feel that the only good research is that which appears in English-language journals. I don't know if that's true or not, but what you just reviewed in your paper from Eastern European journals is important. I'd like to read that literature and I'm curious as to why I can't get my hands on that very rich, descriptive kind of research reporting. I think we shouldn't put the blame for the fact that much research never gets published in the leading alcohol journals so much on the English-speaking researchers as on the gatekeepers, or editors, of the journals, such as the *British Journal of Addictions*, the *International Journal of Addictions*, the *Journal of Studies on Alcohol*, and *Alcohol and Alcoholism Behavior*. As an anthropologist and one who speaks for the value of qualitative research, I know how difficult it is to get those gatekeepers to accept descriptive, qualitative research reports. Acceptance in these journals is often guided by reviewers who demand quantitative methodology. So I think it would be a *tremendous* contribution of the World Health Organization if it could encourage publication of the kind of more descriptive research you talked about today in leading alcohol journals. Actually, I don't think the English-speaking research is the best research. It is good, but I don't think it covers enough of what's going on outside of English-speaking countries. That's a great loss to all of us!

Dr. Marcus Grant: I think Dr. Ames is one hundred percent right! There's very little, however, that WHO can do, and there's a great deal that *you* can do! It is *you*, all of *you*, who are published in these journals. It is you, all of you, and your institutions, who *subscribe* to these journals. The WHO library has one subscription to these journals; you, collectively, have *many* subscriptions. It seems to me that those who subscribe to journals are those who call the tune and that you get the journals you pay for—the journals you deserve!

So, I think there is an opportunity as much for *you* as for me to bring influence to bear upon the editors of these worthy journals, many of whom, I'm sure, would share your sentiments. I'm also duty bound to say that, of course, it is still part of what I perceive as being a somewhat Anglo domination to assume that our job is to make people who write in all these other languages somehow make them accessible in English! Perhaps it might be quite nice if people who spoke English learnt some *other* languages as well!

(Chairperson) Professor Steinglass: One of the impressions I have in listening to the discussion and comparing the discussion for this session to the one for the first two sessions is that there seems to be a lot more emotion being generated about the topics being discussed at this point than there was about the controversy of Type 1 versus Type 2 alcoholism.

I'm struck by the fact that we're obviously carrying out a discussion that's moving increasingly in a political direction at a time when we are trying to take on issues of alcoholism within a community or a mental health context, which was the title for this particular session.

What I wanted to suggest—not as a counter to that trend, but to at least add this perspective as well—is that one of the reasons we take these risks of moving into these areas is because there are *tremendous advantages* in terms of what we can learn by being willing to look at behavior in its natural context, to move into communities, to meet with people in community settings, and also to look at cross-cultural variations in terms of very important behaviors such as drinking behaviors.

It's much easier, from a scientific point of view, to introduce all kinds of controls into studies that try to make study-populations artificially homogeneous. But it's also the case that in the real world these populations don't exist! I think what we're hearing today in these presentations is how *rich* the potential data base and learning experience can be when we actually do look at these cross-cultural differences.

I wonder if I can challenge the panelists at this point to discuss the ways in which the experiences each of them have had might inform other people in their perspective. For example, are there important conclusions or findings coming out of this transition that's occurring within Japan, in taking on a mental health perspective, that would inform the design and strategy for the family coping study?

Are there specific things to be learned from the apparently dramatic deterioration and change in alcoholism and drinking practices in the Indian populations that you've studied, within just that 20-year time frame of the initial impressions to curent impressions, that might also say something about the relative capacity of coping styles to deal with these kinds of problems?

In the spirit of cross-cultural studies, perhaps we can have some cross-cultural dialogue among the speakers to see if they can identify commonalities and differences.

Dr. Marcus Grant: I seem to remember that Dr. Ishii, in his opening remarks for this symposium, emphasized to us that we needed to be doing two things.

First, we needed to be identifying the opportunities that existed for enhancing our understanding through identifying important research questions that could now be answered. Second, he emphasized the extent to which research in this area was not something that should be conducted in isolation—and as I've listened to my colleagues this afternoon, I've certainly been convinced even more of that second item!

In the end, the accumulation of research results, clinical experience, and education and prevention strategies ends up as, *de facto*, a national program on alcohol and/or drug abuse—and national programs cannot exist in isolation. We know that vertical programs fail. We therefore know that an alcohol program that is not part of a national mental health program will *fail*; we know that an alcohol program that is not part of a program of national and economic development will *fail*. It is within that broad perspective that it is possible to become excited about Type 1 or Type 2 alcoholics, just as it's possible to get excited about the "Psycho-Active Substance Use Disorders" chapter of *DSM-IV* or *ICD 10*. These dull, taxonomic questions suddenly take on a vivid reality when you realize that reimbursement payments will be based upon them; when you realize that services will be developed on the basis of them; when you realize that politicians—who read little—will at least read lists!

So, I would think that there's an *enormous* potential here for international collaboration. And I would certainly look forward to hearing comments from any colleagues here about the ways in which they think their experience might contribute to that international effort.

Dr. Senoh: I am the clinician at a psychiatric hospital. Ruth Benedict describes the Japanese culture as a culture based on shame. When thinking about secrecy, Japanese people don't usually think that keeping confidentiality is very important.

However, in recent years in Japan, Alcoholics Anonymous (A.A.) groups have been established. The idea for these groups has come from the United States. There are many branches in Tokyo and all over Japan and they are quite active. And, as the name suggests, they are based on anonymity.

According to the traditional way of thinking, anonymity is very difficult to maintain in Japanese culture. This is theoretically true, but actually it isn't so. A.A. activities based on anonymity have become more popular in Japan recently. When we consider politically depressed or oppressed people, they themselves tend to be anonymous, but when we consider the growth of A.A. group activities, we see that these addicts, even though they have fallen into social and economic insignificance, will take advantage of this very position itself in their course of recovery.

Although it is important to sympathize with these addicts and to reflect on policies that might redress their legal and social position, I get the impression that we clinicians, if we are to continue our work, must feel some optimism that they can recover even though they are at "rock bottom."

The final point is with regard to cocaine use. We import many things from the United States, and they often arrive here five or ten years after starting in the U.S. In Japan, amphetamines were once the main problem, whereas cocaine abuse is presently a most serious problem in the States. So I think cocaine will become a big problem in Japan before too long. We need to watch the development of this situation very carefully. In that sense, it is true that international cooperation is required.

(Chairperson) Dr. Kohno: Thank you. Are there any further comments or questions regarding Dr. Senoh's or Dr. Grant's presentation?

Professor Katoh (Matsuzawa Hospital): Dr. Grant has talked about the family coping system. Of course, I agree that family coping measures are extremely important. However, there are alcoholic patients who are no longer in contact with any family, or who have been thrown out by their families and become homeless. It is very difficult to effectively help homeless alcoholics. What is WHO's future policy towards this kind of homeless patient?

Dr. Marcus Grant: This is a very important question. Clearly, within the context of this symposium, I was focusing only upon the work with which we're engaged with respect to alcoholism and the family. There are at least three other ways in which we are dealing with the wider issue of the treatment of alcohol-dependent persons.

The first is that we have just come to the end of a 10-country study looking at very simple treatment interventions for people who are experiencing alcohol-related problems, including alcohol dependence. The purpose of this study was to assess the relative effectiveness of a variety of *very brief* treatment interventions. Japan was not, in fact, one of the countries involved in that study, but there were 10 countries, including both developing and deveoped countries from all regions of the world.

The results will be published in 1990, but—without wishing to "steal the thunder" of the publication—I can say that the results are most encouraging, in the sense that it does seem that relatively brief interventions can be effective in dealing both with people who are experiencing alcohol-related psychosocial problems and with people who are experiencing the effects of alcohol dependence. That is one study, which I hope will have profound impliations for the delivery of services to *all* alcoholics, whether within or outside families.

Second, Dr. Schuckit this morning made reference to another study which is just beginning, which will be working on issues to do with biochemical markers. These would initially be state-markers, subsequently trait-markers, and eventually predictors of relapse. So this is a very long-term research agenda; perhaps we're talking 10 years before that study will be completed. But we're looking, I hope, at something which will give us a handle on alcohol problems at a very fundamental level.

Third, Dr. Saitoh is involved in a very important piece of WHO work to develop criteria for assessing the quality of care that is offered in drug abuse treatment around the world. As we know, in most countries drug abuse treatment includes alcohol abuse treatment; the two are not differentiated in most countries. The purpose of this work, which began last year in Costa Rica, continued threee or four weks ago in Ghana, and will continue in Indonesia in 1990 and on into 1991, is to establish criteria which can be used in different countries so that national authorities can establish minimum criteria for assessing the quality of care.

WHO is not a regulatory body. We have no *right* to tell any country what to do. We, indeed, have no right to tell a country what they *should* do. But what we can do is provide technical guidance which will enable that country to make decisions for itself. The study in which Dr. Saitoh is involved is concerned with establishing what these criteria are. It is then up to a country to rate these criteria in terms of whether they're *essential* for service development, *advisable* for service development, or *irrelevant* to the situation in that country. Once they have made that rating it is up to them to determine whether or not the current services meet their own standards.

It is interesting that the only schedule completed so far, the schedule for the management of acute withdrawal syndromes, has been pilot-tested in the United Kingdom and in Costa Rica. *Both countries*, one developed, one developing, found that their existing services did not meet the standards that they set for *themselves*.

So, in these three ways, I hope we're addressing the much wider issues to do with the provision of adequate services for those who are alcohol dependent. Let me add that in the final study we're even dealing with those situations where the homeless alcoholics are most likely to come into contact with services—namely, in police stations, in emergency rooms of hospitals, and in other *nonspecialist* settings.

For example, the schedule on the management of acute intoxification will make recommendations of some very simple ideas. For example, every police station should have a tongue suppressor available to prevent intoxicated people dying as the result of inhaling their own vomit. I would guess that very few police stations in *any* country have tongue suppressors. And yet this is an example of very low cost, very simple technology that would, in fact, save lives.

We, as WHO, have no right to tell policemen anything. What we *can* do is set up a mechanism so that the police service decide for themselves that they should have tongue suppressors. In that way, I hope, we find that there are fewer deaths.

This is a very simple example; of course, there would be many more. But I hope it's an indication that although we are engaged in trying to design some rather elaborate and conceptually sophisticated studies, we're in no sense forgetting that we also have a basic responsibility to try to encourage countries to provide for the needs of alcohol- and drug-dependent people who are at the level of primary health care—the level where they first come into contact with the services. That is a pressing need, and one that must be addressed *now*.

(*Chairperson*) *Dr. Kohno*: Thank you very much. I would like to make a comment on Dr. Grant's presentation: WHO can do research and surveys without expensive tools and expensive methods. So, they should be able to handle the programs with less expenses than others. Family intervention, a family approach, is a rather natural method of intervention. Therefore, I think it is essential for the WHO and other international organizations to utilize natural programs. There is a natural family program that observes the cervix or uterus of the female and then can forecast the ovulation period quite accurately. In this way, accurate family planning can be arranged. This, also, is a very inexpensive way of family planning, as well as being a natural family system or coping system. I think this kind of system can be developed for the alcoholism problem, too. We should develop such cheaper and effective methods for the alcoholism problem.

PART IV

ALCOHOLISM AND FAMILY MODELS

In this section, psychiatrists and anthropologists together consider the features of alcoholic family systems.

Dr. Steinglass and his team describe their clinical work and research with families which has contributed to the development of Family Systems Theory and practice.

Dr. Nomura (an anthropologist) and Dr. Ichikawa (a psychiatrist) report their team's findings concerning the process of family therapy conducted with one Japanese family. They highlight the system that revealed itself to the therapy team as it intervened in the family members' communications. Their view is both comparative and cultural, and clarifies some characteristic features of a Japanese family engaged in this type of intervention.

Also from an anthropological stance, Dr. Ames brings us her insights on the effects of recent unemployment on a specific group of workers and their wives. This team's research brings to light a range of environmental and social factors which could trigger alcoholic patterns within families, and also introduces coping methods for this type of situation.

Dr. Saitoh and colleagues report that approximately 25% of the fathers of Japanese wives of alcoholics have themselves experienced a drinking problem. They suggest the possibility of crossgenerational transmission of alcoholism relating to the pattern of mate selection among the daughters from alcoholic families. This discussion also features the pathology of wives of alcoholics in the United States prior to 1970, and its similarity to that presently seen within Japanese wives of alcoholics.

10

Family Systems Approaches to the Alcoholic Family: Research Findings and Their Clinical Applications

Peter Steinglass, M.D.

This selective review of family interaction research into alcoholism focuses on six trends that not only have characterized research done to date, but also point to questions that are likely to dominate the field for the next decade as well. These trends include: a focus on clinical course rather than on etiological issues; a growing interest in biopsychosocial models of alcoholism; an attempt to explicate typologies of alcoholism and alcoholic families; the application of risk versus resiliency models to alcoholism; the use of "goodness of fit" explanatory models in integrating genetic and family environmental data; and the use of family regulatory behaviors as markers of interactional behavior in family/alcoholism research.

These trends are illustrated via a review of the work of two research groups — Steinglass et al., at George Washington University, and Jacob et al., at University of Pittsburgh — and a discussion of likely trends for future research in this area.

Alcoholism, not surprisingly, has traditionally been thought of as a condition of individuals. Although many different perspectives have been brought to bear in hypothesizing factors that might account for the etiology and chronic course of alcoholism, whether the perspective is genetic, biochemical, or psychological, the standard assumption in each perspective is to posit that some defect in the alcoholic individual has lead to the development and perpetuation of the condition.

Juxtaposed against these more prevalent approaches, however, has been a growing interest in family behavioral factors as they influence this most interesting condition. This interest has been fueled by four main factors:

First, the overwhelming majority of alcoholic individuals live in intact families. Over time, most of these families must develop strategies for managing the challenges of chronic alcoholism and their response patterns, therefore, must be considered as possible factors in determining the differential chronic course of the condition.

Second, it is clear that individually-based biomedical models of alcoholism account for at best considerably less than half of the expressed variance in incidence and course of the condition. Therefore, environmental variables must be taken into account to improve explanatory models of alcoholism and surely family behavioral factors are prominent candidates as possible environmental factors.

Third, during the past two decades there has been a dramatic improvement in methods for studying family interaction. These new methods — which have included direct observation of interactional behavior as well as improved techniques of conjoint interviewing — have been applied with dramatic success to other chronic psychiatric conditions (e.g., schizophrenia). Researchers and clinicians trained in these methods have seen in alcoholism another condition that might profit from the application of these sophisticated research techniques.

Fourth, the increasing use of family-oriented treatment approaches to alcoholism and the growing evidence of the efficacy of these approaches have added a wealth of clinical data to more systematic research findings regarding alcoholism and the family. Further, pressure on the part of the non-patient members of alcoholic families for increased services (the dramatic growth of the ACOA movement is perhaps the best example here) has in turn raised interesting questions about not only what types of services to provide, but also about how to most effectively match patient and family type to differential treatment. Hence the growing interest in the development of typologies of alcoholism based at least in part on differences in alcoholic individual/family behavior as an important component in determining effective patient/treatment match.

Several excellent reviews of this family research and therapy literature are now available.[1],[11],[20] Taken in concert, these reviews suggest the emergence of a number of themes that not only characterize research done to date, but point to questions that are likely to dominate the field for the next decade as well. These trends include the following:

— A growing interest in alcoholism as a *chronic condition*. This has meant a movement away from the earlier concern about family characteristics as etiological agents in the development of alcoholism. Instead, the focus has shifted to the role of family factors in the maintenance of chronic drinking behavior.[19]

— A growing interest in *integrative models* that combine biological, individual psychological, and family interactional components. The typical form these models have taken is to focus on family environmental factors that increase or decrease likely continuance of pathological drinking behavior in individuals presumed to be at risk for alcoholism either because of biological (mainly genetic) or psychological factors.

— A growing interest in the development of typologies of family environmental factors in alcoholism maintenance. In particular, there is strong interest in typologies that focus on the relative importance or influence of biological versus environmental factors.[4] This in turn has led to speculation that alcoholic behavior may itself differ dramatically depending upon such factors.

— A growing interest in the application of *risk vs. resiliency* models to alcoholism. These models have become particularly salient in developmental psychology and have been used to address a broad-ranging series of questions related to the course of child and adolescent psychopathology.[15] For alcoholism, the important issue here is the focus not only on factors that place people at risk to develop alcoholism, but, equally important, on the elucidation of factors that protect otherwise at risk individuals from developing the clinical condition.

— A growing interest in *goodness-of-fit* models in understanding the interplay between individual and family level environmental factors in alcoholism. These models derive directly from family systems approaches to alcoholism and take full advantage of an understanding of interaction effects as explanatory variables.[16]

— A growing interest in the identification of specific family level characteristics as part of the assessment and diagnostic process vis-à-vis alcoholism. Included here are not only an elucidation of family-level behaviors associated with the risk versus resiliency issue, but also family behavioral indices useful in the developmental staging of alcoholism during its chronic phase.[19]

What I propose to do in this chapter is to illustrate each of these issues via a selective review of the family research literature. The review is intended to (a) provide an overview of family research strategies currently being applied to alcoholism; (b) present some findings illustrating the trends noted above; and (c) suggest future directions for family research in this area.

FAMILY REGULATORY MECHANISMS AND ALCOHOLISM

A starting point in speculation about the interactive and reciprocal influence of drinking behavior on family interaction and family behavior on styles of drinking has focused on those aspects of family behavior that systems theorists have called family regulatory mechanisms. These mechanisms are a set of behaviors that together are useful in maintaining stability, order and control of family functioning. Our own work has suggested that two constructs of particular usefulness as descriptors of underlying regulatory mechanisms in alcoholic families are the constructs of family temperament and family identity.[19]

At the same time, however, no methods currently exist to directly measure or access these regulatory phenomena. Instead, family researchers have focused on a series of surface-level behaviors which serve as reliable indices of these underlying regulatory structures. The three surface behaviors that have received most attention in alcoholism research are: (1) *daily routines*, such as dinnertime, weekend activities or evening bedtime activities; (2) *family rituals*, such as annual vacations, holiday celebrations or repeated traditions; and (3) *family problem-solving behaviors*, including not only such factors as degree of cohesiveness and coordination in approaching problems, but also whether problem-solving behaviors are fundamentally different in the presence versus absence of alcohol.

A variety of empirical studies conducted both by our research group and by others have suggested that chronic alcoholism is often associated with alterations in family regulatory behaviors. In some instances it appears that repeated drinking behavior itself alters family behavior; but in other instances the family response to chronic alcoholism is the mobilization of specific behaviors that in turn seem to limit the disruptive impact of alcoholism on family life. Hence the interest in models that focus on potential reciprocal influences of alcoholism and family behavior. But of equal importance, these studies demonstrate that by identifying and carefully measuring these behavioral indices of family regulatory behavior (family routines, rituals and problem-solving behaviors), important and replicable findings regarding family factors in alcoholism are beginning to emerge.

Much of this work to date has been carried out by two research groups in the U.S.—the group at the Center for Family Research of the George Washington University School of Medicine (Steinglass and his colleagues) and the group in the Department of Psychiatry at the University of Pittsburgh (Jacob and his colleagues). It is the work of these two research groups that I will use to illustrate how research into family regulatory mechanisms is being operationalized and what kinds of findings and clinical models are beginning to emerge from this work.

Daily Routines

Perhaps the best example to date of a study focusing explicitly on the relationship between alcohol use and daily routines (as a family regulatory behavior) is the home observation study we carried out utilizing an ambitious observational method designed to explicate aspects of family temperamental style as reflected in daily routines.[16] The study was based on the assumption that as families become organized around chronic alcoholism, a reciprocal fit develops between the alcoholic's *type of drinking pattern* and the family's *temperamental style*.

Temperamental style was to be assessed via direct observation of family home behavior, especially how the family organized its use of time and space during routine times at home. Drinking pattern was defined utilizing a developmental model of alcoholism called the family life history model. This model had postulated that as the identified alcoholic moved between phases of active drinking, phases of sobriety, and transitional phases between the two, systemic family behavior would also change in synchrony with this alcohol-related cycle.

The original idea was that family home behavior patterns were most likely highly plastic, and changed as drinking phase changed. However, as will be seen, the study data instead suggested that both alcoholic drinking patterns and family home behavior patterns were highly stable. Thus the associations that were found between drinking styles and family behavioral styles could be best interpreted as a *goodness of fit* between an individual-level characteristic (the type of drinking pattern) and a family-level behavioral characteristic (family temperament as reflected in patterns of daily routines).

The details of the study were as follows: Home observational data were collected from a sample of 31 alcoholic families in which alcoholic family members evidenced one of three different drinking patterns: (a) currently active, highly predictable patterns of daily or weekend drinking (stable wet pattern); (b) episodic, unpredictable binge drinking (alternator pattern); (c) apparent recovery from long-standing alcoholic-level drinking (stable dry pattern). Each family was observed on nine separate occasions, each approximately four hours long, over a period of six months, using a structured observational technique called the Home Observation Assessment Method (HOAM).[17] In the HOAM method, a trained observer is assigned to each spouse for the four-hour observation block and keeps records of family members' physical location, identity of other people with them, physical distance between observed members and others, interaction rates, content of decision-making exchanges, and outcome of verbal exchanges.

A factor analysis of the HOAM data identified five major dimensions of home behavior: (1) intrafamily engagement, (2) distance regulation, (3) extrafamily engagement, (4) structural variability, and (5) content variability (see Figure 1). These dimensions were then used as the dependent variables

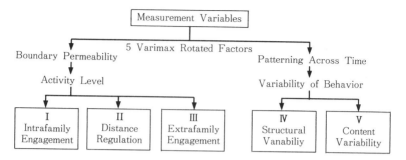

Figure 1

in a series of analyses of variance and discriminate function analytic procedures. The research demonstrated strong associations between alcoholic drinking subtype (stable wet, alternator, stable dry) and home behavior patterns. For example, the discriminate function analysis yielded two discriminate functions, one with a significance level of p = .004, the other with a significance level of p = .04. The discriminate functions plot (Figure 2) graphically illustrates the differences found in the behavior of the three types of families. Further, a one-way analysis of variance indicated that the three alcohol subgroups were significantly different along two of the HOAM factors—distance regulation and content variability.

Taken together, these data support the idea that family regulatory functions reflected in dimensions of daily routines—such as distance regulation and affective expressiveness—differ systematically in conjunction with drinking subtype. This is in essence the "goodness of fit" model we have alluded to above. Another way of describing this process is that alcoholic drinking patterns and family regulatory responses accommodate to each other over a long period of time in the family's history, resulting in a particular family "culture" which exerts considerable influence on the pervasiveness of the alcoholism.

Family Problem-Solving Style

Quite understandably, family researchers have long been interested in how families typically solve problems. The assumption has been that variations in problem-solving style are one of the major factors accounting for differences between functional and dysfunctional families. Two traditions have been used to study problem-solving behavior: (a) laboratory-based behavioral tasks in which the emphasis is on performance patterns of family members (e.g., the Reiss Pattern Recognition Card Sort[13]) and (b) analysis of family

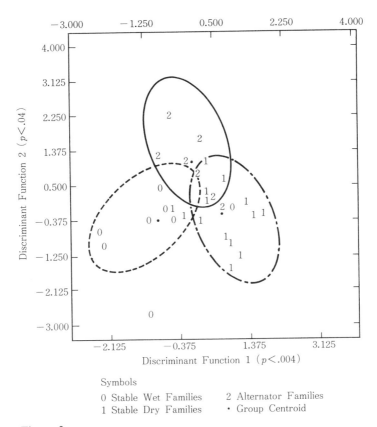

Figure 2

communication patterns using detailed coding procedures applied to inter-actional behavior in response to a problem-solving task. Although a num-ber of studies of problem-solving in alcoholic families have utilized laboratory-based interactional tasks,[10],[18] more recently the focus has been on the use of interactional coding systems applied to problem-solving com-munication patterns. The series of studies carried out by Jacob and his col-leagues is the best example of this research tradition.

Jacob's studies have placed particular emphasis on understanding the ef-fect of drinking behavior on interaction in alcoholic families by (a) examin-ing the contrasts in behavior during alcohol-present and alcohol-absent family conflict resolution discussions and (b) examining the impact of alcoholism on psychological adjustment of family members. In this latter regard, he has attempted to further explore earlier research suggesting that alcohol-related

behaviors may have adaptive as well a maladaptive features by assessing the
temporal relationships between alcohol use and reports of psychologic well-
being on the part of both alcoholic and nonalcoholic spouses in alcoholic
marriages.

In the laboratory-based part of his protocol, families were asked to engage each other in brief discussions of topics based on items derived from
a "revealed difference" questionnaire and from Weiss's Areas of Change
Questionnaire.[23] These discussions were videotaped and subsequently coded using the Marital Interaction Coding System (MICS),[24] a frequently used,
empirical interaction coding system of established reliability. Each family
participated in separate alcohol-present and alcohol-absent sessions during
which they went through the above procedure. Thus contrasts of alcohol-
present versus alcohol-absent behavior were possible. Analyses comparing
these two conditions suggested that marital interaction in alcoholic couples
is more negative and less constructive during the alcohol-present session.

We might say, here, that studies of alcoholic couples in drinking versus
nondrinking laboratory sessions have not always demonstrated a finding of
increased negativity during the alcohol-present state. For example, Frankenstein and his colleagues, although also finding significant differences between
drinking and nondrinking problem-solving sessions, reported that interaction moved in a more *positive* direction during the alcohol-present session.[7]

A second group of findings reported by the Jacob group have addressed
the relationship between alcohol consumption and marital satisfaction in the
alcoholic couples studied.[8] These findings are particularly intriguing because,
as with the Steinglass home observation findings previously discussed, they
again point to the importance of drinking pattern of the alcoholic family
member as a major determinant of the ultimate impact of this drinking on
family life. In a data set of 35 couples with an alcoholic husband, Jacob found
that the amount of alcohol consumed had a different effect on the spouse
depending upon the alcoholic's drinking pattern. Among steady drinkers,
spouses reported more marital satisfaction when alcohol consumption had
risen over the past month, while among binge drinkers, spouse satisfaction
was unrelated to level of alcohol consumption.

In order to understand the covariations of these variables over time, the
Jacob group followed a small group (n = 8) of steady drinkers and their
spouses on a daily basis over a 90-day period, asking them to keep track of
alcohol consumption, psychiatric symptomatology, and marital satisfaction.[6]
Only the steady drinkers were studied because they were the only subtype
who evidenced a significant association between alcohol consumption and
marital satisfaction. Because drinking location was correlated with the binge-
steady categories, four in-home drinkers and four out-of-home drinkers were

selected. The in-home drinkers tended to consume alcohol in a consistent and predictable pattern, while the out-of-home drinkers tended to fluctuate considerably in their consumption patterns.

The most striking finding for the out-of-home group was a five-day lagged negative response reported by the three wives whose husbands had a weekend drinking cycle. It would appear that these scores represent a negative anticipatory response by the wives of their husbands' weekend drinking. Two of the four wives with in-home drinker husbands clearly replicated the cross-sectional findings: An increase in alcohol consumption was associated with an increase in marital satisfaction.

These intriguing findings from the eight-couple sample led the Jacob group to reanalyze the original sample, differentiating three subgroups by drinking style and location: in-home steady drinkers, out-of-home steady drinkers, and out-of-home binge drinkers (very few binge drinkers drink at home). A preliminary report of these analyses suggested important differences in negativity, positivity, and problem-solving success among the three subgroups.[9] The spouses' responses to the binge drinkers are considerably different from the responses to either type of steady drinkers. Binge drinking did not appear to have any adaptive or positive consequences for the family; binge drinkers were clearly more disruptive, evidencing far more psychopathology and sociopathy than the steady drinkers. Family communications among the binge drinkers were generally more negative and aversive; negative remarks were often initiated by the alcoholic. Problem-solving behavior was adversely affected, with the wife showing a decrease in task focus in conjunction with the alcoholic's negativity.

In the *steady in-home* group, communication was far less negative. Further, problem solving actually improved somewhat in the drink condition over the no-drink condition. Strikingly, positive affect increased dramatically during the drinking session for this subgroup. The *steady out-of-home* drinking group was the least stable of the subgroups, sometimes looking more like the binge group and at other times appearing more similar to the steady in-home group. A larger sample will have to be studied to clarify the behavior of this subgroup.

Despite the tentative nature of these findings, these data bear a striking similarity to the Steinglass HOAM results. Selection criteria indicate that Steinglass' Stable Wet and Alternator families are equivalent to Jacob's steady in-home and binge drinkers, respectively. While there is much still to understand in these data, the overall implication is clear: variations in drinking style make a big difference in the way the drinking behavior is viewed by the family. These differences in family response, in turn, largely influence the degree to which alcohol invades family life.

Family Rituals

Family rituals are a set of secular, repetitive behaviors that are acted out in systematic fashion over time and have taken on symbolic importance for the family as reflections of its underlying shared values and goals.[25] Examples of family rituals are holiday and vacation behaviors, dinnertime behavior, child-rearing rituals, etc. It is the research of Steinglass' colleagues, Linda Bennett and Steven Wolin, that has most thoroughly investigated how rituals uniquely regulate behavior in the alcoholic family.

Bennett and Wolin have used family rituals to study two related questions: (1) what role do family environmental factors play in contributing to or protecting family members from intergenerational transmission of alcoholism; and (2) does family behavior concurrent with active drinking influence the impact of alcoholism on children growing up in alcoholic families (the "risk versus resiliency" question).

Bennett and Wolin have carried out two studies looking at the transmission issue. In their first study,[26] they focused on the parental generation and used a semistructured interview to reconstruct the nature of family ritual behavior during that period of time when the alcoholic spouse was engaged in his or her heaviest drinking. The main finding of this study was that in those instances in which families were able to preserve their most highly valued rituals, intergenerational transmission of alcoholism was substantially reduced. Preservation of rituals meant not only that the rituals continued to be enacted, but that they had not been altered to accommodate the needs of the family's alcoholic member.

In their second study,[3] they focused not so much on what was happening in the origin family, but on what happens when an adult child of an alcoholic parent marries and has to deal with the issue of what traditions from his or her family of origin will be perpetuated in the new family. Data were collected from a sample of 68 couples about (a) family life when he or she was a child and (b) present family life. Comparisons of data from these two interviews were used to determine, first, the extent of continuity of ritual behavior from each couple's family of origin versus the development of new ritual behaviors, and, second, how conscious a process this was for the couple. Both these factors proved to be quite powerful predictors of transmission of alcoholism (the criterion variable in a multiple regression analysis). In particular, the degree of *deliberateness* exercised by the couple in choosing *not* to replicate behavior patterns from the alcoholic family of origin proved to be a highly protective factor in diminishing the likelihood of alcoholism developing in this new generation.

Finally, in their most recent work looking at the consequences to children of growing up in an alcoholic family,[2] they have found that although having an alcoholic father clearly is a major risk factor in the development of cognitive and behavioral difficulties in early adolescence, the same factor of deliberateness is again a powerful protective factor in attenuating this impact.

THE INTERFACE OF GENETIC AND
FAMILY ENVIRONMENTAL FACTORS

The above summary of ongoing family interaction research looking into the relationship between family regulatory factors and alcoholism points to the value of using daily routines, family problem-solving behaviors, and family rituals as foci for examining the relationships between chronic alcoholism and underlying systemic properties of families. At the same time, it underscores two trends in our understanding of these relationships that are likely to prove of increasing importance as we move ahead with studies looking at biopsychosocial models of chronic alcoholism. These trends are: (1) the importance of identifying subtypes of alcoholism rather than treating alcoholism as a homogeneous condition; and (2) the role of family environmental characteristics as *protective* factors in helping at-risk individuals to attenuate biological risk for psychopathology.

I want to expand on these two themes by briefly reviewing first, the exciting work of Cloninger and colleagues in developing new typologies of alcoholism based on interactive models of genetic/environmental factors; and second, schizophrenia research also looking at risk/resiliency issues from a family perspective, research that may well presage the next generation of studies in alcoholism and the family.

Genetic Influences on Family Response

The Steinglass and Jacob studies discussed in the previous section demonstrate rather convincingly that alcohol subtype makes a difference in family interaction. But what accounts for the emergence of different drinking patterns? Research currently underway concerning biologically determined alcohol subtypes may provide an additional piece of the puzzle. Cloninger has suggested that neurobiological processes of personality and learning may govern individual differences in patterns of alcohol abuse.[4] Specifically, the *predisposition to initiate alcohol-seeking behavior* appears to be genetically different from the *susceptibility to loss of control* after drinking begins. Alcohol-seeking behavior in adolescence and early adulthood is associated with impulsivity, risk-taking, and a tendency to antisocial behavior; in contrast, loss of control is associated with guilt and fear about dependence on alcohol in individuals who are emotionally dependent, rigid, perfectionistic, and introverted.

Alcoholics with loss of control (Type I) usually begin to have problems in late adulthood after an extended period of exposure to heavy drinking that is socially encouraged; abusers with an inability to abstain (Type II) usually begin to experiment with alcohol early, regardless of external circumstances. Cloninger does not consider these subgroups discrete disease entities, because many alcohol abusers have some features of each type. Rather, the different alcohol-related syndromes are associated with polar extremes of personality traits that vary continuously.

The relevance of the Cloninger findings lies in the diverse triggering effects these inherent biological differences are bound to have on family members. Type I alcoholics are more reactive to their immediate social environment; they tend to be introverted and to drink in order to reduce social inhibition. They tend to feel guilty if intoxication leads to distressing behavior. Type II alcoholics, on the other hand, tend to seek alcohol regardless of their environmental circumstances. Alcohol ingestion does not tend to promote more social interaction; in fact, ingestion is often associated with antisocial acts.

These individually-based genetic differences may help to explain one side of the "fit" described above between the drinker and the remaining family members. The disinhibition experienced by Type I alcoholics may underlie the high-affect alcohol cycles which play an adaptive role in family life. As described earlier, families tend to reinforce these emotionally expressive episodes. Family members of Type II alcoholics, by contrast, would be more likely to become angry or, ultimately, disengaged as a result of the antisocial acts committed by the alcoholic member during drinking episodes. They would be far less likely to reinforce the alcoholic's drinking behavior in any way. Often these families develop completely separate lives from the alcoholic member, excluding him from family activities and decisions.

There is no formula which predicts family response to Type I and Type II alcoholics, and no empirical work to date which explores these relationships in a systematic way. However, these genetic types constitute biological "givens" which present differential challenges to which families must respond. Some genetic subtypes are more likely to engender a receptive family response than others; once triggered, however, these positive or negative family environments either amplify or constrain the further development of drinking behavior. We are likely to see increased interest in the next decade in research that uses typologies of alcoholism based on biological predispo-

sitions combined with sophisticated assessments of family behavioral variables as these "goodness of fit" models are further explored.

Finnish Adoptive Family Study of Schizophrenia

Perhaps the best example to date in the family interaction research literature of a study specifically designed to examine genetic and family environmental factors in the same research design is the Finnish Adoptive Family
Study of Schizophrenia carried out by the psychiatrist Pekka Tienari and
his colleagues. The study attempted to replicate the strategies utilized in the
classical Danish Adoption Studies of Schizophrenia carried out during the
60s and 70s, but adding this time a state of the art assessment of family environmental factors in the adoptee's families.

Tienari and his colleagues utilized a nationwide sample of Finnish women
who had been admitted to a psychiatric hospital for a diagnosis of schizophrenia or paranoid psychosis during the period 1960-70. They were able to identify a sample of 196 offspring of these women who had been adopted by
nonrelated families in Finland before the age of 5 years (73% of the sample
had been adopted before age 2 years). In the ensuing study, these index offspring and their adoptive families were extensively studied, utilizing a protocol that included psychiatric diagnostic interviews of the offspring and
intensive assessments of family environmental variables. These assessments,
which were carried out in the families' homes, took a total of 15 to 16 hours
to complete. A matched control sample of adoptive families in which adoptees' biological parents had no histories of psychiatric hospitalizations for
psychosis were examined utilizing the same intensive assessment procedure.
All assessments were carried out by senior psychiatrists who were blind to
the status of families being assessed.

Critical to our discussion regarding alcoholism and the family are two main
findings that have emerged from the study. First, the Finnish Adoptive Family Study has again confirmed a likely role for genetic factors in the etiology of schizophrenia, thus replicating the earlier Danish and American
adoption studies. But second, the study has also suggested an important role
for family environmental factors in interaction with genetic risk factors as
determinants of ultimate clinical expression of schizophrenia. The details are
as follows:

First, the four psychiatrists who carried out the fieldwork applied a 6-point
scale of level of disturbance to the clinical interview data collected from index offspring with the scale ranging from "healthy" (level 1) to "psychotic" (level 6). Second, the extensive interview material of families was used
to construct a global rating of "family mental health" in which families were

assigned to one of five groups — healthy; mildly disturbed; neurotic; rigid, syntonic; and severely disturbed (chaotic) families.

For our purposes, most intriguing are the findings regarding family environmental variables. Here it turns out that if the adoptive family received a solid clinical rating (either the healthy or mild disturbance category), then a diagnosis of borderline syndrome or psychotic disorder in the adopted offspring was virtually unheard of. (In Table 1, which reports data from the 112 index cases studied as of 12/84, no children raised in "good" family environments had evidence of borderline or psychotic behavior.) These data, taken in concert, are obviously consistent with a conclusion that might be succinctly stated as follows — healthy families seem to have a remarkable ability to protect biologically at-risk offspring from developing full-blown clinical manifestations of their presumed biological inheritance; at the same time even the most disturbed families have a difficult time in influencing their children to such an extent that the children will manifest schizophrenia even in the absence a genetic loading for this condition.

Were we to extrapolate to the alcoholism situation, the interesting speculation would be that family environmental variables most likely exert their influence at the protective end of the risk/resiliency spectrum. That is, in those types of alcoholism thought to have genetic predispositions, we should direct our efforts at identifying family behavior patterns that can help protect offspring from transmission of alcoholism. We will be much less likely to uncover specific family behavior patterns that increase the likelihood of

TABLE 1.

Clinical Ratings of Index Offspring and Their Adoptive Families
(all index cases studied as of 12/84)

Clinical ratings of offspring	*Clinical ratings of adoptive families*					
	Healthy	*Mild disturbance*	*"Neurotic"*	*Rigid syntonic*	*Severe*	*Total*
	1	*2*	*3*	*4*	*5*	
1. Healthy	1	1	0	0	0	2
2. Mild disturbance	5	32	9	3	0	49
3. Neurotic	0	7	8	6	6	27
4. Severe personality disorder	0	3	1	6	6	16
5. Borderline syndrome	0	0	1	5	4	10
6. Psychotic	0	0	1[2]	4	3	8
Total	6	43	20	24	19	112

[1]Collapsing levels 1 + 2 and 4 + 5 in the adoptive family data and levels 1 + 2 and 4 + 5 in the offspring data, $x^2 = 59.321$, $df = 6$, $p < 00005$.
[2]Manic-depressive adoptee.

alcoholism developing given the absence of a genetic predisposition for this condition. At the same time, it is important to underscore that we are talking here primarily about the initial development of alcoholism. Were we to ask a different question — what kinds of factors influence the relative chronicity of alcoholism once it has reached clinical threshold, then we might posit that indeed dysfunctional family patterns are likely to have a major impact on clinical course.

SUMMARY

This brief review of current trends in family interaction research into alcoholism underscores that this is a vibrant area of investigation in which exciting new methods are being applied to sophisticated interactive models of alcoholism with promising results. Further, it is also clear that the advances in our understanding of biological predeterminants of at least some forms of alcoholism benefits family interaction researchers as well, in that these advances help define, with increasing specificity, the characteristics of alcoholism that are critical to control for in research designs intended to elucidate the interface between biological and family environmental factors.

We can also see that family research into alcoholism is following closely along the paths already defined by family research into other chronic psychopathological conditions. Foremost here is the exciting work looking into family environmental factors as determinants of the clinical course of chronic schizophrenia. If we were to extrapolate from this experience, it is not unlikely that the family alcoholism research will soon be suggesting specific aspects of interactional behavior that might be modified via a family therapy treatment approach as an important component of comprehensive alcoholism treatment.

REFERENCES

(1) Ablon J: Literature on alcoholism and the family, In *Recent Developments in Alcoholism*, Volume 2. Edited by Galanter M. New York: Plenum (1984).
(2) Bennett LA, Wolin SJ, Reiss D: Cognitive, behavioral, and emotional problems among school-age children of alcoholic parents. *Amer J Psychiat* 145: 185-190 (1988).
(3) Bennett LA, Wolin SJ, Reiss D, et al.: Couples at risk for alcoholism recurrence: Protective influences. *Family Process* 26: 111-129 (1987).
(4) Cloninger CR: Neurogenetic adaptive mechanisms in alcoholism. *Science* 236: 410-416 (1987).
(5) Cloninger CR, Bohman M, Sigvardsson S: Inheritance of alcohol abuse: Cross-fostering analyses of adopted men. *Arch Gen Psychiatry* 38: 861-868 (1981).

(6) Dunn N, Jacob T, Hummon N, et al.: Marital stability in alcoholic-spouse relationships as a function of drinking pattern and location. *J Abnorm Psychol* 96: 99-107 (1987).

(7) Frankenstein W, Hay WM, Nathan PE: Effects of intoxication on alcoholics' marital communication and problem solving. *J Stud Alcohol* 46: 1-6 (1985).

(8) Jacob T, Dunn NJ, Leonard K: Patterns of alcohol abuse and family stability. Alcoholism: *Clin Experiment Research* 7: 382-385 (1983).

(9) Jacob T, Leonard KE: Alcoholic-spouse interaction as a function of alcoholism subtype and alcohol consumption interaction. *J Abn Psychology* 97: 231-237 (1988).

(10) Jacob T, Ritchey D, Cvitkovic J, et al.: Communication styles of alcoholic and non-alcoholic families while drinking and not drinking. *J Stud Alcohol* 42: 466-482 (1981).

(11) Jacob T, Seilhamer R: Alcoholism, In *Family Interaction and Psychopathology: Theories, Methods and Findings*. Edited by Jacob T. New York: Plenum Press (1987).

(12) Miller WOR, Hester RK: Matching problem drinkers with optimal treatments, in Addictive Behaviors: Processes of Change. Edited by Miller WOR, Hedder N. New York: Plenum Press (1986).

(13) Reiss D: *The Family's Construction of Reality*. Cambridge, MA: Harvard University Press (1981).

(14) Reich T, Cloninger CR, Lewis C, et al.: Some recent findings in the study of genotype-environment interaction in alcoholism, In *NIAAA Research Monogram #5*. Rockville, Md.: NIAAA (1981).

(15) Sameroff AJ: *Principles of development and psychopathology in relationship disturbances in early childhood*. Edited by Sameroff AJ, Emde RN. New York: Basic Books (1989).

(16) Steinglass P: The alcoholic family at home: Patterns of interaction in dry, wet and transitional stages of alcoholism. *Arch Gen Psychiatry* 38: 578-584 (1981).

(17) Steinglass P: The Home Observation Assessment Method (HOAM): Real-time observation of families in their homes. *Family Process* 18: 337-354 (1979).

(18) Steinglass P: The alcoholic family in the interaction laboratory. *J Nerv Ment Dis* 167: 428-436 (1979).

(19) Steinglass P, Bennett LA, Wolin SJ, et al.: *The Alcoholic Family*. New York: Basic Books (1987).

(20) Steinglass P, Robertson A: The alcoholic family. In *The Biology of Alcoholism: Volume 6. The Pathogenesis of Alcoholism: Psychosocial Factors*. Edited by Kissin B, Begleiter H. New York: Plenum (1983).

(21) Steinglass P, Tislenko L, Reiss D: Stability/instability in the alcoholic marriage: The interrelationship between course of alcoholism, family process and marital outcome. *Family Process* 24: 365-376 (1985).

(22) Tienari P, Sorri A, Lahti I, et al.: Genetic and psychosocial factors in schizophrenia: The Finnish Adoptive Family Study. *Schi Bull* 13: 477-484 (1987).

(23) Weiss R: *The Areas of Change Questionaire*. Eugene, Oregon: University of Oregon, Department of Oregon, Department of Psychology (1980).

(24) Weiss R: *Marital Interaction Coding System (MICS): Training and reference manual for coders*. Eugene, Oregon: University of Oregon Marital Studies Program (1976).

(25) Wolin SJ, Bennett LA: Family rituals. *Family Process* 23: 401-420 (1984).

(26) Wolin SJ, Bennett LA, Noonan DL, et al.: Disruptive family rituals: a factor in the intergenerational transmission of alcoholism. *J Stud Alcohol* 41: 199-214 (1980).

PART IV: ALCOHOLISM AND FAMILY MODELS

11

Therapeutic Control and Therapeutic Impasse: Therapists "Hitting Bottom" with an Alcoholic Family

Naoki Nomura, Ph.D
Mitsuhiro Ichikawa, M.D.

This paper illustrates complications that develop as a result of therapists' use of power and control in their encounter with an alcoholic family. Although family therapists are usually concerned with the idea of "changing" the family or the alcoholic, they often end up repeating the same "control game" the family would play — only in the context of therapy settings. The nature of power and control and its limitation in therapy with an alcoholic family is reexamined through a single case study. Similar to alcoholics being powerless over the bottle, this case portrays the therapists' surrender over their power and position for helping the family's evolution. This one-year-long family consultation was carried out as a part of the community case program for alcoholic families in one of the districts of Tokyo.

I. INTRODUCTION

Alcoholic families present a researcher with different aspects of a unitary phenomenon depending on his/her framework and attention. For example, the "outsider's" view and the "insider's" view of why they drink may necessarily offer different dynamics of the family. An "etic" or "outsider's" view of the family may yield the researcher a picture of family as a homeostatic system whereby the members stabilize their bonding via alcohol intake. [14] The alcohol problem is the family's systematic "program," providing a solution for maintaining and organizing the inner chaos. [11] On the other hand, an "emic" or "insider's" view of the family may bring forth descriptions of drinking situations along with explanations for intoxication and individual ways of enacting the group's cultural expectations regarding drinking.[1],[2] Alcohol-related beliefs in one's ethno-religious heritage can hardly be ignored for understanding and treating the family and their alcohol problem.[5]

In therapy with an alcoholic family, the research findings accumulated by the above approaches and others will provide immense help for the practitioners. They will provide both clinical and social backgrounds for assessing the family's inner dynamics and larger molding forces in which the family exist. At the same time, however, there are factors unique to the therapy settings. One of them may be the role of the therapists or the relationship factor between the family and the therapists. In such an encounter, the control of the situation or the exercise of power often becomes one of the central themes for the therapists. Depending upon the approach in family therapy, the idea of control and power may be differently interpreted and put into practice. Generally, strategic and structural approaches seem a bit more power-conscious than other approaches.

In this paper we will discuss the nature of therapeutic control and its limitation with an alcoholic family, using a case example. Our purpose is to explore the epistemology of surrender and powerlessness experienced, not so much by alcoholics, but by the family therapists. We hope to illustrate that the therapists sometimes have to "hit bottom" in order to bring the deadlock in therapy to an end, freeing themselves from entanglement they have created.

Alcoholics Anonymous first recognized the positive implications of "powerlessness" for the recovery of alcoholics. Attempted control over the bottle or one's environment always brings about exasperation and defeat, and continual effort in the same direction simply ends up digging one's own grave. In the A.A. principle, an alcoholic's surrender to a Higher Power is an important step toward recovery. The close affinity between the theology of Alcoholics Anonymous and systems thinking was first elaborated by Bateson,[4] whose theoretical bridge between the two separate fields of thought has had considerable impact upon researchers, and systems-oriented family therapists in particular.

Extending Bateson's view, a number of family therapists also recognized their limitation of control over the patient and his family.[7],[9],[10],[12] Within the frame of limited control by the therapists, Berenson[7] has outlined a therapy procedure with alcoholic families that is congenial to the guidelines of A.A. and related self-help groups. He has addressed an important issue: "how the relationship between the therapist and an individual or family with an alcohol problem replicates, or is isomorphic with, what is happening within the family." That is, the family therapists often become overly invested in "doing something" about the alcoholism and attempt to change the alcoholic or the family in much the same way that the spouse of an alcoholic focuses on and tries to change the drinker.[6] This isomorphism often poses a sticky problem for the therapists, as we will be illustrating in the following case.

II. CASE ILLUSTRATION

This is a story of an alcoholic family and the therapy team, our history of mutual involvement through the course of family therapy which lasted about a year.

1. The Therapy Team

The family-therapy team consisted of six members: two psychiatrists who were alcohol specialists; a nurse from the alcoholic ward; two public health nurses from the city's health center; and an anthropologist with experience in family therapy. One of the psychiatrists (PSY1) was in charge of the patient in the alcoholic ward at the municipal mental hospital. The other psychiatrist (PSY2) worked with the patient's wife. He designed and supervised the alcohol programs at the health center. The public health nurses (PHN1 and PHN2) were responsible for the care of families in their district. When the family was in trouble, these nurses acted as a liaison between husband and wife or between doctors and the family. The anthropologist (ANTH) stayed behind the mirror, working with the interviewer by telephone.

These family sessions were not independent of the district program of the city's health center. Rather, they were incorporated into the long-term care for alcoholic families living in this particular district of Tokyo. Thus, the family sessions program designed by PSY2 and the health center.

2. Mr. J and His Family

Mr. J (age 47) lived with his wife and two sons. His wife was several years younger than he, and the two sons both teenagers. After graduating from high school, Mr. J worked in a company's advertising section for nearly 20 years. He became a habitual drinker at the age of 20. His mother died when Mr. J was 43, and soon he was diagnosed as depressed and hospitalized at a private hospital for about a year. However, no attempt was made to attend to Mr. J's alcohol problems. Mr. J's wife consulted the health center about her husband's alcohol problem, and the public health nurses referred her to the center's educational program. PSY2 also met Mrs. J, and this marked the beginning of the district care, which included the above team.

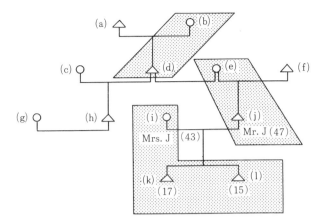

Figure 1. Family genogram.

One day after marriage counseling, a fight erupted between the couple. Mr. J's employer phoned Mrs. J and informed her that Mr. J was no longer wanted at the company. However, Mrs. J kept this information to herself until the next time they were with the marriage guidance counselor, the counselor then also suggesting to Mr. J that he wasn't able to continue work. Returning home, Mr. J furiously accused his wife of ruining his career, and he then threw a knife at the door after Mrs. J left the house. Consequently, Mrs. J left home with her sons and did not return..

The public health nurses had relied upon Mrs. J to obtain their information about her husband. In order to assist Mr. J, the nurses always went through his wife. After this incident, however, this information source was cut off, and the nurses heard nothing concerning Mr. J for two to three weeks. This created enormous anxiety for the nurses, who feared Mr. J's suicide or accidental death. In the meantime, Mr. J began binge-drinking and also searched for his wife and children, but without success. He telephoned his wife's workplace and also his relative ("g" in Figure 1), but Mrs. J continued avoiding him..

Following this, Mr. J telephoned the public health nurse and it was arranged that he and his wife meet at the health center. He also finally agreed to enter the municipal hospital for treatment. Mrs. J and her son returned home subsequently. During his hospitalization, the team members held a case conference and decided to offer the J family some therapy sessions at one-month intervals. The aim was to provide opportunities for all the family to discuss various family problems, including that of divorce.

3. Family Therapy Sessions 1 through 4: Revolving around the Family Genogram

The therapy team first recorded a genogram of the J family, through which a number of crossgenerational patterns were discerned.

Born illegitimately, Mr. J was brought up by his mother's relatives until he was 5 years old. In the meantime, his mother (e) began living with another man (d), who later became Mr. J's stepfather. By the time Mr. J went to junior high school, his household included: his mother (e); his stepfather (d); stepfather's mother (b); stepfather's child by a former marriage (h); and Mr. J himself (j). When Mr. J was in high school, his mother formally married this man (d), and Mr. J found out that the stepfather was not his biological parent. Mr. J asked his mother about his real father, but his mother stubbornly and consistently refused to give him any information.

Mr. J's stepfather was an alcoholic and had frequent fights with Mr. J's mother (e) whenever he got drunk. However, on such occasions, the stepfather's mother (b) would always side with her son (d) and blamed Mr. J's mother for driving him to drink "Because you're bad!" Mr. J frequently had to pick up his stepfather from various places, whenever he became drunk and incapable. Mr. J also went to his stepfather's employer to collect the salary, in order to prevent him from drinking it away..

Mrs. J was first told the full details of her husband's complicated family background upon their marriage. From then on she continuously accused Mr. J of hiding these facts from her.

During the third session, the sons pointed out that when Mr. J's mother (e) had been alive, she had usually mediated between Mr. and Mrs. J when they had a fight. Appearing to criticize what she saw as a too close relationship between Mr. J and his mother, Mrs. J then went on to ask her husband: "What did you think about her intervening in our rows?" Mr. J replied, "I don't know how to answer that. It's natural for a parent to come in as a peacemaker though . . ." The elder son (k) spoke up: "I feel it would have been impossible to build up a good family relationship if grandma always had to step in to stop you two quarreling." Following his brother's point, the younger son (l) said to his mother: "Didn't you feel anything wrong about grandma intervening?"

Mr. J: "I didn't think it was good."

Younger son: "So why didn't you say that?"

Mr. J: "When I had a fight with your father he was always drunk, and even if I said something, it was just repeating the same old issues."

Younger son: "I know no one likes to fight, but you should have done something. That's why I think our family has got like this.''

In the end the younger brother remarked: ''I can see you also were dependent upon grandma, Mom.'' With a short pause, Mrs. J nodded, saying, ''Maybe,'' and everybody fell silent.

The therapy team observed that close mother-son relationships had persisted across generations in this family. These comprised:

1) Mr. J's ''grandmother'' (b) and his stepfather (d);
2) Mr. J's mother (e) and Mr. J (j); and
3) Mr. J (i) and the two sons (k) and (l).

In every case, alcoholism was the linkage that had helped such a relationship to form: an alcoholic male and his overprotective mother confronting the alcoholic's wife.

The team's intervention was aimed at breaking the overly close emotional ties between Mrs. J and the two sons, by encouraging them to speak up against their mother (like the conversation above). Although the son's voicing of critical comments toward their mother was interpreted by the team as a sign of change toward positive involvement with their parents' conflict, the therapy so far had not led to any substantial change in family dynamics. Mr. J continued bout-drinking during this period and again stayed at the municipal hospital for about a month. After being discharged, although he actually wanted to return to the family, he lived alone in an apartment and not with them.

4. Family Therapy Sessions 5 through 10: Revolving around the Family Game

From the fifth session on, the therapy team began paying more attention to the family members' mode of interaction. It became apparent that Mr. J would always be excluded from the decision-making process whenever anything important was discussed in the family. Actual decision-making tended to be done by Mrs. J and the sons. Mr. J's exclusion was understandable considering his incapability during intoxication and the physical separation.

A hypothesis of ''Needing the Unnecessary Father'' emerged from the above observation: the mother and two sons constantly communicated to Mr. J that his existence wasn't necessary in the family's decision-making processes and other important family activities. Therefore, his drinking could be seen as a response to the message that his physical presence was redundant. However, at another level, all the family members required the ''unreliable, powerless father'' in order to sustain leadership of the mother. Mr. J could only challenge this ''powerless situation'' by trying to show his power over, and mark his presence by, alcohol.

(A) "The Alcohol Connection"

In the 7th session, Mr. J unexpectedly informed everyone that he had attended several different job interviews. He hadn't been offered employment, but he stated that it was important for him to be independent. This was a surprise to his wife and children, as well as to the team, as he had never indicated his intentions in any way at all up to this point. It was wondered whether he was genuinely looking for work or just advertising his search as a means of gaining an advantage in the therapy situation.

Another amazing revelation also occurred in this session: it was disclosed that the family knew when Mr. J had been drinking alcohol in the last month, even though they continued to live apart from each other. After much probing, it was finally disclosed that there was, in fact, an unknown communication network in operation, involving people from outside the family.

When Mr. J drank, it was first noticed by the owner of the apartment, who disliked this sort of behavior. Then, the owner complained to the real-estate firm about the client they had placed there. In turn, the real-estate representative then phoned Mr. J's relative — his stepbrother's wife (g) — about the apartment owner's complaint. She would then phone Mrs. J with this information. Thus, his drinking behavior was relayed to his wife, not directly from himself but indirectly via relatives. Mrs. J then would then tell her sons and also the public health nurses.

This was an astonishing finding for both Mr. J and the therapy team. Mrs. J knew of the communication loop and had used it to some extent, as did the children through her. However, Mr. J was shocked to hear that his drinking had been "under observation" in this way. In the case of his job hunt-

Figure 2. "The Alcohol Connection."

ing, no news was relayed via the loop — he alone instigated his job search and declared it to others at the session. However, all of a sudden, the communication loop regarding his drinking was highlighted and a network of considerable size emerged to relay news about the drinker.

Mr. J may not have been consciously aware of this loop, but perhaps intuitively knew that his drinking somehow helped him to "connect" with his family; it was the means of affirming his membership. Likewise, the monthly therapy sessions had brought the family together regularly, affirming that drinking was necessary to continue the family bond.

Surprisingly, it was the therapy team that had been helping the family to reinforce Mr. J's excessive drinking. On the one hand, the sessions had been utilized by the family to maintain their myth of "needing the unnecessary father." On the other hand, the team had been an active member and supporter of the loop, right from the early stages when the public health nurses had used Mrs. J to gain information about her husband.

We, as the therapy team, were blind to the reality mutually created by both the family and the team. Mrs. J tried to gain control of her husband and the whole situation using information from the relative and apartment owner. We also strove to have control over the therapy situation by obtaining information about the drinker from Mrs. J. Thus, the relationship between the family members and that between the therapists and the family was, in fact, isomorphic.

(B) "Playing Drunk"

The therapists intervened as follows: First, they asked Mr. J to leave the room. Mrs. J and the sons were asked to predict whether Mr. J would drink before coming to the next session. They wrote their answers on separate pieces of paper, which were handed to the therapists and sealed. Mr. J then entered the room and the others were asked to leave. The therapists asked Mr. J to "play drunk" — but not actually drink — about once a week at his apartment. He was told that "in this way we can check if the network really works," and requested to keep this a secret. Mr. J tried to stop himself bursting out laughing as he was leaving the therapy room.

At the following two sessions, the therapists asked Mrs. J and the sons, in their father's presence, whether they thought he had drunk in the previous month. Simultaneously, the three pieces of paper were opened which contained their predictions of a month ago. Their answers were mixed — the family's varied responses seemed to indicate that they were getting either no information, or confused information, about their father's drinking and situation. In the meantime, Mr. J visited the real-estate agent and agreed to move out of the apartment within a month so that the agent's complaints ceased.

Interestingly, the family's only source of information about Mr. J's drinking was Mr. J himself. Furthermore, by asking him to play drunk, the team also lost any means of validating Mr. J's statements, rendering themselves powerless over the control of information. Mr. J could choose to play drunk with either alcohol or sobriety. The communication loop had been broken, or at least temporarily retarded, through the therapists' abandoning a part of their control.

(C) "Alcohol Breaking the Alcoholic Patterns"

The 10th session was devoted to the topic of divorce and remarriage — with the intention of possibly saving the marriage. After all, it would seem to the therapists that the ideal partner for Mrs. J would be someone like Mr. J, and vice versa. The session started around 6:30 p.m. Although the overall atmosphere was oppressive, Mrs. J appeared calm and sometimes smiled. Mr. J looked tired and worn out.

Mrs. J remarked that at her company's recent end-of-year party she had drunk alcohol for the first time. She said: "I've avoided alcohol because of my husband's alcoholism. I detested it. But this time I felt like drinking it and so I did. It helped me understand a little bit why he wants to drink." This comment will have greater significance near the end of the session.

The therapists asked what would happen to each member if Mr. and Mrs. J divorced. Mr. J said he would become depressed; the older son said his mother would also become depressed. Regarding the change of family name, the two sons had no objections to using their mother's maiden name.

The therapists then led the family into discussion of the ideal second-marriage partners for the two adults. Mr. J immediately retorted that he had no intention of remarrying. The sons mentioned that their mother was often too stubborn so that her future partner should be "someone healthy who could understand her temperament."

Following these comments, Mrs. J complained that her husband had never explained things clearly to her. So, the therapists suggested that Mr. J should immediately rehearse this sort of hypothetical situation with his wife via role-play. Mrs. J then commented that it wasn't "realistic." Extending this idea of "unreality" further, she objected: "It's been like 'playing at marriage' for the last few months. We come here for a family session once a month and then on the way home my husband and I go together to a restaurant." She further added that she had not been able to cry in front of her husband and that neither of them could empathize with the other.

As Mrs. J repeated her usual complaints about her husband, the therapists became quiet and the session lost pace and liveliness. Gradually, the family grew more depressed and serious as time elapsed, and it became increasingly difficult for the therapists to steer the conversation back to relevant issues. More than two hours had passed. There was a much greater feeling of finality for both family and team; all had a vague notion that this session would be the final one. The two therapists with the family (PSY1 and PHN1) and the three observers behind the mirror (PSY2, PHN2 and ANTH) all felt stuck and helpless. Here, was Mrs. J, full force in her usual pattern, nagging and criticizing her husband. The rest of the family just listened, and Mr. J grew more depressed as time elapsed. The therapists were silenced and a real feeling of "Here she goes again" hit the team. At this point, the therapy team had used up all their resources, having been driven into a tight corner.

It took a long and oppressive time for the team to think of a way out of this situation. One of the team behind the mirror (ANTH) proposed that Mrs. J should drink alcohol. Another (PSY2) suggested that they use tea to represent alcohol. The former's suggestion prevailed, on the understanding that using tea wasn't "realistic." One of the therapists (PSY1) returned to the observation room at that time and also agreed with the idea of offering Mrs. J alcohol. A bottle of beer was purchased on the street and taken into the room with a plastic cup. The team members suggested that the wife should drink this in front of her husband. Mr. J was asked to open the bottle and pour it for his wife. The family looked shocked and were speechless.

At the therapist's request, Mrs. J drank half the bottle. She became even more talkative and emotional over her complaints about her husband.

PSY1 returned to the observation room and PSY2 took over. Using a more confronting style and approach, he asked the couple to once again discuss their feelings about divorce. Since Mr. J insisted that he didn't want a divorce, the interviewer pressed him to explain precisely why. It was clear to the team that an expression of his love was the thing that the wife badly sought, but she considered this impossible to obtain from him.

Mr. J's first response to the therapist's question had been, "I don't want a divorce because of the children." This sounded unconvincing to both the therapists and Mrs. J.

Mr. J wasn't able to express affection to his wife, neither was she able to receive it. Telephone calls from the observation room became frequent. The new interviewer was very much directed by the team behind the mirror. Once again pressed by the therapist, Mr. J admitted that his real reason for not wanting a divorce was his love for his wife. PSY2 immediately responded by saying, "Don't tell me — tell her!" Forced into it, Mr. J said to his wife in a wavering voice: "The reason . . . is because I love you."

Unable to speak, Mrs. J started crying, pressing her handkerchief to her eyes.

Following the team's directions, the therapist praised Mr. J for expressing his feelings, and also praised Mrs. J for crying in front of her husband.
The therapist said to her: "Don't you feel like drinking more?" With rising
confusion and perhaps frustration, she replied: "Yes. Yes! I feel like throwing this right at him!" and immediately threw the remaining beer at her husband. Mr. J was soaked, as well as the sofa behind him. He wiped his face
with his handkerchief, weakly saying, "Oh, that's terrible!," and Mrs. J dis-
solved into tears again.

Mrs. J turned on PSY2 loudly and angrily, accusing him of unfairly making her drink. She insisted that her tears weren't genuine. She then said to
Mr. J: "Why can't you say things without other people's help?! It's not fair!
I've gone through agony because you never explained things clearly to me.
I was patient only because I loved you. If you don't change, I'm most certainly going to divorce you!" The sons remained quiet throughout this exchange. The therapists commented on the fact that they had now both
expressed their feelings openly, and suggested that it might be too early to
make any decisions about divorce.

To close the session, PSY1 entered the therapy room and indicated to the
family that this was the final session, and that in future therapy — if they
wished it to continue — the children should be excluded.

5. Afterwards . . .

A few months after the last session, Mr. and Mrs. J agreed to divorce.
Then, Mr. J was hospitalized because of a subdural hemorrhage and had
an operation. He recovered and is presently at a rehabilitation facility in
Tokyo. Mrs. J continues to live at home with her two sons, and has the same
job.

The team's tentative evaluation of the results of therapy are the following:

a) The couple were able to discuss their marital problems and decide to
divorce, which they would not have found possible before therapy.

b) Mrs. J is moving satisfactorily toward her own independence. Her involvement in and dependence on the city's support programs for alcohol
abusers and their families is now minimal.

c) Mr. J's dependence upon the loop decreased significantly, although not
entirely. He no longer needed to maintain his relationship with the family
through alcohol. He has now settled into life in the rehabilitation center and
is seeking financial independence.

d) Throughout the therapy, the children witnessed their parent's love and
conflict. We hope this will be meaningful in their future lives.

e) The therapy team later suggested family sessions for Mr. J and his sons.

This was due to the team's concern about the cross-generational transmission of alcoholism in the J family line. The family have not, so far, responded to our proposal for further therapy. This suggests that either they find little need for therapy or that they have given up on the therapy team. Either way, the family keep their distance, indicating their independence from network personnel.

f) The family inevitably noted the number of different personnel and professionals involved in therapy team, as well as the larger care-system, which had worked for their benefit. We trust this will be of value to them.

III. DISCUSSION

The J family's case is neither a model for successful family therapy nor a case for which we began with clear guidelines in advance. Rather, it was exploratory in nature, and the therapists received as great an impact as the family themselves upon the closing of the therapy. We, the therapy team, held on to our cherished value of therapeutic control and its framework that we were the observers and had power to change others. Through our sessions with the J family, however, we realized that it only reflected our hubristic view similar to the alcoholic's pride. For the alcoholic, A.A. aptly explains, "trying to use willpower is like trying to lift yourself by your bootstraps." The therapists' attempt for control would simply and up following in the family's steps, consequently getting into a therapeutic impasse.

1. The Therapists Relinquish Control

The J Family was in the control game and suffering from addiction to control. The isomorphism between the wife and the husband and between the therapists and the family was most clearly seen in the communication loop called "the Alcohol Connection," which included members outside the family as well as the therapists. Through this loop, it was "discovered" that the therapists were no longer detached observers but a part of the ongoing description of the therapy process, inseparable from the shared domain of actions.

Mrs. J was able to monitor her husband's alcoholic behavior via the Connection; and the public health nurses and the other team members received information about the drinker via Mrs. J. She thought she was observing her husband; and the therapists thought they were observing the family.

In order to control Mr. J's drinking, the therapists needed information about him. Mrs. J was the primary source of information for the therapists. The harder we tried to obtain information from Mrs. J, the more effectively the Alcohol Connection was able to operate. Our desire to change the drinker and the family simply reinforced the communication loop.

The therapy team wanted to change the way messages were relayed along the loop. The team intervened and ordered Mr. J to play drunk once a week at his apartment. We prescribed this with a considerable humor to make the communication loop parodylike. Mr. J, usually quite a gloomy person, was almost bursting out laughing upon leaving the therapy room. But the therapists didn't notice at the moment that the consequence of this prescription would deprive the therapists of their control of information. We later realized that we had inadvertently relinquished control over Mr. J and the Connection; that is, we had no way of knowing whether Mr. J was actually drinking or not. The only source of information about Mr. J's drinking was now Mr. J himself. The therapists ended up creating their own parody.

His drinking had been the major issue throughout the sessions, and to stop him drinking should be one of the primary aims of the therapy, yet it was our mistake — but a lucky one — that we made the issue irrelevant.

Mr. J had to drink in order to remain as a member of the family, since he was branded as "the Unnecessary Father." But now he knew he was the focus of Mrs. J's and the therapists' attention — he turned in to a "Necessary Man" instead. After Mr. J found himself as a necessary member and with his own choice to drink or not to drink, the former function of his drinking became also irrelevant for him.

When we surrendered control over the information, the communication loop itself began to disappear.

2. The Therapists Relinquish Their Position

Our illusion of control died hard. Even though the family game along with the loop had been significantly modified, the therapy team still considered that they could have influence over the couple's marital issues. The topic of divorce had been perpetually brought up by Mrs. J since her initial contact with the therapy team. The team, in turn, hoped to be able to save the marriage if they could. In retrospect, this part of the team's effort was overshooting the target, but at that moment the therapy team were preoccupied in "doing something" about this grave family issue. It was the therapists' momentum that had lasted for a period of one year in this direction. Our role preoccupation was difficult to change.

Up until the stage of the family game, that is, the Alcohol Connection, the therapists found it possible to be of help to the family. But once the alcoholic issue turned to that of a personal one between husband and wife, it was beyond our capacity. The alcoholic game had been the couple's major preoccupation in the history of their relationship. Once that game aspect had been taken away, the couple had to come face to face with their essential problems as individuals. This could have been more painful than the continuation of the alcoholic game.

At the final session, Mrs. J remarked that her husband had never explained things for her; that she had not been able to cry in front of her husband; that neither of them could empathize with the other.

These problems of compatibility between husband and wife came out after the alcoholic game fell apart. The therapists found themselves utterly helpless. Whether the couple should start all over again together or reach divorce and find their own ways is a personal issue that the therapists could not direct or influence. Mrs. J began nagging and complained about her husband's lack of explanation and sympathy, but everybody in the setting was ineffectual. Mr. J was powerless over his wife's accusations and he was getting increasingly depressed. Mr. J, too, was in fact powerless over the control of Mr. J's individual characteristics. The therapists were powerless over the essentially private issues between the two people. We didn't know how to move. This was our therapeutic impasse. Our own hubristic belief in power and control as therapists made us enter an unwanted territory and imprisoned us. The therapists had to find a way out of this self-locking situation to "undevelop" a property that they had once developed (cf. 3).

Hitting bottom as therapists, we prescribed a paradox exclusively to ourselves: How can we tell the family that we can no longer serve as therapists? To answer this at the setting of therapy would be a doublebind. Finally, we used our "power" to make Mrs. J drink alcohol in front of her husband and to ask Mr. J to help her drink by opening the bottle and pouring it for her. This was to deny our existential meaning as therapists, since the role of the therapists should be to direct individuals away from intoxication.

The therapists relinquished the therapists' position by encouraging alcohol — but with reversed roles: making the "intoxicated, violent wife" and the "enabling husband."

The team attemped a solution through alcohol, and the family took the "material" to invent a new reality. Alcohol had meant so much for the J family in their family history: it pained all the family members for a long time; yet the family bond was maintained because of it; the family was incorporated into the district program because of alcohol problems; Mrs. J received so much social support and respect for her difficult position as wife of an alcoholic and mother. Mrs. J's throwing alcohol at her husband would have many layers of meaning, symbolic as well as ironic.

Mrs. J had always performed a "good girl" act for the therapists (particularly for PSY2). Under the influence of alcohol, however, she turned on

PSY2 loudly and angrily, accusing him of unfairly making her drink. Mrs. J changed her stance toward the therapists for the first time and was able to get out of her identity of nice client.

Through these sessions, the J family had a chance to work out their own destiny and to evolve from being a family with stalemated alcohol problems to one which could chose therapy, marriage or divorce. And, the therapists had a chance to recognize their limitation of therapeutic control.

REFERENCES

(1) Ablon, Joan. The significance of cultural patterning for the "alcoholic family." *Family Process*, 19, 127-144 (1990).
(2) Ablon, Joan. Irish-American Catholics in a West Coast metropolitan area. In: *American Experience wih Alcohol*, edited by L. Bennett and G. Ames. New York: Plenum Press (1985).
(3) Ashby, Ross. *An Introduction to Cybernetics*. London: Methuen (1956).
(4) Bateson, Gregory. The cybernetics of "self": A theory of alcoholism. In *Steps to an Ecology of Mind*. New York: Ballantine (1972).
(5) Bennett, Linda and G. Ames (Eds.). *The American Experience with Alcohol: Contrasting Cultural Perspectives*. New York: Plenum Press (1985).
(6) Bepko, Claudia, J. Krestan. *The Responsibility Trap: A Blueprint for Treating the Alcoholic Family*. New York: The Free Press (1985).
(7) Berenson, David. The therapist's relationship with couples with an alcoholic member. In: *Family Therapy of Drug and Alcohol Abuse*, edited by E. Kaufman and P. Kaufmann. New York: Gardner Press (1979).
(8) Alcoholics Anonymous: From surrender to transformation. *The Family Therapy Networker*, 11, 25-31 (1987).
(9) Boscolo, Luigi, G. Cecchin, L. Hoffman and P. Penn. *Milan Systemic Family Therapy: Conversations in Theory and Practice*. New York: Basic Books (1987).
(10) Hoffman, Lynn. Beyond power and control: Toward a "second-order" family systems therapy. *Family Systems Medicine*, Vol. 3, No. 4, 381-396 (1985).
(11) Julius, Eloise and P. Papp. Family choreography: A multigenerational view of an alcoholic family system. In *Family Therapy of Drug and Alcohol Abuse*, edited by E. Kaufman and P. Kaufmann Press (1979).
(12) Palazzoli, Mara, L. Boscolo, G. Cecchin and G. Prata. *Paradox and Counterparadox: A New Model in the Therapy of the Family in Schizophrenic Transaction*. Northvale, NJ: Jason Aronson (1978).
(13) Steinglass, Peter, S. Weiner, J. Mendelson and C. Chase. A systems approach to alcoholism: A model and its clinical application. *Archives of General Psychiatry*, 24, 401-408 (1971).
(14) Steinglass, Peter, D. Davis and D. Berenson. Observations of conjointly hospitalized "alcoholic couples" during sobriety and intoxication: Implications for theory and therapy. *Family Process*, 16, 1-16 (1977).

12

A Cultural Approach to Conceptualizing Alcohol and the Family

Genevieve M. Ames, Ph.D.

This paper presents conceptual guidelines for identifying cultural and socioenvironmental risk factors that have causal and thereby preventive significance for heavy and problem drinking at the family level. These issues are discussed on the basis of results of a recent study of families from a high-risk population of unemployed workers. For purposes of collecting demographic and drinking level data, a survey of husbands and wives was conducted in a sample drawn from 6000 workers who lost their jobs when an auto assembly plant closed in 1982. Using ethnographic techniques, in-home interviews and observations were then carried out with 30 families: 15 families with heavy drinking fathers, and 15 with moderate drinking fathers. Results show a relationship of heavy or moderate drinking practices to features of cultural and family background and present-day family, workplace and community environments. Strategies are presented on how this conceptual approach and the research findings can be used for primary prevention of alcohol problems.

INTRODUCTION

In recent years a handful of researchers utilizing anthropological methods and theories have identified aspects of cultural environments that put families at risk for alcoholism and alcohol-related problems.[1],[3],[8],[12] This relatively new development in alcohol and family theorizing parallels contributions from other disciplines where advances have been made towards identifying genetic and psychological risk factors. With a realization that fam-

---

Research and preparation of this article were supported in part by National Institute on Alcohol Abuse and Alcoholism Research Center grant AA06282 to the Prevention Research Center, Pacific Institute for Research and Evaluation.

ily aspects of alcohol and problem drinking are complex, and cannot be isolated to any one disciplinary approach, the present paper presents guidelines for identifying cultural linkages to family drinking practices.

Cultural dimensions to alcohol and the family complement and, in some cases, build upon existing family models that have emerged from the varying perspectives of stress theory,[14] transactional analysis,[24] behavioral learning theory,[21] longitudinal family development,[26] and family systems theory.[11],[27],[28],[10],[25] In particular, the approach presented here complements the family systems model which provides understandings of psychological and developmental factors affecting the alcohol-troubled family.

Findings from the study reported on here illustrate the usefulness of cultural understandings for purposes of primary prevention. There is little doubt that existing family and alcoholism models have made significant contributions that are of use for treatment. However, treatment, like law enforcement, is a remedial response only to highly visible problems after they occur—not before.[13] There is a corresponding demand to develop theoretical guidelines for identifying risk factors that may be of causal and, thereby, preventive significance for the development of family drinking practices.

An impediment to this goal is the lack of empirical research documenting the influence of cultural and otherwise socioenvironmental characteristics of the family, community, and workplace on drinking patterns and alcohol problem development. An understanding of drinking in the context of these integrated cultural environments presents an opportunity to determine if otherwise "healthy" individuals are distinguishable in the early stages of drinking careers, before drinking becomes problematic, and if they are distinguishable, how such problems can be prevented within the framework of environmentally oriented programs for prevention.

THEORETICAL ISSUES

Any attempt to explain what is meant by cultural dimensions of family drinking practices must begin with the relevancy of the concept of culture to such understandings. In 1871, Tylor, a founding father of anthropology, defined culture as "that complex whole which includes knowledge, beliefs, art, morals, values, law, customs, attitudes, language, and any other capabilities and habits acquired by humans as a member of society."[29] This classic definition of what culture consists of is simplified in a contemporary one that states: "Culture is that which is learned, shared and transmitted continually in a process of formulation, change and reformulation."[9] That process of learning, sharing, and transmitting—and to some degree changing—knowledge, beliefs, values, and so forth takes place throughout an individual's lifetime. It occurs through normal socialization processes in early life experiences in the family home and thereafter in concert with family and other social institutions of an individual's cultural milieu.

These academic definitions of the content and process of culture are relevant to understanding the interrelationship between culture, alcohol, and the family because they take into account that attitudes, beliefs, and behaviors emerge from and reflect interaction with environments both outside and inside the family setting. Cultural components of family life can play a significant role in the development of drinking patterns and whole family response to drinking problems, when and if they emerge. All families, however defined, are bearers of the culture of the larger social groups in which they live. Likewise, families develop their own culture as it is situationally determined by historical background and by the roles, personalities, and interactional patterns of their immediate social unit. A cognizance of the significance of both external and internal family culture is critical to an understanding of alcohol troubled families.[4],[2]

In recent years, two studies by anthropologists using ethnographic research methods have demonstrated the influence of cultural factors on family drinking practices and family responses to problem drinking. In a study of unlabeled Irish-Catholic families, Ablon[1] found that heavy drinking of fathers was the cultural norm and met with little family resistance. Family adaptations to the father's drinking reflected culturally defined patterns related to personal social networks, employment situations, and residency patterns.

In a similarly designed study of middle-class Protestant families with an alcoholic mother,[3],[4] I found that entirely different responses to parental drinking abided, but these too stemmed from cultural circumstances. In accordance with their religious beliefs and cultural expectations concerning alcohol use, heavy drinking was viewed as unacceptable behavior. "Alcoholism" was conceptualized as a condition brought on by weakened will or flawed character and thereby seen as a moral rather than a medical problem. Under pressure for cultural conformity, and to avoid being socially ostracized by church and community peers, families were compelled to build physical and social boundaries that protected both the mother and the family unit from outside view. As the mother's drinking became ever more deviant and secretive, a family culture evolved that accepted the alcoholic drinking as normative behavior within the boundaries of family life.

In both of these studies, cultural dimensions influenced the family tendency to support, rather than resist, the continuance of problem-drinking practices of one of its members. These findings support the basic tenets of the existing "alcoholic family system"[25] where psychological dimensions of familial alcoholism support the maintenance of the drinking behavior.

Family systems theory as applied to alcohol dependency tends to frame the family as a bounded social unit with its own internal system of balance and homeostasis in interpersonal relations.[27],[28] In these families, the drinking behavior is often balanced into the ebb and flow of family life. However, a consideration of cultural factors of family drinking practices presents another dimension to family systems theory in the recognition that the family is just one of several linked, open systems that influence individual drinking patterns and family's response to drinking. The present paper offers a conceptual approach that identifies and explicates cultural factors that put families at risk for developing and thereafter maintaining problem drinking once it occurs.

Recognizing that alcohol beliefs and behaviors develop in the context of different but interrelated cultural and social systems, how do we identify linkages among systems that may be of causal significance for drinking problems? That question is addressed with conceptual guidelines for examining three environmental dimensions that may influence family drinking practices, including family response to heavy or problem drinking of one of its members. Two of these dimensions are concerned with external influences on family drinking, and the third with internal influences. The third dimension was not applied to the analysis of the data reported on here.

The first dimension considers linkages of childhood cultural patterning and socialization to alcohol use (in other words, early life environment) to present drinking practices. An examination of the cultural background of parents, including ethnic, religious, and familial experiences, informs us of specific factors that may affect individual drinking levels. For example, early life involvement in certain religious denominations, ethnic communities, or kinship rituals offers protection or puts people at risk for heavy and problem drinking in later life. We also examine the drinking pattern in the families of origin of parents in our research population, the relationship between our parent respondents and their heavy drinking parent, if one existed, as well as recollections of whole family responses to heavy or problem drinking.

The second dimension examines the relationship between present cultural environment and family drinking practices. At this step, we look at the level of involvement in community, church, workplace, and leisure activities, and the degree to which these linkages influence the development of heavy or moderate drinking. Social groupings of a particular collectivity, bonded together by kinship, ethnicity, religion, or other social factors, often share cultural profiles for certain beliefs and behaviors, including alcohol beliefs and behaviors. However, as people move in and out of social situations that are external to their primary cultural groupings, they may be confronted with subtle or overt pressures to adhere to cultural profiles about drinking that either complement or radically depart from their own socialization to alcohol. For example, drinking practices of a particular workplace culture may be integrative or socially functional for one family member, but at the same time at odds with family traditions and values. It is important to document ways in which, families respond to these external pressures on drinking practices, because it is through that process of adaptation that a family develops a culture—or system—that either supports or inhibits heavy drinking practices.

The third dimension, which, to some degree, integrates cultural with certain psychological dimensions of the existing family systems approach,[27],[28] examines internal influences on drinking practices that support the maintenance of heavy or alcoholic, drinking practices, once they have developed. Here we look closely at family role expectations, role reversal or compensations, reciprocal exchanges around needs of individual family members, and adaptive responses to individual drinking practices as they differ between families with moderate or heavy drinking levels. This level of conceptualizing, which focuses on characteristics of individual families, has been applied to data analysis in a previous study.[3],[4]

METHOD AND SAMPLE

Data in this paper are drawn from an anthropological study conducted between 1984 and 1987. The project was designed to examine cultural factors influencing drinking practices of blue-collar families. The research design was divided into two stages, combining standard survey methods with qualitative, open-ended interviews and in-home observations. In the first stage, we conducted a survey in a population of 6000 workers who lost their jobs due to closure of an auto assembly plant. The sample was drawn from a list of bargaining unit members provided by the union. The survey included screening questions concerning demographic data, certain family variables, drinking levels, and drinking problems. Because the study focused on workers and their families, we asked that only married couples with at least one child living at home complete questionnaires.

Following analysis of the survey, we randomly selected 30 couples for inclusion in the second stage of the study, the in-home interviews and observation. The primary question of the study was whether familial and cultural environments in heavy drinking families (those at risk for alcohol problems) could be distinguished from moderate drinking families (those not at risk) on the basis of individual, familial, and cultural characteristics. To keep our families as homogeneous as possible, differing only on the basis of the husband's drinking, we controlled for ethnicity (all families were white) and age (husband/father was between 30 and 55). We excluded abstaining and alcoholic men from this pool, but selected 15 families with a heavy drinking father, and 15 families with a moderate drinking father. Heavy drinking was defined for the whole sample as drinking at least 50 drinks in the previous month plus drinking six or more drinks in one day at least once during the month. However, the drinking level of most heavy drinkers was much higher, some as high as 180 drinks a month. Moderate drinking included all other drinkers, excluding abstainers.

Because of the complexity of conducting multilevel research, we relied heavily on methodological techniques that preserve as much as possible the natural, ongoing processes of everyday life. Each family was visited on at least four occasions by the same two researchers. In the course of these visits, husbands, wives, and children over the age of 13, participated in semistructured, open-ended interviews concerning their individual and family history, current family, church and working experiences, the effects of layoff and unemployment, and family drinking history. All interviews were tape recorded, transcribed verbatim, coded and analyzed according to emerging thematic categories. This paper is one of a number that reports findings of both the survey and the in-home interviews.[6],[5],[15],[18]

RESULTS AND DISCUSSION

The correlation of familial and sociocultural factors we found to be related to drinking levels in our population is illustrated in Figure 1. At the far

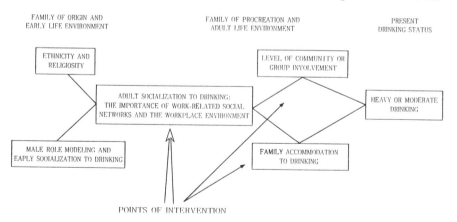

Figure 1. Cultural Patterning and Socialization to Alochol Use in a White, Blue Collar Population.

left of the diagram are those ethnic, religious, and intrafamilial patterns that affect individuals' socialization to alcohol. Ethnicity and early-life religious involvement were relatively unimportant in this population, and did not appear to significantly affect adult drinking levels. On the other hand, most of our heavy drinkers were socialized to heavy alcohol use at home, or came from unstable and chaotic family backgrounds. These are factors that have been related to heavy drinking in other literature on the development of adult drinking patterns.[19],[7]

At the center of the diagram is the workplace which, for this population, emerged as a high-risk environment for heavy alcohol use. At the right are those contemporary community and family processes that may inhibit, promote or permit the development of alcohol problems. This report focuses on suggested precursors to alcohol problem development from the family of origin, and in the workplace and community environments.

Drinking Practices

The literature on economic conditions and alcohol use suggests that unemployed individuals tend to drink more than employed and report more drinking-related problems.[17],[23] However, we immediately discovered that the exact opposite was the case here: Men reported reducing their consumption substantially, often from heavy to moderate levels, subsequent to the layoff (see Figure 2). Our in-depth interviews revealed that certain characteristics of the workplace environment and work-related social networks played a central role in the development and maintenance of heavy drinking practices before the layoff, and that drinking had become a symbolically important and normative behavior for a significant proportion of the workplace.

Analysis of interviews of both husbands and wives from both heavy and moderate drinker groups produced strong evidence that drinking regularly took place in the workplace, and that drinking subcultures developed and were maintained. The fact that drinking on the job was considered normative behavior was substantiated further by the degree of physical availabiliy of alcohol. The heavy drinkers in our sample reported that in the normal course of daily routines at work they often drank at their work station, during lunch breaks, and after work in parking lots, nearby bars, or in selected homes where cohort drinking was tolerated by wives. Those who worked the swing shift began their drinking with their car pool on the way to work. Alcohol was brought into the plant concealed in lunch box thermos jugs, coat pockets, or in boots. Most workers preferred spirits because they were easier to bring in than beer or wine, and could easily be disguised by pouring into coffee cups or soft drink containers. By their own reports and that of

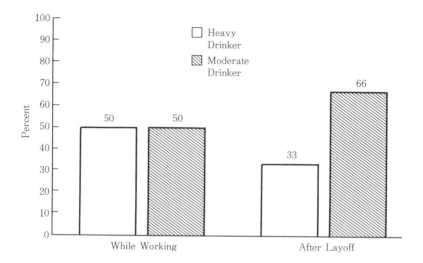

Figure 2. Changes in Drinking as a Function of Leaving Work Environment.

their wives, most of the heavy drinkers had a routine weekday cycle of drinking by day in work or work-related environment and recovering or sleeping it off at home.

Linkages of Drinking Patterns to Workplace Factors

In addition to the workplace drinking patterns and physical availability factor, we identified several organizational characteristics of the subject plant that permitted a heavy drinking subculture to flourish. First, most of the 6000 workers in this large plant worked more than 40 hours a week; overtime was mandatory and routine. Men spent most of their waking lives, often six days a week, in this plant which on any one shift had the population of a small town. Thus, there were always ample numbers, times, and opportunities to socialize with coworkers.

Second, wages for this work are relatively high and the benefits exceptional. Many workers were often bound to the company from young adulthood to retirement, thus permitting the evolution of strong and active social networks. In addition, the nature of assembly work and workers' response to it indicates a high degree of boredom and alienation. Workers looked for activities that would help them get through the day. For our heavy drinking group, these were social activities where alcohol played a central role.

Third, as mechanization in this industry increased, the physical and time demands of specific jobs decreased. In some jobs, a proficient worker could do an hour's worth of work in 15 to 20 minutes. Many workers had the balance of the hour to socialize and, if they wished, drink.

Fourth, although neither management nor union leaders were explicitly in favor of drinking on the work site, action against such behavior was inhibited by the structure of company-union negotiations. Disciplinary action against individuals caught drinking on the job was often averted when local union officials threatened to enforce safety grievances against the company or sabotage the assembly line, thereby affecting the production quotas and deadlines.

In terms of identifying a focus for intervention, it would appear that the analysis could end here. The implications are obvious: Change the structure and organization of this workplace, and consumption among workers will decrease. However, many workers who worked alongside of those who drank heavily were not vulnerable to the drinking subcultures of the workplace, maintaining moderate drinking patterns despite environmental pressures to do otherwise. This suggests that the workplace alone cannot be considered the cause of heavy drinking. The fact that many men did not drink at work or after work suggests there were other environmental factors that led to a decision not to drink, clearly most difficult in this heavy drinking environment. To clarify these issues, we looked for linkages of other social and cultural environments to the husbands' drinking practices.

Linkages of Drinking Patterns to Family of Origin Factors

Current thinking on the relationship of early life factors to heavy drinking of males centers on three major areas of cultural and family environments. These are: ethnicity, religiosity, and male role modeling. In the present sample, where all but three of the husbands and wives were of Northern or Central European heritage, with an almost equal split between Catholic and Protestant backgrounds, ethnicity and religion proved to be relatively unimportant in relation to drinking patterns. However, the role modeling for positive socialization to drinking appeared to have causal significance (see Table 1).

Literature on adolescent and young-adult drinking suggests that the relationship of young men with their parents, particularly their fathers, and the stability of the family of origin during childhood are related to problem drinking.[30],[31] There are two aspects of this hypothesis. The first concerns the socialization of individuals to the positive aspects of heavy drinking, or, more accurately, patterns of social activities where heavy drinking was common,

TABLE 1.

**Selected Demographic Variables, Risk Factors and
"Protective" Factors by Drinking Status**

	DRINKING STATUS	
VARIABLES	*HEAVY*	*MODERATE*
Family of Origin Risk Factors		
1) % (N) Reporting poor or no relationship with father/male role model while growing up[a]	47 (7)	20 (3)
2) % (N) Reporting growing up in a sociocultural environment where heavy drinking was common and not stigmatized	67 (10)	13 (2)
Contemporary Social Network Risk Factors		
3) % (N) Reporting that majority of friends were met at work or in work-related contexts	93 (14)	20 (3)
4) % (N) Reporting that the majority of leisure time spent outside home is in context of predominantly male peer groups	67 (10)	0
5) % (N) Reporting that the majority of leisure activities were work rather than family oriented	87 (13)	20 (3)
Protective Factors		
6) % (N) Reporting a strong background in religions where adult drinking is discouraged[b]	7 (1)	20 (3)
7) % (N) Reporting a strong and current involvement in a religion (any denomination)	0	20 (3)
8) % (N) Reporting participation in non-work related groups, clubs, or organizations	7 (1)	60 (9)
Demographic Variables		
9) % (N) of first-generation migrants to Northern California area	80 (12)	60 (9)
10) % (N) Working at manufacturing plant		
4-5 years	0	27 (4)
6-10 years	33 (5)	0
11-15 years	20 (3)	33 (5)
>15 years	47 (7)	40 (6)
11) % (N) Reporting strong ethnic upbringing and/or current ethnic affiliation	27 (4)	7 (1)
12) % (N) whose fathers were working class[c]	87 (13)	93 (14)

(Continued)

Table 1. (Continued)

Summary Measures		
Mean number of risk factors stemming from family of origin environment (composite of #'s 1, 2, and 6 above)	2.1[d]	1.1[d]
Mean number of risk factors stemming from current work and work-related social networks and leisure activities (composite of #'s 3, 4, 5, and 8 above)	3.4[e]	.8[e]
Mean number of "symptomatic drinking" problems reported in lifetime[f]	3.7[g]	.3[g]

[a] Percentages reflect proportion of those within each drinking group that report each characteristic.

[b] In this case these were Pentecostal, Baptist, and Mormon denominations.

[c] Men considered working class were those who had no more than a high school education and who worked as laborers, transportation workers, or skilled or unskilled craftsmen for the majority of their working lives.

[d] $t = 3.42; p < .01$

[e] $t = 7.87; p < .01$

[f] Individuals were queried as to frequency with which the following problems occurred: 1) I awakened the next day not able to remember some of the things I had done while drinking; 2) I skipped regular meals while I was drinking; 3) I tossed down several drinks fast to get a quicker effect from them; 4) I took a few quick drinks before going to a party to make sure I had enough; 5) I took a drink the first thing when I got up in the morning; 6) My hands shook a lot in the morning after drinking; 7) I could not stop drinking before becoming intoxicated; 8) I was sick because of drinking (nausea, vomiting, severe headache, etc.).

[g] $t = 4.70; p < .01$

not stigmatized, and did not disrupt family life. As indicated in Table 1, in our sample, 67% of the heavy drinkers grew up in homes where heavy drinking behavior of the father was permitted, not stigmatized and not carried out with disruptive effect on family life. By comparison, only a minority of the moderate drinkers — 13% — report any positive socialization to drinking. Interestingly, where the heavy drinking of the parent of our moderate drinking fathers was perceived negatively, particularly where it caused significant family disruption, it appeared to lead the individual to make a deliberate and conscious decision not to drink. None of the heavy drinkers reported having alcoholic fathers at home while they were growing up, but three of the moderate drinkers did, and these three clearly credited the severe family disruption caused by their father's drinking to their decisions as adults to drink lightly.

The second aspect has to do with flawed or non-existent male role modeling; that is, where there is no male parent or parent surrogate (uncle, grandfather, stepfather), or where the relationship between parent and son is a very poor one. Although the literature on role modeling and parenting is essentially atheoretical, the implication is that the absence of a strong male role model in the family of origin makes the individual somewhat more prone to peer influences, especially those in the contexts of school and work.

Because the focus of our interview on family history was more on socialization to drinking behavior and attitudes in the family than on family interactional or psychological issues, our data do not lend themselves to direct analysis of the psychological aspects of our respondents' families of origin. However, we did note some interesting patterns in our data which suggest that the lack of an effective male role model made individuals susceptible to peer pressures for heavy drinking. For example, comparison of informants' self-reported relationships with their fathers suggests that an absent father, the lack of a close, affective relationship with a father or father figure, or an abusive, domineering or rigid father was related to later heavy drinking. Forty-seven percent of our heavy drinkers reported such relationships with their fathers, while only 20% of the moderate drinkers reported such a relationship.

Linkages of Drinking Patterns to Community Factors

Level of involvement in community and voluntary organizations, particularly those that led to the development of nonwork-related social networks for both men and their wives, emerged as a major difference between moderate and heavy drinkers. Table 1 shows that 93% of the heavy drinkers, compared to 20% of moderate drinkers, had minimal to no involvement in nonwork or community-related social activities. Sixty percent of moderate drinking families reported that they were involved in formal or informal group activities (outside of work) on a regular basis.

The social network for 93% of the heavy drinking group that was limited to work peers creating a continuum of on-the-job, off-the-job social interaction where heavy and frequent drinking occurred. In addition to the workplace, social activities of heavy drinkers took place in the Union Hall, in one another's homes on weekends, or infrequently in restaurants. At all of these events, drinking was the major focal point of activity. While 67% of the heavy drinkers reported that the majority of their leisure time outside the home was predominantly with all-male peer groups, not one of the moderate drinkers reported such (see Table 1). Thus, leisure activities of heavy drinking groups tended to be male oriented; wives and children were seldom included in the father's exclusive social life.

By contrast, moderate drinkers resisted pressures to drink on and off the job with coworkers from early on in their work experience, made a concerted effort to establish social networks outside the work environment, and in most cases in the context of local community activities, voluntary organizations, and church functions. In the process of actively pursuing these types of activities, family units established a diversified social network, one that may have offered protection against heavy drinking in that it superseded work-related drinking networks.

In summary, our interviews revealed that identifiable environmental factors promoted or enabled the development of strong drinking networks. The heavy drinkers, who appeared to be vulnerable to such networks, shared similarities in other areas, including positive socialization to heavy drinking in their family of origin, nonexistent or flawed male role models, maintenance of almost exclusively all-male and work-related social networks, low to no involvement in social activities with their families, and no involvement in activities outside of work, such as in the context of church, community, or voluntary organizations. In contrast, moderate drinking individuals exhibited a number of characteristics that appeared to offer protection against participation in the drinking groups, including negative socialization to heavy drinking and existence of an effective male role model in early life, and involvement in community, church, and voluntary organization activities, most often in company of spouse and children.

IMPLICATIONS FOR PREVENTION

In this paper, I attempt to accomplish several goals. The first is to present cultural dimensions to conceptualizing alcohol and the family, the second is to present results of a study that empirically supports the significance of that approach, and the third is to illustrate the importance of a cultural-environmental approach for prevention of alcohol and drug abuse. Since I have already addressed the first and second goals, I will now speak to the third one: implications for prevention.

As the results of the study reported here indicate, when the family is the focus of research and intervention, the linkages of families to other environments must be considered. We have found several important factors in such environments that may have causal and, thereby, interventive significance. However, if the goal of primary prevention of alcohol problems is to alter the environment in such a way that risk factors for heavy and problem drinking are removed or minimized, we are immediately confronted with problems of scale. Where might intervention occur at the family level that will have the greatest impact? Do we focus on the individual whose alcohol beliefs and behaviors derive from early family role modeling and socialization, and later in primary peer groups? On the family unit that may promote levels or styles of drinking by incorporating such behavior into the family system?

On the workplace where frequent alcohol use is influenced by a prevailing tolerance for drinking, certain characteristics of the work environment, and drinking-focused social networks? Or on the community which, according to our results, has the potential to offer families social opportunities that they can participate in as a unit, and where drinking is not the central focus of activity? (For other prevention purposes, communities also share responsibility for physical and social availability of alcohol.) Let us view these possibilities in terms of action.

It is questionable whether findings on an individual's family of origin or on present family life have any direct application to intervention. Clearly, it is impossible to change factors of an individual's childhood and difficult to intervene in contemporary family life, particularly in relation to role modeling and family stability. However, knowledge about family characteristics that place individuals at risk alert clinicians on what to look for in their client assessments and help prevention planners to develop more effective prevention strategies, especially in the context of educational programs. The inclusion of family characteristics in educational prevention programs may be especially beneficial to parent groups, churches, schools, and organizations.

It is reasonable to assume that industries and smaller workplaces alike should take action in reducing environmental risks that lead to unhealthy behavior such as heavy drinking, and in increasing responsibility for quality of life for workers and their families. With the understanding that each workplace is different, and problems are complex, general examples of such actions would be as follows: (a) to identify specific working conditions that appear to have causal significance of workplace drinking, and if possible, change the work environment to one that reduces reasons and opportunities to drink; (b) to change the organizational structure, including social and physical control of alcohol, to one that inhibits rather than promotes drinking habits, and (c) sponsor special events and recreational activities that include families as a way of breaking up all-male heavy drinking networks. We have elaborated on possibilities for workplace prevention in other reports.[6]

The community, perhaps in cooperation with local industries, could take a role in reducing work-related drinking by providing alternative and culturally relative opportunities by which families can develop and sustain "healthy" friendship networks, wherein drinking is not the focus of activity. In the population where this study took place, many of the families were found to be socially disoriented due to migration and geographic mobility. There were few mechanisms — other than the workplace — by which people could seek out and participate in social activities. In terms of critically needed prevention strategies for both alcohol and drugs, cultural restructuring of community life may be an idea worth pursuing.

To conclude, our research findings highlight the importance of understanding the linkages of family life to other cultural environments in relation to their drinking patterns. Such linkages, as we have found here, form the avenues for increasing the probability of reducing the incidence of alcohol problems.

REFERENCES

(1) Ablon J: The significance of cultural patterning for the alcoholic family. *Family Process* 19:127-144 (1980).
(2) Ablon J, Ames G: Culture and family, In *Toward a Science of Family Nursing*. Edited by Gillis C, et al. Menlo Park: Addison Wesley Publications, Inc. (1989).
(3) Ames G: Problem drinking and middle class protestant culture: The family experience, In *The American Experience with Alcohol Contrasting Cultural Perspectives*. Edited by Bennett L, Ames G. New York: Plenum Press (1985).
(4) Ames G: Maternal alcoholism and family life: A cultural model for research and intervention. Ph.D. dissertation in Medical Anthropology, University of California, San Francisco and Berkeley (1982).
(5) Ames G, Janes C: Drinking, social networks and the workplace, In *Alcohol Problem Intervention in the Workplace Assessing Strategic Alternatives*. Edited by Roman P. Westport, Quorum Books (1990).
(6) Ames G, Janes C: Heavy and problem drinking in an American blue collar population: Implications for prevention. *Social Science and Medicine* 25(8):949-960 (1987).
(7) Bennett L, Ames G: *The American Experience with Alcohol: Contrasting Cultural Perspectives*. New York: Plenum Press (1985).
(8) Bennett LA, Wolin SJ, Reiss D et al.: Couples at risk for alcoholism transmission: Protective influences. *Family Process* 26:111-129 (1987).
(9) Berreman G: Lectures in cultural anthropology. Berkeley: University of California (1979).
(10) Bowen M: Alcoholism as viewed through family systems theory and family psychotherapy. *Annals New York Academy of Sciences* (1974).
(11) Ewing JA, Fox RE: Family therapy of alcoholism, in *Current Psychiatric Therapies*, Vol. 8. Edited by Masserman, JH. New York: Grune & Stratton (1968).
(12) Gilbert MJ, Cervantes RC: Mexican Americans and alcohol. University of California, Los Angeles, Spanish Speaking Mental Health Research Center Monograph 11 (1987).
(13) Holder H: Control issues in alcohol abuse prevention: Strategies for states and communities, In *Advances in Substance Abuse, Behavioral and Biological Research Series*. Greenwich: JAI Press (1987).
(14) Jackson JK: The adjustment of the family to the crisis of alcoholism. *Quarterly Journal of Studies on Alcohol* 15(4):562-586 (1954).
(15) Janes C, Ames G: Men, blue collar work and drinking: Alcohol use and misuse in an industrial subculture. *Culture, Medicine and Psychiatry*, 13: 245-274 (1989).
(16) Janes C, Ames G: The family as a focus of primary prevention. National Council on Alcoholism Forum, San Francisco, CA (1986).
(17) Johnson P, Armor DJ, Polich S et al.: U.S. adult drinking practices: Time trends, social correlates and sex roles. U.S. National Technical Information Service,

Springfield, VA (1977).

(18) Klee L, Ames G: Reevaluating risk factors for women's drinking: A study of blue collar wives. *American Journal of Preventive Medicine* 3(1):31-41 (1987).

(19) Marshall M (Ed.) Beliefs, behaviors, and alcoholic beverages: A cross-cultural survey. Ann Arbor, MI: University of Michigan Press (1979).

(20) Olson S, Gerstein DR: Alcohol in America: Taking Action to Prevent Abuse. Washington, DC: National Academy Press (1985).

(21) Paolino TJ, McCrady BS: The Alcoholic Marriage: Alternative Perspectives. New York: Grune & Stratton (1977).

(22) Ratcliffe J, Wallack L, Fagnani F et al.: Perspectives on prevention: Health promotion vs. health protection, In *The End of an Illusion: Future of Health Policy in Western Industrialized Nations*. Berkeley: University of California Press (1984).

(23) Smart RG: Drinking problems among employed, unemployed, and shift workers. *J Occup Med* 21:731 (1979).

(24) Steiner CM: *Games Alcoholics Play*. New York: Grove Press (1971).

(25) Steinglass P: The alcoholic family at home. *Arch Gen Psychiatry* 38:578-584 (1981).

(26) Steinglass, P: A life history model of the alcoholic family. *Family Process* 19(3):211-226 (1980).

(27) Steinglass P, Weiner S, Mendelson J: Interaction issues as determinants of alcoholism. *Am J of Psychiatry* 128:55-60 (1971a).

(28) Steinglass P, Weiner S, Mendelson J: A systems approach to alcoholism: A model and its clinical implications. *Arch Gen Psychiatry* 24:401-408 (1971b).

(29) Tylor EB, Primitive Culture: *Researches into the Development of Mythology, Philosophy, Religion, Art and Custom*. London: John Murray, Ltd. (1871).

(30) Zucker RA, Barron FH: Parental behaviors associated with problem drinking and antisocial behavior among adolescent males, In *Research on Alcoholism: Clinical Problems and Special Populations*. Edited by Chafetz ME. Washington: U.S. Government Printing Office, DHEW Pub. No. (NIH) 74-675 (1973).

(31) Zucker RA, Noll R: Precursors and developmental influences on drinking and alcoholism: Etiology from a longitudinal perspective, In *Alcohol Consumption and Related Problems, Alcohol Monograph Number 1*, p. 289, Washington: U.S. Government Printing Office, USDHHS, NIAAA (1982).

13

Marriage Patterns of Females from Alcoholic Families in Japan

Satoru Saitoh, M.D.,

Anthony Dalby, C.Q.S.W.

Kiyoshi Nagano, M.D.

Ichiro Tezuka, B.A.

Yuji Noguchi, Ph.D.

Forty-five married, male alcoholics who were hospitalized in an alcoholism rehabilitation ward and their wives were asked to complete a prepared questionnaire concerning their parents, spouses and children, and were then interviewed individually concerning their marital situation. Problem drinking (with alcohol dependence strongly suspected) was present in 55.6% of the subjects' parents, while in the spouses' parents it was noted in 24.4% (50% of fathers). This prevalence of problem drinking is far higher than those expected from epidemiological studies in Japan.

Spouses whose fathers had evidence of problem drinking had a higher tendency of "passivity" and "withdrawal" regarding their selection of spouse and marital relationships, had a stronger tendency to be the major breadwinner in the family and had more complaints about their mental and physical health than spouses from nonalcoholic families.

INTRODUCTION

In recent years Systems Theory has been widely accepted. This views not only a couple's individual personalities and problems but also their interactional patterns and the ways these contribute to the overall picture—how the family both uses and maintains problem drinking in their relationships. From such observations we have seen that all family members are affected by all problems, creating a family system.[39]

Thus, in the alcoholic family, both the spouse and the children share in the results of alcohol abuse and contribute to the maintenance of the problem. In such a situation the children of alcoholic couples learn the mode and style of interactional patterns of their parents and may well, in turn, transmit this to their own offspring.

Therefore, we focus upon the daughters of alcoholics raised in such families in Japan. Many daughters do not become alcoholics but nevertheless may go on to marry a man with a history of alcohol abuse. They have, it appears, a greater susceptibility to repeat the harsh problems they knew in their mother's life and their own childhood. Such women take a critical role in transmitting the alcoholic role to the next generation.

In consideration of the psychopathology of such females, Paolino and McCrady[28] cited a report by Gaertner,[14] from the late 1930s. Gaertner investigated 15 wives of alcoholics, 2 of whom were daughters of alcoholics, and 1 niece, raised by her alcoholic uncle. Black[5] states:
"... *Adult children of alcoholics have many identities. First and foremost, they are just that ... adult children of alcoholics. Second, they may be the spouse or former spouse of an alcoholic. Third, they may be the alcoholic themselves. Fourth, they could be any combination of the three ...*" From her quote we can see that, in the U.S.A., it is known that daughters of alcoholics marry alcoholic spouses. However, we also need to consider the effect of cultural differences: Will there be any obvious differences in Japanese homes due to different cultural expectations?

Finally, what percentage of daughters of alcoholics actually go on to become spouses of men with alcohol problems? And what specific features might they have which distinguish them from other women who marry alcohol abusers? This study seeks to address such questions.

SUBJECTS

The subjects were 45 alcoholics (referred to as IPs, "identified patients") and their wives who were admitted to Kuriharma National Hospital in the first half of 1981 and had undergone the 3-month ARP Program (Alcoholism Rehabilitation program). Subjects were chosen sequentially from the time of their admission, and their wives had also consented to take part.

Average age of the alcoholics was 44.6 (32-61 y.o.) and their wives 42.1 (28-59 y.o.) Each alcoholic had an average drinking history of 24 years; 24% had a previous history of hospital admission for alcoholism. Average duration since IP's first drink was 24 years. Socioeconomic status: 15.6% were white-collar workers, 22.2% were self-employed (or family-employed); 48.9% were blue-collar workers. 2.2% were irregularly employed. Unemployed, on government benefit, were 11.1%. These characteristics were representative of the alcoholics admitted to the Kurihama Hospital.[34] Average duration of marriage was 17.6 years (8 months – 45 years). For 38 couples (84.4%) it was their first marriage. In 2 couples both partners had previously been married; in 4 cases it was the subject's second marriage and in 2 the wife's second marriage.

Of the total number of 180 parents of the subjects and their wives, the father was still living in 38.9% of cases and the mothers in 46.6%.

Average age of fathers was 66 (56-74 y.o.) and that of the mothers 68 (50-80 y.o.). Of the original 180 parents, 20 fathers (22.2%) and 56 mothers (62.2%) were still alive. In 42% of the cases both parents had died before either the subject or the wife had reached the age of 15. There were 6 IPs who experienced loss of both parents (either due to death or separation) before 15 years of age; 17 IPs experienced loss of father, 3 experienced loss of mother. In total, 26 (57.8%) experienced early parental loss.

Among IPs' spouses, 2 experienced loss of both parents before age 15. Early loss of father was known by 14, early loss of mother by 3. The total was 19 (42.2%).

The number of children totaled 98 (average 2.2 per family). There were 4 childless couples, 1 of which had a stepdaugher. Of the original number, 83 children were blood-related to both parents. After omitting children aged 3 or under, 79 children were observed (male 33, female 46). Of these, the average age of males was 16.6 (range: 4-34 years), and females 14.5 (range: 4-32) years.

METHOD OF INVESTIGATION

Questionnaire

First, two weeks after the IP's admission, both the IP and his wife were each requested to fill in and return a questionnaire and return this a week later. The questions differed for the two groups. There were questions concerning general family history.

The wife was asked to give information about her parents' drinking history, as well as te drinking history of the IP and herself. Wives were given the opportunity to show their wishes to continue their marriage, and asked to indicate any mental or physical abuse experienced during marriage.

Both were asked to indicate any behavioral problems of their children aged between 3-20 years.

Investigational Interview

Individual and joint interviews of IPs and wives were held. In the individual interviews, subjects were asked about their general marital relationship, sexual relationship, and why they had married their spouse.

Determining Problem Drinking among Parental Generation

The above questionnaire also gave opportunity for the highlighting of alcohol-related problems within the parental generation. Replies such as "he got violent when drunk," "he certainly drinks like an alcoholic." "drink killed him," "he was in hospital because of alcohol," indicated such problems within the parental generation.

The IPs whose parents exhibited alcohol-related problems were classified as the "A-Group." Their wives with such parents were known as the "Alpha group." Other IPs were known as the "Non-A group," and similarly, wives whose parents had no history of drink problems were known as the "non-Alpha group."

In order to fully analyze the influence of the parental generation's drink problems upon the IPs and their wives, we made a full history of the life/marriage/health situation of IPs with parental-generation drinkers, and cross-matched this against the histories of those IPs whose parents experienced no such problems.

RESULTS

Parental Generation: Problem Drinking and Marital Situation

Of the IPs' fathers, 24 had a previous history of problem drinking; 3 of the IPs' mothers also had the same. Of the above numbers, both parents of 2 IPs had a history of problem drinking. The total number of the parental generation of IPs having identified previous histories of drinking episodes was 25.

The analysis of the IPs' wives indicated that 11 of them had fathers indicating prior history of alcohol abuse/problem drinking. None had mothers with such prior history.

As stated previously, the A-group consisted of 25/45 people (55.6%).

The Alpha group comprised 24.4%. There is no statistically significant difference when cross-matching and comparing the [A-to Non-A] and [Alpha to Non-Alpha] groups (See Table 1).

TABLE 1.

Cross-Match of Mate Selection, Comparing Groups

[Number] %

Groups of Wives	Groups of IPs		Total
	A	Non-A	
Alpha	[6] 54.5	[5] 45.5	[11] 100.0
	24.0	25.0	24.4
Non-Alpha	[19] 55.9	[15] 44.1	[34] 100.0
	76.0	75.0	75.6
Total	[25] 55.6	[20] 44.4	[45] 100.0
	100.0	100.0	100.0

X^2-Test: Not Significant

TABLE 2.

Life History and Marital Status of IPs and Wives

[Number] %

Life history and marital situation Groups	IP			WIVES		
	A [25]	Non-A [20]	☆	Alpha [11]	Non-Alpha [34]	☆
(1) Parental loss before age 15	[15] 60.0	[11] 55.0	··	[8] 72.7	[11] 32.4	**
(2) Lives on public assistance	[3] 12.0	[2] 10.0	··	[1] 9.1	[4] 11.8	··
(3) Arranged marriage	[10] 40.0	[8] 40.0	··	[6] 54.5	[12] 35.3	··
(4) First marriage	[22] 88.0	[17] 85.0	··	[10] 90.9	[32] 94.1	··
(5) Aware of drinking problems before marriage	[6] 24.0	[5] 25.0	··	[7] I63.6	[4] 11.8	***
(6) Sexual dysfunction within marriage	[18] 72.0	[17] 85.0	··	[11] 100.0	[24] 70.6	***
(7) Wife is a main income provider within the home	[8] 32.0	[7] 35.0	··	[7] 63.6	[8] 23.5	**
(8) Manifest problems in children	[15] 60.0	[12] 60.0	··	[10] 90.9	[17] 50.0	··
(9) Satisfied with the marriage	[10] 40.0	[5] 25.0	··	[8] 72.7	[7] 20.6	***
(10) No intention to divorce	[11] 44.0	[10] 50.0	··	[8] 72.7	[13] 28.9	**

☆ X^2-Test: *** $P < 0.01$ **$P < 0.05$ *$P < 0.1$ ·· Not Significant

IPs and Wives: Life History and Marital Situation

The life history and marital situation of IPs and their wives was investigated, in the light of the previous histories of problem drinking found among the parental generation. Results are as shown in Table 2. As to IPs, there were no obvious differences between the A and Non-A groups.

On the other hand, concerning their wives, statistically significant differences are noticed between Alpha and Non-Alpha groups. The Alpha groups show a significantly large proportion of them had experienced parental loss before age 15 (see Table 2). Also, a clear percentage showed a history of marriage to a male with a history of problem drinking prior to marriage. Plus, the Alpha group had a larger percentage of sexual dysfunction within marriage. Many Alpha group wives were the main income-provider within the home. Finally, many Alpha group wives stated they were satisfied with their marriage and had no intention to divorce (See Table 2).

Range and Frequency of Alcohol Problems

The IPs were investigated regarding the range and frequency of alcohol-related problems, in light of the parental generations' histories of problem drinking. Results were as shown in Table 3.

TABLE 3.
Range and Frequency of Alcohol Problems

[Number] %

Problems / Groups	IPs			Wives		
	A [25]	Non-A [20]	☆	Alpha [11]	Non-Alpha [34]	☆
Violence during intoxication	[11] 44.0	[11] 55.0	··	[6] 54.5	[16] 47.1	··
Drunk & disorderly	[16] 64.0	[17] 85.0	··	[8] 72.7	[25] 73.5	··
Absenteeism	[20] 80.0	[16] 80.0	··	[9] 81.8	[27] 79.4	··
Unemployment	[10] 40.0	[8] 45.0	··	[2] 18.2	[16] 47.1	··
Taken into custody by police	[8] 32.0	[4] 20.0	··	[2] 18.2	[10] 29.4	··
Drunken driving	[9] 36.0	[1] 10.00	**	[4] 36.4	[6] 17.6	··
Serious physical damage due to drinking	[20] 80.0	[17] 85.0	··	[9] 81.8	[28] 82.4	··
Alcoholic psychosis	[7] 28.0	[10] 50.0	··	[7] 63.6	[10] 29.4	··
Paranoid delusion of jealousy	[2] 8.0	[4] 20.0	··	[3] 27.2	[3] 8.8	*

☆ x^2-Test: **$P < 0.05$ *$P < 0.1$ ·· Not Significant

Among the IPs, a significantly large number had histories of drunken driving offenses.

Among Alpha group wives, a significantly large number of them had experienced being accused or attacked by their husbands, due to the husbands' paranoic tendency towards jealousy.

Mental Health of IPs' Wives

All of the IPs spouses undertook the Japanese version of C.M.I. (Cornell Medical Index). This was comprised of 24 questions concerning physical and/or mental symptoms. Prominent physical symptoms revealed included "Stiff neck & shoulders" (at 57.8%, significantly greater than other symptoms); this was followed by "insomnia" (33.3%); gastrointestinal disorders (31.3%) and headache (28.9%). Other symptoms included hypochondriacal tendency (26.7%), fatigue upon awaking (20%), menstrual problems (20%). Non specific malaises such as "flu," fevers, aches, etc. comprised 15.6% (see Table 4 on p. 210).

Psychologically, of the three most significant symptoms, 35.6% expressed dependency needs (e.g., "I always feel a real longing to share my problems with someone"), while 20% stated they became "very easily angered" and 17.8% were in a depressed state. Seven wives (15.6%) had expressed suicidal feelings in the past, 3 wives (6.7%) stated they were suffering from neurosis. There were 2 (4.4%) healthy wives, with no reported symptoms.

In Table 4, items numbered 1-16 indicated physical problems, those numbered 17-24 reported psychological symptoms. "Healthy" was classed as no more than 3 physical symptoms, or 0 psychological symptoms.

Using the above guidelines, 13 wives (28.9%) were healthy 32 wives (71.1%) indicated 4 or more physical symptoms or some psychological symptom. Ten wives (22%) manifested some clinical psychological disturbance such as anxiety or hypochondriacal state. These were sociophobia (1); depressed state (3); depression or anxiety attack (with history of abuse as a child) (1); schizoid personality disorder (1). These symptoms increased in severity in relation to the amount of alcohol abuse within the family.

In comparison, Alpha group wives exhibited much higher frequency and range of symptoms than the Non-Alpha group. As Table 3 shows, there were statistically significant differences in such items as gastrointestinal disorders, neck and shoulder stiffness, headaches, menstrual problems, fatigue, hypochondriacal tendency, insomnia, dependency, previous history of neurosis and obsessional thinking.

TABLE 4.

Physical and Mental Symptoms of Wives

[Number] %

Symptoms	Groups	Total		Alpha		Non-Alpha		
		[45]	%	[11]	%	[34]	%	☆
(01) Choking		[3]	6.7	[0]	0	[3]	8.8	··
(02) Palpitation		[11]	24.4	[2]	18.2	[9]	26.5	··
(03) Short of breath		[7]	15.6	[1]	9.1	[6]	17.6	··
(04) Nausea		[3]	6.7	[2]	18.2	[1]	2.9	··
(05) Gastrointestinal disturbances		[14]	31.3	[8]	72.7	[6]	17.6	***
(06) Stiff neck/shoulder		[26]	57.8	[11]	100.0	[15]	44.1	***
(07) Headache		[13]	28.9	[7]	63.6	[6]	17.6	***
(08) General 'flu' symptom		[7]	15.6	[2]	18.2	[5]	14.7	··
(09) Menstrual problems		[9]	20.0	[6]	54.5	[3]	8.8	***
(10) Tiredness		[13]	28.9	[7]	63.6	[6]	17.6	***
(11) Exhausted upon awakening		[9]	20.0	[4]	36.4	[5]	14.7	··
(12) Nonspecific physical complaint		[2]	4.4	[0]	0	[2]	5.9	··
(13) Hypochondriacal tendency		[12]	26.7	[7]	63.6	[5]	14.7	***
(14) Insomnia		[15]	33.3	[7]	63.6	[8]	23.5	**
(15) Excessive smoking		[6]	13.3	[2]	18.2	[4]	11.7	··
(16) Excessive drinking		[0]	0	[0]	0	[0]	0	~
(17) Dependency need		[16]	35.6	[7]	63.6	[9]	26.4	**
(18) Depression		[8]	17.8	[4]	36.4	[4]	11.7	*
(19) Thinking of suicide		[7]	15.6	[3]	27.2	[4]	11.7	··
(20) History of suffering from neurosis		[3]	6.7	[3]	27.2	[0]	0	***
(21) Previous admission to psychiatric hospital		[0]	0	[0]	0	[0]	0	~
(22) Easily becomes angry		[9]	20.0	[1]	9.1	[8]	23.5	··
(23) Obsessive idea		[2]	4.4	[2]	18.2	[0]	0	**
(24) Irrational fear		[0]	0	[0]	0	[0]	0	~

☆ X^2-Test: *** P<0.01 **P<0.05 *P<0.1 ·· Not Significant

Items of CMI-Japanese version equivalent to the symptoms in this table as follows, (01) B-11 (02) C-31, 32 (03) C-33 (04) D-48 (05) D-54 (06) E-67 (07) E-78, 79 (08) E-82, H-1 01 (09) H-99 (10) I-108 (11) I-110 (12) J-117 (13) J-121-123 (14) L-139 (15) L-142 (16) L-144 (17) M-154 (18) N-158, 160, 161 (19) N-162 (20) O-168 (21) O-170 (22) Q-180, 182, 184, 185, 186 (23) R-193 (24) R-194.

Emotional and Behavioral Disturbance in IPs' Children

The behavioral and emotional situation of a total of 79 children (Males = 33, females = 46, all blood-related) of IPs was investigated.

Findings: Of 36.7% (29: m16, f13), at least one of the following behaviors was exhibited: aggressive tendencies toward their parents, restlessness and lack of attention, hypersensitivity and nervous tic. Anorexic state, school maladaptation/truancy, juvenile law-breaking, asthmatic attack and enuresis. (See Table 4).

Frequency reporting showed:

Intrafamilial tensions and hypersensitivity towards parents in 13 children (16.5%).

School maladaptation/truancy = 10 (12.7%)

Enuresis = 8 (10.1%)

Asthmatic attack = 8 (10.1%)

Violence towards parents = 4 (5.1%)

Alcohol abuse = 2 (2.5%)

Absconding from home = 2 (2.5%)

Juvenile law-breaking = 1

Anorexic state = 1

Abused child at age 5 y.o. by mother = 1

The 2 alcohol abusers were male high school students, 1 with a history of school truancy and juvenile lawbreaking.

Investigation by gender shows that males have a higher percentage (48.5%) than females (28.3%).

Investigation by household showed that 41 families had at least one blood-related child, 27 of which (65.9%) exhibited some type of behavioral disturbance (physical or mental).

Findings showed 18 blood-related children from Alpha groups. Of these, 11 (61.1%; m5, f6) showed some kind of mental or behavioral disturbance. From 61 such children (m25, f36) from 34 Non-Alpha house holds, 18 children (29.5%; m11, f7) showed similar patterns of disturbance. Statistically significant differences showed in the frequency reporting of both groups (see Table 5 on p. 212).

Investigation by type indicated that children of Alpha groups have an overall higher frequency of emotional/behavioral disturbance in all items. Violence toward parents and school problems are notably higher among Alpha households.

Following the above data, let us now consider some of the charcteristics of females from alcoholic families who have themselves become spouses of alcoholics. This will be followed by a) summary of the features of Alpha type wives and b) case history.

Features of Wives from Alcoholics' Families

It was clear that the Alpha group members had a higher tendency of "passivity" and "withdrawal" in the area of selection of their spouse and marital relationships. They had a strong tendency to be the "major bread winner"

TABLE 5.
Emotional and Behavioral Disturbance of Children

[Numbers of Children] %

Groups	Total	Alpha	Non-Alpha	
Disturbances	*[79]*	*[18] 100.0*	*[00] 100.0*	☆
Disturbance of all kind	[29] 36.7	[11] 61.1	[18] 29.5	**
Intra-familial tensions	[13] 16.5	[4] 22.2	[9] 14.8	··
Violence towards parents	[4] 5.1	[4] 22.2	[0] 0.0	***
Absconding from home	[2] 2.5	[2] 11.1	[0] 0.0	**
School maladaptation/truancy	[10] 12.7	[5] 27.8	[5] 8.2	**
Juvenile law-breaking	[2] 2.5	[1] 5.6	[1] 1.6	··
Alcohol abuse	[2] 2.5	[1] 5.6	[1] 1.6	··
Asthmatic attack	[5] 6.3	[2] 11.1	[3] 4.9	··
Enuresis	[8] 10.1	[3] 16.7	[5] 16.7	··

☆ X^2-Test: *** $P < 0.01$ **$P < 0.05$ *$P < 0.1$ ·· Not Significant

in the family. Their physical and mental health was significantly poorer than wives from the Non-Alpha group. Their children, also, experienced a higher incidence of emotional and behavioral disorders than children from other groups.

DISCUSSION

From Alcoholic Family to Alcoholic's Wife

After observing 45 wives of alcoholics in Japan, the following facts emerged:

Some wives had shown an apparent lack of concern or interest in the selection of their spouses. Only 2 had actively considered the type of future husband they wanted. Others had married without such apparent concern. Thirty-one had married totally passively, seeming to look more at their immediate situation or emotional needs of love, indifferent to the importance of the decision; 5 stated they had accepted marriage proposals very shortly after experiencing a broken relationship.

Eleven stated that, prior to the marriage, they had realized already that their spouse had a drink problem; 6 of these 11 had come from homes where the father was a problem drinker, and thus realized what problems they could well experience in the future. This seemed particularly strange, but we must say that many of the above attitudes concerning finding a spouse seemed very unusual.

However, in the U.S.A., certain clinicians had formally reported that some women seemed to be pathologically drawn towards difficult lives, and that this feeling was prevalent also among female spouses of American alcoholics.

Paolino, and McCrady, [28] pointed out that the first dissertation focusing upon the psychopathology of female spouses of alcoholics was by Gaertner,[14] in the late 1930s. Gaertner stated that of 15 wives of alcoholics, 8 had chosen spouses whom they already knew had problems with alcohol. Two wives were themselves daughters of alcoholics and 1 other had been raised by an uncle known to have drink problems. The difficulties they would experience were well known to these women, so their choice of spouse is again very illogical to onlookers.

Twelve of the 15 were from broken homes and experienced much difficulty during their upbringing. Gaertner[14] reports they had developed acute super-egos and, controlled by their punitive feelings, ". . . have such masochistic impulses, which only finds pleasure in such difficulties, so that it seems this misery makes them happy . . ." These wives had not achieved full development of sexual maturity, and did not seemed to want to exercise any real choice concerning their partner. They tended to dislike sexual intercourse following marriage.

However, they appeared very eager to control their husbands both socially and/or economically. Six of the 15 provided the main source of income, while all had a job and contributed to maintaining the household and children instead of their dysfunctional husbands.

As cited above, Gaertner's description is similar to that of our investigation, especially with regard to Alpha-group wives. Thus, both Gaertner and ourselves found some correlation regarding the features of couples in alcoholic families, irrelevant of generation or culture. Further findings in the U.S.A. during the 1950s also stressed such tendencies among spouses of alcoholics. [4],[8],[12],[13],[22],[26],[41]

These reports were characterized by their psychoanalytic stance, which can be summarized as follows:

Females who marry alcoholics have a specific leaning or psychopathological tendency to do so. This psychopathology is not the result of the marriage but rather is the result of their nurturing environment prior to marriage. This theory has become known as the *"disturbed personality theory"*[11]). Such behavior as cited according to this theory is considered very persuasive and can attract certain personalities. This is seen clearly in the above descriptions of marriages in alcoholic families.

However, other researchers,[18],[19] have criticized the disturbed personality theory, stating that ". . . (this theory) has one fatal deficit. It does not believe the stressful effects of being married to an alcoholic are responsible for the wives' pathological behavior. Thus, 'personality' theorists have not

accounted for the effect of the couple's interaction . . ." Some researchers
have labeled this the *Stress theory*.

Stress theorists have seen the wife's physical and/or psychological symptoms as a stress reaction to her husband's alcoholism. They state that these
symptoms frequently manifest themselves in relation to the husband's degree
of alcohol consumption.[3],[17],[19] Representing these stress theorists, Edwards[11] insists that ". . . there is no single personality tendency which can
categorize spouses of alcoholics . . ." Such reviews[1],[2],[11],[17] have been
prevalent since the 1960s, and the disturbed personality theory was strongly
believed to be "a pseudoscientific, fatalistic discussion . . ."

Since the 1970s, however, the "systems approach" has been used in the
study of alcoholic families, including direct observation of interaction between alcoholic couples (especially direct observation of interaction during
intoxication) This is now seen as a major research method.

The Family Systems Theory stresses the importance of understanding not
only the individual pathology of the "identified patient," but also the effect
that this individual's behavior creates within the whole family. There is now
realization that the family members seek to adjust their own behavior patterns, both consciously and unconsciously, in order to adapt to the "problem
member." This, in itself, often creates skewed familial behavioral and communication patterns which, in turn, may lead to other family members individually acting out in reaction to the build-up of dysfunctional familial
behaviors.

Family members may not necessarily fall into the same types of problem
behaviors as the originally identified patient. Thus, although they are under
greater risk, an alcoholic's children are not themselves bound to become
problem drinkers, but may exhibit other forms of dysfunction. However,
as indicated by the various tables throughout this report, the members within an alcoholic family are more prone to experience a greater number of
health, behavioral, and communication problems because all members are
ineluctably involved in and affected by each other's actions and reactions.

The role of the family therapist is to help the family by pointing out the
existence of this damaging family system, and work with as many of the family as possible in creating new healthy interactions in place of the old.

Via such recent research, the systems approach has pointed out deficits
within the two theories mentioned previously. Thus, the disturbed person-
sality theory is criticized for focusing only upon the wife's pathology, as is
the stress theory for considering only the husband's pathology.

Since the development in the 1980s of the family therapy approach to alcoholic families, researchers[28] have been observing behavioral and emotional
disturbance in many children.[20],[23],[43] The mode of interpersonal relation-

ships between parents and children was observed, and once again the lifestyle of alcoholics' wives was considered. However, this time, attention didn't narrow in on individual psychopathology but rather or the alcoholic family system, including the drinker and the children thus affected.

Cross-generational Transmission of Alcoholism, and the Alcoholic's Daughter

We found that 56.7% of the alcoholic subjects and 24.4% of their wives have parents with histories of problem drinking, while 27 (of whom 24 are fathers) of the 90 blood-related parents of alcoholic subjects were recognized as problem drinkers. Overall total is therefore 30.0%, and 53.3% of fathers. On the wives' side, 11 (all fathers) of the 90 blood-related parents were recorded as problem drinkers. This means that 12.2% of all parents and 24.4% of the wives' fathers are similarly classified.

In Japan, the ratio of problem drinkers among the general adult population (20 years and older) is estimated as 2-3% (males 3-5%). Of this, males aged 40-50 years account for 10.7%, males aged 51-60 account for 6.7% and males 61 and over account for 6.8%.[32],[33] From these figures we can ascertain that the prevalence ratio of problem drinkers is very high, both among the blood-related parents of our alcoholic subjects and also among their wives.

Many observers pointed out the notably high alcoholism rate found in the alcoholic's ancestral family line and also the offspring of alcoholic subjects.[10] Recent adoption studies are revealing the presence of "genetic factors."[6],[7],[9],[15] This biological factor may explain the high ratio of drink abuse in the subjects' parents; however, only the rearing environment could be attributed to the high ratio of alcohol problems among spouses' parents, with the alcoholic couple possibly transferring their interpersonal communication patterns to the next generation. Thus, through this process, the daughters of such couples "learn" much of their way of life, including the mode of relationships and spouse selection.

Zucker[44] and Penick[30] insisted that psychological and environmental factors both influence the cross-generational transmission of alcoholism. In this respect, the report of Wolin et al.[43] is vital, as the authors insisted they could verify the cross-generational transmission of interactional styles between alcoholic couples. They observed genograms of 10 alcoholic couples spanning 4 generations. In 7 out of the 10, they established cross-generational transmission of alcoholism occurring from grandparents to grandchildren. In this investigation, Wolin et al. discovered the same interactional styles or patterns among couples in every generation.

Other authors have also cited the specific tendency of children of alcoholics to select spouses with similar problems: Lemert, [25] Paolino et al.,[29] and Rimmer and Winokur[31] have all reported quite high findings (42%) of alcoholism prevalence in both first- and second-degree family members of spouses of alcoholics—similar to our data. Rimmer and Winokur[31] entitled such marriages "assortative mating."

In this report we have tried to determine the specific tendencies related to mate selection and sexual relationships (passivity and withdrawal) among 11 wives whose fathers were problem drinkers. We observed that their physical and mental health, as well as that of their children, was much more disturbed than those wives whose fathers had no history of alcohol abuse. Although it is impossible to determine the exact cause of these tendencies— whether derived from genetic, physical or environmental origins—we may say that such tendencies are substantially influenced by the interactional patterns of their parents.

In alcoholic families, daughters tend to be strongly influenced and guided by their mothers, as their fathers are usually either deceased, absent, or considered dysfunctional because of their drinking behavior. These daughters also are likely to be dragged into the "battle zone" of their parents' interaction, perhaps being forced to take a "pseudocounselor" stance as they listen to the mother's complaints about her husband. Sometimes this has been known to create a father hatred, although sometimes the opposite has occurred and the mother has been criticized strongly by the daughter for her "heartless attitude." The daughter has then taken a protective role for the alcoholic father, for whom she feels great pity.

Yet, whatever the situation, the daughter has great difficulty in achieving the sort of positive and normal detachment from the parents that is required during the adolescent process. Thus, as adults, these young women frequently have an inflated sense of their apparent responsibilities to be carers. Therefore, in the process of perhaps consciously or otherwise looking for someone to care for, they are apt to enter into an unsuitable marriage. From this point on, they tend to lead lives similar to their mothers.

Alcoholics' Daughters and the Road Back to Recovery

Daughters from alcoholic families, who have themselves married problem drinkers, may particularly need to learn that their longings for internal stability will not be achieved merely by aspiring to control and influence others. In order to change their previous controlling style of behavior, their preoccupations of caring for others (notably their husbands and families in Japan) need to be replaced with an appropriate level of self-care, and care by others. Instead, they need to permit themselves to pursue their own happiness, their own potential. However, because of their intense need to nurture others, such thinking may be very difficult for them to learn.

We are supporting such women here via alcoholism-related community support systems or special encounter groups based around community health centers.[34] Such an example is cited by Nomura, during this symposium.

During these programs, clients—that is, wives of alcoholics—become more aware of their own problems, and gradually gain a new idea of the need for a change of orientation. It is necessary that we, the "helping professionals," avoid at all costs being inappropriate enablers to these clients. Their independence and maturity will only be from within themselves, not through the control of therapists or counselors. Therapists need to be very aware of the myth of therapeutic power, and be extremely alert to the clients' abilities of spontaneous recovery. Indeed, the most suitable means of client recovery might be through such as a suitable self-help group. *Al-Anon* and several other specialized organizations do exist in Japan as self-help groups for alcoholics' family members. However, regrettably, there is a real scarcity of such groups for the children of alcoholics. *Alateen* meetings are supported by Al-Anon members, but their range is limited and they are not well known. Only very recently has the need for a self-help group for adult children of alcoholics been realized by a few enlightened citizens' groups. Helping professionals are very hopeful at this development, but we must curb our enthusiasm to provide inappropriate enabling, and be merely excited onlookers.

CONCLUSION

1) This paper concerns Japanese females raised in alcoholic families, who themselves went on to marry alcoholics. We investigated such areas as their marital interaction, their mode of spouse selection, sexual relationships with their husbands, state of health and range and frequency of emotional and/or physical disturbances among themselves and their children, in comparison to those Japanese wives of alcoholics whose fathers had no history of problem drinking.

2) Forty-five married, male alcoholics were hospitalized in the Alcoholism Rehabilitation Ward of Kurihama National Hospital. They and their wives were requested to complete prepared questionnaires concerning their parents, spouse and children, and then individually interviewed concerning their marital situation.

3) Problem drinking (with alcoholism strongly suspected) was present in the subjects' parents in 25 out of 45 cases (24 in the father, 2 in both cases and 1 in the mother), while in the spouses' parents it was 11 out of 45 (24.4%), all fathers. This prevalence of problem drinking is far higher than that made

clear from epidemiological studies in Japan (the ratio being 2-3% in general population, and 6-10% in male population aged over 40).

4) The high frequency of problem drinking observed among the subjects' parents may be explained by genetic factors, but only the rearing environment could the high ratio of alcohol problems among spouses' parents, the alcoholic couple possibly transferring their interpersonal communication patterns to the next generation. Thus, through this process, the daughters of such couples "learn" much of their way of life, including mode of relationship and spouse selection.

5) The authors divided the 45 spouses into 2 groups. One, entitled the "Alpha group," consisted of 11 wives from alcoholic families (i.e., alcoholics' daughters). The other, entitled the "Non-Alpha group," comprised those daughters whose fathers had no history of alcohol-related problems. It was seen that the Alpha group wives exercised much more "passivity" and "withdrawal" concerning spouse selection and marital relationship. Further, their own and their children's health was in many aspects inferior to that of the Non-Alpha group.

6) Daughters from alcoholics' families tended to be strongly controlled and guided by their mothers, as their fathers were rendered dysfunctional via alcohol. It was conjectured that they mirrored the marital interactions of their parental generation in their own relations, i.e., that they tend to need to take the role of carer and controller of others.

These controlling styles of behavior need to be changed in favor of those which permit them their own happiness and potential. This can occur only from within themselves, and not through the control of therapists. Suitable self-help groups for adult children of alcoholics, the necessity of which is only just being realized in Japan, might prove the most adequate means of recovery for these females.

REFERENCES

(1) Ablon J. Family structure and behavior in alcoholism: a review of the literature. In *The Biology of Alcoholism, Vol. 4.* Edited by Kissin B. and Begleiter H. New York: Plenum Press (1976).

(2) Bailey M. Alcoholism in marriage—a review of research and professional literature. *Q.J. Stud. Alcohol* 22: 81-97 (1961).

(3) Bailey M, Haberman P, Alksne H. Outcome of alcoholic marriages: Endurance, termination or recovery. *Q.J. Stud. Alcohol* 2: 610-623 (1962).

(4) Baker SM. Social casework with inebriates. Alcohol, Science & Society. New Haven. *Q.J. Stud. Alcohol Lecture 27* (1945).

(5) Black C. *It Will Never Happen to Me.* Denver: Medical Administration Company (1982).

(6) Bohman M, Sigvardsson S, Cloninger CR. Maternal inheritance of alcohol abuse:

Cross-fostering analysis of adopted women. *Arch. Gen. Psychiat.* 38: 964-999 (1981).

(7) Cadoret RJ, Cain C, Grove WM. Development of alcoholism in adoptees raised apart from alcoholic biological relatives. *Arch. Gen. Psychiat.* 37: 561-563 (1980).

(8) Clifford BJ. A study of the wives of rehabilitated and unrehabilitated alcoholics. *Social Casework* 41: 457-460 (1960).

(9) Cloninger CR, Bohman M, Sigvardsson S. Inheritance of alcohol abuse: Cross-fostering analysis of adopted men. *Arch. Gen. Psychiat.* 38: 861-868 (1981).

(10) Cotton NS. The familial incidence of alcoholism: a review. *Q.J. Stud. Alcohol* 40: 89-116 (1979).

(11) Edwards P, Harvey C, Whitehead PC. Wives of alcoholics: A critical review and analysis. *Q.J. Stud. Alcohol* 34: 112-132 (1973).

(12) Fox R. *The alcoholic spouse.* Neurotic interaction in marriage: Chapter 15. (Edited by Eisenstein VW.) New York: Basic Books (1956).

(13) Futterman S. Personality trends in wives of alcoholics. *J. Psychiat. Social Work* 23: 37-41 (1953).

(14) Gaertner ML. *The Alcoholic Marriage: A Study of 15 Case Records and Pertinent Psychoanalytic Writings.* Thesis, New York School of Social Work: New York (1939).

(15) Goodwin DW, Schulsinger, F, Hermansen L et al. Alcohol problems in adoptees raised apart form alcoholic parents. *Arch. Gen. Psychiat.* 28: 238-243 (1973).

(16) Goodwin DW and Guze SB. Heredity & alcoholism. In *The Biology of Alcoholism Vol 3. Clinical Pathology.* Edited by Kissin B. & Begleiter H. New York: Plenum Press (1974).

(17) Haberman PW. Psychological test score changes for wives of alcoholics during periods of drinking and sobriety. *J. Clinical Psychology* 20: 230-232 (1964).

(18) Jackson JK. The adjustment of the family to the crisis of alcoholism. *Q.J. Stud. Alcohol* 15: 562-586 (1954).

(19) Jackson JK. Alcoholism and the family: Society, culture and drinking patterns. Edited by Pitmann DJ and Snyder CR. New York: Wiley (1962).

(20) Jacob T, Favolini A, Meisel S. et al. The alcoholic's spouse, children and family interactions: substantive findings and methodological issues. *Q.J. Stud. Alcohol* 39: 1231-1251 (1978).

(21) James JE, Goldman M. Behavior trends of wives of alcoholics. *Q.J. Stud. Alcohol* 32: 373-381 (1971).

(22) Kalashian MM. Working with the wives of alcoholics in an out-patient clinic setting. *Marriage and Family Living* 21: 130-133 (1959).

(23) Kaufman E. The future of family therapy of substance abusers. In *Substance Abuse and Family Therapy.* Edited by Kaufman, E. New York: Grune & Stratton (1985).

(24) Kaij L. *Alcoholism in Twins: Studies of the Etiology and Sequels of Abuse of Alcohol.* Stockholm:: Almquist & Wiksell (1960).

(25) Lemert EM. Dependency in married alcoholics. *Q.J. Stud. Alcohol* 23: 590-602 (1962).

(26) Lewis ML. The initial contact with wives of alcoholics. *Social Casework* 35: 8-14 (1954).

(27) Orford J. Alcoholism and marriage: the argument against specialism. *Q.J. Stud. Alcohol* 36: 1537-1560 (1975).

(28) Paolino TJ, McCrady BS. *The Alcoholic Marriage: Alternative Perspectives.*

New York: Grune & Stratton (1977).
(29) Paolino TJ, McCrady BS, Diamond J. Statistics on alcoholic marriages: an overview. *Int. J. Addict*: 1285-1294 (1978).
(30) Penick FD, Read MR, Crowley PA. Differentiation of alcoholics by family history. *Q.J. Stud. Alcohol* 39: 1945-1948 (1978).
(31) Rimmer J, Winokur G. The spouses of alcoholics: an example of assortative mating. *Dis. Nerv. Syst.* 33: 509-511 (1972).
(32) Saitoh S, Ikegami N, KAST (Kurihama Alcoholism Screening Test) and its applications. *Japan. J. Stud. Alcohol* 13: 229-237 (1978).
(33) Saitoh S. Alcohol dependence syndrome in clinical gerontology. Edited by Matsushita, M, Tokyo. Joho Kaihatsu Kenkyusho (1983) (in Japanese).
(34) Saitoh S. Clinical data on alcoholics visiting the alcoholism treatment unit of Kurihama Hospital in 1980. In *Handbook of Alcohol Problems*. Edited by Saitoh S et al. Tokyo: Kongo Shuppan Inc. (1984) (in Japanese).
(35) Saitoh S, Noguchi Y, Ikegami N. Report on the community-based program at the Setagaya Health Center. In *Biomedical Aspects of Alcohol and Alcoholism*. Edited by Kamada D. et al. Tokyo: Gendaikikakushitsu Publishing (1988).
(36) Steinglass P, Weiner S, Mendelson JH. A systems approach to alcoholics—a model and its clinical application. *Arch. Gen. Psychiat.* 24: 401-408 (1971).
(37) Steinglass P, Weiner S, Mendelson JH. Interactional issues as determinants of alcoholism. *Amer. J. Psychiat.* 128: 275-279 (1971).
(38) Steinglass P, Davis DI, Berenson D. In-hospital treatment of alcoholic couples. Paper presented at the APA 128th annual meeting, Anaheim, California (1975).
(39) Steinglass P. Experimenting with family treatment approches to alcoholism-1950-1975: A review. *Family Process* 15: 97-123 (1976).
(40) Steinglass P. An experimentl treatment program for alcoholic couples. *J. Stud. Alcohol* 40: 159-182 (1979).
(41) Wahlen T. Wives of alcoholics: four types observed in a family service agency. *Q.J. Stud. Alcohol* 14: 632-641 (1953).
(42) Winokur G, Reich T, Rimmer J. et al. Alcoholism III: diagnosis and familial psychiatric illness in 259 alcoholic probands. *Arch. Gen. Psychiat.* 23: 104-111 (1970).
(43) Wolin SJ, Steinglass P, Sendroff P. et al. Marital interaction during experimental intoxication and the relationship to family history. In: *Experimental Studies of Alcohol Intoxication and Withdrawal*. Edited by Gross M. New York: Plenum Press (1975).
(44) Zucker RA. Parental influences upon drinking patterns of their children. Alcoholism problems in women and children. Edited by Greenblatt M, Schuckit MA. New York: Grune & Stratton (1976).

Part IV: Discussion

(*Chairperson*) *Dr. Motoi Hayashida*: Thank you for those presentations. Are there any questions for either Dr. Steinglass or Dr. Nomura?

(*Chairperson*) *Professor Whittaker*: Perhaps I might start? Dr. Steinglass, I have a couple of questions about methodology. Did you consider what the effects of the observers were on the families? And secondly, were the families volunteers?

Professor Steinglass: This is a good starting question. We are often asked about the impact of observers upon families. Also, Dr. Nomura described a situation in which there were observers in a clinical setting and paid particular attention to the relationship between the family and the observing team as the therapy unfolded.

In training the observers in this system, one of the steps that we characteristically used was to have each observation team, after they had gone through initial training, come to *my* home and observe *my* family! What I found most useful about that was that I could see what it was like to be on the "observed" end of that dichotomy. At the time, my children were about the ages of seven and 10, or perhaps a little younger. What we found was that the first time we were observed it was very much a curiosity and we were clearly paying attention to the process of being observed. By the third observation session, the observers had "faded into the woodwork," as we say. We were able to treat them as if they were workers in the household, there to do a job, but not people that we had to interact with.

From a clinical point of view, what was particularly useful to us was that we found that, at least initially, the process of being observed made us more observant of ourselves. And I came away from that experience wondering about the ways in which research projects like the one I described to you have therapeutic value as well as research value. We were particularly impressed by this when we went back to study the same group of families two years later and found that, almost without exception, the alcoholic members of these families had stopped drinking. When we asked them what therapy programs they had been in that had brought this about, they said that they hadn't been in any therapy programs, that it was being in the research project that had been the major stimulus to the change in their family.

Thus, the growing interest in clinical interventions that have used aspects like observation teams can be thought of as extensions of research methodology into the clinical setting. We shouldn't assume there is a distance or a difference between doing systematic research and doing systematic clinical work in which one is paying very careful attention to the observations that you're making in a clinical situation.

Professor Whittaker: Second point had to do with volunteers. You're using a biased sampling, aren't you, because you're getting people who knew . . .

Professor Steinglass: These were all research volunteers. They were recruited for the study largely through advertising and, what we call in the States, Public Service Announcements on radio or television. The advertisement went something like this:

Is alcohol a problem in your family?
If so, you may be eligible for an important study at the George Washington University Medical Center! Please call the following number if you are interested.

That was the way we recruited our subjects. Therefore, this was not, by any means, a representative sample of families in which we tried to develop the sample in some systematic fashion. Nevertheless, there's a growing conviction among family researchers that the parallel in findings coming out of a number of these different studies—our studies, the studies of the Jacob group, and others—suggests that these are solid findings that deserve our attention.

(*Chairperson*) *Dr. Motoi Hayashida*: May I ask one question about your sampling? Did you have certain requirements about the family constellations, the number of family members, etc.?

Professor Steinglass: We worked only with families in which there were two spouses. That was a minimum: two spouses. We also worked with two-generation families, but we also had a number of childless couples in the studies.

One of the very severe problems or challenges in doing family interaction research is the difficulty in being able to develop samples that are homogeneous in terms of family characteristics. This has been particularly true in the United States. If you're looking for a sample that has a husband and wife, one or two children, first marriage, it sometimes seems there might be only three families left in the United States that actually meet those criteria! So we wind up having to relax these criteria as the study goes along. What we've been encouraged by is the finding that, when you work with heterogeneous groups of families and have an interesting idea about how to divide the sample of families into subgroups, then some of the most powerful findings come out of that process of subdivision. In contrast to some of the studies that were described yesterday where the focus was on individuals and all the data were collected from one person, making it possible to control for homegeneity of the sample—we've used this other approach and then have actually found that it has worked to our advantage in helping us understand the importance of family typology as a factor in the differential clinical course of alcoholism.

(*Chairperson*) *Dr. Motoi Hayashida*: Thank you. Does anyone have any questions for Dr. Nomura?

Question: Yes, I have three questions. The first one is related to the previous one, and concerns *agreement*. Family members have different expectations for the family therapy. What is the goal of family therapy? Unless it is clearly explained, then the problems will be worsened and this will lead to destruction of the family. So I'd like to know what agreement is reached with the family before the family therapy.

The second question: Who was the leader in the family sessions or the program?

The third question: After the family became independent and able to decide its own direction, you said that you felt the surrender of power and position of the family therapists. However, I believe the goal of the family session is the independence of the families. Therefore, I don't think you should feel the surrender or failure in the therapy. The throwing of beer at the husband is acting out and, I think, one example of the success of family therapy.

Doctor Nomura: To answer the latter questions first: We didn't feel surrender or failure because of the independence of the family. We wanted to *control* the family; that was our paradigm. However, we came to realize that that was impossible and we deviated from the paradigm; the independence or evolution of the family was not related to our feeling of failure or impasse.

Who was the leader of the family sessions? Well, I am an anthropologist; I am not the leader. PSY1 and PSY2 were both involved. PSY2 was involved in the designing of the program of the public health centers and PSY2 was involved in the very beginning of the family sessions, with the participation of PSY1 and myself. So there was no fixed leader in these family sessions.

As to agreement for the family sessions, I would like to ask Dr. Ichikawa to explain.

Dr. Ichikawa: Those family sessions were a part of the district program. Mr. J's wife came to the public health center, and asked about her husband's alcohol problem. That was the beginning of the start of the session. Mr. J was hospitalized. Meanwhile, we had a case conference about whether we were going to have family therapy or not. I was in charge of the hospitalized husband and I mentioned to him about our interest in offering family therapy to him and his family. He agreed to this. Also, his wife asked her sons about this and there was agreement.

Question: Whether it was successful or not, there must have been some kind of rationale for recommending drinking alcohol in the session. Would you explain some of the reasons why you did this?

Doctor Nomura: We had no reasons! The tenth session was the last session and it was very intensive and oppressive. We were looking for a way of changing and evolving, not only for the family but for us too. We felt *we* were stuck. There needed to be some radical shift, or action to break that pattern. But, of course, it is not proper to ask Mr. J to drink and thereby make Mrs. J the enabler again. We reversed that.

It is just like the alcohol connection that caused Mr. J to drink, but from his own volition. The idea of the social orientation regarding his family and other people *changed*. So, returning to your point, I don't think we had a clear, logical reason to do this.

Dr. Ichikawa: Let me supplement what Dr. Nomura stated. While it is not limited to family therapy, there are some changes in the therapies in clinical situations. There are two types: first-order change and second-order change. As to the first-order change, somehow we can predict the consequences. The second-order change cannot be predicted.

We were in the final session and we were in an impasse. We wanted to make a change. However, what we wanted was a second-order change, which is unpredictable. Of course, the family has a certain direction and has its own evolution, and the family therapy session was involved in that direction. We wanted to do something different, to introduce some changes in that evolution. Alcohol had played a very important role in this family's dynamics; therefore, we utilized alcohol.

In 1973, Dr. Steinglass conducted a study on couples. The research environment at that study permitted the drinking of alcohol. I think that was a very important study. In the case of A.A., alcohol is not permitted in the sessions. However, our study was completely different and we wanted to have some kind of changes in our situation.

(*Chairperson*) *Dr. Motoi Hayashida*: Do we have any questions for Drs. Ames and Saitoh?

Question: This isn't really a question, but more a comment on Dr. Ames' work, tying in a bit with Dr. Steinglass' work.

Living in Japan and being married to a Japanese man, I get firsthand experience of the high-risk factors you described. What you said for heavy drinkers is the *norm* for Japan. There are no friends outside of work, except if you meet old high-school or college friends once or twice a year. Moreover, after-work intimacy is encouraged by drinking at bars. It is very important to be able to ultimately share your grievances over alcohol, because anything you say when you drink is forgiven. So, it's a forum for Japanese workers under stress to finally relieve some tension. Moreover, it's *required*. If your boss says, "We'll go and have a drink," you don't say no, you *do* it.

How that ties in with the marriage satisfaction of heavy, steady drinkers and their wives is interesting; you learn to cope with your husband coming home late and drunk. First, with anger, and then with resignation. It's the way the *society* is, you can't change it. We're not talking about a company; it is *life* here in Japan.

So you develop a routine as a wife with kids, and you learn to get your kids' schooling done and bath and bed. You may hope he comes home after 10.00 p.m. so you can get two hours to yourself. And if he does come home earlier, you don't want him! You give him messages as a wife: "Can't you go out?" and "Yes, you're going out—great!"

So, a drunk husband after a long commute and a 14-hour day is easy to handle! No sexual demands. You get him in the bath, you put him to bed, he passes out; it's great! He brings his paycheck home, it's fine! *That's* why there's so high a percentage of sexual disturbances! There isn't much sex with a drunk guy like that. Sex is over the drink, flirting with the "mama-san," the bar lady, that's the sex; it's all in the mind.

(*Chairperson*) *Dr. Motoi Hayashida*: I see about one-third of the men in this audience are smiling. The others are *not* smiling! (*Laughter among audience*)

Dr. Ames: I'd like to respond to that. You know, when you give a paper like this, there's so much rich data that you haven't time to present. I also interviewed the wives, and we're in the process of developing papers about the wives of the heavy drinkers.

I don't think the situation you've just described is unique to Japan, I don't know the percentages of heavy drinkers in Japan. In our factory of 6,000 people, I think it was 28% or so who were heavy drinkers, which really is a large percentage because that's higher than the norm for heavy drinkers in the United States.

The wives' stories of their experience with heavy-drinking husbands were very similar to the account you gave. Men who work the "swing shift" between 3.00 p.m. to midnight sometimes drink with co-workers until four or five in the morning!

In the same way you described here in Japan, it is also true in the United States, or at least in this factory, that when a supervisor asks you to drink with him, you feel obligated to drink with him, especially if it's your foreman.

Of course, the stories from the children in our families were the most interesting and, in some cases, pathetic. The family lifestyle that emerges with a heavy-drinking parent becomes the norm for them; heavy-drinking lifestyles tend to go from one generation to the next. It's so much the norm that they think this is the way things are. This becomes evident from answers to questions about the relationships with their fathers or the things they do with their fathers: "Does your father help you with your homework? What do you do with him on Saturdays?" When I asked a young adult what he did with his father, he said, "One time, when I was 12 years old, my father took me fishing." And he thought it wsa remarkable that his father took him fishing one time, when he was 12 years old! Other than that, he couldn't recall any special activity with his father. The lack of involvement of heavy-drinking fathers in family life was prevalent among that group. Of course, the moderate drinkers' lives are different. They do have more involvement with their wives and children. Perhaps you were speaking of the minority of heavy drinkers here in Japan?

Question: I found Dr. Saitoh's presentation extremely interesting. One of the things I found terribly disturbing was the statistics at the beginning of our booklet, as well as the statistics he mentioned that only two to three percent of Japanese are alcoholic!

I find that number just unbelievable, because I ride the Tokyo train system every night and that certainly is not what I see going on around me! I think that what is happening here in Japan is that the people who are labeled "alcoholic" are those who have fallen out of the fabric of society and become so *chronically* unable to work and carry on the Japanese tradition that they are then seen as outcasts and labeled "alcoholic." The people who are carrying on their lives and at least managing to work are considered only "heavy drinkers."

I know that in the States, where I do extensive work in this area, the people I ride the trains with in Japan every night would be considered alcoholic. Their behavior and the marriage patterns that the previous questioner has described are very alcoholic patterns!

I see Japan where we in the States were 20 years ago, with so much denial! I hope you can take your heads out of the sand before it is too late and see the problems that alcohol produces in the family and will produce in your country! And perhaps you can then avoid some of the things that have subsequently happened to us. You really don't want to go through the problems we are experiencing now with this disease!

Dr. Saitoh: As to the two to three percent you mention, I should like to comment on the incidence of alcoholism in Japan.

It depends on the *definition* of the disease. The definition can be different from culture to culture. The drinking pattern in Japanese culture is *clearly* different from that of European countries or that of the United States. It is quite natural to have that kind of difference. The drinking pattern of European countries or the United States is not the only drinking pattern in the world. The Japanese people are agricultural people from their origin; as the seasons change, many people will get together and have a festival and to drink with each other. And many Japanese people will go to sleep after they've drunk a lot. Of course, some people will go on to become binge-drinkers, but it is quite rare that fights or violence occur after heavy drinking.

This kind of drinking continued after the urbanization of Japan, and many males drink every night after work is over. But this is not a problem of the drinking itself, but rather a problem of the relationship between the husband and wife. There is some intermediate place between the workplace and the home and there is a peer relationship which is centered around drinking. This is a very specific characteristic of Japanese culture.

Why do many males who have wives and children go to bars and other drinking places? This may be very difficult for foreigners to understand. However, Japanese wives understand why their husbands drink after work. Not all, but some Japanese males do go to "mama-san," the bar ladies, and when they go to such places, their childlike needs are often pampered to and they find their mothers' characteristics in the hostesses, enabling them to play the child's role. Once they return home, they know they will have to play the father's and husband's roles. Since they are rather reluctant to take such roles, they would rather remain at bars or other drinking places. These kinds of cultural, psychological problems should be, of course, a topic for future research!

As to the figure of two to three percent of Japanese being alcoholics, this is a consistent figure according to the epidemiological study we have designed to discover the level of alcoholism. In the United States they have the M.A.S.T. test. We have in Japan the equivalent K.A.S.T. test—a method devised by the Kurihama National Hospital for alcoholism. We also have an interview per 1000 subjects and so this should be quite a reasonable means for discovering the percentage of alcoholism.

Question: In regard to cultural and historical aspects, what is important to remember, I believe, is that alcoholism isn't born overnight, it takes time to develop. Because of that, children and family members are influenced. Therefore, it is necessary, I believe, to identify the problems at a very *early* stage in order to come up with appropriate measures. I think this is most important.

Dr. Saitoh: I would like to comment further on this point. Of course, to come up with measures to cope with alcoholism at earlier stages is what we have been doing for many years. Dr. Grant from the WHO and Dr. Nomura both indicated that the community activities of the public health centers have been making progress in this regard. Foremost are the short-term programs which offer a lot of assistance to women and to wives. In the past, therapy focused upon hospitalization, but I think such community-level activities are also effective. This sort of brief family intervention has been conducted and wives who have undergone treatment as family members have been able to reflect upon their behavior as wives of alcoholics and their roles as wife and caretaker of the husband. I think they have been starting to change *themselves*.

Question: Dr. Saitoh, you mentioned that daughters tend to be protective and they tend to marry alcoholic men. But are there many cases where the opposite occurs—that they most certainly would never marry alcoholic men? What data are there to support such instances?

Dr. Saitoh: Daughters do sometimes feel an affinity to their drinking fathers. However, there are other types of daughters who would not wish to marry drinking men. This is true, but in the long run some daughters find that the husband they married because he didn't drink later goes on to become an alcoholic. So, we cannot discuss only those daughters who decide not to marry men who go on to become alcoholics.

PART V

THERAPEUTIC APPROACHES TO THE ALCOHOLIC FAMILY

To begin this section, Professor Motoi Hayashida reviews and evaluates the family therapy approach from the standpoint of a psychiatrist in the clinical field. He relates work with adolescent children brought up in Japanese alcoholic family systems, and focuses on their physical and psychological pathology.

Three more reports outline concrete therapeutic approaches: Dr. Nakamura, a psychiatrist, and Ms. Endo, a social worker, indicate the value of their counseling program conducted in private practice in Tokyo. Next, Dr. Kazumi Nishio, a clinical psychologist, details the case study of one of her clients from an alcoholic family. She indicates the reasons for introducing various therapeutic interventions and charts their effectiveness. Finally, Dr. Claudia Black, a clinician working with Adult Children of Alcoholics (ACA) in the United States, gives insight into the problems manifest within an alcoholic family and the complex survival roles played out by each family member within the alcoholic system.

14

Our Experiences in Family Therapy

Motoi Hayashida, M.D., Sc.D.

The author presents a commentary on the concept of alcoholism as a family disease. He then argues that not all problems affect the rest of the system, so that solution of such a problem need not involve the rest of the system. Similarly, not every problem is definable by forces within the system and may be subject to forces from outside. The author provides a few caveats for the therapist since, on entering the system in any capacity, the therapist takes the risk of becoming part of this ecological system. Various forms of family therapy are reported in favorable terms, but caution is advised. Comprehensive treatment of the patient and his/her family addresses those issues under the familial influence, as well as those issues relatively independent of such influence. One should not be blinded by a single-minded approach in the real world. Lastly, the author briefly touches on the state of art in family treatment at the Philadelphia VA Medical Center.

1. ALCOHOLISM AS A FAMILY DISEASE

Alcoholism affects not only the individual who suffers from it, but also those who live with him.* Conversely, it is possible that a dysfunctional family may perpetuate the alcoholism. For example, if the family is an emotionally closed system and attempts to keep the problem of alcoholism within the family's boundary, its impact may be quite severe upon members of the family and the alcoholic himself. The more psychologically vulnerable individual members of the family are, the more severely will they be affected by abusive drinking in the family. The modes in which each member of the

---

*The alcoholic is referred to as "he" and the nonalcoholic as "she" in this article, but the genders of these individuals can be either male or female.

family will be affected differ and are determined not only by the characteristics of the stress and each member's mode of defense but also by her role within the existing family structure.

One basic way of dealing with alcoholism in the family is for the spouse to overidentify with the abuser and internalize his psychological and behavioral disturbances, which then may lead her to develop depression and extreme anxiety. On the other hand, as a consequence of overcompensation for her intensified sense of insecurity, she may strive to be a superachiever at home, at work, or in school. But when the alcohol-abusing individual gives up drinking and shows signs of recovery, this forms a new source of conflict for her. With loss of her previous focus, she may experience a profound sense of emptiness and anger.

Another member may choose to project her own preexisting emotional vulnerability out onto the alcohol-abusing member and engage actively in a caretaking or "scapegoating" role for the latter. By so doing, she may temporarily experience a reduction of her own preexisting anxiety, accomplish a sense of control over the alcoholic, and even find the entire experience fulfilling. This is the type of individual who is commonly referred to as "an enabler." She can, however, become hypercritical of the alcoholic, causing him to have a relapse of drinking, and then come to the rescue for him, thereby unconsciously "enabling" him to continue his drinking.

With this type of individual, the drama revolves around the alcoholic member while she may remain completely devoid of insight into her own personal difficulties. Not surprisingly, then, it can be extremely threatening to this type of individual should the alcohol-abusing member decide to give up drinking and begin to recover. If this happens, she could no longer blame the alcoholic for her own problems, or take care of her projected (or triangulated) problems through the alcoholic, but would have to face her own emotional vulnerabilities.

With some individuals, the modes of dealing with alcoholism may not be fixed and these two modes of responses discussed above may be employed alternately, depending upon a variety of factors such as the magnitude of the disturbances of the alcohol-abusing member and the psychological strength of family members at a given moment. This situation may lead family members to develop ambivalent attitudes towards the alcoholic member.

There are a number of other emotional and behavioral responses among adults and children alike that may arise in the alcoholic family. These symptoms are manifestations of complex but recognizable maladaptive responses. They may be psychological (denial of problems, depression, anxiety, shame, guilt, etc.), communicational (emotional withdrawal, lack of or ineffective communications, frequent verbal fighting, etc.), behavioral (sexual abuse, physical violence, substance abuse, delinquency, forced pseudo-maturation, perfectionism, etc.), and other symptoms (sleep disorders, etc.).

So long as abusive drinking takes place in the the family, affected members of the family will attempt to adapt to it—rarely, however, realistically, and more often detrimentally. The failure to deal with it realistically will often result in the perpetuation of the problem of abusive drinking in the family and will often lead to various serious long-term consequences. Some of these problems may even be handed over to the next generation. Problems associated with so-called "adult children of alcoholic parents" attest to this. Quite logically, then, one reaches the realization that alcoholism may truly be a "family disease."

2. IDENTIFICATION OF PROBLEMS IN THE FAMILY IN THE THERAPEUTIC CONTEXT

How we conceptualize clinical problems that we see in our alcoholic patients, their family members, or their whole family will have significant therapeutic implications. The opening section of this article has highlighted the fact that many of the problems associated with the problem of alcohol abuse in the family are not simply the problems of the alcohol-abusing member, but involve two or more members, or even the whole family, in such an intricate manner that one's problems are linked with others' problems. This is the core concept of alcoholism as a family disease.

However, not all problems we encounter are shared by all members of the family or even alcohol-related. Even if one considers that all alcohol-related problems are theoretically shared by all members in an ecological sense, one still needs to examine the specific nature and extent of the involvement of the problems in the family.

Some problems are inherently associated with the family as a social institution. Thus, one might consider them "institutional problems." Problems associated with the formation, development, and dissolution of a family are such problems. Individuals exist as members in this institution and, likewise, are faced with their own evolving tasks and problems. These problems may or may not be related to the problem of alcoholism.

Cultural, ethnic, and gender problems will compound the clinical picture of the problems presented. Here, therapeutic implications go beyond the scope of the field of alcoholism.

Psychological problems associated with alcohol abuse and alcoholism have gained much attention in recent years and have produced a number of popularized terms to describe not only characteristics of emotional states, response patterns, and behaviors, but also techniques of therapeutic interventions.

"Enabling," "healing the child within," "adult children of alcoholics," "co-dependency," "co-alcoholic," "distancing," "detachment," "see-saw phenomenon"[8] are examples. These terms have contributed to the identification of some of the key elements involved in the respective characteristics of emotional states, behavioral responses, and therapeutic mechanisms, which in turn have benefited both professionals and public alike, but may have misled them to oversimplify the problems involved, on the one hand, and give the impression, on the other hand, that alcoholics have uniquely alcoholism-specific problems that must be dealt with by uniquely alcoholism-specific therapeutic techniques.

Apart from a long list of psychological and behavioral dispositions and responses to the problem of abusive drinking in the family, there are some primary diagnosable psychiatric conditions among the alcoholic and his family members. Identifying these problems early in treatment would be extremely important. The problems range from personality disorders such as antisocial personality, to major psychiatric conditions such as depression, schizophrenias, and anxiety disorder. Major depression is particularly common in female members of the alcoholic family. These are discrete diagnoses defined in the American Psychiatric Association's Diagnostic Statistical Manual III, Revised. The therapist should be aware of these conditions in the therapeutic context.

One may also conceptualize the problems of the alcoholic family in terms of "family reactivity types," rather than focus on problems or specific patterns of interactional behavior in the family. This has been advocated by Kaufman and Pattison.[6],[7] They acknowledge that these family types each have different needs for treatment.

Four family reactivity types are described. The first type is called "the functional family system, the family with an alcoholic member," and is characterized by relatively isolated drinking behavior by an alcoholic spouse, leaving the rest of the family functionally almost intact. Kaufman notes that this type is equivalent to Steinglass's "stable wet" family. There is, however, a good deal of denial and emotional isolation in this type of family.

The second type is called "the neurotic enmeshed family system, the alcoholic family," and is characterized by "enmeshed" (or interlocked) relationships among family members in which communication is often not direct among them, and everyone feels guilty and responsible for each other, particularly for the alcoholic and his drinking. Kaufman states that such marriages are often highly competitive; that the partners see themselves giving in to each other; that the one who gives in most loses his sense of self and is vulnerable to drinking; and that these spouses find their lives totally preoccupied with the alcoholic and have been labeled "co-alcoholic."

Kaufman and Pattison's third type is called "the disintegrated family system, family separation and isolation" and is characterized by progressive deterioration from a reasonable vocational function and family life to the loss of job and self-respect, with associated family instability and, finally, separation and alienation from the family. They note that this type of alcoholic usually presents at hospitals or clinics without any family or any recent family contact and that usually he requires immediate physical support in terms of room, food and clothing.

The fourth and last type is called "the absent family system, the long-term isolated alcoholic" and is characterized by the total loss of family of origin early in the drinking career. Kaufman notes that such persons usually have never married or have had brief, fleeting relationships. They may have relatives or in-laws with whom they maintain perfunctory contact, but rarely have close friendships, and their social or vocational skills are minimal.

"Mainstream family systems approaches" championed by Steinglass and others[9] focus on the problems of an alcoholic family as those of a behavioral system organized with alcoholism as a central organizing principle. Family systems approaches have been responsible for generating a rich fund of information both on functional and dysfunctional families through their unique methodological approaches. However, much work still seems to remain to be done so that this information can be utilized by the clinician in his day-to-day clinical practice.

Bohman, Cloninger et al.'s studies[1],[2],[3],[4] of adoptees in Sweden have identified two types of genetic predisposition to alcoholism—milieu-limited (Type I) and male-limited (Type II). These two groups of alcoholics may require different treatment goals and approaches. If so, identification of these alcoholics become an important future clinical issue.

3. RELATIONSHIP OF THE THERAPIST TO THE PATIENT AND HIS FAMILY

A word needs to be said about the relationship of the therapist with the alcoholic and his family. Obviously, certain types of relationships will enhance treatment outcomes and others may sabotage them. The therapeutic relationship that the clinician forms with the alcoholic and his family is quite different from the traditional client-therapist relationship.[10]

In the traditional relationship, the therapist and client ally themselves to fight against the client's problem. Here, the client's problem now becomes the client-and-therapist's common problem. But in the case of the treatment of the alcoholic, the situation may require a different approach. The traditional approach would remind us of the familiar situation that often happens in the alcoholic family. This is a déjà vu. It is striking to see how much this situation resembles the situation where the spouse of the alcoholic has decided that her husband's problem is her problem and has come to the rescue mission for him. When the alcoholic husband relapses unexpectedly despite her concern and interventions, it affects the alcoholic and the spouse alike, with various feelings including anger, disappointment, revenge, guilt, and overcompensation. At times, this serves, in fact, to perpetuate the problem of alcoholism.

In the case of the therapist-patient relationship, this kind of reaction can take the form of countertransference. This is exemplified by a case in which a resident physician demonstrated his irate feelings when he found his alcoholic patient lying in one of the hospital ward beds, the very morning after he discharged him. After this alcoholic left the hospital, he drank heavily and returned to the hospital, whereupon the night on-call physician had decided to readmit him to the same ward. What ensued was sad. This patient was embarrassed in public by the resident physician's outburst of anger, which the doctor obviously was unable to control, packed up his belongings and walked off the ward, almost unnoticed. Guilt on the part of this resident physician after his dramatic display of anger was evident by the way he covered his head with his hands. Everything was over by then.

The point here is that it would be counterproductive if one must rely on one's patients and their family for one's sense of career success and well-being. One needs to dissociate oneself from the success or failure of one's patients and their families. When the therapist provides his therapeutic support to the alcoholic patient, it will be directed not so much to whether or not he has maintained abstinence from alcohol, as to his sincere efforts to reach his own goals. Nor must one permit the patient to develop dependency on the individual therapist, but rather on the treatment programs of a facility, and, if the patient so desires, on more permanent support organizations such as AA, Al-Anon, etc.

To allow the alcoholic and family to develop false expectations from the therapist, and then let them down when they return to seek help would be disastrous. Thus, from the beginning of therapy, it would appear sensible to let them know about what they can and cannot expect from the individual therapist. Also, one should discourage forming a lasting therapeutic alliance. It is a matter of simple prevention of the formation of an unproductive countertransference and a matter of maintenance of a detached therapeutic effectiveness.

Gurman and Kniskern[5] have identified a set of therapist (as opposed to technique) factors that appear to be predictably associated with poor marital and family therapy outcomes: "The available evidence points to a composite picture of deterioraiton in marital-family therapy being facilitated by a therapist with poor relationship skills who directly attacks 'loaded' issues and family members' defenses very early in treatment, fails to intervene in or interpret intrafamily confrontation in ongoing treatment, and does little to structure and guide the opening of therapy or to support family members. Such a style is even more likely to be countertherapeutic with patients who have weak ego-defenses or feel threatened by the nature or very fact of being in treatment."

4. FAMILY THERAPY STRATEGIES

The most pertinent question seems to be what would be the best method of treating the alcoholic and his family. The next question would be whether or not there are alternate methods of treatment that would be comparable in effectiveness but less costly. These questions, however, are not answerable in reality unless one defines the questions in specific terms.

There are reports to indicate that some treatment approaches seem to enhance existing treatment outcomes. Some reports appear to address multiple outcome measures in contrast to one measure such as abstinence. Outcome studies of family therapy are still in their infancy. In general, involvement of the family, whether they are the indexed patient's spouse, children, or the entire family, seems to improve treatment outcome. It is not the intent of this article to review the family therapy outcomes.

Technical factors in contrast to therapist's factors that may adversely affect treatment of the alcoholic and his family include insufficient appraisal of psychiatric problems of individual members of the family. Some alcoholics may be extremely strongly bonded, often dependently or symbiotically, to either parents or spouse, and often react violently or become suicidal when forced to separate through a therapeutic intervention. An example is a middle-aged alcoholic male tragically ending his life by lying across the railroad track and getting run over by a train. This incident was precipitated when his wife rejected him at a critical time. Another middle-aged male, also an alcoholic, with a borderline personality disorder with paranoid tendencies, made repeated threatening telephone calls to his treatment team believing that he was under pressure from the staff to break off his ties with his aging mother with whom he had long maintained a symbiotic relationship.

Depression is extremely common among female spouses of alcoholics and often needs to be treated with antidepressant medications. Sometimes, this may be secondary to the spouse also being a heavy drinker. Therapeutic intervention here needs to be extremely tactful. It seems best to leave her alone for several months and simply encourage the primary alcoholic to concentrate on his own recovery efforts before a possible intervention may be planned.

Future improvement of family therapy depends a good deal on well-designed clinical research. It is obvious that if some treatment method is effective without doubt, any elaborate research project would not be necessary. However, such a situation is rare. The less clear-cut the efficacy of a treatment measure, the more careful and larger the research project need to be. Research projects ought to be designed in such a way that some credible and clinically useful conclusions could be obtained at the conclusion of the projects. Cost factors involved in a treatment method will need to be considered as they continue to be a critical factor in this age of cost-containment.

Elucidation of clinically useful typologies of alcoholism may shed light on more rational treatment approaches to the problem involved. As mentioned earlier, Cloninger[4] advocates different treatment goals for Types I and II alcoholics, which is promising.

5. CURRENT STATUS OF OUR FAMILY TREATMENT

At the Philadelphia VA Medical Center, one of the major alcohol and drug treatment and research centers in the U.S., we have been making serious efforts to improve our treatment effectiveness, including family treatment. I have chosen the term "family treatment," because our programs do not currently limit ourselves to traditional family therapy approaches, but rather involve a variety of family-related treatment approches. All new patients will have their families evaluated by one of the two social workers. Basic data then are collected, which include their living conditions, family constellations, extended family arrangements, marital history, cohabitation information, early history of family of origin, familial history of alcoholism and substance abuse as well as of psychiatric disorders, history of delinquency, legal and social agency involvements, history of attendance at AA, Al-Anon, Alateen, and other self-help groups, religious affiliations and current church activities, status of children, etc. All patients are systematically evaluated for family treatment interventions and many of them enter treatment with social workers. Referrals to social workers for patients already enrolled in the programs are made by primary case managers for a variety of reasons.

Our patient population is primarily of low socioeconomic class and most of the patients and their families belong to Kaufman and Pattison's[6] third reactivity type, with some families belonging to their second and fourth types. Kaufman[7] notes that "The use of family intervention might seem irrelevant in such a case (the Disintegrated Family System — Family Separation and Isolation). However, many of these marriages and families have fallen apart only after years of severe alcoholic abuse. Furthermore, there is often only "pseudoindividuation" of the alcoholic from marital, family, and kinship ties. These families cannot and should not reconstitute during the early phases of rehabilitation. Thus, the early phases of treatment should focus primarily on the individual alcoholic. When abstinence and personal stability have been achieved over several months, more substantive family explorations can be initiated."

He further states that "family intervention is not aimed at treatment of the alcoholism, since we must assume that meaningful family interaction can be considered only after abstinence and major steps toward personal rehabilitation have been achieved. Rather, the focus of family therapy will have to be on the exploration of the ruptured roles and relationships and the establishment of new family, rules and roles. In contrast to the 'here-and-now' approach used with the enmeshed neurotic family (the second type), it is necessary to review the past and plan for the future with the disintegrated family system."

This author concurs with Kaufman's view for this group of patients and what we have been doing for our patients is for the most part consistent with his views. Family sessions tend to be five or seven sessions for the majority of cases, but there are cases which have been followed for more than a year. For the entire family to attend a session, then, is rather an exception, but most frequently sessions are conjoint couples with one or two children attending. Nearly 80% of appointments are kept by these individuals.

External self-help groups such as Al-Anon, Alateen, Adult Children of Alcoholic Parents, etc., are regularly attended by our patients and their families and complement our programs well.

In addition, Family Night held once a month provides families and friends of the patients an opportunity to meet with the staff. Educational lectures, discussion groups, question-answer sessions, and films and videotapes are featured. This program has been well attended.

Furthermore, family problems are often dealt with by alcoholics attending any of the three levels of group therapy sessions (2-3 times a week for up to 2 years) or patients attending the Day Hospital Program (6 hours a day, 5 days a week for a month). Psychodrama sessions are conducted whenever appropriate during group therapy sessions, in dealing with family or interpersonal issues.

Our approaches to family therapy are at this point of time summarized as eclectic.

REFERENCES

(1) Bohman, M; Sigvardsson, S; Cloninger, CR. Maternal inheritance of alcohol abuse. *Archives of General Psychiatry.* 38:965-969 (1981).

(2) Bohman, M; Cloninger, CR; von Knorring, AL; Sigvardsson, S. An adoption study of somatoform disorders. III. Cross-fostering analysis and genetic relationship to alcoholism and criminality. *Archives of General Psychiatry.* 41:872-878 (1984).

(3) Cloninger, CR; Bohman, M: Sigvardsson, S. Inheritance of alcohol abuse. *Archives of General Psychiatry.* 38:861-868 (1981).

(4) Cloninger, CR. Genetic and environmental factors in the development of alcoholism. *Journal of Psychiatric Treatment and Evaluation.* 5:487-496 (1983).

(5) Gurman, AS; Kniskern, DP. Deterioration in marital and family therapy: Empirical, clinical and conceptual issues. *Family Process.* 17:3-20 (1978).

(6) Kaufman, E; Pattison, KL. Differential methods of family therapy in the treatment of alcoholism. *J. Studies on Alcohol.* 42:951-971 (1981).

(7) Kaufman, E. The current state of family intervention in alcoholism treatment. In: *Advances in the Psychosocial Treatment of Alcoholism*, by Galanter, M; Pattison EM. Monograph series of the American Psychiatric Press., Inc. 1-15 (1984).

(8) Saitoh, S. Alcoholism and the family. In: *Alcohol Clinical Handbook* (Jap.) Ed. by Saitoh, S; Takagi, T. Tokyo: Kongo Shuppan, 376-397 (1982).

(9) Steinglass, P. with Bennett, LA; Wolin, SJ; Reiss, D. *The Alcoholic Family*, pp. 381. New York: Basic Books (1987).

(10) Vaillant, GE. Dangers of Psychotherapy in the Treatment of Alcoholism. In: *Dynamic Approaches to the Understanding and Treatment of Alcoholism*, edited by Bean, MH; Zinberg, NE. 36-54. New York: Free Press (1981).

15

Treatment of Psychiatric Illnesses in Adolescents with Alcoholic Parents

Kenji Suzuki, M.D.

Hiroaki Kohno, M.D.

*Three studies were performed on the treatment of psychiatric ill-
nesses in adolescents with alcoholic parents in Japan. (1) One outlined the problems of children with alcoholic parents in Japan.
Many emotional problems were found in children with alcoholic
fathers without divorces, and they also showed related psychosomatic and adaptation disorders. Many cases of child abuse, delinquency and school phobia were observed among children from
alcoholic families with a high divorce rate. (2) In a survey of psychiatric illnesses in adolescents, many cases of borderline personality disorders were found among adolescents with alcoholic
parents. (3) Treatment of psychiatric illnesses in 24 adolescents
with alcoholic fathers was discussed, and it was found that resolv-
ing their borderline personality organization and aggression, as
well as the strong conflict with their fathers, is the basic principle
of such treatment, and that family therapy is also important for
alcoholic families.*

I. INTRODUCTION

It is well known that children with alcoholic parents have various problems,
and many studies have been performed on such problems including those
by Newell[23] and Nylander.[13] In Japan, only the research team at the Kurihama National Hospital, including the author, is studying children with alcoholic parents. Knowledge concerning such children is lacking and measures
to help them are insufficient in Japan.

In this paper, the problems facing children with alcoholic parents in Japan
are first outlined, followed by a description of the characteristics of psychiatric

illnesses in adolescents with alcoholic parents. Treatment of such illnesses is also discussed.

Three studies are included in this paper. The first consists of a summary of two studies on children with alcoholic parents which have already been reported.[28],[29] One was a study on children of alcoholic male parents without divorces admitted to Kurihama National Hospital, and the other was a study on children with alcoholic parents under the care of a Child Guidance Center. The second study involves psychiatric research on psychiatric illnesses of adolescents with alcoholic parents who were among the adolescents treated at Kurihama National Hospital. The third study is on the treatment of psychiatric illnesses in adolescents with alcoholic fathers.

II. SUBJECTS AND METHODS

Part 1

The A group consisted of 107 children with nondivorced alcoholic fathers admitted to Kurihama National Hospital over a period of 13 months in 1985 and 1986. These children ranged in age from 4 to 18, and the study was conducted by interviewing their mothers. These interviews focused on the home life of the children, their mental and physical health, and their adaptation to society.

The C group consisted 107 control children from families with no alcohol-related problems living in Yokosuka City. Their age range was also 4-18 and the survey was conducted in the same way as in the A group.

The B group consisted of 34 children with parents with alcohol-related problems who were cared for at a Child Guidance Center over a 16 month period in 1985 and 1986. The age range was 4 to 17, and these 34 children accounted for 32% of the 106 children surveyed. The survey was conducted by interviewing the case workers. The contents of the survey were the same as those for the A group. The alcohol-related problems of the parents were based on the WHO concept.

The home life, the mental and physical health of the children, and their adaptation to society were compared among the A, B and C groups.

Part 2

The subjects were adolescents with psychiatric illnesses treated at the Kurihama National Hospital. They ranged in age from 11 to 25. The survey period was four years from 1984 through 1987. They consisted of 31 adolescents with alcoholic parents among the 254 examined during this period. Family life and the diseases concerned were compared between the alcohol group of 31 patients with alcoholic parents and the nonalcohol group of 223 patients without alcoholic parents. The traditional names were used for the psychiatric diseases diagnosed in the adolescents, but the DSM-III concept of borderline personality disorders was used. The number of diagnoses was limited to within three.

Part 3

Twenty-four cases which could be observed for at least one year were selected from among the adolescents with psychiatric diseases with alcoholic parents treated by the author over a 7-year period. All of these 24 subjects had alcoholic fathers. The psychological and behavioral characteristics and the problems encountered in the treatment of these psychiatric illnesses, as well as the methods of family therapy for the alcoholic families, were analyzed.

III. RESULTS AND DISCUSSION

1. Outline of the Problems of Children with Alcoholic Parents in Japan

Tables 1 to 4 show a comparison among the A group (children with alcoholic fathers without divorces), the B group (children from families with alcohol-related problems who were cared for at a Child Guidance Center) and the C group (control children).

Table 1 is a general comparison between the A and C groups. There were 107 children in both groups and the average age was 13.5. The C group had slightly more males, and there were no divorces in the 62 families in both groups. The socioeconomic class was significantly lower in the A group (X^2 test, $p < 0.01$).

Table 2 shows comparison of the mental and physical problems and the social adaptation of the children in the A and C groups. There were many more emotional disorders in the A group than in the C group; 31% vs. 3%, a significant difference (X^2 test, $p < 0.01$). The emotional disorders included aggression, hypersensitivity, anxiety, fear and depression. The A group also showed significantly more behavioral disorders, 12% vs. 4% (X^2 test, $P < 0.01$). The behavioral disorders included tic, restlessness and violence. There were also significantly more neurotic symptoms in the A group; 19% vs. 8% (X^2 test, $p < 0.05$). These neurotic symptoms included the psychosomatic syndrome (headache, abdominal pain, nausea, and diarrhea), neurosis, and eating disorders. Developmental disorders were significantly more common in the A group; 22% vs. 8% (X^2 test, $p < 0.01$). The developmen-

TABLE 1.

Outline of A Group (Children of Hospitalized Nondivorced Alcoholic Fathers) and C Group (Control Children)

	A group	*C group*
Children		
Number	107	107
boys	54	67
girls	53	40
Age range	4-18	4-18
Average age	13.5	13.5
Families		
Number	62	62
Ratio of broken families	0	0
Socioeconomic class**		
high & middle	48%	97%
low	52%	3%

A group vs. C group ** $p < 0.01$

TABLE 2.

Comparison of Psychosomatic Symptoms between A Group and C Group

Psychosomatic symptoms	*A group*	*C group*
Emotional disorders**	31 (%)	3 (%)
Behavioral disorders*	13	4
Neurotic symptoms*	19	8
School phobia	4	4
Other school difficulties	13	5
Developmental disorders**	22	8
Delinquency	5	3
Oral difficulties	21	20
Allergies	21	17

A group vs. C group ** $p < 0.01$ * $p < 0.05$

tal disorders included premature infancy, developmental retardation, and mental retardation. There were no significant differences between the A and C groups in school phobia, other school difficulties (isolation, victim of violence, rule violations), delinquency (police problems, drug abuse), oral difficulties (thumb-sucking, nail biting, obesity) and allergies (asthma, allergic dermatitis, rhinitis).

From Tables 1 and 2, it was evident that children with alcoholic fathers show more emotional disorders, behavioral disorders, neurotic symptoms and developmental disorders than the controls.

Table 3 shows a general comparison between the A and B groups, which

TABLE 3.

General Comparison between A Group and B Group
(Children of Alcoholic Families in a Child Guidance Center)

	A group	B group
Children		
Number	107	34
boys	54	19
girls	53	15
Age range	4-18	4-17
Average age	13.5	12.8
Families		
Number	62	32
Presence of parent in home		
both present	100 (%)	25 (%)
one present	0	41
one natural, one step	0	25
other	0	9
Socioeconomic class		
high & middle	48 (%)	44 (%)
low	52	56

consisted of 107 and 34 children, respectively. The average ages were 13.5 and 12.8. There were 62 and 32 families, respectively, and major differences in the family conditions. None of the families in the A group had experienced divorces, but there were many broken families in the B group. Only 25% of the families in the B group had no divorces. Single parent families accounted for 41%, families with remarriages for 25%, and other types of families, (children and grandparents, children only) for 9%. There was no difference between the two groups in socioeconomic class. Among the 32 families in the B group with alcohol-related problems, the source of these problems was the real father in 23, the real mother in five, the real mother and father in three and the stepfather in three.

Table 4 shows a comparison of the children's problems in the A and B groups. A major difference was seen in emotional disorders between the A and C groups, but there was no difference between the A and B groups (35% vs. 34%). However, in the B group, there were high frequencies for school phobia (24%), delinquency (44%), and developmental disorders (44%). Compared with children from families with no alcohol-related problems at the Child Guidance Center, children from families with alcohol-related problems showed higher frequencies of school phobia and delinquency, but not of developmental disorders. Although it is not shown in the table, five of the 34 children in the B group had suffered child abuse. Two of these five children

TABLE 4.

Comparison of Psychosomatic Symptoms between A Group and B Group

Psychosomatic symptoms	A group	B group
Emotional disorders	35 (%)	34 (%)
Behavioral disorders	12	21
Neurotic symptoms	19	18
School phobia	4	24
Other school difficulties	13	15
Developmental disorders	22	44
Delinquency	5	44
Oral difficulties	21	18
Allergies	21	12

had been subjected to both violence and sexual abuse.

It is evident from Tables 3 and 4 that children with alcoholic families cared for at the Child Guidance Center had complex family problems in addition to the alcohol-related problems of their parents, and they included many cases of school phobia, delinquency and child abuse.

The following points can be noted from the above results: (1) children with alcoholic parents often have emotional disorders, behavioral disorders, neurotic symptoms and developmental disorders, and (2) children from alcoholic familities with severe domestic problems often show school phobia, delinquency and child abuse.

These results concerning the problems of children from alcoholic families in Japan are not much different from those which have been reported in the United States and Europe. Nylander[24] reported that children with alcoholic parents often have psychiatric illnesses and school difficulties. Mik[20] and Cork[6] found that children of alcoholics show pride which is easily wounded, dependence, and violent behavior. Morrison[22] and Goodwin[8] reported many restless children among those with alcoholic parents. Mik,[20] Mackey,[18] Lewis,[15] Chafetz,[5] and others have reported on the delinquency of children of alcoholics. Young,[32] Smith,[25] and others have reported cases of child abuse by alcoholic parents.

School difficulties have been pointed out by Nylander,[24] Chafetz,[5] Haberman,[12] Aronson,[3] etc. School phobia was stressed in the results of the present survey because a high percentage of school phobia is seen in children and adolescents in psychiatric clinics in Japan and school phobia has become a major social problem.

Compared with previous reports, the present study was characterized by the problems of children from alcoholic families without divorces, and it was clear that the problems become more serious in children from alcoholic families with divorces.

The author feels that the most important disorders in children from alcoholic families are emotional disorders. It appears that neurosis, delinquency, disturbances in interpersonal relations, and other problems are derived from emotional disorders in accordance with differences in family conditions. This assumption led to the next study on adolescents from alcoholic families.

2. Characteristics of Psychiatric Illnesses in Adolescents with Alcoholic Parents

Tables 5 and 6 show a comparison of psychiatric illnesses in adolescents treated at the Kurihama National Hospital between the alcohol and nonalcohol groups. Thirty of the 31 adolescents in the alcoholic group had alcoholic father and one had alcoholic father and mother.

TABLE 5.

Comparison of Adolescents with Psychiatric Illness between Alcohol Group and Nonalcohol Group

	Alcohol group	*Nonalcohol group*
Number	31	223
male	12	114
female	19	109
Average age	18.2	19.3
Inpatients	48%	31%
Broken family**	48%	12%
Family on welfare**	19%	2%
Mother with psychiatric illness*	19%	4%

TABLE 6.

Comparison of Diagnosis of Psychiatric Illness of Adolescents between Alcohol Group and Nonalcohol Group

	Alcohol group	*Nonalcohol group*
Schizophrenic disorders	16 (%)	27 (%)
Affective disorders	10	9
Neurosis, psychosomatic disease	23	24
Organic brain disorders	10	9
Alcohol, drug dependence	19	13
School phobia	26	14
Eating disorder	10	8
Borderline personality disorder**	36	9

Alcohol group vs. nonalcohol group **p<0.01

A general comparison between the alcohol and nonalcohol groups is shown in Table 5. In a comparison between 31 cases in the alcohol group and 223 cases in the nonalcohol group, the mean ages were 18.2 and 19.3; the mean age in the alcohol group was slightly lower. More cases in the alcohol group, 48% vs. 31%, received inpatient treatment. Significantly more cases in the alcohol group, 48% vs. 12%, lost their father or mother before the age of 15 (X^2 test, $p < 0.01$). There were also significantly more cases, 19% vs. 2%, of welfare families in the alcohol group (X^2 test, $p < 0.01$). Psychiatric illnesses in the mothers were also significantly more common, 19% vs. 4%, in the alcohol group (X^2 test, $p < 0.05$).

Table 6 shows a comparison of the diagnosed diseases. Borderline personality disorders were seen in 36% in the alcohol group and 9% in the nonalcohol group; there were significantly more in the alcohol group (X^2 test, $p < 0.01$). There were more cases of school phobia in the alcohol group and more of schizophrenia in the nonalcohol group. No differences were seen for the other diagnoses.

From Tables 5 and 6, it was evident that adolescents with psychiatric illenesses and with alcoholic parents had many family problems in addition to their alcoholic parents, including broken homes, economic difficulties, and psychiatric illnesses among the mothers, and many were diagnosed as borderline personality disorders.

Little research has been done on psychiatric illnesses in adolescents with alcoholic parents. The only report has been that of Keaney[13] who found more cases of acting out, suicidal tendencies, and police problems in cases being treated in clinics than in controls.

The fact that there are many borderline personality disorders in alcoholic families presents an interesting problem. In familial studies on borderline personality disorders, Loranger[17] and Andorulonis[2] reported that many of the fathers were alcoholics. However, there have been many reports, including those of Gunderson,[11] Stone,[27] Loranger,[16] Akiskal[1] and Soloff,[26] that many of the parents with borderline personality disorders have affective disorders. On the other hand, Winokur[30],[31] proposed the concept of depression spectrum disease, and discussed the relation between alcoholism and affective disorders. From these familial studies, it appears that alcoholism, borderline personality disorders and affective disorders probably all have a genetic relation.

In a study on the historical development of borderline personality disorders Masterson,[19] Grinker,[9] Gunderson,[10] Bradley,[4] Frank[7] et al. reported on disturbances in the relations between the patients and their parents when they were young children. Disruptions of the family system in alcoholic families result in disturbances in the parent-child relationships in the children, and this explains why there are so many borderline personality disorders in alcoholic families.

This study indicated that there are many cases of borderline personality disorders among children from alcoholic families, which presents problems related to both the genetics of alcoholism and family relationships.

3. Treatment of Psychiatric Illnesses in Adolescents with Alcoholic Parents

Table 7 shows results for 24 cases which were treated or followed up by the author for at least one year. All 24 of these cases had alcoholic fathers and the cases with alcoholic mothers excluded. The ages ranged from 11 to 27, with a mean age of 17.9. There were 12 males and 12 females, and 18 (75%) were treated as inpatients. Thirteen of the cases came from broken families. At the time of initial treatment, 14 of the adolescents were living with their alcoholic fathers. Two of these were from homes with fathers only and one was from a home with the real father and a stepmother. Among the 14 fathers, five had already stopped drinking and nine continued problem drinking. In both of the homes with fathers only, the fathers continued to drink. Alcoholic fathers were not present because of deaths or divorces in 10 cases. Eight of these adolescents lived with their mothers only, and two of them had married, but both had experience living with stepfathers because their mothers had remarried.

The diagnoses were schizophrenia in four cases, affective disorders in two cases, neurosis in two cases, school phobia in six cases, alcoholism in three cases, drug dependence in one case, eating disorders in three cases, mental retardation in one case, and borderline personality disorders in eight cases.

It was noteworthy that 17 of these cases, including eight with borderline personality disorders, showed borderline personality organization (splitting, projective identification, and abandonment of anxiety) as proposed by Kernberg[14] and by Masterson.[19] This indicates that even though the types of diseases differ, psychological conditions resembling borderline personality disorders are widespread among psychiatric diseases in adolescents with alcoholic parents. From now on, it will be necessary to include methods for the treatment of borderline personality disorders in the treatment of psychiatric illnesses in adolescents with alcoholic parents. The author uses the method of Masterson[19] in which efforts are made to make the patients aware of their own emotions and increase their self-control by way of confrontation and an interpretation of abandonment of anxiety. Nine cases which underwent systematic psychotherapy received this type of treatment. Among these adolescents with alcoholic parents and psychiatric illnesses, 16 showed poor control of aggression. They included cases of violence, temper tantrums,

TABLE 7.
Intensive Therapy of Adolescents of Alcoholic Fathers

Case number	age	sex	Diagnosis	Broken family	B.P.O.*	Aggression	Delinquency	In-patient	Conflict*	Family therapy	Psychotherapy
1	17	♂	B.P.D.*	+	+	+	−	+	−	−	−
2	13	♂	School phobia	+	+	+	+	+	+	+	−
3	11	♂♀	School phobia	+	+	+	−	−	+	+	−
4	15	♀	Schizophrenia	+	+	+	−	+	−	−	+
5	16	♀	Manic depressive psychosis	+	+	+	+	+	+	−	+
6	24	♀	Eating disorder, B.P.D.	+	+	+	+	+	+	−	+
7	20	♂	Manic depressive psychosis	−	−	−	−	−	+	−	+
8	27	♂	Alcoholism, B.P.D.	+	+	−	−	+	+	−	+
9	21	♂♀	Schizophrenia	−	−	−	−	−	−	−	−
10	16	♀	Neurosis, B.P.D.	−	+	+	+	+	+	+	−
11	16	♀	Drug dependence	−	+	+	+	+	+	+	+
12	12	♂	School phobia	−	+	+	−	−	−	+	+
13	14	♂♀	Neurosis	+	−	+	−	+	+	+	−
14	26	♀	Schizophrenia	+	+	+	+	+	+	+	−
15	25	♂	Drug dependence	+	+	−	+	+	+	+	+
16	21	♀	Neurosis, B.P.D.	−	+	+	−	−	+	+	+
17	15	♀	School phobia	+	+	+	−	+	+	−	+
18	17	♂	Mental retardation	−	+	−	−	+	−	−	−
19	21	♂	B.P.D.	+	+	+	−	+	+	−	−
20	14	♂	School phobia	−	−	+	−	+	+	−	−
21	20	♀	Alcoholism, Eating disorder, B.P.D.	−	+	−	+	+	+	+	+
22	16	♀	Schizoprenia	+	+	+	−	+	−	−	−
23	19	♀	Alcoholism, Eating disorder, B.P.D.	−	+	+	+	+	+	−	−
24	14	♂	School phobia	−	−	+	−	−	+	+	−

*B.P.O. Borderline personality organization   B.P.D. Borderline personality disorder   Conflict: Conflict with father wrist cutting, and suicide attempts. Seven cases had delinquency problems. These cases showed difficulties in coping with acting out during therapy. Their aggression was decreased by therapy which made them aware of their own emotions and increased their self-control.

Nineteen of the adolescents experienced conflict with their alcoholic fathers. Four of them showed fear, 10 showed anger, insincerity and animosity, and five of them viewed themselves to be the same as their fathers. Strong conflict with their fathers resulted in disturbance in their emotional development. Conflict with fathers was decreased through an understanding of alcoholism and objectification of their fathers.

Table 8 shows a summary of family therapy. Family therapy was performed in 11 cases and not used in 13 cases. This therapy involved joint sessions with the families in nine cases and counseling for the mother in two cases. Among the nine cases with joint sessions, two cases were families with mothers only and only the mother and child attended. Three of the sessions included fathers who had already stopped drinking and four sessions fathers who continued problem drinking. The reasons why family therapy was not performed in 13 cases were the severity of the psychiatric illness of the patient in four cases, rejection of the problem by the drinking fathers in four cases, rejection of the problem by the mothers in three cases and disability of the mothers in four cases. Among the 14 cases living with alcoholic fathers, seven underwent family therapy, while four of the 10 not living with their alcoholic fathers participated in such therapy.

There are three important points concerning family therapy. The first is that it provides the participants with accurate knowledge concerning alcohol-related problems and all members of the family tackle the problem together. Second, the family cooperates in getting the alcoholic father to stop drinking and maintain his abstinence. Third, it restores communication among

TABLE 8.
Family Therapy of 24 Adolescents of Alcoholic Fathers

Family therapy 11 cases	
family session	9
father continues to drink	4
father already abstinent	3
family of mother and children	2
counseling for mother	2
No family therapy 13 cases	
rejection by father	4
rejection by mother	3
disability of mother	4
serious illness of patient	2

family members and improves disturbed relationships within the family. Family therapy was based on the system family therapy of Minuchin.[21]

However, long-term treatment was necessary for changes to occur in alcoholic families. At least one year was required for the alcoholic father to maintain his sobriety and for family relationships to change.

Therefore, the treatment of psychiatric illnesses in adolescents with alcoholic parents should involve not only solving the problems of the adolescent, but also solving the problems of the alcoholic family as a whole.

These 24 cases have been followed up for one to five years. The illnesses have been alleviated or treatment has been completed in 11 cases, eight of which underwent family therapy. These figures indicate how difficult it is to treat psychiatric illnesses in adolescents with alcoholic families.

Ala-teen has just started to become active in Japan and only two of these 24 patients participated in Ala-teen. In the future, group sessions of families including children for family treatment will be started.

REFERENCES

(1) Akiskal HS: Subaffective disorders: Dysthymic, cyclotymic and bipolar II disorders in the "Borderline" realm. *Psychiatr Clin North America* 4: 25-45 (1981).
(2) Andrulonis PA, Glueck BL and Stroebel CF: Organic brain dysfunction and the borderline syndrome. *Psychiatr Clin North America* 4: 47-66 (1981).
(3) Aronson H. Gilbert A: Preadolescent sons of male alcoholics. *Arch Gen Psychiatry* 8: 235-241 (1963).
(4) Bradley SJ: The relationship of early maternal separation to borderline personality in children and adolescents: A pilot study. *Am J Psychiatry* 136: 424-426 (1979).
(5) Chafetz ME, Blane HT and Hill MJ: Children of alcoholics: Observations in a child guidance clinic. Quart J Stud Alcohol. 32: 687-694 (1971).
(6) Cork RM: *The Forgotten Children: A Study of Children with Alcoholic Parents*. Don Mills, Ont, Canada, General Publishing Co. (1969).
(7) Frank H and Paris J: Recollections of family experience in borderline patients. *Arch Gen Psychiatry* 38: 1031-1034 (1981).
(8) Goodwin DW, Schulsinger F and Hermansen L: Alcoholism and the hyperactive child syndrome. *J Nerv Ment Disease* 160: 349-353 (1975).
(9) Grinker R, Werble B and Drye R: The borderline syndrome. New York, Basic Books (1968).
(10) Gunderson JG and Kerr J: The families of borderlines. *Arch Gen Psychiatry* 37: 27-33 (1980).
(11) Gunderson JG and Eliott GR: The interface between borderline personality disorder and affective disorder. *Am J Psychiatry* 142: 277-288 (1985).
(12) Haberman PW: Childhood symptoms in children of alcoholics and comparison group parents. *Journal of Marriage and the Family* 28: 152-156 (1966).
(13) Keaney TR and Taylor C: Emotionally disturbed adolescents with alcoholic parents. *Acta Paedopsychiatry* (Basel) 36: 215-221 (1969).
(14) Kernberg 0: *Borderline Conditions and Pathological* Narcissism. New York: Ja-

son Aronson (1976).

(15) Lewis OL, Shanok SS, Grant M, et al: Homicidally Aggressive Young Children: Neuropsychiatric and Experimental Correlates. *Am J Psychiatry* 140: 148-153 (1983).

(16) Loranger AW, Oldham JM and Tulis EH: Familial transmission of DSM-III borderline personality disorder. *Arch Gen Psychiatry* 39: 795-799 (1982).

(17) Loranger AW and Tulis EH: Family history of alcoholism in borderline personality disorder. *Arch Gen Psychiatry* 42: 153-157 (1985).

(18) Mackey JR: clinical observation on adolescent problem drinkers. *Quart J Stud Alcohol* 22: 124-134 (1961).

(19) Masterson JF: *Treatment of the Borderline Adolescent: A Developmental Approach*. New York: Wiley-Interscience (1972).

(20) Mik J: Sons of alcoholic fathers. *Brit J Addiction* 65: 305-315 (1970).

(21) Minuchin S: *Families and Family Therapy*. Cambridge, Harvard University Press (1974).

(22) Morrison JR and Stewart MA: A family study of the hyperactive child syndrome. *Biol Psychiatry* 3: 189-195 (1971).

(23) Newell N: Alcoholism and the father-image. *Quart J Stud Alcohol* II: 92-96 (1950).

(24) Nylander I: Children of alcoholic fathers. *Acta Paediatrics* (Stocholm) 49 (Suppl. No. 121): 1-134 (1960).

(25) Smith SM, Hanson R and Noble S: parents of battered babies: A control study. *Br Med Journal* 4: 388-395 (1973).

(26) Soloff PH and Millward JW: Psychiatric disorders in the families of borderline patients. *Arch Gen Psychiatry*, 40: 37-44 (1983).

(27) Stone MH, Kahn E and Flye B: Psychiatrically ill relatives of borderline patients: A family study. *Psychiatric Quarterly* 53: 71-84 (1981).

(28) Suzuki K, Higuchi H, Muraoka H, et al: Psychosomatic disorders in the children of alcoholic fathers. *Jpn J Alcohol & Drug Dependence* 22: 25-40 (1987).

(29) Suzuki K, Ono K, Higuchi S, et al: Children of alcoholics: Cases from a Child Guidance Center. *Seishin Igaku*, 30 (10): 1089-1098 (1988).

(30) Winokur G, Cadoret R, Dorzab J, et al: Depressive disease. *Arch Gen Psychiatry* 24: 135-144 (1971).

(31) Winokur G, Morrison J, Clancy J, et al: The Iowa 500: Familial and clinical findings favor two kinds of depressive illness. *Comprehensive Psychiatry* 14: 99-106 (1973).

(32) Young L: *Wednesday's Children. A Study of Negrect and Abuse*. London: McGraw-Hill (1964).

16

Therapeutic Effects of Counseling on Wives of Alcoholics

Michio Takemura, M.D.

Yuko Endo, B.A.

In a one- to two-year follow-up study, 39 wives of alcoholics answered questions about the present status of problems they had when they first visited the counseling program. At the time of the initial session, most of their husbands were still drinking, and were not receiving professional therapy.

Treatment planning was based on the family evaluation of each client. Forty-one percent of the wives attended counseling only one or two times and only 31% of them attended more than 10 sessions.

Overall improvement of the initial problems, especially violence within the family, was excellent. Prognosis was usually good if the clients found support in other people even when they stopped the counseling in early stages. This study confirms that there can be recovery of the alcoholic family if at least one family member takes action and contacts a helping resource.

INTRODUCTION

Many studies demonstrate the efficacy of family therapy in the treatement of alcoholism. Most of them use concurrent therapy for alcoholics and spouses[4],[6],[7] or multiple-couples' group therapy[1],[2],[3],[5],[8] as the modality of the therapy. That means they mostly deal with the families of "dry phase" alcoholics who have already participated in therapy. However, the most difficult time for the family is the period when the alcoholic is still continuing to drink and to deny alcohol-related problems. They will not ask for or follow any usual advice to see a professional or experienced person. These families of "wet phase" alcoholics are the primary clientele of the Harajuku

Counseling Room.

The most important period in the treatment of alcoholics is that of family intervention, including establishment of working relationship with the client, judgment of emergency, their education and confrontation appropriate to the unique situation of the client and the alcoholic. It is essential to appreciate the client's condition and apply flexibly various treatment techniques such as individual session, educational session, group session. We made a one to two years follow-up study of those wives who visited the counseling room to ask for help with the anxiety and troubles caused by the alcoholic husband. This paper examines the efficacy of counseling wives of alcoholics.

SUBJECTS AND METHOD

1. Facility

This study was made at the Harajuku Counseling Room (HCR), a private counseling office in Tokyo. The HCR was opened in June 1983 for the clinical practice of addiction problems. The HCR offers psychotherapy, without using drug or physical therapy. It cooperates with several outpatient clinics and hospitals for clients who need medical treatment. At the HCR, the majority of clients are family members of alcoholic or drug-dependent individuals in treatment rather than the substance abuser. Most clients seeking treatment at this facility are individuals under high stress because of their relationship with the substance abusers. The focus of therapy at the clinic is offering treatment and support to this individual, not to treat the substance abuser. Table 1 demonstrates the details of clients who visited the HCR between Ocober 3rd 1983 and August 25th 1988. Alcoholism-related clients comprise 53.7% of all clients and 63.2% of them are the family member of the alcoholic.

The approach at the HCR is eclectic but educational therapy and family

TABLE 1.
Number of Clients with Addiction Problems

Diagnosis	Identified Patient	Family	Total
Alcoholism	361 (46.3)	621 (59.2)	982 (53.7)
Eating Disorder	304 (39.0)	211 (20.1)	515 (28.2)
Drug Addict	26 (3.3)	89 (8.5)	115 (6.3)
Cross-Addict	31 (4.0)	40 (3.8)	71 (3.9)
Others	58 (7.4)	88 (8.4)	146 (8.0)
Total	780 (100.0)	1049 (100.0)	1829 (100.1)

(%)

therapy-oriented group sessions are a central part of the therapy. There are about 10 types of group sessions per week at the HCR, but the following two group sessions are ones that most wives of alcoholics are recommended to attend.

1. *Educational Program*: This consists of eight lecture-type sessions teaching alcohol-related problems. In attendance are alcoholics, their family members, and people working with alcoholics. Usually, the wives of alcoholics comprise more than half of those attending. The themes of these sessions are physical and mental complications of alcoholism, addictive behavior patterns, social problems, interpersonal relationships of the alcoholics and his (her) family, and self-help groups and the value of their use in treatment.

2. *Wives' Group*: This is a special group for the wife of the alcoholic. The number of sessions is 12 for one series. In this group the entanglements associated with a relationship with an alcoholic are defined and discussed.

Other specified groups are also available as needed. Most group sessions are held once a week, with sessions of 90 to 120 minutes. Average number in attendance is 15 to 20 for the educational group and 10 to 15 for the wives' group. Almost every client makes first contact by telephone. The clients are informed about the contract terms at that time. Payment is made before the session. Cancellation is allowed three days prior at no charge. In the intake session of about 90 minutes, case history is taken, their motivation to ask for professional help is encouraged, and the principle of the therapy of alcoholism is discussed. The clients are asked for permission to be contacted by the staff of HCR as the need arises. The second session is an orientation interview in which a flexible therapy program is proposed to meet the needs of a client. These two preliminary sessions might be finished in one session or divided into three sessions or more. Most of the clients are encouraged to make their visit known to the family, including the identified patient. In the case of the wives of alcoholic, usually an educational program is recommended in the orientation session. Generally, they attend the wives' group sessions after the educational group finishes or during the same period. This is a standard course that many wives follow but individual sessions or medical treatment is recommended in the case of an emergency or if the client's anxiety is severe.

Recovery of each client is evaluated and the treatment planning is discussed regularly at the staff meeting.

2. Subjects

Sixty-three wives of alcoholics visited HCR between June 1st 1987 and May 31st 1988. Eleven of them refused any contact from the therapist. One client was so mentally unstable that no valid information was obtained in the intake session which was the last contact. Therefore, a questionnaire was sent to 51 clients. They were asked to answer questions about the status of their alcohol-related problems by mail in June 1989, one to two years after the initial interview. Twenty-three replies were received in a month. Sixteen of the remaining 28 clients gave their answer in a telephone interview. No information was reported from the remaining 12 clients. Thirty-nine replies were analyzed with demographic data obtained from the patients' case record.

The age of clients was 45.1 ± 8.2 (average $\pm$ standard deviation) and that of alcoholic husband was 47.8 ± 9.9 at the time of the first session. As for family formation, 10% of the clients were living with a husband only, 74% with a husband and children, and 15% with extended family. Public health centers or mental health centers were first referral agencies in 31% of the cases, clinics or hospitals for 38% of the clients. Except for 5 cases in the hospital, most of the alcoholics were still drinking (about 79%), were not receiving professional help (84%), were not attending self-help groups (84%), and were attending neither a professional therapy nor a self-help group (69%) at the time of their wife's first visit to the HCR.

There was no significant difference between the 24 excluded cases and 39 included cases regarding the above-mentioned data.

The number of sessions they attended was 1 to 2 in 41% of cases, 3 to 10 in 28% of cases, and 11 or more (highest 45) in 31% of cases. The attendance rate of the clients who refused the contact from the HCR was rather low, with only 1 to 2 sessions attended in 55% of such cases.

3. Questionnaire

The questionnaire consists of 5 questions, of which the #1 question is the most important part. In #1, clients are requested to evaluate in five grades the present status of initial problems which were marked already by the HCR staff. The mark sheet is omitted. Indications and problem items are included here.

    #1. When you visited the Harajuku Counseling Room for the first time, your problems were as follows. Please indicate present status by marking the appropriate column.

    ☐ Completely resolved;   ☐ Positive change;
    ☐ No change;   ☐ Slight negative change;
    ☐ Negative change.

    Problems: 1. Violence in family; 2. Unemployment; 3. Money borrowing or refusal to provide family financial support; 4. Refusal to work or poor attendance; 5. Trouble in work place, absenteeism, or lateness. 6. Criminal

activity; 7. Trouble with neighbors or others; 8. Physical or mental problems;
9. Doubt of mental competency; 10. Communication problems between husband and wife; 11. Separation or divorce; 12. Womanizing by husband;
13. Relationship difficulties between father and children; 14. Relationship
difficulties between client and family of husband; 15. Acting out by children; 16. Drinking problem of children; 17. Relationship difficulties between
client and parents and siblings; 18. Mental instability of client; 19. Client
seeking help to prevent entanglement in husband's drinking problem;
20. Client seeking methods of dealing with husband's behavior;
21. Husband's behavior unchanged by his attending self-help group;
22. Husband's behavior unchanged by hospitalization/treatment.

 #2.   Please list any new problems that have emerged since treatment
started.

 #3.   Please answer the following questions about your husband.
a) Has he received treatment?
    ☐ In-patient hospitalizations;   ☐ Out-patient treatment;
    ☐ Attended only one treatment session;   ☐ No treatment received.
    If he is under treatment, what hospital or clinic is it?

---

b) Is he attending any self-help group?
    ☐ Yes. (Please specify. _____)
    ☐ No.
c) Is he drinking now?
    ☐ Complete abstinence;   ☐ Partial abstinence;
    ☐ Drinking less;   ☐ Drinking with less problem behavior;
    ☐ Drinking continued;   ☐ Unknown.
d) How is his social situation?
    ☐ Working (☐ full-time;   ☐ part-time);
    ☐ Not working with some social activity (☐ volunteer work;
    ☐ social movement)
    (Please specify. _____)
    ☐ No social life.
 #4.   How is your mental status?
    ☐ Excellent;   ☐ Good;   ☐ Normal;
    ☐ Stressful;   ☐ Extremely stressful.
 #5.   Do you participate in any alcohol-related program?
    ☐ Yes. (Please specify. _____)
    ☐ No.

RESULTS

A. Initial Problems

The five most frequent problem items that were mentioned in the first interview of 39 wives of alcoholics were the physical and mental condition of their husband (24 cases), violence by an alcoholic husband (22), relationship difficulties between father and children (21), communication problems between husband and wife (20), and relationship difficulties between client and husband's family (15).

This tendency was almost same for the 11 wives who refused contact from HCR staff. A relatively high rate (8 cases) of complaint of difficult relationship between father and children was observed in this group. Such differences were not seen in the other 12 clients refusing to reply to the questionaire, with whom the HCR could not establish contact.

TABLE 2.

Cases of Each Status for Each Initial Problem One to Two Years after the Start of Counseling for Wives of Alcoholics

Initial Problem No	Number of Cases (n=39) → (scale 5, 10, 15, 20, 25)
8	◎ ○ ○ ○ ○ ○ ○ ○ ○ ○ ○ ○ ◑ ◑ ◑ ◑ ◑ ▼ ▼ ▼ ▼ ▼ ● ⑦
1	◎ ◎ ◎ ◎ ◎ ◎ ◎ ◎ ◎ ◎ ○ ○ ○ ○ ○ ○ ○ ○ ◑ ⑦ ⑦
13	◎ ◎ ○ ○ ○ ○ ○ ○ ○ ○ ◑ ◑ ◑ ◑ ◑ ◑ ◑ ▼ ▼ ● ⑦
10	◎ ◎ ○ ○ ○ ○ ○ ○ ○ ○ ◑ ◑ ◑ ◑ ◑ ⑦ ⑦ ⑦ ⑦ ⑦ ⑦
14	◎ ◎ ◎ ○ ○ ○ ○ ○ ○ ○ ◑ ◑ ◑ ◑ ◑ ◑
5	◎ ◎ ◎ ◎ ◎ ○ ○ ○ ○ ○ ◑ ⑦ ⑦
15	◎ ◎ ◎ ◎ ◎ ○ ○ ○ ○ ○ ◑ ▼ ▼
17	◎ ◎ ○ ○ ○ ○ ○ ◑ ◑ ◑ ◑ ▼
18	◎ ◎ ○ ○ ○ ○ ○ ◑ ◑ ◑ ● ⑦
4	◎ ◎ ◎ ◎ ○ ○ ◑ ◑ ◑ ● ⑦
7	◎ ◎ ◎ ○ ○ ○ ◑ ⑦ ⑦
22	◎ ○ ○ ○ ◑ ◑ ⑦ ⑦
3	◎ ◎ ◎ ◎ ○ ◑ ◑
21	◎ ○ ○ ◑ ◑ ⑦
6	◎ ◎ ◎ ○ ◑ ⑦
11	◎ ◎ ○ ◑ ⑦
12	◎ ◎ ◎ ◎ ⑦
16	◑ ◑ ◑ ▼ ▼
19	◎ ○ ○ ○ ○
20	◎ ○ ○ ○ ○
2	◎
9	◑

Legend:
- ◎ Completely Resolved
- ○ Positive Change
- ◑ No Change
- ▼ Slight Negative Change
- ● Negative Change
- ⑦ No Answer or Not Applicable

B. Present Status of Initial Problems

Table 2 demonstrates the present status of initial problems. Positive change is seen in almost every problem item except for the drinking problem of children, which was unchanged or showed a slight negative change. Excellent results were obtained concerning violence in the family. Ten out of 22 clients reported that the violence was completely resolved and 9 other wives indicated a positive change. For husband's physical or mental conditions and father-children relationship, the effect was mild and about half of clients indicated positive change.

The following figures (C to I) were compiled from the questionnaires received from the 39 wives of alcoholics.

C. New Problems

(New problems that emerged since treatment started)

ITEMS	# of CASES
1. Physical symptom of husband	4
2. Hospitalized	3
3. Mental symptom of husband	3
4. Divorced	3
5. Separated	2
6. Considering divorce	2
7. Drinking problem of children	2
8. Financial problem	2
9. Husband died	1*

Fifty-one-year-old alcoholic husband died of cerebral infarction.

D. Treatment

(Treatment that the alcoholic husbands have received)

ITEMS	# of CASES
1. In-patient hospitalization	2*
2. Attending outpatient treatment	14*
3. Attended only one treatment session	1
4. No treatment received	14
5. No answer	8

Sixteen patients were receiving medical treatment, with 10 receiving therapy from a physician and only 4 being treated by an alcoholism specialist.

E. Self-helf Group

(Self-help groups that the alcoholic husbands were attending)

ITEMS	# of CASES
1. A.A.	1
2. Danshukai*	3
3. Other self-help group	1
4. Not attending	28
5. No answer	6

Japanese style self-help group for alcoholics and their families

F. Drinking Status

ITEMS	# of CASES
1. Complete abstinence	7
2. Partial abstinence	2
3. Drinking decreased	10
4. Drinking with problem behavior decreased	9
5. Drinking continued	5
6. Unknown	1
7. No answer	4
8. Died	1

G. Social Situation

ITEMS	# of CASES
1. Full-time job	22
2. Part-time job	4
3. Not working with some social life	1
4. No social life	4
5. Died	1
6. Hospitalized	2
7. Unknown	2
8. No answer	3

H. Wife's Mental Status

ITEMS	# of CASES
1. Excellent	5
2. Good	9

3. Normal   15
4. Stressful   5
5. Extremely stressful   1
6. No answer   4

I. Alcohol-Related Program

(The alcohol-related program that the wives of alcoholics were attending at the time of study)

ITEMS	# of CASES
1. Attending*	15
2. Not attending	20
3. No answer	4

PROGRAMS	# of CASES
① Danshukai	5
② Public Health Center	4
③ Al-anon	3
④ Hospital-supported meeting	3
⑤ HCR	2
⑥ AKK**	2
⑦ ASK***	1
Total*	20

*Three wives were attending two or more programs
**AKK: Citizens' Network on Addiction Problems
***ASK: National Citizens' Association on Alcohol Problems

DISCUSSION

Analysis of the demographic data of the 39 subjects and their initial problems draws the profile of clients and their family. Most of them are middle-aged (average 45 years old) housewives from a nuclear family (74%) who are suffering from their husband's continued drinking (about 87%). They are anxious about their husband's physical and mental condition (62%), and being bothered by the violence of husband (56%). They are worrying about the relationship between father and children (54%), as well as about troubles in communication between husband and wife (51%). Most of their husbands do not participate in any alcohol-related programs or therapy (69%). They are introduced to HCR either by clinics or hospitals (38%) or by public health centers (31%). Forty-one percent of clients attended the HCR only one or two times and only 31% attended more than 10 sessions.

Considering the varying number of sessions attended, improvement of clients' initial problems is outstanding (Table 2). Because 41% of clients attended only one or two sessions, this high recovery rate means that some basic change has occurred in the clients or the improvement continued after the session. This is true for both the counseling to the wives of alcoholics and in the family intervention. Even in one or two preliminary sessions, clients sometimes find that there are people who understand their pain and who know how to deal with these troubles. They are encouraged to seek resourses and ask for help. If the clients find someone whom they can trust, the prognosis is usually good. In fact, 38% of wives were attending alcohol-related programs one to two years after the first interview. Since the therapists in HCR introduce those programs and most of sessions are group based, clients become familiar with such information. Therefore attending the HCR sessions means that clients are connected to the helping network. The alcoholic family makes the problem open to the outside world through the clients. This is a radical change for the alcoholic family. The positive attitude encouraged in the HCR sessions will be expressed in other parts of their interpersonal relationship. A 48-year-old client attended only 4 sessions and dropped out. But she wrote in the questionnaire that she disclosed her husband's alcohol problems to all her relatives. She indicated that his violence had been completely resolved and that all of her initial problems changed positively except the husband's physical condition.

On the contrary, the prognosis tended to be relatively poor when clients gave up any hope of recovery. For example, a 60-year-old wife thought after the intake session that her 71-year-old husband was too old to recover and cancelled the second session. She indicated that all of her initial problems had changed negatively one year later. A 50 year-old client gave up her husband and decided to get divorced after the first visit and did not appear at the second session. Her mental status was indicated in her report as bad and her childrens' alcohol problems as getting worse.

Prognosis of the mental conditions of client and children was good if the client found help from other people, even when her husband died or when she got divorced or separated.

Excellent improvement was found in the item of family violence (Table 2). This result strongly supports the idea that a wife can usually avoid her husband's violence if she takes action to get professional help and changes her communication with the alcoholic husband. It is said that the relationship between the alcoholic and his family is not a one-way relationship. This is especially the case in a family violence.

Since the clients of this treatment study are the wives of the alcoholic, the therapeutic effects spread to the family through the wives. Therefore, the effects on the personal pathology of an alcoholic husband and his relationships with other members are indirect and mild compared to the direct effect on the problems reflecting the client's anxiety and attitude. That might be the reason for the mild effects on the drinking status of her husband, his physical and mental condition, and the relationship between husband and children.

The score of the drinking problem of the children, which was the only study item that had a negative change, suggests that a problem shift or a shift of the wives' attention from the husband to the children may have occurred.

These good results might reflect the satisfaction of the clients with the HCR program. Data of wives' mental status also suggest that the clients benefit from counseling since most of them were obviously extremely stressed when they contacted the HCR for the first time.

Because of the HCR's location in a fashionable district in Tokyo and the lack of insurance for payment of session fees, the clients of the HCR do not represent the average population of alcoholics in Japan. Although a sliding scale fee system is applied, most clients are middle or above-middle class, having employed family members. That might be one of the factors of this overall good result. That also explains the fairly good social situation of the alcoholic husbands (56% of alcoholic husbands had a full-time job).

This study confirms the excellent therapeutic effect of counseling on wives of alcoholics. It suggests that there can be family recovery if at least one family member tries to take action and contact a helping resource. A well planned controlled study would be required to substantiate our findings.

REFERENCES

(1) Burton, G., Kaplan, H.M. & Mudd, E.H.: Marriage counseling with alcoholics and their spouses. *Br. J. Addict.* 63: 151 (1968).
(2) Cadogan, D.A.: Marital group therapy in the treatment of alcoholism. *Q. J. Stud. Alcohol.* 34: 1187 (1973).
(3) Corder, B.F., Corder, R.F. & Laindlaw, N.L.: An intensive treatment program for alcoholics and their wives. *Q. J. Stud. Alcohol.* 33: 1144 (1972).
(4) Ewing, J.A., Long, V., & Wenzel, G.G.: Concurrent group psychotherapy of alcoholic patients and their wives. *Int. J. Group Psychother.* 11: 329 (1961).
(5) Gallant, D. M., Rich, A., Bey, E. et al.: Group psychotherapy with married couples: a successful technique in New Orleans Alcoholism Clinic patients. *J. La. State Med. Soc.* 122: 41 (1970).
(6) Gliedman, L. H., Rosenthal, D., Frank, J.D. et al.: Group therapy of alcoholics with concurrent group meetings with their wives. *Q. J. Stud. Alcohol.* 17: 655 (1956).

(7) Smith, C. J.: Alcoholics: Their treatment and their wives. *Br. J. Psychiatry.* 115: 1039 (1969).
(8) Steinglass, P., Davis, D. & Berenson, D.: Observations of conjointly hospital-ized "alcoholic couples" during sobriety and intoxication: implications for the-ory and therapy. *Family Process* 16: 1 (1977).

17

Psychotherapeutic Treatment of Alcoholic Families — Broad-Spectrum Intervention

Kazumi Nishio, Ph.D.

Psychotherapeutic treatment of alcoholic families using broad-spectrum interventions for different subgroups in the family is described. The case example illustrates methods used to treat an adult child of an alcoholic (ACA) and her family when alcoholic members were resistant to receiving outside help themselves.

Initial psychotherapy was focused on an ACA until she regained her self-esteem sufficient to deal with potential alienation from alcoholic members.

The next step was to improve her marriage through couples therapy, followed by family therapy in the absence of resistant alcoholic members.

When the family members were ready to confront the alcoholics, a meeting was arranged by a therapist. Inpatient treatment and AA attendance were prescribed for the alcoholic. Subsequently, family therapy, including the alcoholic members, was employed to break the cycle of multigenerational effects of alcoholism and to strengthen the unity of the family.

INTRODUCTION

Alcoholism has been connected with severe family problems such as spouse and child abuse,[2],[3] depression and suicide.[5]

The recent Adult Children of Alcoholics (ACA) movement in the United States[6] has created an awareness of the fact that being raised in an alcoholic family has had far-reaching negative effects on the family member(s) even when the presence of severe family problems is not apparent.

The dynamics of growing up in an alcoholic family in which inappropriate defense mechanisms and coping styles[1] are developed have impaired many people's healthy functioning as adults.

Broad-spectrum interventions are indicated as valuable for treatment of alcoholics and their families.[4]

In the treatment of chronic alcoholic families and resistant alcoholic family members, utilization of individual, couple and family therapy approaches is designed not only to provide recovery for individual alcoholic members but to establish healthy relationships and better communication among all family members.

Some broad-spectrum interventions include education, giving information, utilizing outside support groups, in-depth psychotherapy, intensive experiential group therapy, and homework assignments such as reading germane literature and listening to tapes on the dynamics of alcoholism.

CASE STUDY

The case example presented here involves use of a wide range of treatment methods with an ACA, her family, and family of origin.

This family consists of three generations, Debby (36 years), her husband Tom (40 years), Debby's mother (68 years), stepson (20 years), and daughter (18 years). At this time, Debby, her husband, stepson and daughter lived together in one household. Debby's mother lived apart but in the same town. Debby came to therapy because she wanted her mother and her stepson to stop drinking.

Debby has tried to stop her mother and stepson from drinking alcohol by pleading, threatening, pouring alcohol down the sink, hiding liquor in the house, taking them to an alcohol treatment center, all without success. Both her mother and stepson deny that they have alcohol problems. Debby's father died six years ago from an alcohol-related illness. Debby has been married to her second husband, Tom, for 7 years. This marriage, like her first marriage, has been rocky and troublesome.

Debby exhibited typical co-dependent behavior such as covering up the shameful behaviors of mother and stepson and doing chores for them when they were too intoxicated to perform these by themselves. She also bailed the stepson out of jail when he was arrested for drunken driving, and helped her mother to pay her debts when the mother had spent all her money on alcohol.

The daily drama of these alcoholics was becoming her main preoccupation.

TREATMENT PLAN

A treatment plan was devised to achieve these goals: to help Debby function better as an individual adult; to develop a stronger couple's relationship; to achieve for her mother and stepson alcoholic detoxification; and to establish healthy communication among family members.

The sequence of the treatment plan is as follows:

1. Initially not to treat her mother or stepson as they are not motivated to recover, although this was Debby's goal as stated in her presenting problem.
2. Treat Debby for her co-dependency and ACA issues to increase her sense of self and develop strength to withstand potential loss of relationship with her alcoholic mother and stepson.
3. Al-Anon, ACA meetings, and women's support group for Debby are recommended to augument psychotherapy and give support to Debby, who feels isolated.
4. Treat Debby's current relationship problems with her husband and strengthen the marriage, as Debby and her husband relate to each other in co-dependent ways, one of the characteristics of an ACA relationship.
5. Involve other nonalcoholic members from current and original families to cooperate in the treatment plan.
6. A loving confrontation with alcoholic mother and stepson by united nonalcoholic family members.
7. Detoxification and 30 days of inpatient treatment for mother, who is in the advanced stage of alcoholism and in poor health, and 30 days of outpatient treatment program (for economic reasons) for the stepson, who is in good health and in the early to middle stage of alcoholism.
8. Attendance at A.A. meetings for mother and stepson.
9. Upon completion of the alcoholic treatment programs, family therapy is prescribed for all family members to deal with effects of alcoholic behavior and communication problems, to enhance healthy family unity and break the multigenerational cycle of alcoholism.

TREATMENT

Treatment of Debby as an ACA started with encouragement to attend self-help groups such as ACA meetings and Al-Anon meetings as well as a women's support group (assertive training group) and weekend intensive experiential workshops. Relevant books and tapes were lent. These outside helpers are part of the comprehensive broad-spectrum treatment. Information on

ACA issues, including mistrust, nonawareness of subtle feelings, difficulty in intimacy or having fun, was supplied to Debby. Explorations were made of patterns of seeking approval, making harsh judgments of self, overreacting to situations, having low self-esteem, feeling an extreme sense of responsibility and excessively controlling others. Debby's compulsive eating disorder was discussed from an ACA point of view.

These explorations were made by way of a series of questionings and exhibition of empathic interpretations.

Examples of questions by the therapist:

"Knowing you are an ACA, what do you expect from yourself when your husband is not taking care of his business?"

"When you find yourself excessively helping your husband, what kind of feelings do you experience inside of you?"

"How do you see yourself responding when your son blames you?"

"What kind of coping styles do you use to deal with your son's blaming?"

"If as a child you constantly used to take care of your alcoholic father and mother, do you sense any connection in your way of taking care of your husband and your stepson?"

Examples of empathic interpretation:

"It is no wonder that you cover up for your mother and stepson. When you were a child, you must have felt ashamed whenever your parents got drunk and made a scene in public. As the first-born responsible girl, you were accustomed to covering up your parents' mess!"

"You may not be able to respond to your husband rationally when his voice gets a little loud. It is very natural that you suddenly become like a little girl when your husband yells at you in the way your father did."

"You say you eat food compulsively. It's understandable if you use food to numb your uncomfortable feelings whenever all this family stress comes up."

After Debby had had three months of once-a-week psychotherapy, her husband was invited to couple therapy. Debby made it clear to him that the marriage might not survive unless he too put forth effort to improve the relationship. Although the husband was initially reluctant to participate in conjoint therapy, within six months he and Debby learned to sufficiently develop their communication skills to be able to hear each other and support each other.

The basic communication skills taught included active listening for five minutes without interruption, plus taking turns speaking and accurately guessing underlying feelings and intentions when the partner speaks. Debby and her husband's co-dependent behavior regarding their dealing with his son was also an issue for therapy.

When the husband-wife relationship became strong enough, Debby's mother's drinking problem was brought up. Debby was instructed to get cooperation from her adult brother and sister. A therapy session was held to explain the dynamics of their alcoholic family and why setting limits are important if anything is to change.

The plan of loving confrontation was carried out as follows: As it was felt that their mother might die prematurely from an alcohol-related illness or by an accident caused by excessive drinking, Debby and her siblings prepared a will to be signed to take care of assets and debts after their mother's death.

Debby and her siblings expressed to their mother their love and explained they had reached emotional bankruptcy. They told their mother that to protect their own sense of well-being, from now on they would neither call her nor accept her calls unless the mother decided to go to a treatment center. They would help any way they could, including giving financial support, provided the mother decided to receive treatment. They were not forcing her to get outside help, but were offering mother a choice. If alcohol is that important in her life, they told her, they do not have the right to force her to stop drinking. Rather, this is the last act of love because they see what alcohol is doing to her physically and mentally. They can no longer face the daily pain of seeing the deterioration of their valued mother. Alcoholism is a disease, not a moral weakness. Any disease has to be treated to be cured. If mother sincerely wishes to recover and decides to go to an inpatient treatment center which has a strong family involvement programs, she should call them. Otherwise, this is their last meeting together.

Right after this meeting, Debby's siblings had the urge to call their mother in fear of mother's suicide. This was discouraged as this might be regarded as a lack of seriousness on the part of Debby and siblings. If mother commits suicide instead of choosing treatment, that also is her choice as she is already making attempts at slow suicide by drinking tremendous amounts of alcohol. Debby and siblings stated that to carry out this plan was one of the hardest things they had to do in their lives.

As a result, the mother decided to go to a 28-day treatment center and followed this up with family therapy and AA meetings. Debby and her husband stopped rescuing their son from all kinds of problems he had created and asked him to leave their house. Their daughter, as well as relatives, also took a strong stand toward him. Their son then decided to get help for his drinking problem.

Family therapy sessions have been in progress from Debby's mother and stepson came back from the treatment center. They are also attending AA meetings three times a week. It took approximately one year since the start of Debby's treatment to get to this point.

The family members are hopeful that they will not transmit alcoholic-related dysfunctional behaviors to the next generation.

Appropriate use of as many and varied methods as possible is often the key to the successful treatment of alcoholic families.

Note: Among broad-spectrum treatment methods, loving confrontation should not be chosen in all situations. For example, if the family has reached the point where the family members do not care about the alcoholic members, this kind of confrontation is contraindicated. If, also, an alcoholic member is an isolated drinker who has already cut ties with other family members, loving confrontation may not be appropriate. As family wills are often volatile issues, the use of these wills, as in the present case, would have to be carefully evaluated to obviate a real threat of suicide.

REFERENCES

(1) Black, C.: *It Will Never Happen to Me*. Denver: M.A.C. (1981).
(2) Hindman, M.: Child abuse and neglect: The alcoholic connection. *Alcohol Health and Research World*, I, 2-7 (1977).
(3) Hindman, M.: Family violence. *Alcohol Health and Research World*. I, 1-11 (1979).
(4) Miller, W.R. & Hester, R.K.: The Effectiveness of Alcoholism Treatment: What Research Reveals. In W.R. Miller & N. Heather (Eds.), *Treating Addictive Behaviors Process of Change*. New York: Plenum Press (1986).
(5) Winokur, G.: Alcoholism and depression in the same family. In D.G. Goodwin and C.K. Erickson (Eds.), *Alcoholism and Affective Disorders: Clinical, Genetic and Biochemical Studies*. New York: SP Medical and Scientific Books (1979).
(6) Woititz, J.: *Adult Children of Alcoholics*, Pompano Beach, Fla: Health Communications. Inc. (1983).

18

Effects of Family Alcoholism

Claudia Black, M.S.W., Ph.D.

The words which best describe living in an alcoholic family are
"inconsistency" and "unpredictability." When structure and con-
sistency are not provided by the parents, children will find ways
to provide it for themselves. The oldest child often becomes a
"responsible child" who takes on many of the household and
parenting responsibilities; the younger child often becomes an
"adjuster," who finds it much easier to exist by simply adjusting
to whatever happens. Other children may become the placater who
becomes very skilled at listening and showing empathy. However,
some other children act out and display delinquent behavior which
typifies the state of the family. A child in an alcoholic family tends
to have a well-developed denial system about his feelings and his
perceptions of what is happening in the home.

There are between 28 and 34 million children and adults in the United States who are unique. They are unique in that they are more likely than any other identifiable group to become alcoholic. They are the people who grew up, or are presently being raised, in alcoholic families.

While one of the clearest indicators of a smoothly working family is consistency, the words which best describe living in an alcoholic family are inconsistency and unpredictability. It is my premise that what a spouse or child does while living in an alcoholic environment is done because at the time it makes sense to each of them. As the problems surrounding alcoholism cause more and more inconsistency and unpredictability in the home, the behavior of the nonalcoholic family members typically becomes an attempt to restabilize the family system. Members of this family system act and react in manners which make life easier and less painful for them.

In most well-functioning families, one finds emotions being expressed clearly and each person being given the opportunity to share feelings. Emotions are accepted by an attentive group which offers understanding and support.

Family members can freely ask for attention and give attention to others in return.

In a home beset with alcoholism, emotions are repressed and become twisted. Emotions are often not shared and, unfortunately, when they are expressed, it is done in a judgmental manner placing blame on one another.

While constructive alliances are part of the healthy family, adult members of an alcoholic family often lack alliance. If alliances are demonstrated, they are destructive and usually consist of one parent and a child (or children) against the other parent.

Families have rules which need to be verbalized and to be fair and flexible. Rules such as "no hitting," or "everyone will have a chance to be heard," lead to healthier functioning within a system. In alcoholic family structures, should rules be established, they are not based on a need for healthy protection but instead are built on shame, guilt or fear. Rather than a verbalized rule which says, "There will be no hitting," there is an unspoken, silent rule which says, "You won't tell others how you got that bruise."

Many times there are clearly defined roles within the family. It is typical for adults in the family to divide or share the roles of being the breadwinner and the administrator—the one who makes the decisions within the home. Children raised in homes where open communication is practiced and consistency of lifestyles is the norm usually have the ability to adopt a variety of roles, dependent on the situation. These children learn how to be responsible, how to organize, how to develop realistic goals, to play, laugh and to enjoy themselves. They learn a sense of flexibility and spontaneity. They are usually taught to be sensitive to the feelings of others and are willing to be helpful to others. These children learn a sense of autonomy, but they also learn how to belong to a group. Children growing up in alcoholic homes seldom learn the combinations of roles which mold healthy personalities. Instead, they become locked into roles based on their perception of what they need to do to "survive" and to bring some stability to their lives.

I. SURVIVAL ROLES

Children need consistency and structure. As an alcoholic progresses into alcoholism and the co-alcoholic becomes more and more preoccupied with the alcoholic, children experience decreasing consistency and structure in the family unit and their lives become less and less predictable. Some days when dad is drinking, no disruption or tension occurs, but on other days when he is drinking, he becomes loud, opinionated, and demanding in his expectations of the children. Mom, at times, reacts to this disrupting behavior by being passive and ignoring it; other times, she makes arrangements for the children to go to the neighbors until dad goes to bed or she tells them to go outside and play until she calls for them. The children don't know what to expect from dad when he drinks, nor do they know what to expect from mom when dad drinks.

1. Responsible Child

When structure and consistency are not provided by the parents, children will find ways to provide it for themselves. The oldest child, or an only child, very often becomes the responsible one in the family. This child takes responsibility for the environmental structure in the home and provides consistency for the others. This is the nine-year-old child who is referred to as "nine years of age going on 35," or "the 12-year-old going on 40." From the onset of alcoholism in the family, this child has been an adult. It is the seven-year-old putting mom to bed, the nine-year-old getting dinner ready every night, the 12-year-old driving dad around because dad is too drunk to drive himself. This responsible role is a role in which the child seldom misbehaves, but rather takes on many of the household and parenting responsibilities for the other siblings and, very possibly, for the parents.

Whether or not responsible children are directed into this role, or more subtly fall into it, it is typically a role which brings these children comfort. Playing the responsible role provides stability in the life of this oldest, or only, child and in the lives of other family members. They practice this role so consistently that they become very adept at planning and manipulating. In order to provide the structure they seek, they often manipulate their brothers and sisters. This ability to organize, to affect others, to accomplish goals, provides these children with leadership qualities—qualities which get them elected as class leaders, captains of teams, etc.

Responsibility, organization, setting and achieving goals are attributes which are encouraged and rewarded both at home and at school. Obviously this is not the kind of behavior which results in these children being sent to school counselors or gets them punished by their parents.

These responsible children have learned to rely completely on themselves. It is what makes the most sense to them. They have learned the best way to achieve stability is to provide it for themselves. They cannot consistently rely on mom or dad. The unpredictability and inconsistency of their parent's behavior are the destructive elements.

Children also come to believe other adults will not be available to them when help is needed. Typically, they believe most adults are not capable, nor astute enough, to provide any insight or direction for their personal lives. Youngsters interpret this to mean others don't care or aren't very sensitive.

Such messages are internalized by the children, yet possibly never consciously acknowledged.

Being goal-focused allows this responsible child a diversion from the family pain.

2. Adjuster

When others in the home provide structure (typically, an older sibling, mom, or dad), younger children may not find it necessary to be responsible for themselves. The child called the adjuster finds it much easier to exist in this increasingly chaotic family situation by simply adjusting to whatever happens. This youngster does not attempt to prevent or alleviate any situation. The child doesn't think about the situation or experience any emotions as a result of it. Whatever happens, when it happens, is simply handled. The adjuster's thinking is "I can't do anything about it anyway," which in the child's mind seems to be a fairly realistic attitude. Professionally, this child would be described as detached and noninvested in the family unit.

The adjuster is less visible within the family structure. This is the child who most likely goes to his room unannounced, who spends less time at home and more time with his friends; this is the family member who seems oblivious to the conflicts and emotions at home.

Adjusting children find it wiser to follow and simply not draw attention to themselves. This behavior is less painful for these children and makes life easier for the rest of the family as well. The role of the adjuster is permeated with denial, without the focus on others. It is this lack of attention to others which makes adjusters appear to be more selfish. Acting without thinking or feeling is typical behavior of the true adjuster.

3. Placater

In every home there is usually at least one child who is more sensitive—one who laughs harder, cries harder, and seems to be more emotionally involved in everyday events. The placater's behavior is usually acknowledged as a matter of fact. In the alcoholic home, the placating child is not necessarily the only sensitive child in the home, but is the one perceived as the "most sensitive." The placater finds the best way to cope, in this inconsistent and tension filled home, is by acting in a way which will lessen his own tension and pain, as well as that of other family members. This child spends his childhood years trying to "fix" the sadness, fears, angers and problems of brothers, sisters, and certainly, of mom and dad.

The placater becomes very skilled at listening and at demonstrating empathy, and is well liked for those attributes. The placater never disagrees. Being a placater is safe. These children are highly skilled at diverting attention from themselves and focusing it onto other persons. If they allowed themselves to risk self-disclosure, they would have to deal with their own reality, and experience the pain of that reality.

4. Acting-out Child

Most children raised in alcoholic homes react to the turmoil in their lives in a way which does not draw negative attention to them or to their family. Yet a number of them, approximately 20 percent of children in alcoholic homes, draw attention to themselves through negative behavior. Instead of behaving in a manner which brings greater stability into their lives, or at least in a way which does not add to the turmoil, "acting-out children" often display delinquent, problematic behavior which typifies the state of the family. Acting-out children will cause disruption in their own lives and in the lives of other family members. In doing so they will often provide distraction from the issue of alcoholism.

If there is a delinquent child in the family, it is often easier for parent to focus on that child and the ensuing problems created rather than worry about dad's or mom's alcoholic drinking. Such children are the ones who are doing poorly or dropping out of school, getting pregnant in mid-teens, drinking at a younger age than other children, abusing other drugs and exhibiting other socially unacceptable behavior.

Unfortunately, thousands of these acting-out children don't get help and, for those who do, the help they get is only for their problematic behavior, or for being part of an alcoholic family system which is the basis of their behavior.

The reality is *all* children in alcoholic homes are negatively affected. *All* children need to be addressed.

II. DENIAL

In my direct work with children, my experience is that by the time a child in an alcoholic family reaches the age of nine, he has a well-developed denial system about both his feelings and his perceptions of what is happening in the home. Again, children in alcoholic homes do whatever they possibly can to bring stability and consistency into their lives. The role adoption described assists these children in coping, but in the meantime they, too, need to develop a denial system. For the young child, that means "pretending things are different than how they really are."

Children learn the *Don't Talk* rule. They learn it isn't safe to talk honestly about what is occurring. They learn that nothing positive happens when one acknowledges the truth. The following are a variety of reasons children learn at a young age to repress both their feelings and their perceptions.

Children learn to deny because:

They have been told not to talk about what is occurring at home.

They believe they are being disloyal to their parents should they talk. They believe they are betraying their family members.

They have been told that what they see is not the way it is. Their perceptions have been discounted and they no longer trust their perceptions.

They don't have the language in which to describe their experiences.

Others are not talking. They have no models for talking honestly.

These children have also learned a second major rule: *Don't Trust*. To trust means investing confidence, reliance, and faith in another. Confidence, reliance, and faithfulness are virtues often missing in alcoholic families. Children need to be able to depend on their parents to meet their physical and emotional needs in order to develop trust. In alcoholic environments, parents are not consistently available to their children either by being drunk, physically absent, or mentally and emotionally preoccupied with alcohol or with the alcoholic.

The single most important ingredient in a nurturing relationship — in any relationship — is honesty. No child can trust, or be expected to trust, unless those around him are also open and honest about their own feelings. Alcoholics lose this ability to be honest as their disease progresses. As the alcoholic continues to drink, he has to rationalize his negative behavior and he has to do it extremely well in order to continue his drinking. An alcoholic's life is consumed with feelings of guilt, shame, anxiety, and remorse, causing him to drink all that much more to attempt an escape. It becomes a never-ending circle because of the psychological need to drink and a physical addiction to alcohol. Enabling parents are fearful of being honest with their children. They don't want them to experience the same pain they are feeling and they don't want to acknowledge that the problem exists in the first place.

While children in alcoholic homes can and do survive, problems arise in their lives because their environmental circumstances have made it impossible for them to feel safe and secure, or to rely on or trust others. Trust is one of those vital character building blocks children need in order to develop into healthy adults. Being raised in an alcoholic family structure often denies or distorts this portion of a child's development.

The family rules of *Don't Talk* and *Don't Trust* teach children it isn't safe to share feelings. Being isolated with feelings of fear, worry, embarrassment, guilt, anger, loneliness, etc. leads to a state of desperation, of being overwhelmed. Such a state does not lend itself to survival, so the children learn other ways to cope. They learn to discount and repress feelings. These children build walls of self protection. Family members deny and minimize situations and feelings in order to hide their own pain.

III. ADULTHOOD

Whatever children learned in the family system they take with them to adulthood. What was survival for the first several years of their life is what will often cause problems for them in their adulthood.

Reaching young adulthood, children of alcoholics go on about their lives continuing to applaud themselves for being survivors. The oldest, or only, child, the one who became the little adult, continues into the grown-up world carrying a lot of responsibility. The ability to be responsible has many strengths—the ability to take charge, to make decisions, to set goals.

But this adult-age person, who has come to be known as the "adult child" experiences increasing anxiety, has become tense, and often feels separated from others by an invisible wall. During their adolescent years, the children who adopted the responsible role were so busy being young adults there was little time for them to be children. As a result they did not have the time to learn child developmental skills. As adults, they have become rigid and lacking in flexibility. They need to be in charge; they do not know how to follow. They didn't learn to listen or to ask for input. They have a need to be in control and live with great fears of being out of control. They did not learn spontaneity or creativity. They are often depressed and don't understand why. They feel much loneliness, anxiety, and fear.

Adult adjusters find it easier to avoid positions where they need to take control. They have become adept at adjusting, at being flexible and spontaneous. They have neither a sense of direction nor a sense of taking responsibility for the direction they would like their lives to take.

Adjusting children have found life to be a roller coaster in that they feel they have no options and no power with which to respond to situations. They did not learn that choices were available to them. They are fearful of making decisions. Oftentimes, they had so little practice making decisions that they do not know how. They are afraid to initiate. They continue to walk through life not being invested and, therefore, not feeling the pain.

The placater child who was busy taking care of everyone else's emotional needs is often the warm, sensitive, caring, listening child. This is a well-liked child. He or she grows up continuing to to take care of others, either personally or professionally.

Placaters have never seriously considered what they want; rather, they are forever discounting their needs. They have trained themselves to be concerned only with providing for others. If we cannot ask ourselves what our own wants are, we cannot direct ourselves to obtain them.

Again, it is relatively easy to understand why these children develop depression as adults. Although they appear to be living their lives the way they want, they still feel apart from others; they feel lonely. They don't have equal relationships with others and they always give too much and refrain from putting themselves in a position to receive.

The acting-out child, the one who was constantly in trouble and caused problems, will continue to find conflicts in early adulthood. These people are not capable of feeling good about themselves. They have been unable to interact with others in acceptable ways and have been unable to express their own needs or have them met. They know their anger, but they know little else. They are more apt than other children to begin using and abusing alcohol and other drugs at an early age. They are more prone to become alcoholic than the other children in the family.

Some children may clearly fit into one or more of these four roles. Some will exhibit traits of all four roles. A percentage will change and adopt different roles as they grow older. Whatever roles children adopt, there are gaps in development and growth. Gaps are the emotional and psychological voids which occur as a result of the unpredictable and inconsistent parenting in alcoholic homes. For most children, the gaps are issues related to control, trust, dependency, identification, and expression of feelings. These factors will affect the now adult children in 1) involvement in relationships, 2) depression, 3) continuance in an alcoholic or otherwise dysfunctional system via marriage, or 4) the progression of their own addictive/compulsive behaviors.

What is so important to remember is that these are children who grow up with chronic powerlessness. They live a life of fear and loneliness. They have come to believe that they are responsible for the problems in the home and/or they are responsible for alleviating the family problems. In attempting to stabilize the family through their role and adopting the rules of survival, they ultimately come to learn that "no matter what they do, it is never good enough." This leads them to move into adulthood with a sense of shame. Shame is the belief that there is something inherently wrong with who they are. It is the belief that they are defective. Best summarized, "Guilt is when you make a mistake, shame is when you believe you are the mistake."

Almost always when one pulls away the layer of shame, abandonment is at the foundation. That abandonment may be either physical or emotional. In most alcoholic homes the abandonment is on a chronic basis.

In spite of how good these children often have the ability to look, shame becomes a core issue for them in their life and is to be addressed in their recovery.

Shame manifests itself in a variety of ways:

1) For some adult children their shame is manifested in their being extremely controlling. Control compensates for their sense of powerlessness and inadequacy. Controlling behavior is a direct attempt to compensate for the sense of being defective. To control feels powerful. When you have power over another you feel less vulnerable to being shamed. To control is an attempt to see that no one ever shames you.

2) In contrast to being controlling, many people who live with shame take on a victim stance. They have difficulty setting limits. They don't believe in their own worth. They are always giving other people the benefit of the doubt and are willing to respond to the structure others set. They don't recognize they have needs. Ultimately, this produces a depressive and victimlike stance in life.

3) Rage is shame bound. When we express rage, we feel most powerful. We no longer feel inadequate and defective. Rage also keeps people away so they do not see one's inner wounded self that the child believes is so ugly.

4) Shame is often the basis of perfectionism. Highly perfectionistic people are usually people who a) as children were raised with unrealistic expectations on the part of the parents that the child internalized for himself and b) children who needed to do things right in order to get approval from their parents and to lessen fears of abandonment. Perfectionism is a shame-based phenomenon because the child learns that "no matter what we do, it is never good enough."

5) Shame produces compulsive behaviors. Childhood behaviors that were comforting point one toward adult escapes that often become compulsive for the adult. These adult behaviors included:

Compulsive Exercising
Compulsive Spending
Workaholism
Compulsive Extramarital Affairs

One makes friends with one's escape behaviors. These actions initially feel good and powerful and there are minimal negative consequences. But, in time, people come to depend on escape behavior to relieve their sense of unworthiness.

6) Shame is an integral part of addictive behaviors.

People eat, drink, and use other drugs to comfort their loneliness, to medicate their anger, fears, and sadnesses. They eat, drink, and/or use drugs to anesthetize their shame. They often use and abuse to feel more powerful. This does not make one food-ddicted or chemically dependent, but it fuels their psychological dependency, which in turn leads to addiction.

7) The ultimate act of shame is suicide. I am hopeless, I am unworthy. I don't deserve to live.

Acoholism is a living nightmare. It is not possible to be in an alcoholic family and not be negatively affected. Yet, there is much that can be done. Alcoholism treatment, as it has been developed in the United States, has made it possible for millions of alcoholics to get sober. The self-help groups of Alcoholics Anonymous, Cocaine Anonymous, and Narcotics Anonymous have helped millions of people become clean and sober and maintain a recovery process. The miracles for the alcoholic can also be miracles for the family members. Understanding the family members' process offers a direction for intervention and treatment and for children of alcoholics, young and adult, a choice about how they live their lives.

Part V: Discussion

(*Chairperson*) *Dr. Marcus Grant*: This afternoon we're going to be focusing upon therapeutic approaches. What this means is that after the broad, scientific and other considerations we have discussed, we will turn our attention to the ways in which the *existing* services can respond more effectively to individuals and to families experiencing problems as a result of alcohol consumption.

I do not wish to limit in any way the discussion tha will take place this afternoon. However, after reading through the papers that have been prepared, I think it clear that the first lesson we will have to learn—the first fact that we will have to take into account—is that there is no *one* way of dealing with individuals or families experiencing such problems; there are *many* ways.

These ways will differ according to the discipline from which people come, whether they are psychologists, psychiatrists, social workers, nurses, primary health care workers. They will differ also because of the culture in which they have to operate: the same psychologist, for example, working here in Japan, would have to do things which are different from what he or she would have to do if working in Botswana or Cuba or Peru or the United States of America. So, there may be many reasons, cultural reasons and reasons to do with a therapeutic tradition, that will condition the way in which a response if offered by any individual therapist.

From my point of view—that is to say, from the point of view of the World Health Organization—what we are interested in is building bridges between these different traditions. I do not in my heart believe, nor do I think the evidence supports the view, that any one of these professions is necessarily any better or any worse that any other. Psychologists are no more the key to the truth on how to conduct family therapy than are psychiatrists, social workers, or family therapists. *All* have something to contribute.

Collaboration between disciplines is something that you will often hear people saying is to be encouraged. I've yet to meet anybody who says they think collaboration is a bad thing. But very frequently, the people who say that they're in favor of collaboration are rather poor at doing it themselves. What we all need to remember, as we enter a discussion such as this, is that "collaboration" doesn't just mean telling people what you do; it also means learning from people what they do. Collaboration means *giving something up* as well as *giving something to* other people. And it is always easier to give a gift than to receive a gift. The people who are the most courteous are those who are the best at receiving compliments, as well as the best at giving them.

I think that we should try to keep our minds as open as we can, and try to recognize that everyone has something to contribute and that everybody can learn from everyone else. That, I think, is what collaboration is about: between disciplines, between countries, and between therapeutic approaches.

(*Chairperson*) *Dr. Yoshimatsu*: We will first discuss the three fascinating presentations from Drs. Hayashida, Suzuki and Takemura. Perhaps Dr. Hayashida would like to add some comments?

Dr. Hayashida: I should like to deviate from the main topic that I presented today and relate to you something I've been pondering over in recent years. Let me first give you an idea of the composition of our rehabilitation programs. We conduct a two-year outpatient program for our alcoholic patients. Initially, they come to a day hospital for five days a week from 9.00 a.m. to 3.00 p.m. for one month. The day hospital is open only during the day. After this first month, they continue to visit and attend group therapy sessions two or three times a week, either during the day or evenings. This treatment phase is divided into two stages: an intermediate group that lasts for five months and the advanced group that lasts one year. After that, they are followed up once a month for six months as the final stage of rehabilitation. They are then discharged with the recommendation that they continue to attend AA meetings indefinitely.

What I have been noticing recently is that when these people are discharged, they tend to be very stable as regards their alcoholism. However, some of them do rather poorly as regards their social life, particularly in the area of forming heterosexual relationships. I fear that our unit may not have been doing its job so effectively in this area, for various reasons. Perhaps we focus too much on individual patients' issues and not enough on their relationships with the opposite sex. It is astonishing that, after two years of rehabilitation, some of them continue to entertain rather archaic and distorted ideas about women. This is evidenced by middle-aged, recovering alcoholics dating women in their early twenties, by men continuing to live with their aging mothers, by men being unable to assume parental or spousal roles in their families, or by men being unable to acknowledge women other than as sex objects.

I am aggrieved that this is the state of many men leaving our unit after two years of therapy. We are not sure whether we will be able to fully prepare our patients to play a more adequate heterosexual role. Many of these men do come from broken families of origin and have also experienced the break-up of their own marriage. So, what sort of therapy should we provide for them? Should we look into their past more actively and do more reconstructive therapy? Many of them have virtually no idea of what constitutes a mature and healthy heterosexual relationship. There is no frame of reference.

Another related point concerns Alcoholic Anonymous. I don't like to criticize the great contribution that A.A. makes to recovery. I do appreciate all the good work that they, and other similar organizations, are doing. However, A.A. may not be fully aware of the issues I'm raising here. A.A. often asks recovering alcoholics to refrain from forming intimate relationships with persons of the opposite sex for at least one year, and to concentrate on their own recovery from alcoholism. That is all well and good, but what will they do afterwards?

Is one answer to this question for us to extend our programs beyond two years? That doesn't sound realistic. In fact, I would rather shorten the programs, if possible, not extend them! I've been worried about this issue. I'd value hearing from the audience as to how we can approach and solve this most important problem in the future.

(*Chairperson*) *Dr. Yoshimatsu*: I think this is a very improtant and relevant concern for the treatment and well-being of clients. If you have any comments, advice or suggestions for Dr. Hayashida, please let him know. Meanwhile, are there any about questions to Dr. Suzuki?

Dr. Nagano (*P.R.I.T.*): I have a question concerning borderline personality. You have stated that alcoholic fathers often have "borderline" sons and daughters. If so, what are the differences in clinical features between the children diagnosed as exhibiting borderline personality disorder whose fathers are alcoholics, compared to those children with the same diagnosis, but whose fathers are not alcoholics?

Dr. Suzuki: Many of our patients are adolescents. We need to help the parents to understand their children. Also, we have to ask family members to pay attention to the father's alcohol problem. While we are treating these adolescents, we would also like to treat the alcoholic problem of the father in conjunction. You might say that it is impossible to do this simultaneously. Well, when the adolescent has a borderline personality disorder, he or she is treated just the same whether the father is an alcoholic or not. It doesn't make much difference. However, the child with an alcoholic father frequently shows much more acting-out and aggressive behavior in a very severe manner and is prone to be diagnosed as having borderline personlity disorder.

We conducted research on 24 children who had alcoholic fathers, of whom eight children were aged over 16. We continued to obtain updated information about the symptoms of their disorders over two years. We found that their personality structures remained unchanged, but symptoms got better in several cases.

Dr. Nagano: May I ask you another question, please? Borderline personality disorder is primarily identified by identity problems. It is my opinion that the Alcoholic Children of Alcoholic (ACA) movement may help solve such identity problems of the alcoholic children. What is your opinion about this?

Dr. Suzuki: Projective identification problems are frequently observed in children whose fathers are alcoholics. In my presentation, I reported the characteristics of borderline personality disorder, and there are a mixture of other problems. Thus, these children have difficulty in being accepted by society.

The common psychic structure of children with an alcoholic father is the *borderline personality organization*, as I mentioned in my presentation. The ACA movement reports on the psychic structure of ACA's and I think there are some common features between borderline personality organization characteristics and ACA. I believe that the ACA movement will become more popular in the future.

Out of 24 cases, two are presently attending Ala-teen in Yokohama. However, the Ala-teen Yokohama organization is presently not so well known or organized, so it is rather difficult for them to have group therapy sessions—partly due to instability of the ACA organization itself. However, in Japan, ACA will become more and more important.

Dr. Saitoh (P.R.I.T.): If I remember correctly, around 15% or 16% of alcoholic patients are diagnosed as having borderline personality disorder. Yet, in your data, this figure was 30%, which seems very high. Perhaps this means that there needs to be a clearer definition of just what is borderline personality disorder?

Dr. Suzuki: The concept of Borderline Syndrome may differ from researcher to researcher. In addition, the relation between Borderline Syndrome and Borderline Personality Disorder (B.P.D.) is not yet defined clearly. I agree with Dr. Spitzer's concept of Borderline Syndrome, but his concept is too broad. So, in this report, the B.P.D. diagnosis was based upon DSM-III criteria. It is generally believed that one must be cautious in diagnosing B.P.D. in adolescents. I agree with this belief. Recently, some researchers in Japan have been using the Diagnostic Interview for Borderline (DIB) test (Gunderson) to determine such diagnoses. I compared *DIB* and *DSM-III* and I found very little difference between the two criteria. However if the B.P.D. should last for a long period of time, then I have to question myself as to whether my own diagnosis of this disorder was in fact really B.P.D. So, you were right to point out this important issue.

(Chairperson) Dr. Yoshimatsu: I'd like to comment about adolescents: This is a period when there are a lot of adjustments and growing pains, so I think

we have to be very careful, to be much more cautious about diagnosing adolescents as having B.P.D.

Do we have any comments or questions to our third speaker, Dr. Takemura?

Dr. Matsuo (*Komatsu Hospital*): Japanese people tend to buy a lot of products, but not a lot of information. They don't pay much to obtain information. But I was amazed that you actually *charge* at your counseling room. I believe sessions vary between minutes to two hours, right? You said that unless cancellation of a session is advised at least three days in advance, you charge the full amount due. I'm very much interested in how you do this.

Dr. Takemura: In the interest of clarity, perhaps I should ask Ms. Endo to come up here and explain this, please.

Ms. Endo (*Chief, Harajuku Counseling Room*): For the initial consultation, the fee is ¥5,000 for 90 minutes, and for individual sessions it is ¥5,000 for 30 minites. So, for one hour it is ¥10,000. In addition to individual sessions, we also conduct family sessions, and we have different charges for these. For example, ¥12,000 per hour and ¥20,000 for up to two hours. We also have group programs; for the educational program, one session is 90 minutes and costs ¥3,000. For other group programs, each two-hour session is either ¥2,500 or ¥3,000. Usually, we have an eight-session "lump sum" contract and ask for payment in advance for group programs.

Dr. Ichikawa (*Narimasu Kohsei Hospial*): In Tokyo, Harajuku Counseling Room, I believe, is one of the state-of-the-art counseling offices, and there are other places, public health centers, for example, which also conduct such programs. Wives make up many of the clients there, also. It seems that there are a good many cases in which the alcoholism has decreased after the wives have participated in these courses.

However, there are some cases in which the alcoholism does not decrease at all, and many of those cases seem to come on to our hospital. There were several problems mentioned by the speakers: One is that the drinking may have stopped, but the family members still are dysfunctional and unhappy. Another is deterioration in adolescents or children. Sometimes, also, the wives attend such educational sessions, but nothing changes in the home. These are the three types of family situations.

So, it seems there are some families which do very well and others which don't respond well at all. What differences in therapy would you offer these different types of families or wives?

Dr. Takemura: Perhaps I should ask Ms. Endo to respond to this.

Ms. Endo: The Harajuku Counseling Room started only six years ago; therefore, the overall number of clients is not great. Also, we look only at the prognosis of husbands and wives. We've just started to look at the differences between the prognosis of the two counseling situations, and need to do so much more closely in the future.

For the past year only, we have examined the prognosis. As Dr. Ichikawa mentioned, in the third pattern where the wives were relieved of their difficulties—in particular, intrafamily violence, which was the most urgent problem—the husband's alcoholic condition continued unabated. So I think we may need to elucidate further exactly what sort of approaches we should take for the wives. And maybe we shouldn't confine ourselves just to wives, but should go one step further to intervene at the level of the couple's interaction. However, this is our present situation.

(Chairperson) Dr. Marcus Grant: Now we shall be discussing two papers— by Drs. Kazumi Nishio and Claudia Black—which look in somewhat different ways at issues concerning alcoholic families.

I remember that the very first time I heard the term "Adult Children of an Alcoholic" was in a bus in Palm Springs in California, where I was sitting besides a woman called Migs Woodside—who has turned out to be an important person in the area of alcoholism. She was very cross with me because I was at that time unfamiliar with the term!

This was perhaps seven years ago. So, perhaps my ignorance then was pardonable. Certainly, it would not any longer be pardonable. This is a concept that has become very much more important in thinking about alcohol problems in the U.S.A. and has come to have some influence in other parts of the world as well. Thus, it is a very important focus for this final session.

Now I would like to call for questions addressed to Dr. Nishio and Black.

Dr. Motoi Hayashida: Dr. Black, in my presentation I implied that what you're talking about is not specific with the children of alcoholics or substance abusers. I believe that what you have described can be be encountered in other types of children. For example, in a family where the man and wife *constantly* fight, *constantly* disagree, do you think children growing up in such a family would be just like what you have described so beautifully?

Dr. Claudia Black: Yes . . . and let me elaborate! I believe what I said is very generalizable to many other troubled families. I think the dynamics are loss on a chronic basis—not on a situational basis, but on a *chronic* basis. It is easy to see how this is generalizable to the battering home, the sexually abusing home, the home in which mental illness is present.

Sometimes the source of dysfunction is not so identifiable. The dynamics that will often be there, in addition to the chronic loss, are rigidity, isolation both emotional and social, and denial—and when I say denial, you may want to think of the terms "minimizing," "discounting," and "shame." The reason that I have taken this stance with children from alcoholic homes is that for years people have ignored the alcohoic family and the child in that family. If I keep talking about this is the framework of children of alcoholics, people are less likely to ignore them.

For years, people have talked about dysfunctional, unhealthy family systems, but for years they have ignored the alcoholism within that system.

Dr. Kazumi Nishio: I'd like to add something: The recent movement of ACA—Adult Children of Alcoholics—also includes many people from dysfunctional families. When you go to ACA meetings, you will hear some people say, "I'm so-and-so, ACA." Also, they say, "I'm so-and-so and an Adult Child of a *dysfunctional* family." These people come together; some are from incestuous families, with the father very cold, workholic, violent, and so on. Different kinds of adult children get together in these ACA meetings. The dynamics of dysfunction are very similar.

Question: I am a children's therapist. However, there are two aspects to treatment: that offered by the physician and that offered by the family, or from the patient him or herself. So, there are two categories of therapy.

I'm rather impressed that even a very young child involved within a family with very serious dysfunctional conditions has the power—the *natural* power—to survive. Therapy, therefore, is to *support* their power to live. So, I have learnt a lot from our presentations and I'm grateful.

Dr. Claudia Black: I wanted to comment that in working with children of any age it is important to *validate* and support their strengths. In working with adult children, so often they will tend to become critical of what they did as children and refer to that as their "co-dependent behavior," with a negative connotation.

What was survivorship for them then may no longer be working in their adulthood. When they were children, survivorship was a strength and I think they should be able to feel good about that. Some of the work in addressing children is certainly to validate what their strengths are about, but these are children who've had to respond in *vacuum* and they don't perceive options available to them. Also, so many times they've learned their strengths out of *fear*. So, I would hope, in the treatment process, they will learn, will have opportunity to practice those skills in a nonfrightening environment, in order to associate a greater sense of safety and positiveness with those skills.

Again, I would like to emphasize that a child needs very much to be commended. we know what it is they didn't learn, and we will help them to focus on those areas, but I wouldn't necessarily point out all that they're not learning. Often we point to family members and tell them how *sick* they are. Children can't do much with that information that's positive. There really isn't any direction for them to go with that where they can feel good about who they are. So, I would go back to how we can support these children and at the same time teach them what they haven't have an opportunity to learn.

Question: I have a question for both of you: I am providing therapy for pathological children from alcoholic families. You are handling healthy children. ACAs are rather healthy children, adult children, who've grown up in alcoholic families. And when I'm working with pathological children, I think it's very important to help them change their thinking or increase their awareness of emotional reactions towards their parents. This is very important for their treatment. So, I think it's very important to educate them to change their attitude toward their parents. At first, I teach them that their parents have a disease, that alcoholism is a disease. We should teach them this.

However, in your case the children may have very complex and subtle feelings towards their parents. What kind of key concepts do you provide to these ACAs in order to help them change their attitude towards their parents?

Dr. Claudia Black: I believe that, before one can forgive others, one has to explain and express one's emotional truth and feelings. Before I, as a 12-year-old or a 20-year-old, in my *heart* accept my parents as having a disease and before I have any level of forgiveness for our experiences, I typically have to be able to own in full—to honestly speak out and try to grasp, understand—what my experience has been. Education gives children an understanding. So many ACAs *want* to understand their parents, *want* to forgive their parents and *want* everything to be fine as it once was (or how it has never been, but they have fantasized), and want to *pass over* their own work.

As treatment people, sometimes we have a tendency to move Adult Children to forgiveness too quickly. Before they can forgive, they must own their fears, sadnesses, embarrassments and angers. This does not have to be imparted directly to the parent, but it does need to be identified and spoken about by the Adult Child. The purpose is not to cast judgment and/or blame. It is to allow the Adult Child to speak the truth of his or her own experience— to open and express his full feelings.

Let me also talk about the fact that, in working with more pathological children in the States, we tend to see them as being disruptive in the school system and we see them as they get involved with the court system. In the United States, in many, many cities—not all—schools are actively participating in setting up support groups for what are termed "high-risk children."

Often, that will mean the child from the chemically dependent family system, in which these children are now being helped: to speak their truth, take responsiblity for what they *do* with those emotions; to learn better problem-solving skills, because they have very poor problem-solving skills or are in a vacuum. These children are being taught how to set healthier limits for themselves; how not to react but to think through before they do something. So, our schools are taking some responsibility.

Also, though not as actively as our schools, mental health professionals involved in the court systems are beginning to identify the child of an alcoholic in the court system and attempting to refer that child to an appropriate resource rather than to scapegoat the child. Many of the psychiatric treatment programs are developing a curriculum not just for children from alcoholic homes but also for children from violent homes as well. I think that every child in a psychiatric facility has come from a troubled home, so I'm wondering why they have to develop a separate curriculum to do that. I think that all children in such facilities could use this additional work.

Dr. Kazumi Nishio: I think it is really difficult for children in a dysfunctional family to respond any way but very negatively! They are in a very, very *powerless* position—the parents tell them what to do, what not to think, how to respond. So these children really don't have a lot of power. Therefore, asking children to understand and excuse their parents' disease of alcoholism may not be a great service to children. Understanding and forgiveness by children come only after a great deal of therapeutic work. So, my approach would be to provide a model for children, where they can find different kinds of models besides mother's or father's alcoholic models. Also, we should be teaching *very healthy communication skills* outside of the home. As Dr. Black said, in the group setting there are lots of opportunities these days— at least in the United States. I'm sure you can do it in Japan too.

Dr. Claudia Black: Wherever somebody has access to children, they have access to intervene in the life of a child from an alcoholic system. How you do that will vary according to where you're at: what I do as a neighbor to this child, what I do as the librarian in the school library, what I do as the school bus driver or the clergy person or the nurse—these will all vary, but if we each take responsibility for being willing to impact a child, then throughout our community a child will find resources.

Question: Dr. Black, I am a psychologist in a children's hospital working with children similar to those you describe in your work. In some cases, children do not understand their own feelings. You mentioned that education is very important. Pelase give more details about the kind of education we should provide.

Dr. Claudia Black: I'm going to bypass the part about talking about education, because I think we're talking about going *beyond* just education. I have best been able to teach a child to better identify his feelings with experiential forms of therapy. For example, I use art therapy (my first book was concerned about children's art therapy, entitled *My Dad Loves Me, My Dad Has A Disease*). I'm not a certified art therapist, but I think a sound counselor can bring art into the counseling session. Just try not to interpret, but allow the children to interpret for himself. *Art therapy* is a wonderful tool to use with teenagers and young children.

Collage work, where you work from magazines, is a form of art therapy where children take pictures, words, and portions of words to create a picture statement about some aspect of their experience. There are also *role-playing, psychodramatic techniques*. I've also created a *stamp game*, which I'll tell you about so you can create your own version, as it's hard to get from the United States. There are eight different-colored pieces of paper, representing various feelings: The red symbolizes any form of anger; the yellow is anything that is positive; the black represents fear; and the white is a "wild card" that can represent any feeling not covered by the others. I use this a lot with people of any age to help them connect with their feelings.

Most of the time children respond to things that are tangible. When I began, there was no specific training. You can create media and resources. It means you have to have a willingness to give up a little control. Having come from an alcoholic home, I like to be in control, so if *I* can do it, *you* can do it! These techniques give children something tangible to work with so they feel a little bit of distance and safety, and it is easier for them to talk. For example, when a child comes to see me, I'll say, "How was your weekend?" and he will go to the cards, pick them up, and say, "Three blues and a black!" Then I'll have him talk about the three blues and a black, and the more he picks up of a color, the more he feels that feeling that weekend.

I take that game into all kinds of variations. I use *feeling lists*. I may have already made up the feelings list, depending upon the length of time I'm going to be working with the child—if it's short, I give him one; if it's long, I have him create one. We use that list from which I ask him to begin to clarify his feelings:

"What is it you're feeling right now?"

"I don't know,"

"I want you to pick a word. What is it you're feeling right now?"

"I don't know!"

"Of these words, which come the closest?"

So again, we work it out that way. In terms of helping children to understand what they're feeling, I've had to create somevery tangible ways in order for them to do that.

Dr. Kazumi Nishio: I also use a feelings list and I do *sand-tray therapy*. They can express their feelings a little more easily when they use their animals, dolls, or whatever—not themselves, but they're talking about themselves through these sand-box toys.

Another thing I do is I take children for walks. I cook with them (I have a facility where we can cook together). So we do lots of things together and I show my emotion. They can see a range of emotions—feeling intimate and feeling good, as well as experiencing disappointment and other kinds of emotions. That's how I've developed my therapy techniques.

Dr. Claudia Black: In that way, you become a positive model?

Dr. Kazumi Nishio: Yes, I think modeling is one of the main forms for my therapy techniques. In provides safety, and is a positive method for me.

(Chairperson) Dr. Marcus Grant: Dr. Hayashida, I think you said you had a second question.

Dr. Hayashida: This is about feelings, but first I need to give a little account of one of my therapy sessions:

I was running a therapy group one day, and it so happened that this was the day that my co-therapist, who'd been with us for six months, was going to leave, it was her last day.

I opened the session. Usually, I don't say much, but wait for the members to say things. One patient talked about the time he had received a "Dear John" letter from a girlfriend who left him. Another patient talked about a former counselor we had had with us who was a very rigid, straightforward person, *very* dogmatic, aggressive. Yet, this patient had very fond memories of him.

I was confused about why all this sort of thing was coming out in the group; I didn't know what was going on! But it dawned on me that the most significant thing for that day was that our co-therapist was leaving. I suddenly wondered, "Are they talking about her, maybe?" and then it all "clicked."

In fact, the patient I just mentioned felt that his "girlfriend" was deserting him. This was her last day, and it reminded him of the girlfriend who had left him. The other member was reminded to the good relationship he'd had with this former counselor—but also with this particular co-therapist.

At this point in the session, our co-therapist was feeling very hurt. She looked empty. This was her last day and yet nobody had acknowledged that or said anything! So, I decided to make an interpretation, and said, "Are we talking about *her* today, when we're talking about a *Dear John* letter and past memories of a former counselor? Are we really talking about her?'' Then, everybody understood this truth. In fact, our co-therapist was overwhelmed and began to cry.

Now, let me share my thoughts with you. I thought the group members were clearly capable of expressing their feelings about the departure of our co-therapist. She had been much involved with us in many ways over the months, arranging many things for them and being very helpful. And yet, they were not able to describe their feelings about her directly. However, the *affect* they had about her was very appropriate, I believed.

Now, is that what you mean by "They don't know the language"?

Dr. Claudia Black: Yes, that's exactly right. In your case they were *physically* closer to their feeling than others often will be. That's often true, also, of Adult Children; they will have tears in their eyes and say that they're not feeling anything. And I will point out that they're actually much closer to their feelings than they're recognizing. I'll say, "How are you feeling?" as somebody is pounding his fist on a table and he'll say, "Fine. Why?" I'll say, "Do you know how you're feeling?" and he'll continue to pound and I'll continue to ask: "Are you aware that your fist is pounding on the table?" and he'll look at it and say, "No," and continue to pound. They're *with* their anger, it's very visible, but they don't have the language with which to describe it.

So, yes! In that kind of setting they're very close to their feelings, and I think we can begin to give them that language—by just verbiage back: "Sounds like you're feeling angry"; "Sounds like you're feeling she's deserting you"; "You're feeling alone"; "You're feeling scared." We give them that language.

Some people have a difference kind of therapy—the *educational* approach. The educational approach *isn't* a didactic lecture; a lot of that education is through conversation. Such conversaton when somebody begins to talk about their *Dear John* letter when the therapist is leaving the group would be to say, "How is that feeling—the one you experienced when you got that letter—similar to what you're experiencing with our therapist leaving today?" "What is the feeling you felt then?" ("I didn't feel anything") "Well, sounds like today you have a lot of feelings and I think you should work with that."

That's what I mean about giving them the language. At some point, you are educational: "Sounds like you're angry," "Sounds like you're lonely," etc.

(Chairperson) Dr. Marcus Grant: May I suggest that Dr. Black and Dr. Nishio sum up with a final comment?

Dr. Claudia Black: I've spent a lot of time talking about children who look good. It's very *easy* to continue ignoring that population of people.

Yet, in the United States we're seeing them chronically depressed, in need of psychotherapy, suicidal, with a greater preponderance of eating disorders—bulimia, anorexia. We're seeing them become addicted to alcohol and other kinds of drugs and we're seeing a lot of hurtful, compulsive-type behaviors.

I urge you not to ignore the young child when you have access to him or her. When they're young—under nine years of age—I think this is truly prevention. As they get older, we have to undo a denial process and also teach them what they have already *not* learned. Again, the alcoholic has an opportunity for recovery and I can't see any reason why that can't be true for the child, as well.

Dr. Kazumi Nishio: I'm very excited about the ACA movement. I hope Japan also will increase in this area and develop its own ACA movement. It is said that 80% of people come from dysfunctional families—that means practically all of us. So, we shouldn't really disconnect ourselves from our patients, we should really look into *ourselves* to see what kinds of dysfunctional things *we* have or do, what kinds of families *we* come from. We should really be in touch with *that* part of us to be able to work with people wo are coming from dysfunctional and alcoholic families.

(Chairperson) Dr. Marcus Grant: I'll make one quick closing comment: The whole point of a meeting such as the one we've been involved in for the last two days is, presumably, to improve our own practice . . . to make us better at doing the things we do. I think that during this last session we've been privileged to hear some very illuminating, stimulating, creative, and—I hope—provocative accounts that will help us all to do just that.

(Chairperson) Dr. Yoshimatsu: I would like to thank all the participants for their contributions over the past two days, and also for their active involvement in this session. I should now like to ask Dr. Nobukatsu Katoh, Coordinator of the Organizing Committee of the 4th International Symposium and Director of the Matsuzawa Hospital, to make his closing remarks.

Dr. Katoh: On behalf of the Organizing Committee of this symposium, I would like to thank all of you who attended this symposium on *Alcoholism and the Family*.

It is a very serious problem that family members of alcoholics, especially children, are at relatively high risk of developing alcoholism. It is apparent that alcoholism can constitute a major source of stress for family members.

Thus, what we have heard during this symposium has been—and will continue to be—very significant and helpful in helping us form strategies to overcome this serious disease. We have heard many new facts regarding the genetic and environmental factors relating to alcoholism and the family. However, we still have to increase our research in this area. International cooperation will be critical in ensuing continued breakthroughs, in order for us to understand the cultural differences and similarities occurring in this disease. Therefore, further international exchanges are strongly required in the future.

The success of this symposium was mainly due to the contributions of our distinguished guests from abroad, so I would like to thank them, in particular. I hope you have enjoyed your stay in our country, brief though it may have been.

Finally, I should like to express my appreciation to the members of the Psychiatric Research Institute of Tokyo, especially to the Director, Dr. Ishii. Thank you all again. I hereby declare this symposium closed.

Name Index

Subject Index

AA, *see* Alcoholics Anonymous
Aborigines, 143
Absent family system, 235
Absolute difference, between pair of twins, 44
Abstinence, total, 106
ACA/ACOA, *see* Adult Children of Alcoholics
ACTH, *see* Adrenocorticotropin hormone
Acting-out child, 276, 279
Addictive behaviors, 280
ADH, 92
Adjuster, child as, 275, 278
Adolescents, with alcoholic parents; *see also* Child(ren)
   effects on, 98-105
   treatment of psychiatric illnesses in, 241-252
Adopted men, cross-fostering analysis of, 62-64
Adopted women, cross-fostering analysis of, 64-66
Adoption study(ies), 4-5
   and classification of alcoholism, 59-69
   Stockholm, 61-64, 68
Adrenocorticotropin hormone (ACTH), 9, 53
Adult alcoholic dependence, development of, by men, 75, 76
Adult children of alcoholic families, 278-281
   case example of, 266-271
Adult Children of Alcoholics (ACA/ACOA), 156, 204, 229, 239, 266-271, 285, 287, 288, 294
Adulthood, young, alcoholism in, personality in childhood as predictor of, 67-68
Adult variables, as more result than cause of alcoholism, 73-74
Advances in Alcohol and Substance Abuse, 59
Africa, 128
Age of onset, 79-80
Agreement, as to expectations, 223
Ainu Tribe, 144
Al-Anon, 217, 236, 238, 239, 262, 268
Alaska, Native populations in, 127-128, 132-134, 135, 136
Alaskan Eskimos, 91, 95, 127-128, 132, 133, 140; *see also* Native American *entries*
Alateen, 217, 239, 285
Alcohol abuse
   inheritance of susceptibility to, 62
   risk for, *see* Risk *entries*
Alcohol and Alcoholism Behavior, 146
"Alcohol and Family Health: An International Review of the Effects and Outcomes of Excessive Drinking," 97

"Alcohol Breaking the Alcoholic Patterns," 180-182
"The Alcohol Connection," 178, 183, 184
Alcohol dependence
   development of
      culture of parents and, 74-75
      by men, 75, 76
      environmental factors and, 36-37
      twins with, 24-37
Alcohol Dependence (303.90), 14, 15
Alchoholic(s)
   daughters of, *see* Daughter(s)
   wives of, therapeutic effcts of counseling on, 254-264; *see also* Marriage patterns
Alcoholic family(ies)
   cultural approach to, 187-201
   Family Systems approaches to, *see* Family Systems *entries*
   "hitting bottom" with, 172-186
   international perspectives on, 97-112
   in Japan, marriage patterns of females from, 203-218
   and mental health, 95-151
      discussion of, 140-151
   therapeutic approaches to, *see* Therapeutic *entries*
Alcoholic father, substance use patients with, CNV of, 13-22
Alchoholic parents, *see* Parental *entries*
"Alcoholic personality," vii
Alcoholics Anonymous (AA), 52, 121, 136-137, 148, 173, 183, 224, 236, 238, 268, 281, 283, 284
Alcoholism
   adult variables as more result than cause of, 73-74
   classification of, 59-69
   cross-generational transmission of, and alcoholic's daughter, 215-216
   definition of, 226-227
   environmental factors and, *see* Environmental factors
   as family disease/disorder, 3-11, 231-233
   and family models, 153-228
      discussion of, 221-228
   family regulatory mechanisms and, 157-165
   genetics and, *see* Genetic *entries*
   incidence of, in Japan, 226
   and Native American family, 127-138, 140-142, 145
   paternal, *see* Paternal alcoholism
   predictor of, personality in childhood as, 67-68

302

Stockholm Adoption Study, 61-64, 68
Stress theory, 213
Study, proposed WHO, on natural family
    coping methods, 110-112
Subjective Mental Index (SMI), 42, 43-44
Subjective Physical Index (SPI), 42, 44
Substance use patients, with alcoholic father,
    CNV of, 13-22
Subtypes, *see* Type 1 alcoholism; Type 2 al-
    coholism
Suicide, 281
Sun Dance, 142
Survey on counseling at public heatlh centers
    in Tokyo, 95, 117-125
Survival roles, 273-276
Susceptibility, to loss of control, 165-166
    inheritance of, in adoption study, 62
Sweden, 57, 59-69, 104, 235
Swedish Medical Research Council, 59
Swedish Temperance Boards, 61, 62
Switzerland, 102, 108, 109
Symptoms
    physical and mental, of wives in marriage
        pattern study, 209, 210
    psychosomatic, in adolescents with alcohol-
        ic parents, 243-244
Syrians, 74
Systems Theory, 203

TAST, *see* Tokyo University ALDH2-Pheno-
    type Screening Test
Team, therapy, 174
Temperamental style, 159
Temperance Act (Sweden), 62
Temperance Boards, Swedish, 61, 62
Tests, psychological, 16-17
Theoretical issues, in cutlural approach,
    188-191
Theory, on treatment of alcoholism, 3
Therapeutic approaches, to alcoholic family,
    229-295
    discussion of, 282-295
Therapeutic context, identification of
    problems in family in, 233-235
Therapeutic control
    giving up of, 291
    and therapeutic impasse, 172-186
Therapeutic effects of counseling, in wives of
    alcoholics, 254-264
Therapist(s)
    "hitting bottom" of, with alcoholic fami-
        ly, 172-186
    relationship of, to patient and his family,
        235-237
Therapy, *see also* Intervention; Treatment art,
    291

family, *see* Family therapy
    sand-tray, 292
Therapy team, 174
Tlingit, 128 , 132-133
Tokyo, survey on counseling at public health
    centers in, 95, 117-125
Tokyo Metropolitan Matsuzawa Hospital, vii,
    148, 294
Tokyo 12-year-old Twin Registry, 38, 42, 56
Tokyo University ALDH2-Phenotype Screen-
    ing Test (TAST), 25, 38, 40, 41, 42, 46-47
Total abstinence, 106
TPQ, 51
Treatment, *see also* Intervention; Therapeu-
    tic *entries*
    family, current status of, 238-239
    at HCR, 260
    of psychiatric illnesses, in adolescents with
        alcoholic parents, 241-252
Treatment Institute, Belgrade, 100
Tribal Resolution No. 313-87-CR, 136
Tsukuba University, 129
Twin Registry, 38, 42, 56
Twins
    case study of, 24-37
    drinking behavior in, 38-42
    genetic study of ALDH in, 86, 87
    lifestyles in, 42-45
Twin studies, 4, 5
Type 1 alcoholism, 51, 56, 59, 63, 64, 65,
    66-67, 68, 79, 90, 92, 146, 147-148, 166,
    235, 238
    characteristics of, 68-69
    personality and, 66-67
Type 2 alcoholism, 51, 56, 59, 63-64, 65-66,
    67, 68, 79, 90, 92, 146, 147-148, 166, 235,
    238
    characteristics of, 68-69
    personality and, 66-67
Type of drinking pattern, 159
Typology, validation of, in adoption study,
    64-66

USSR, 99-100, 105, 142 143
United Kingdom, 150; *see also* Great Britain
Unites States, 8, 55, 56, 61, 67, 74, 75, 98,
    106-107, 108, 109, 128, 134, 136, 145,
    153, 158, 204, 212-213, 222, 225, 226-227,
    246, 266, 272, 281, 282, 287, 290, 291,
    294
University of Hamburg, 129
University of Pittsburgh, 155, 158
University of Tokyo, *see* Tokyo University

Vacuum, children and, 288